T0214915

Communications
in Computer and Information Science   **1235**

Commenced Publication in 2007
Founding and Former Series Editors:
Simone Diniz Junqueira Barbosa, Phoebe Chen, Alfredo Cuzzocrea,
Xiaoyong Du, Orhun Kara, Ting Liu, Krishna M. Sivalingam,
Dominik Ślęzak, Takashi Washio, Xiaokang Yang, and Junsong Yuan

Editorial Board Members

Joaquim Filipe 🆔
  Polytechnic Institute of Setúbal, Setúbal, Portugal
Ashish Ghosh
  Indian Statistical Institute, Kolkata, India
Igor Kotenko 🆔
  *St. Petersburg Institute for Informatics and Automation of the Russian
  Academy of Sciences, St. Petersburg, Russia*
Raquel Oliveira Prates 🆔
  Federal University of Minas Gerais (UFMG), Belo Horizonte, Brazil
Lizhu Zhou
  Tsinghua University, Beijing, China

Nirbhay Chaubey · Satyen Parikh ·
Kiran Amin (Eds.)

Computing Science, Communication and Security

First International Conference, COMS2 2020
Gujarat, India, March 26–27, 2020
Revised Selected Papers

Springer

Editors
Nirbhay Chaubey (iD)
Ganpat University
Gujarat, India

Satyen Parikh (iD)
Ganpat University
Gujarat, India

Kiran Amin (iD)
Ganpat University
Gujarat, India

ISSN 1865-0929   ISSN 1865-0937 (electronic)
Communications in Computer and Information Science
ISBN 978-981-15-6647-9   ISBN 978-981-15-6648-6 (eBook)
https://doi.org/10.1007/978-981-15-6648-6

This Springer imprint is published by the registered company Springer Nature Singapore Pte Ltd.
The registered company address is: 152 Beach Road, #21-01/04 Gateway East, Singapore 189721,
Singapore

Preface

This volume contains the papers presented at the First International Conference on Computing Science, Communication and Security (COMS2 2020), held at the beautiful campus of Ganpat University, India during March 26–27, 2020. COMS2 2020, perhaps the first of its kind, was organized in India wherein the invited guests, keynote speakers, dignitaries, session chairs, paper presenters, and attendees joined a two-day international conference online from their homes through zoom. The online conference forum brought together more than 80 delegates including leading academics, scientists, researchers, and research scholars from all over the world to exchange and share their experiences, ideas, and research results on the aspects of Computing Science, Network Communication, and Security.

The conference was virtually inaugurated on the first day by the National Anthem "Jana Gana Mana" with the online presence of academic leaders and luminaries: Dr. Mahendra Sharma, Pro-Chancellor and Director General of Ganpat University; Dr. Rakesh Patel, Pro-Vice Chancellor of Ganpat University; Dr. Amit Patel, Pro-Vice Chancellor and Executive Registrar of Ganpat University; Chief Guest Dr. D. P. Kothari, Former Vice Chancellor, VIT University, India; Guest of Honor Dr. Himanshu Mazumdar, a well-known scientist and currently head of, Research and Development at Dharmsinh Desai University, India; and Invited Guest of Honor Dr. Mohit P. Tahiliani, National Institute of Technology, India; which declared the conference open for further proceedings.

There were three plenary lectures covering the different area of conference: Dr. D. P. Kothari addressed the delegates by providing them an insight about qualitative research and PhD pursing areas, insisting that the constant updating of technical knowledge in new research areas is necessary for national development and academic growth. Dr. Himanshu S. Mazumdar graced the conference and delivered a plenary session talk on "Big Data and Machine Learning in Life Science."

Dr. Mohit P. Tahiliani also gave a special plenary session talk on "Networking using Network Namespaces in Linux."

The conference accepted 27 papers as oral presentations (out of 79 full papers received and critically peer reviewed using the Springer OCS System), which were received online during the two days. The conference committee formed three session tracks: (i) Artificial Intelligence and Machine Learning; (ii) Network, Communication and Security; and (iii) Computing Science. Each session track had four session chairs, all expert professors in their fields and from reputed universities in India and abroad. The selected papers come from researchers based in several countries including Australia, Brazil, Canada, the USA, Colombia, Russia, Peru, Saudi Arabia, Bangladesh, and India. All the accepted papers were peer reviewed by three qualified reviewers chosen from our conference Scientific Committee based on their qualifications and experience. The proceedings editors wish to thank the dedicated Scientific

Committee members and all the other reviewers for their contributions. We also thank Springer for their trust and for publishing the proceedings of COMS2 2020.

The conference was organized by the Ganpat University as a well reputed State Private University established through the Government of Gujarat State Legislative Act No.19/2005 on April 12, 2005, and recognized by the UGC under the section 2(f) of the UGC Act, 1956, having a campus which spread over more than 300 acres of land with world class infrastructure and more than 10,000 students on campus. In consideration of its contribution to education in a short period of time, the university has been given Permanent Membership of Association of Indian Universities (AIU), New Delhi, besides having a membership from Association of Commonwealth Universities (ACU), UK, and International Association of Universities (IAU), France. Ganpat University offers various unique, quality, industry-linked and sector-focused Diploma, Undergraduate, Postgraduate and Research level programs (professional and non-professional) in the field of Engineering, Management, Computer Applications, Pharmacy, Sciences, Commerce & Social Science, Architecture, Design & Planning, Maritime Studies, Law, etc.

In a nutshell, the conference was full of fruitful discussions, igniting the spirit of research. It was indeed a remarkable, memorable, and knowledgeable virtual conference. The success of this COMS2 conference edition means that planning can now proceed with confidence for the Second International Conference on Computing Science, Communication and Security (COMS2 2021) scheduled for February 2021 at Ganpat University, India.

March 2020

Nirbhay Chaubey
Satyen Parikh
Kiran Amin

Organization

Scientific Committee

Ganpatbhai Patel (Patron-in-Chief & President)	Ganpat University, India
Mahendra Sharma (Pro-chancellor)	Ganpat University, India
Rakesh Patel (Pro-vice Chancellor)	Ganpat University, India
Amit Patel (Pro-vice Chancellor)	Ganpat University, India
Rajen Purohit	Ganpat University, India
Akshai Aggarwal	University of Windsor, Canada
Shri. A. R. Dasgupta (Retd Dy Director)	Space Application Centre, ISRO, India
Rajkumar Buyya	The University of Melbourne, Australia
K. S. Dasgupta	DAIICT, India
Dipak Mathur	IEEE Asia Pacific Region 10
Sartaj Sahni	University of Florida, USA
Kevin Dami	University of Detroit, USA
Mohammed Atiquzzaman	University of Oklahoma, USA
Om Prakash Vyas	IIIT, Allahabad, India
Kiran Amin	Ganpat University, India
Satyen Parikh	Ganpat University, India
Hemal Shah	Ganpat University, India
Nirbhay Chaubey	Ganpat University, India
Rakesh D. Vanzara	Ganpat University, India
Girish Patel	Ganpat University, India
Hamid R. Arabnia	University of Georgia, USA
Bala Natarajan	Kansas State University, USA
Sanjay Madria	Missouri University of Science and Technology, USA
Arvind Shah	Georgia Southwestern State University, USA
P. Balasubramanian	Nanyang Technological University, Singapore
Rutvij H. Jhaveri	Pandit Deendayal Petroleum University, India
Sabu M. Thampi	IIITM-K, India
Shyam Iyer	Dell EMC, USA
Virendra C. Bhavsar	University of New Brunswick, Canada
Xing Liu	Kwantlen Polytechnic University, Canada
G. Sahoo	Birla Institute of Technology, India
Savita R. Gandhi	Gujarat University, India

Sabyasachi Chakraborty	Inje University, South Korea
Ammar Muthanna	Saint Petersburg State University of Telecommunications, Russia
Gua Xiangfa	National University of Singapore, Singapore
Ashraf A. M. Khalaf	Minia University, Egypt
Pahlaj Moolio	Pannasastra University of Cambodia, Cambodia
Mudassir Khan	King Khalid University, Saudi Arabia
Lal Bihari Barik	King Abdulaziz University, Saudi Arabia
Ahmed M. Elmisery	Waterford Institute of Technology, Ireland
Moharram Challenger	University of Antwerp, Belgium
Dimiter G. Velev	University of National and World Economy, Bulgaria
Tran Cong Hung	Posts and Telecommunication Institute of Technology, Vietnam
Anand Nayyar	Duy Tan University, Vietnam
Pao-Ann Hsiung	National Chung Cheng University, Taiwan
Seyyed Ahmad Edalatpanah	Ayandegan Institute of Higher Education, Iran
Aws Zuheer Yonis	Ninevah University, Iraq
Moharram Challenger	International Computer Institute at Ege University, Turkey
Noor Zaman Jhanjhi	Taylor's University, Malaysia
Irdayanti Mat Nashir	Universiti Pendidikan Sultan Idris, Malaysia
Jing Rui Tang	Universiti Sains Malaysia, Malaysia
Jing Rui Tang	Universiti Pendidikan Sultan Idris, Malaysia
Zaliza Hanapi	Universiti Pendidikan Sultan Idris, Malaysia
Encik Ong Jia Hui	Tunku Abdul Rahman University College, Malaysia
Muhammad Asif Khan	Qatar University, Qatar
Sandeep Kautish	LBEF CAMPUS, Nepal
Amrita Mishra	IIIT, Naya Raipur, India
Amit Kumar Gupta	DRDO, Hyderbad, India
Satyabrata Jit	IIT (BHU), India
Pratik Chattopadhyay	IIT (BHU), India
Amrita Chaturvedi	IIT (BHU), India
Aruna Jain	Birla Institute of Technology, India
Sarang C. Dhongdi	BITS Pilani, India
Amit Kumar Singh	IIT (BHU), India
R. Kumar	SRM University, India
B. Ramachandran	SRM University, India
Iyyanki V. Muralikrishna	J.N. Technological University, India
Apurv Shah	M. S. University, India
Bhushan Trivedi	GLS University, India
Manoj Kumar	Infliblnet University Grants Commission, India
U. Dinesh Kumar	IIM, Bangalore, India
Saurabh Bilgaiyan	KIIT, Deemed to be University, India
Raja Sarath Kumar Boddu	Jawaharlal Nehru Technological University, India
Kiran Sree Pokkuluri	SVECM, India
Devesh Kumar Srivastava	Manipal University, India

P. Muthulakshmi	SRM University, India
R. Anandan	VELS Pallavaram, India
Amol Dhondse	IBM India Software Labs, India
R. Amirtharajan	SASTRA Deemed University, India
Deepak H. Sharma	K. J. Somaiya College of Engineering, India
Padma Priya V.	SASTRA Deemed University, India
Ravi Subban	Pondicherry University, India
Parameshachari B. D.	Visvesvaraya Technological University, India
Rakhee	Jawaharlal Nehru Technological University, India
Nilakshi Jain	University of Mumbai, India
Archana Mire	University of Mumbai, India
Sonali Bhutad	University of Mumbai, India
Anand Kumar	Visvesvaraya Technological University, India
Jyoti Pareek	Gujarat University, India
Sanjay Garg	Nirma University, India
S. D. Panchal	Gujarat Technological University, India
Madhuri Bhavsar	Nirma University, India
Vijay Ukani	Nirma University, India
Mayur Vegad	Gujarat Technological University, India
N. M. Patel	Gujarat Technological University, India
J. M. Rathod	Gujarat Technological University, India
Maulika Patel	Gujarat Technological University, India
Nikhil Gondalia	Gujarat Technological University, India
Priyanka Sharma	Raksha Shakti University, India
Digvijaysinh Rathod	Gujarat Forensic Science University, India
Kalpesh Parikh	Intellisense IT, India
Balaji Rajendran	CDAC, Bangaluru, India
Mehul C. Parikh	Gujarat Technological University, India
G. R. Kulkarni	Gujarat Technological University, India
Snehal Joshi	Veer Narmad South Gujarat University, India
Ambika Nagaraj	Bengaluru Central University, India
Amol C. Adamuthe	Shivaji University, India
Shrihari Khatawkar	Shivaji University Kolhapur, India
Ashok Solanki	Veer Narmad South Gujarat University, India
Aditya Sinha	CDAC, Pune, India
Harshal Arolkar	GLS University, India
Binod Kumar	University of Pune, India
Maulin Joshi	Gujarat Technological University, India
Vrushank Shah	Indus University, India
Manish Patel	Gujarat Technological University, India
Ankit Bhavsar	GLS University, India
Seema Mahajan	Indus University, India
S. K. Vij	ITM University, India
Vishal Jain	BVICAM, New Delhi, India
D. B. Choksi	Sardar Patel University, India
Paresh Virpariya	Sardar Patel University, India

Priti Srinivas Sajja	Sardar Patel University, India
C. K. Bhensdadia	Dharmsinh Desai University, India
Vipul K. Dabhi	Dharmsinh Desai University, India
N. J. Kothari	Dharmsinh Desai University, India
Narayan Joshi	Dharmsinh Desai University, India
M. T. Savaliya	Gujarat Technological University, India
Vinod Desai	Gujarat Vidyapith, India
Himanshu Patel	Babasaheb Ambedkar Open University, India
Chhaya Patel	Gujarat Technological University, India
Jignesh Doshi	Gujarat Technological University, India
Bhaveshkumar Prajapati	Gujarat Technological University, India
Nisha A. Somani	Gujarat Technological University, India
Desai Archana Natvarbhai	Gujarat Technological University, India
Akhilesh Ladha	Nirma University, India
Jaymin K. Bhalani	Gujarat Technological University, India
Ashok Jetawat	Motivational Society of Achievers, India
Jeegar Trivedi	Sardar Patel University, India

Organizing Committee

Paresh M. Solanki	Ganpat University, India
Ajay Patel	Ganpat University, India
Ketan Patel	Ganpat University, India
Pravesh Patel	Ganpat University, India
Savan Patel	Ganpat University, India
Jigna Prajapati	Ganpat University, India
Keyur Jani	Ganpat University, India
Ketan Sarvakar	Ganpat University, India
Chirag Gami	Ganpat University, India
Ravindra Modi	Ganpat University, India
Sweta A. Dargad	Ganpat University, India

Contents

Network, Communication and Security

Computing Science

Artificial Intelligence and Machine Learning

Applications of Classical and Deep Learning Techniques for Polar Bear Detection and Recognition from Aero Photography

Mikhail A. Nakhatovich[1,2] (iD), Ilya Y. Surikov[1,2] (iD), Vladimir Chernook[3] (iD),
Natalia Chernook[3] (iD), and Daniil A. Savchuk[1,2(✉)] (iD)

[1] Peter the Great St. Petersburg Polytechnic University (SPbPU), Polytechnicheskaya 29,
195251 St. Petersburg, Russia
dsavchuk@itsociety.su
[2] ITSociety LTD, Diagonalnaya 4-1-170, 194100 St. Petersburg, Russia
[3] Autonomous Non-Commercial Organization «Ecological Center «ECOFACTOR», 11/1-10 N
Neyshlotskiy Lane, 194044 St. Petersburg, Russia

Abstract. The problem of detecting polar bears on the image taken from the plane is essential for ecologists who are tracking the disappearing population of the arctic inhabitants. The main challenge for this problem is to detect the white bear on the white ice. This paper covers the approaches which have shown valuable results for contrast objects captured from the plane, like cars, ships, and many others, instead of the polar bears that look blurry on the ice. However, the introduced approach based on both statistical and machine learning methods made it possible to build a tool that increases the semi-automatic bear detection rate a dozen times. The source data consists of 7360 × 4912 px aerial images, each image covering about the 21600 sq.m. of ice. On average, only one bear appears on every 1000 photos. The best-fit parameters for the solution gave a result of about 100% by recall metric and 51% by precision metric. The main strength of this solution is that it allows for finding almost all bears with a moderate amount of false-positive detections.

Keywords: Polar bear detection · Image processing · Deep machine learning · Transfer learning · Object detection · Augmentation

1 Introduction

A polar bear is at the top of the trophic pyramid in the Arctic and is an integral indicator of the state of the entire Arctic ecosystem. Therefore, regular instrumental monitoring of the polar bear population is outstandingly important. The main parameters of the population's state are the number and distribution of animals that can be obtained during regular aerial surveys. The main problem of detecting polar bears in aerial photography is the masking color and peculiar heat-protective fur, which makes these animals poorly visible in photos and IR images. After accounting flights, specialists have to process hundreds of thousands of aerial photographs manually, and the processing lasts for years.

© Springer Nature Singapore Pte Ltd. 2020
N. Chaubey et al. (Eds.): COMS2 2020, CCIS 1235, pp. 3–15, 2020.
https://doi.org/10.1007/978-981-15-6648-6_1

The distribution density of polar bears in the spring on ice is low, and, as a rule, just one bear (sometimes with cubs) appears in several thousand of the processed photographs. Given such a low density, it is critical not to miss a single picture with polar bears.

The problem of detecting polar bears on images taken from a plane is an object detection task in aerial images. The detection of an object in aerial photography is complicated since objects in aerial photographs are tiny. Also, the light conditions such as the angle of observation, camera settings, fog, and daylight conditions are essentially affecting factors that could be detected in aerial photography. Finally, the main difficulty of the task is that the color of the object almost matches the background color.

The automatic recognition system (ROI generation system) is performed in this work and based on a combination of statistical methods in a row with machine learning, which allowed to achieve high accuracy with a small training dataset. An additional complication of the task was that no bear should have been lost, so machine learning models must have about 100% recall metric.

The main objective of this paper is to describe an approach that uses the combination of classic computer vision methods and deep learning to enhance the overall result.

1.1 Previous Work

The existing solutions that provide the automatic location of objects in aerial photographs can be divided into three categories, which are distinguished by the use of deep learning. Methods from the first category [1–6] are based on statistical computer vision methods and basic machine learning algorithms. The main idea is to get the segmentation of possible candidates, and then clarify the result (refine the boundary of the desired object) using classic computer vision methods. For example, in work [2], mean-shift clustering is used for segmentation and a circle-frequency filter for filtering. The problem with such approaches is that they show low accuracy and hardly ever used in their pure form today.

The second category of methods uses deep learning. Deep learning has shown remarkable successes in image recognition in recent years. Convolutional neural networks (CNNs) have been successfully applied in the field of object detection in aerial photographs [7–10, 12]. The resolution of aerial photographs can reach 10000×10000 pixels, which prevents the use of a neural network for the entire image at once. Therefore, for sufficiently large images, sliding windows are used to obtain lower resolution images without loss of information. Object detection architectures can be divided into two categories: single-stage and two-stage. The difference is that two-stages architectures (Region-based) firstly classify potential objects into two classes: foreground and background. Hence, such models have lower performance but higher scores [11]. In paper [12] Faster R-CNN [13] and Yolo [14] architectures are compared on a car detection from aerial photographs task. A modified version of Faster R-CNN was applied in [8] for detecting vehicles. The rotation-invariant CNN model was introduced in [9]. An additional rotation-invariant layer applied to AlexNet made it better in the performance of object detection.

Finally, the third group of methods uses classic computer vision algorithms in a row with deep learning models, namely CNN. There are two main ideas across this group. The first idea is to extract the feature map from the image using CNN and then, based on the obtained map, define object class using classic machine learning algorithms. In paper [15], AlexNet is used for feature extraction and SVM for classification. The second idea is quite similar to the idea of the statistical methods, but CNN is used to clarify if the object belongs to the desired class. In this paper, statistical analysis is used to propose regions of interest (ROIs), and CNN is used as the classifier of the proposed region.

2 The Input Data

The aerial survey of polar bears was carried out in the Russian part of the Chukchi Sea from April 18 to May 18, 2016. The survey was performed from a flight altitude of 250 m, during the daytime, mainly between 10- and 17-h local time. The dataset consists of 30 thousand high-resolution (7360 × 4912 px) photographs of the iced sea surface. Each image covers an area of 180 × 120 m. Illumination of the ice surface changed depending on the height of the sun and on the weather (sun, cloudiness, haze, fog). The example of the input image is presented in Fig. 1.

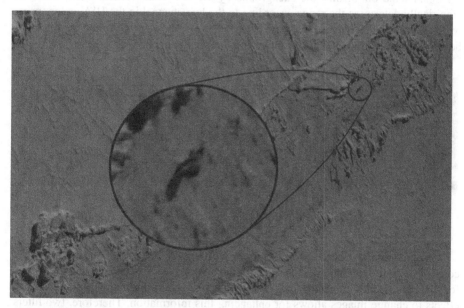

Fig. 1. A quarter of the input data example. A bear is only 50 × 50 px.

Since the density of the bears is usually low (one bear per 30–70 km of flight), 30 photographs with polar bears detected during the preliminary manual data processing were used for the train the neural network.

3 General Approach

The pipeline for image processing consists of several steps was developed. The main requirement for the pipeline was to add new steps easily or modifying existing ones. A scheme of the pipeline is presented in Fig. 2.

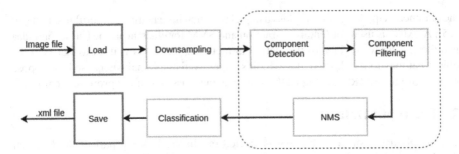

Fig. 2. Image processing pipeline.

In the first step, the image is compressed to a resolution two times smaller than the original. The compression allows for increasing the speed of image processing without losing important information.

Bears stand out against the background by the hue value. Hence, it is possible to empirically determine the range according to the hue channel in the HSV color space, which contains the color value of the bears. Figure 3 shows an example in which the bear is separated from the background using the hue channel.

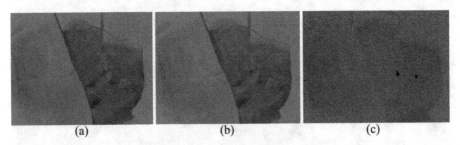

Fig. 3. (a) RGB image; (b) HSV Value channel image; (c) HSV Hue channel

On some images, some conditions make it difficult to determine a bear only by the color of its coat. For example, the sun shines from the back of the bear; the bear is in a fog. The fur visually turns gray, but it still contains useful information. Using standard effects to change images allows for enhancing this information. Therefore, two filters are applied to the original image:

1. "Light" filter: increased gamma correction, contrast, brightness, saturation, light, and sharpen.
2. "Sharp" filter: increased saturation and sharpen.

For each of the filters, a range on the hue channel can be determined. The examples are provided in Fig. 4. In images with the bear heavily lit by the sun, the snow around the bear also acquires a yellowish tint, which interferes with the correct segmentation by color. To avoid this, in addition to the hue range, the value range filter in the HSV color space is applied:

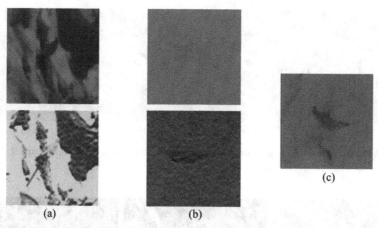

Fig. 4. Examples of images with bad weather conditions and effects allowing to highlight bear: (a) bear in shadow – "light" filter; (b) bear in fog – "sharp" filter; (c) normal image – default params

The result of segmentation is a map of ROIs – a black-and-white image on which areas of potential bears are marked in white (Fig. 6(b)).

The connected components of the image are found using the result of the previous step. The next step is to filter the found areas. Since the flight altitude is constant, the size of the bears does not significantly differ in aerial photographs. Therefore, the filtering of connected components is based on their size and shape. While components processing, next filters are applied to recline noises:

– component area;
– an aspect ratio of the rectangle built around component;
– component occupancy inside rectangle;

Adaptive Gaussian thresholding [16] is performed inside each rectangle on the grayscale, hue, and blue channels (Fig. 5). Next, for each channel, the percentage of black inside the rectangle is checked. If the value is out of an empirically selected range, it is discarded as noise. Thus, such noises as part of a block of snow or a highly illuminated surface are reclined. Figure 6 (c) illustrates the result of the component filtration.

The filtering result is a set of ROIs, which are the possible locations of bears. After filtering, detection results on three images (original and with filters) are combined, and the non-maximum suppression (NMS) technique is applied to unite the intersecting regions.

However, there are landscapes with objects that cannot be distinguished from bears based on the previously mentioned signs. A CNN-based classifier is used to eliminate them.

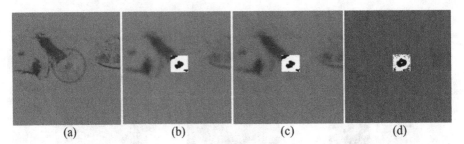

Fig. 5. Adaptive binarization: (a) source image; (b) blue channel; (c) grayscale channel; (d) hue channel.

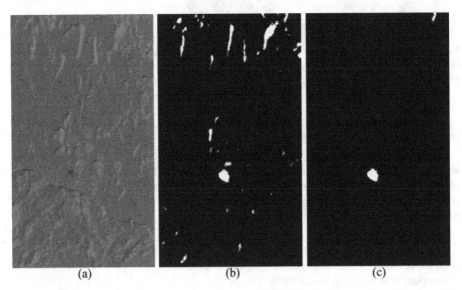

Fig. 6. Image processing stages: (a) source image; (b) ROIs after component detection; (c) component filtration result

3.1 Dataset

From the original image, 128 × 128 squares were cut for training the classifier. Some of them contain bears, while others are the ice surface (noise). As clippings of noise were selected, those areas that were segmented as bears after applying statistical methods.

Since the number of bears in the pictures is tiny, we had to deal with imbalanced classes dataset. Moreover, the task is complicated by the fact that the recall rate for bears must be as higher as possible since each bear is crucial for estimating the population density.

Ordinary augmentation, such as rotations and flips was not enough to achieve the necessary results, so we have expanded our dataset using simple method: for each bear, several images were added to the dataset, in which the bear was in different parts of the image (in the center, at the corners), as well as all kinds of rotations of these images. An example of various instances presented in the dataset for one bear is shown in Fig. 7. Such a method allows increasing precision metric by 0.39 compared with ordinary augmentation.

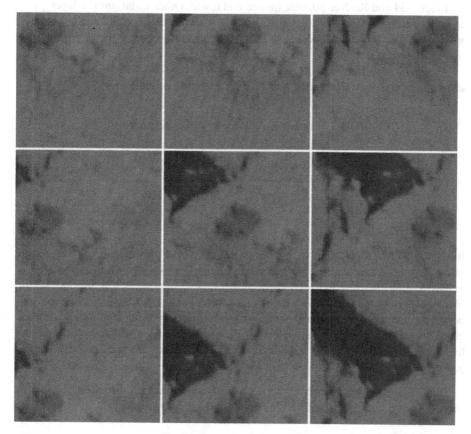

Fig. 7. Augmentation example.

Thereby, a training classification dataset consists of 4320 images: 2160 of them are augmented bears, other – noises of various types.

The test dataset for classification contains 1152 images, of which 576 are augmented 8 test bears. The best results are presented as the best shot from cross-validation over all possible permutations of given bears with 8 bears taken as a validation base set. The cross-validation showed results are closely distributed from one to another run with general fluctuation, not more than 3% in Recall and 15% in Precision.

3.2 Classification

ResNet. The first method of bears classification, which was tried in the course of research is Residual Network (ResNet) [17] – a state-of-the-art neural network used as a backbone for many computer vision tasks. It is pre-trained on the ImageNet dataset, so training this model even on an own small dataset can lead to good results. The output layer of this network was replaced to perform the task of one-class classification.

ResNet-34 and ResNet-50 were trained and tested. Other variations (18 layers, 101 layers) have shown worse results. The results of classification on train and test dataset are presented in Table 1. Models have been trained for 100 epochs; the best result was chosen from each training.

As can be seen from Table 1, ResNet-50 showed better results. Using this method allows throwing away most of the noise, while not losing a single bear.

Table 1. Comparison of using ResNet architectures.

	Recall	Precision
ResNet-34	1	0.273
ResNet-50	**1**	**0.419**

ResNet + SVM. In addition to the use of ResNet as the classifier, it can be used to extract features from the image. Then classic machine learning algorithms can be applied to classify objects using image features. One of these algorithms is a Support Vector Machine algorithm [18, 19] with the regularization parameter C, which compromises between correctness on a training set and maximization of the decision function's margin. This algorithm was chosen as one of the classic methods which are effective in high dimensional spaces. The params for SVM were chosen empirically: RBF kernel, gamma = 1/n_features, C = 1.0.

Table 2 shows the comparison between ResNet pre-trained on ImageNet and pre-trained ResNet with additional training on the collected dataset.

Table 2. Comparison of using ResNet architectures with SVM.

	Recall	Precision
Pre-trained ResNet-34 + SVM	0.778	0.055
Pre-trained ResNet-50 + SVM	0.806	0.071
Trained ResNet-34 + SVM	1	0.424
Trained ResNet-50 + SVM	**1**	**0.507**

Faster R-CNN. The other way to classify bear on the image is to try to detect them using CNN. If the model finds a bear on the ROI, then it is classified as a bear. Pre-trained on ImageNet dataset Faster R-CNN was chosen as one of the most widely used state-of-the-art architecture, which shows high accuracy even when training on a small dataset.

Two training approaches have been tested: one-class object detection (only bears) and two-classes (bears and noise). It turned out that training on two-classes object detection performs better. The results are provided in Table 3.

Table 3. Comparison of using Faster R-CNN with different numbers of classes.

	Recall	Precision
Faster R-CNN one-class	1	0.234
Faster R-CNN two-class	**1**	**0.456**

2 VAE+SSIM. The idea of using several Variational Autoencoders (VAEs) for classification task was proposed in [20]. The main idea is to exploit the primary objective of VAE (generation) for classification. For each class, VAE is trained in an unsupervised way. Then to find out which of the classes the object belongs to, the image is passed through every trained VAE, and then the SSIM index is calculated between input and output. The classifier operation scheme is presented in Fig. 8. The class whose VAE showed the best generation result (the largest SSIM index) is the class of the object. The process repeats 5 times to improve the prediction, and then the class that is chosen more times is selected as a predicted class.

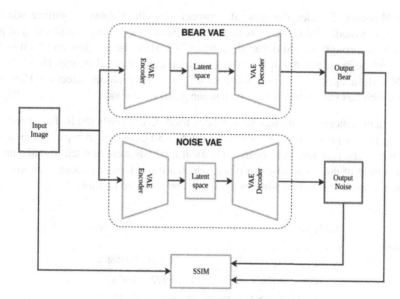

Fig. 8. 2 VAE approach scheme.

Two VAE were trained for polar bear detection task: one for bear generation, and one for noise. Figure 9 shows the autoencoders' results. It can be seen that the autoencoder trained on bears generate output looks like a bear at the bear as the input while output from noise does not seem like a bear. However, not all the images are handled well. In most cases, the region with the noise is not so different from the region with the bear. So, the output from the VAE trained on bears is quite similar to the input noise.

The training metrics for this approach are presented in Table 5.

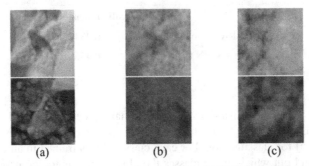

Fig. 9. Autoencoders results: (a) input region; (b) result of VAE trained on bears; (c) result of VAE trained on noises.

Thus, several approaches were tested for the classification task. ResNet-50 pre-trained on ImageNet and trained on the own dataset has shown the best result.

Sliding Window. Besides the general approach described above, a sliding window method was tested. The key idea is to put a 'window' on an image and run that part of the image through trained object detection CNN, slide the window and do it again. It is one of the most popular ways to process high-quality aerial images [8, 9]. Faster R-CNN with Inception v2 has been chosen as a model for object detection. However, this approach has shown worse results than the general approach.

Also, a modification with ResNet has been tried. Every predicted by Faster R-CNN bounding box is passed through a trained ResNet-50 classifier to reject some noises which have been recognized as bears. Statistical methods were applied to make up the dataset consist of noises of different types, which are similar in characteristics to bears.

The results of the sliding window approach are provided in Table 4.

Table 4. Comparison of sliding window methods results.

	Recall	Precision
Faster R-CNN	0.972	0.076
Faster R-CNN + ResNet50	**0.972**	**0.271**

4 Experiments

4.1 Performance

The developed approach has shown the ability to process the input data and find bears almost without lossless. Due to a large amount of data that needs to be processed, the performance of the trained model is an important issue while using an approach to investigate the ecological state during the plane expedition. The developed method should be able to process the 20 000 source images for 8 h on average using three laptops in parallel. 8 h is the time between possible arctic daytime flights. Table 5 provides the comparison of the mean image process time (including all steps of the pipeline). Computer params: Intel Core i5-8400, GeForce GTX 1080 Ti, and 16 GB RAM.

The system allows the assessor to look through the data ten times faster and more accurately when the exact number of bears needed. This statement has been tested with an independent group of 5 experts, who tried to find 3 bears on 100 photos with and without our approach that point assessor to the place in the image where bear possible could be. All experts have never seen the dataset even before.

4.2 Accuracy

Precision and Recall were chosen as the primary metrics for the validation of our approach. The Precision and Recall of a predicted set of bears' and a set of real bears' are calculated as:

$$Precision = \frac{TP}{TP + FP}; Recall = \frac{TP}{TP + FN} \tag{1}$$

where TP are the true positives, FP - false positives, and FN - false negatives. Precision shows how many selected items are relevant, and Recall shows how many relevant items are selected.

Table 5 shows a comparison of the best results of using different methods for the classification of ROIs and the mean computational time T.

Table 5. Comparison of classification best results.

	Recall	Precision	<T > , sec.
Without classification	1	0.015	3.81
ResNet-50	1	0.419	3.86
Trained ResNet-50 + SVM	**1**	**0.507**	**3.90**
Faster R-CNN two-class	1	0.456	5.81
2 VAE + SSIM	1	0.041	4.32
Sliding window (Faster R-CNN + ResNet50)	0.972	0.271	4.36

Analyzing Table 5, it was concluded that the ResNet-50 + SVM method shows the best ratio of accuracy and speed. However, other methods tested are also applicable for solving the desired problem, although more regions with ice are detected as bears (Precision metric is lower). Table 6 provides the results for each step of the pipeline for the best method.

Table 6. Number of ROIs after each stage.

Stage	Number of ROIs
Component detection	1151849
Component filtering	2902
NMS	2425
Classification with the best method	71

5   Conclusions

The approach developed has shown the ability to be used as a reliable helper for counting and locating the polar bear appearances on aerial photography.

A lot of general techniques have been tried with valuable customizations developed. The best results with a 100% recall metric and a 51% precision metric have been shown by pipeline, including statistical ROI preparation step finalized with Trained ResNet-50 as feature extractor and SVM as classifier. The best approach shows the appropriate performance of 3.9 s on average for each photo, which makes it possible to use the method for performing calculations of 20 000 photos in 8 h (by three portable workstations) between flight sessions to collect statistics for correcting future flights.

The roadmap of this solution is to collect more data containing bears and incrementally increase the accuracy of the model and finally build a fully automatic tool for bear detection. To further improve the results on this task, it is recommended to speed up the ROI search algorithm. Most of the time, the system takes to process three images (2 filters and the original), so it would be better to find a filter that is universal for all cases, which allows you to process one image instead of three.

References

1. An, Z., Shi, Z., Teng, X., Yu, X., Tang, W.: An automated airplane detection system for large panchromatic image with high spatial resolution. Optik – Int. J. Light Electron Opt. **125**(12), 2768–2775 (2014)
2. Bo, S., Jing, Y.: Region-based airplane detection in remotely sensed imagery. In: 3rd International Congress on Image and Signal Processing, pp. 1923–1926 (2010)
3. Cai, H., Su, Y.: Airplane detection in remote sensing image with a circle-frequency filter. In: International Conference on Space Information Technology, p. 59852T (2005)
4. Moranduzzo, T., Melgani, F.: Automatic car counting method for unmanned aerial vehicle images. IEEE Trans. Geosci. Remote Sens. (TGRS) **52**(3), 1635–1647 (2014)

5. Yu, X., Shi, Z.: Vehicle detection in remote sensing imagery based on salient information and local shape feature. Optik – Int. J. Light Electron Opt. **126**(20), 2485–2490 (2015)
6. Shi, Z., Yu, X., Jiang, Z., Li, B.: Ship detection in high-resolution optical imagery based on anomaly detector and local shape feature. IEEE Trans. Geosci. Remote Sens. (TGRS) **52**(8), 4511–4523 (2014)
7. Li, K., Cheng, G., Bu, S., You, X.: Rotation-insensitive and context-augmented object detection in remote sensing images. IEEE Trans. Geosci. Remote Sens. (TGRS) **56**(4), 2337–2348 (2018)
8. Tang, T., Zhou, S., Deng, Z., Zou, H., Lei, L.: Vehicle detection in aerial images based on region convolutional neural networks and hard negative example mining. Sensors (Basel, Switzerland) **17**(2), 336 (2017)
9. Cheng, G., Zhou, P., Han, J.: Learning rotation-invariant convolutional neural networks for object detection in VHR optical remote sensing images. IEEE Trans. Geosci. Remote Sens. (TGRS) **54**(12), 7405–7415 (2016)
10. Tayara, H., Chong, K.T.: Object detection in very high-resolution aerial images using one-stage densely connected feature pyramid network. Sensors (Basel, Switzerland) **18**(10), 3341 (2018)
11. Huang, J., et al.: Speed/accuracy trade-offs for modern convolutional object detectors. In: IEEE Conference on Computer Vision and Pattern Recognition (CVPR), pp. 3296–3297 (2017)
12. Aerial Images Processing for Car Detection using Convolutional Neural Networks: Comparison between Faster R-CNN and YoloV3. https://arxiv.org/abs/1910.07234. Accessed 29 Dec 2019
13. Ren, S., He, K., Girshick, R., Sun, J.: Faster R-CNN: towards real-time object detection with region proposal networks. IEEE Trans. Pattern Anal. Mach. Intell. (TPAMI) **39**(6), 1137–1149 (2017)
14. Redmon, J., Divvala, S., Girshick, R., Farhadi, A.: You only look once: unified, real-time object detection. In: IEEE Conference on Computer Vision and Pattern Recognition (CVPR), pp. 779–788 (2016)
15. Wang, Y., Wang, A., Hu, C.: A novel airplane detection algorithm based on deep CNN. In: Zhou, Q., Gan, Y., Jing, W., Song, X., Wang, Y., Lu, Z. (eds.) ICPCSEE 2018. CCIS, vol. 901, pp. 721–728. Springer, Singapore (2018). https://doi.org/10.1007/978-981-13-2203-7_60
16. Wang, Y., Fang, B., Lan, L., Luo, H., Tang, Y.: Adaptive binarization: a new approach to license plate characters segmentation. In: International Conference on Wavelet Analysis and Pattern Recognition, pp. 91–99 (2012)
17. He, K., Zhang, X., Ren, S., Sun, J.: Deep residual learning for image recognition. In: IEEE Conference on Computer Vision and Pattern Recognition (CVPR), pp. 770–778 (2016)
18. Cortes, C., Vapnik, V.: Support-vector networks. Mach. Learn. **20**(3), 273–297 (1995)
19. Evgeniou, T., Pontil, M.: Support vector machines: theory and applications. In: Paliouras, G., Karkaletsis, V., Spyropoulos, C.D. (eds.) ACAI 1999. LNCS (LNAI), vol. 2049, pp. 249–257. Springer, Heidelberg (2001). https://doi.org/10.1007/3-540-44673-7_12
20. Rezaeifar, S., Taran, O., Voloshynovskiy, S.: Classification by re-generation: towards classification based on variational inference. In: 26th European Signal Processing Conference (EUSIPCO), pp. 2005–2009 (2018)

Floor Plan Recognition and Vectorization Using Combination UNet, Faster-RCNN, Statistical Component Analysis and Ramer-Douglas-Peucker

Ilya Y. Surikov[1,2] ⓘ, Mikhail A. Nakhatovich[1,2] ⓘ, Sergey Y. Belyaev[1] ⓘ, and Daniil A. Savchuk[1,2(✉)] ⓘ

[1] Peter the Great St. Petersburg Polytechnic University (SPbPU), Polytechnicheskaya, 29, 195251 St. Petersburg, Russia
[2] ITSociety LTD, Diagonalnaya 4-1-170, 194100 St. Petersburg, Russia
dsavchuk@itsociety.su

Abstract. The floor plan recognition and vectorization problem from the image has a high market response due to the ability to be applied in such domains as design, automatic furniture fitting, property cost estimation, etc. Several approaches already exist on the market. Many of them are using just statistical or deep machine learning methods capable of recognizing a limited set of floor plan types or providing a semi-automatic tool for recognition. This paper introduces the approach based on the combination of statistical image processing methods in a row of machine learning techniques that allow training robust model for the different floor plan topologies. Faster R-CNN for the floor object detection with a mean average precision of 86% and UNet for the wall segmentation has shown the IoU metric results of about 99%. Both methods, combined with functional and component filtration, made it possible to implement the new approach for vectoring the floor plans.

Keywords: Floor plan analysis · Image processing · Deep machine learning · Transfer learning · Object detection · Augmentation

1 Introduction

The floor plan recognition and vectorization aim are to produce the standard vector format file (*.svg, *.dxf) describing the topology of the floor plan captured by the camera or by scan from the photo, print, or screenshot. Sometimes, especially for the old building – architecture documentation could be presented only in paper form, this is a problem for the digital property market. The method proposed in this paper allows recognizing and reconstructing the vector format of the floor plan that could be useful for 3D reconstruction, property price calculations, and design proposals, and so on. At the moment existed solution could be described as three following types:

© Springer Nature Singapore Pte Ltd. 2020
N. Chaubey et al. (Eds.): COMS2 2020, CCIS 1235, pp. 16–28, 2020.
https://doi.org/10.1007/978-981-15-6648-6_2

1. Manual.
2. Could be any vector tool like CorelDraw, AutoCAD.
3. Semi-automatic.
4. Making some preprocessing before the user could fix things manually. Have a bunch of drawbacks cause some complicated cases could probably save not so much time rather than Manual methods.
5. Automatic.
6. Methods that consume only the image and returning the vector output file. Nothing must be done manually.

Mostly all automatic solutions use only deep learning or only statistical methods applicate to specific cases or datasets with known image conditions and structure. The primary purpose of this paper is to describe an approach that uses the combination of methods like computer vision, computational geometry, statistical analysis, and deep learning to enhance the general result metrics and make an approach independent on which type of plan used and what image conditions were to predict.

Our main contributions are summarized as follows:

- We proposed the approach that allows us to recognize and vectorize floor plans of different topology and different image conditions with a better IoU indicator than presented in other papers.
- We have shown an approach of enlarging small dataset using back perspective transform with physical photography. This approach has shown an increase in 1.5% in the IoU indicator and allowed us to build the solution robust to shadows.

1.1 Previous Work

The introduction part of this paper has denoted that there are three general types of vectorization methods: manual, semi-automatic, and automatic.

The manual methods are usually general vector graphics software for developing the floor plan itself, for example, AutoCAD, CorelDraw, etc.

The investigated semi-automatic methods have many different approaches implementing the idea of the vectoring plan. Some methods used just for the preprocessing based on thresholding [1]. A bit more advanced methods starting from the thresholding and after this, switching to the edit mode, where the preserved object could be placed over the source image [2].

The essential type of methods in the context of this paper – is an automatic approach. One of the first published solutions for floor plan vectoring is based on statistical methods (blurred shape model, k-means, A*) [3]; the example result of vectoring depicted in Fig. 1.

Convolutional neural networks (CNNs) have been successfully applied in many fields, so as in the field of plan recognition. The wall segmentation approach [4] using the Fully-Convolutional Networks (FCN) shown the result of 89.9% by mean IoU metric. The example results presented in Fig. 2. As it could be observed, the best results have been achieved with FCN-2s. The approach in this paper is also based on CNN, and the UNet [5] has been chosen for this problem. It has a higher number of parameters than

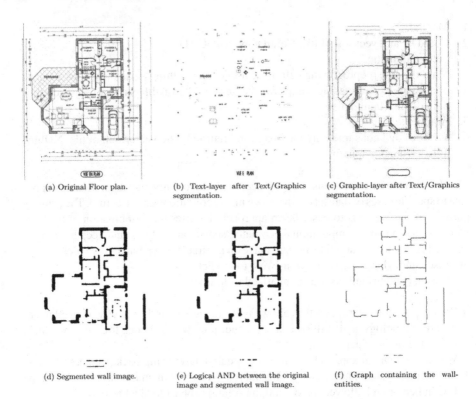

(a) Original Floor plan.

(b) Text-layer after Text/Graphics segmentation.

(c) Graphic-layer after Text/Graphics segmentation.

(d) Segmented wall image.

(e) Logical AND between the original image and segmented wall image.

(f) Graph containing the wall-entities.

Fig. 1. Complete flow of wall recognition process in [3] (Image from [3]).

FCN, but, shows better accuracy. The comparison between architectures on different datasets is presented in Table 3. Since the real-time solution of this problem is not the main goal, the performance of the neural network was not considered.

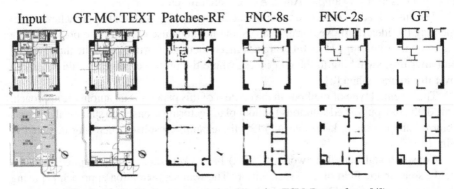

Fig. 2. Example plan segmentation [4], using FCN (Image from [4]).

The UNet architecture is used in [6] for door and wall recognition, but modified version U-Net+DCL, where the baseline UNet's deconvolution layers were replaced with a simplified version of pixel deconvolution layers for segmentation. The best result in the wall recognition task in this paper is 0.799 by mean IoU metric.

The object detection approach for filtering floor plan using Faster R-CNN [7] was applied in paper [8]. In this work, Faster R-CNN was chosen for object detection too since it shows high scores with fast convergence. They have achieved a mean average precision of 0.86, and a mean average recall of 0.92 on a dataset including 12 classes of objects.

2 The Floor Plan Datasets

The work has been performed for the specific type of plan named BTI (Bureau of Technical Inventarization), so 700 floor plan images have been collected from public real estate websites. The dataset consists mainly of scans, but private testing revealed that user input is usually a photo with different lighting conditions. An example of the user input is shown in Fig. 3.

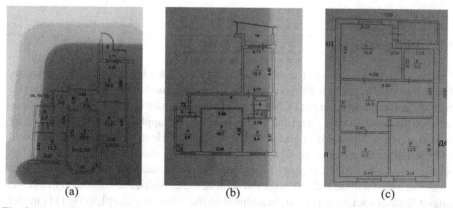

(a)   (b)   (c)

Fig. 3. Example of user input while private testing: (a) cascade shadow example; (b) sharp shadow border; (c) noised smooth shadow.

An approach based on inverse perspective transformation [9] was applied to build a model capable of recognizing floor plans in images with different lighting conditions, as well as to increase the number of images in the dataset. Some of the labeled plans were printed with ArUco markers from the OpenCV library [10] at a fixed distance from them. Each of the printed photos was captured 10 times in different viewpoints; an example of a photo is shown in Fig. 4(b). Markers are accurately detected by OpenCV function, so based on their coordinates, the perspective transformation matrix to the vertical plane is calculated. The layout of the original floor plan (Fig. 4(a)) is converted to the layout of the printed using an inverse matrix of the perspective transform. Then the image is cropped, and the markers are erased using the bilinear interpolation algorithm. An example of the result is presented in Fig. 4(c). Thereby, the dataset was increased to 2000 images.

Training on this expanded dataset made it possible to increase the accuracy of the IoU indicator by 3%, and to train a model resistant to shadows.

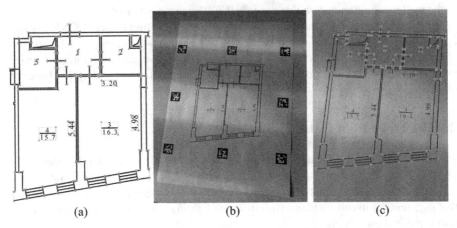

| (a) | (b) | (c) |

Fig. 4. (a) original image with labels; (b) photo; (c) the result of the transformation.

3   Architecture

2 neural networks were used for solving the problem: UNet for semantic segmentation. The U-Net architecture is built upon the Fully Convolutional Network (FCN), and the two main differences comparing to FCN are that UNet is symmetric and the skip connections between the downsampling path and the upsampling path apply a concatenation operator instead of a sum. These skip connections intend to provide local information to the global information while upsampling. The UNet architecture is used in this paper since it has been successfully applied to many image segmentation tasks, and it does not require a dataset of a dozen thousands of images to achieve high results. Pre-trained on ImageNet dataset ResNet backbone is used. In addition to the UNet, the DeepLab3+ [11] model was tested as one of the state-of-the-art models for image segmentation, but results turned out to be worse than the UNet ones. The results were compared using the Intersection over Union (1).

As a model for object detection, pre-trained on ImageNet dataset Faster R-CNN was chosen as one of the most widely used state-of-the-art architecture, which shows high accuracy even when training on a small dataset. It uses Region Proposal Network (RPN) to reduce computational time and make a good accuracy as their predecessor method. Faster R-CNN spread out in many pieces of research in object detection [12–14].

4   General Approach

The pipeline for image processing consists of several steps was developed. The main requirement for the pipeline was to add new steps easily or modifying existing ones. A scheme of the pipeline is presented in Fig. 5.

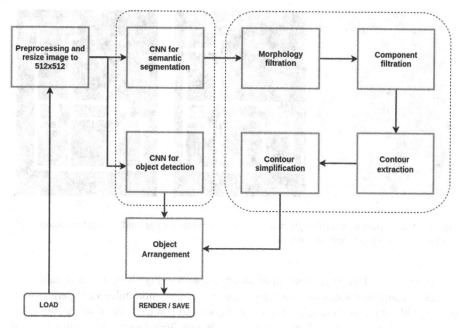

Fig. 5. Image processing pipeline.

The trained neural network consumes 512×512 RGB images as an input. In the first step, the image is resized from the original shape to the desired one. If the image is larger than required, compression is performed so that the bigger side has a length of 512. After that, the image is supplemented to shape 512×512. To avoid the appearance of image borders, next algorithm to blur the edges was applied to each of the smaller sides:

Algorithm 1. Removing image borders

Inputs: source I - image size m, n

Outputs: image 512x512 free of noize near the border

```
1:   I←scaled(I,512 / max(m,n)) #scaling
2:   w ←(max(m,n)- min(m,n)) / 2 #width of strip
3:   I[0:w] ← AVG(I[w]) #extrapolation of empty space up to
     512x512
4:   I[m - w: m] ← AVG(I[m-w])
5:   blur_w ← 10
6:   I[w-10:w+10] ← blur(I[w-10:w+10])#removing border
7:   I[m-w-10:m-w+10] ←blur(I[m-w-10:m-w+10])
```

This method avoids the appearance of artifacts near the border in segmentation results, as shown in Fig. 6.

If the original image is smaller than required, the same algorithm is applied but using upsampling. The scaling result is processed by two neural networks.

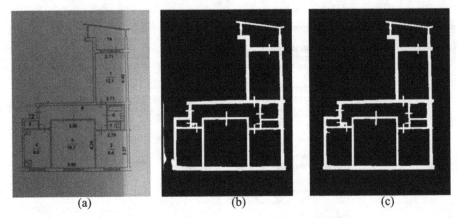

Fig. 6. (a) floor plan photo; (b) segmentation result for white background; (c) segmentation result for background with smoothed borders.

An example of the segmentation result can be seen in Fig. 7(b). It is noticeable that the result contains noise and little gaps in the walls. The morphological operations of erosion, dilatation, and closure with a 3×3 core and connectivity of 4th are used for eliminating this noise as well as inaccuracies. Figure 7(c) depicts the result of neural network pixel noise removal.

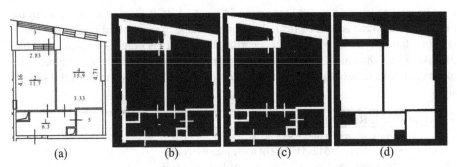

Fig. 7. (a) floor plan; (b) UNet segmentation result; (c) morphological filtration; (d) component filtration.

Based on the previous step, the connected components of the image are built and semantically representing the rooms. Morphological operations as above are applied to get rid of small defects at the border, such as part of a door segmented as a wall, but using scalable empirical constants depending on the size of the door, since it is standard and varies in small intervals of 600–1000 mm. Further, component filtration is used to remove connectivity components that are not rooms Fig. 7(d).

Based on the room components, an approximation of the components by the contours is used. Since the approximation is rough due to the pixelated source border, there is a need to simplify contours. So, Ramer – Douglas – Peucker algorithm is used [15] with the parameter $\varepsilon = 1.0$ (the parameter was selected empirically, with any increase contours are distorted on most images, with any decrease there are no changes in contours). The algorithm reduces the number of points in the contour, thereby removes steps at non-parallel walls and also rectifying the corners of rooms, as shown in Fig. 8.

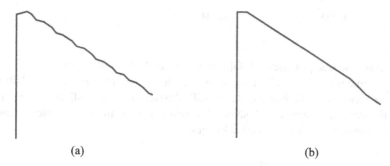

(a)   (b)

Fig. 8. (a) component contour; (b) simplification result using Ramer – Douglas – Peucker algorithm.

Using the obtained contours of the rooms (internal walls borders), as well as the borders of the external walls obtained at the segmentation stage, the 1px-wide middle line is found using the Thinning Algorithm [16]. Hereupon, the wall thickness could be found.

The result of simplified contours in a row with the result of object detection is used to arrange doors, windows, and other objects. Doors and windows are placed by the method of intersecting segments, so they become part of the wall. A K-D tree [17] is constructed for reducing the enumeration of segments when searching for intersections.

5 Experiments

5.1 Performance

The developed approach has shown the ability to process user input that does not correlate with the training data. The group of methods from start to result works for 2–3 s using the following configuration: Intel Core i5, GeForce GTX 1080Ti, and 16 GB RAM, which allows recognizing incoming plans in production environments without long delays.

5.2 Accuracy

The test set contains 300 different plans, both scans and photos. There were deep learning tasks: semantic segmentation and object detection. Table 1 shows the mean average precision (mAP) score [18] for object detection using Faster R-CNN.

Intersection over Union (IoU) with threshold = 0.7 was chosen as the main metric for the validation of the segmentation model. The IoU of a predicted set of wall pixels and a set of true wall pixels is calculated as:

$$IoU = \frac{TP}{TP + FP + FN} = \frac{|X \cap Y|}{|X| + |Y| - |X \cap Y|} \tag{1}$$

Table 1. Faster R-CNN mAP score at different IoU thresholds.

IoU threshold	mAP, collected dataset	mAP, collected dataset expanded with photography
0.5	0.852	0.860
0.75	0.735	0.744

where TP are the true positives, FP false positives, and FN false negatives.

As aforementioned, the UNet model is used for semantic segmentation. Different backbones were tried: ResNet-34, ResNet-50, ResNet-101. They all showed approximately the same accuracy, but ResNet-50 turned out to be the best. Table 2 shows a comparison of the results for these backbones.

Table 2. Comparison of different backbones for UNet.

	ResNet-34	ResNet-50	ResNet-101
IoU, test images	0.986	0.989	0.985

Model weights are updated using binary cross-entropy soft-dice loss (2) with dice weight (dw) = 0.7, where P - predicted, T – target:

$$BCESoftDiceLoss(P, T) = (1 - dw) * BCE(P, T) - dw * SoftDice(P, T) \quad (2)$$

Also were tried Lovasz loss [19] and a sum of losses (3), but unfortunately, it did not improve the results.

$$SummLoss = 0.8 * WBCE + SoftDice + Lovasz \quad (3)$$

The IoU metric obtained on the test set of source data presented in our dataset is presented in Table 3. The results of training on the public floor plan dataset [20] are also presented. The public dataset contains 5000 images with labels for segmentation; 1000 of them were used for training, 200 for validation, and 3800 for testing.

Table 3. IoU score for different neural network architectures.

	IoU, collected dataset	IoU, collected dataset expanded with photography	IoU, public dataset
FCN-2s	0.951	0.947	0.945
DeepLab3+	0.944	0.933	0.922
UNet	0.974	0.989	0.975

Examples of the recognition results of test images are presented in Fig. 9, while results from private testing are shown in Fig. 10.

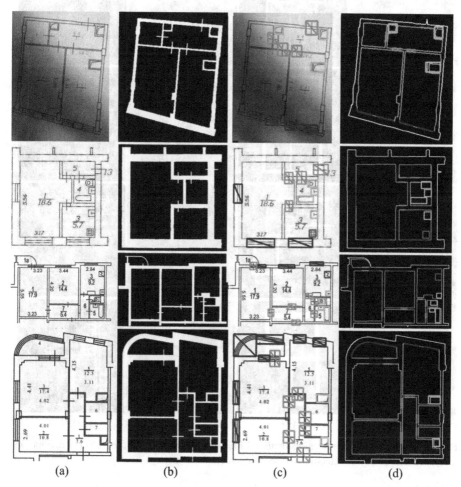

(a)   (b)   (c)   (d)

Fig. 9. Recognition system results on test images: (a) source image; (b) UNet segmentation; (c) Faster-RCNN object detection; (d) resulting vectorization.

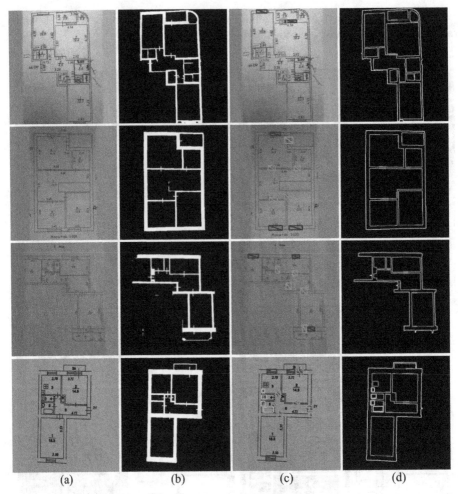

(a)   (b)   (c)   (d)

Fig. 10. Recognition system results on users' images: (a) source image; (b) UNet segmentation; (c) Faster-RCNN object detection; (d) resulting vectorization.

6   Conclusions

The developed approach allows recognizing and building vector representation for the floor plan using the combined methods of deep learning (semantic segmentation with UNet, object detection with Faster R-CNN) in a row with statistical methods (morphology, component filtration, and Ramer - Douglas - Peucker algorithm). The segmentation has shown an accuracy of about 99% by the IoU metric, while object detection has shown 86% by the mAP metric. Also, the dataset enlargement approach using a back-perspective transform was tested. This way of augmenting the dataset introduces natural spatial noise to the image that reduces risks of overfitting and allows make the processing algorithm more robust to shadows. The method developed performs the whole data processing for one input for about 2 s. It allows using this approach for cloud-based recognition systems or any other productive deployment.

References

1. PlanTracer. http://www.plantracer.ru. Accessed 26 Oct 2019
2. PlanCAD. System of automated design of floor plans https://sapr.ru/article/18006. Accessed 26 Oct 2019
3. de las Heras, L.-P., Ahmed, S., Liwicki, M., Valveny, E., Sánchez, G.: Statistical segmentation and structural recognition for floor plan interpretation. Int. J. Doc. Anal. Recogn. (IJDAR) **17**(3), 221–237 (2014). https://doi.org/10.1007/s10032-013-0215-2
4. Dodge, S., Xu, J., Stenger, B.: Parsing floor plan images. In: Fifteenth IAPR Conference on Machine Vision Applications (MVA) (2017)
5. Ronneberger, O., Fischer, P., Brox, T.: U-Net: convolutional networks for biomedical image segmentation. Comput. Res. Repository (2015)
6. Yang, J., Jang, H., Kim J.: Semantic Segmentation in architectural floor plans for detecting walls and doors. In: 2018 11th International Congress on Image and Signal Processing, BioMedical Engineering and Informatics (CISP-BMEI), Beijing, China, 2018, pp. 1–9 (2018). https://doi.org/10.1109/cisp-bmei.2018.8633243
7. Ren, S., He, K., Girshick, R., Sun, J.: Faster R-CNN: towards real-time object detection with region proposal networks. In: The IEEE Conference on Computer Vision and Pattern Recognition (CVPR) (2015)
8. Ziran, Z., Marinai, S.: Object Detection in Floor Plan Images. In: Pancioni, L., Schwenker, F., Trentin, E. (eds.) ANNPR 2018. LNCS (LNAI), vol. 11081, pp. 383–394. Springer, Cham (2018). https://doi.org/10.1007/978-3-319-99978-4_30
9. Borgefors, G.: Distance transformations in digital images. Comput. Vis. Graph. Image Process. **34**, 344–371 (1986)
10. OpenCV. https://opencv.org. Accessed 26 Oct 2019
11. Chen, L.-C., Zhu, Y., Papandreou, G., Schroff, F., Adam, H.: Encoder-decoder with atrous separable convolution for semantic image segmentation. In: The European Conference on Computer Vision (ECCV), pp. 801–818 (2018)
12. Zhu, B., Wu, X., Yang, L., Shen, Y., Wu, L: Automatic detection of books based on faster R-CNN. In: Third International Conference on Digital Information Processing, Data Mning, and Wireless Communication (DIPDMWC), pp. 8–12 (2016)
13. Zhang, H., Du, Y., Ning, S., Zhang, Y., Yang, S., Du, C.: Pedestrian detection method based on faster R-CNN. In: 13th International Conference on Computational Intelligence and Security (CIS), pp. 427–430
14. Xu, Z., Wu, Z., Feng, J.: CFUN: combining faster R-CNN and U-net network for efficient whole heart segmentation. In: The IEEE Conference on Computer Vision and Pattern Recognition (CVPR) (2018)
15. Ramer, U.: An iterative procedure for the polygonal approximation of plane curves. Comput. Graphics Image Process. **1**(3), 244–256 (1972)
16. Gonzalez, R., Woods, R.: Digital Image Processing, pp. 541–545. Addison-Wesley Publishing Company (1992)
17. Bentley, J.: Multidimensional binary search trees used for associative searching. Commun. ACM **18**(9), 509–517 (1975)
18. Beitzel, S.M., Jensen, E.C., Frieder, O.: MAP. In: Liu, L., Özsu, M.T. (eds.) Encyclopedia of Database Systems. Springer, Boston (2009). https://doi.org/10.1007/978-3-540-29678-2_3313

19. Berman, M., Rannen Triki, A., Blaschko, M.: The Lovász-Softmax loss: a tractable surrogate for the optimization of the intersection-over-union measure in neural networks. In: The IEEE Conference on Computer Vision and Pattern Recognition (CVPR) (2018)
20. Kalervo, A., Ylioinas, J., Häikiö, M., Karhu, A., Kannala, J.: CubiCasa5K: a dataset and an improved multi-task model for floorplan image analysis. In: Felsberg, M., Forssén, P.-E., Sintorn, I.-M., Unger, J. (eds.) SCIA 2019. LNCS, vol. 11482, pp. 28–40. Springer, Cham (2019). https://doi.org/10.1007/978-3-030-20205-7_3

Predicting Passenger Flow in BTS and MTS Using Hybrid Stacked Auto-encoder and Softmax Regression

Archana M. Nayak[1]([✉]) [iD] and Nirbhay Chaubey[2]([✉]) [iD]

[1] Gujarat Technological University, Gujarat, India
er.archananaik@gmail.com
[2] Ganpat University, Gujarat, India
nirbhay.chaubey@ganpatuniversity.ac.in

Abstract. In recent era, the deep learning techniques are effectively applied and achieved an amazing result in numerous fields. Meanwhile, for the past few years the transportation industry also gets modernized due to the influence of big data. With these two trending topics, the traditional issue found in transportation industry while predicting the passenger flow is again taken into consideration in this method for solving the issues in passenger flow forecasting. In this method, the passenger flow prediction for both Bus Transit System (BTS) and Metro Transit System (MTS) mode of transportation is carried out. The gathered passenger details is clustered by dynamic clustering as summer, winter, weekend, weekdays and public holidays. Initial cluster centroid selection is enhanced by Tabu search algorithm, which furthermore improves the performance of dynamic clustering algorithm. Following this clustering, the stacked auto-encoder (SAE) with softmax regression (SR) classifier is introduced for prediction purpose. Finally, the Root Mean Square Error (RMSE), and Mean Absolute Percentage Error (MAPE) of the Cluster-SAE-DNN (Proposed) method is compared with SAE-DNN based prediction approach. The implementation for this prediction process is carried out in Matlab. Final results illustrate that this proposed method provide high prediction result with less error rate than SAE-DNN.

Keywords: Passenger flow · Dynamic clustering · Stacked auto-encoder · Softmax regression · Tabu search

1 Introduction

Passengers flow can be predicted by analysing the data collected from bus administration framework, automatic ticket gate, observation camera, and additional big data from prevailing bus stop structure [1]. Due to various factors accurate prediction of passenger flow is quite challenging. One of the main factors is chaotic nature of the transportation system [2]. Various techniques are available for forecasting the passenger flow problems. Generally the transport forecasting techniques are separated into two categories, namely parametric and non-parametric [3]. The parametric based techniques has very limited

© Springer Nature Singapore Pte Ltd. 2020
N. Chaubey et al. (Eds.): COMS2 2020, CCIS 1235, pp. 29–41, 2020.
https://doi.org/10.1007/978-981-15-6648-6_3

models by reason of time delayed variables on linear assumption. The non-parametric techniques have a main advantage of tracking the non-linear characteristic of traffic flow. It examines and provides the non-linear relevance among the input and output variables without using any extra components [4]. The transportation framework administrations require passenger flow forecast which is used to make the decision on transportation arrangements and operation planning [5]. The transportation planners can take proper decisions along with additional valuable information after analyzing the data in a sufficient manner [6]. In BTS, the current practise followed by the operators reveals that the manual data-collection process are expensive and also suits mostly for small scale [7]. A real time system is required to predict and observe the passenger flow when the bus is moving for improving the quality of bus facility. Most essential factor for managing the bus operation and dispatching of real-time transportation is passenger count. With this, the timetable for bus operation is adjusted by transit operators, likewise vehicle is also scheduled. By this factor, the operation management (e.g., reduce bus bunching) and service planning for bus are improved [8].

The public transport authorities have to enhance the service quality for increasing the passengers by including set of planning and functional procedures, signal superiority of transport, network optimization of transport, and passenger details [9]. It gains essential importance in the transportation organization and also it is identified as a most important basics to make the decisions on operation planning and transportation pattern [10]. Some frequently used forecasting techniques are: expert prediction model, time-series model, neural network, regression analysis, grey prediction model, exponential smoothing and trend extrapolation method [11].

Recently, the traffic flow is identified as a major issue in big cities. To relieve this pressure, number of transportations are given for public [12]. Normally used public transportation in various cities is buses. Predicting the flow of passenger in the moving bus with the real-time model is very much useful to improve the quality of services provided by bus [13]. Predicting the passenger flow in transportation is the base for design, manufacture, process and improvement of a transportation system [14]. The two important factors that affect the performance of passenger flow prediction were input influenced factors and modeling technique [15]. According to the historical data forecasting estimates the statement of events in future as well as significantly essential in several disciplines like meteorology, finance, industry, to reduce the amount of gas emission which results in a decrease in pollution rates, Public safety and so on [16–19].

The main contribution of this work is: here the passenger flow prediction is carried out with SAE-SR classifier. With, this hybrid classifier the accuracy of entire prediction process gets improved. The SAE is normally applied for feature extraction, it precisely extract the features from available data. So, this SAE is applied in this prediction process. Similarly, the SR also applied in this process for prediction. With the SAE features, the SR performs the prediction process. The prediction of passenger flow during weekdays, weekends, summer, winter, etc. are essential as this prediction process has a significant influence over the transportation system. Large flow of passengers may improves the income of transportation industry.

Our paper is structured as: some literature works are reviewed in Sect. 2; the discussion for the proposed work is presented in Sect. 3, finally the outcomes of this prediction process is discussed in Sect. 4 and the entire work is concluded in Sect. 5.

2   Related Work

Yu et al. 2018 [20], developed a novel prediction method by investigating the connection between the traveller stream of a station and its surrounding region's factors. Initially, the city was separated into various regions to accurately identify the factors that were affecting the passenger flow. Subsequently, the fuzzy processing and membership degree concept were introduced to solve the issues produced by the fuzziness of the bus stops attraction scope. Finally, based on Xgboost the prediction method was launched for passenger flow.

The most essential component of ITS, was passenger flow forecasting. To enhance the forecasting accuracy Li et al. 2018 [21], combined both symbolic regression and ARIMA model. The complexity patterns that were obtained beneath the data structure was captured after obtaining the unique strength from this every single model. An increase in prediction step increases the superiority of this method.

Hu et al. 2019 [22], introduced a re-sample Recurrent Neural Network (RRNN) model to forecast the traffic flow of passenger on MRT system. RNN approach was introduced to develop a method to predict the passenger traffic, here the forecast phase was changed as classification task. But, the training dataset is ended up in imbalanced manner, so RRNN was introduced to overcome this dataset imbalance problem.

Lijuan and Rung 2017 [23] have developed a (passenger flow on hours) prediction model along with the aid of deep learning models. They have included some temporal features like days in a week, the hour in a day, and so on. Further, the features have both inbound and outbound. Those features were combined, and they have also trained as varied 'Stacked Auto-Encoders (SAE)' in the initial stage. Next, to this, a pre-trained SAE was utilized to prime the supervised Deep Neural Network (DNN) along with the passenger flow, which was considered as the data label for second phase (stage).

3   Proposed Methodology for Passenger Flow Prediction

The major objective of this proposed (Cluster-SAE-DNN) approach is to analyse diverse approaches to execute this passenger flow estimation for Surat city data. With this passenger details, the passenger flow for summer, winter, public holidays, weekend, and for week days are predicted by this proposed method. The historical data for this method is taken from Surat city dataset. The passenger flow for both BTS and MTS are predicted by this method. In this paper we develop an intelligent passenger flow estimation for public transport system. Initially, we collect the passenger amount from the historical data. The proposed clustering algorithm follows Tabu search algorithm to enhance the clustering performance through the selection of initial cluster centroid. The process of selecting the initial centroid for clustering gets affected therefore the solution may easily get trapped in local optimum. The flow diagram of proposed (Cluster-SAE-DNN) methodology is depicted in Fig. 1.

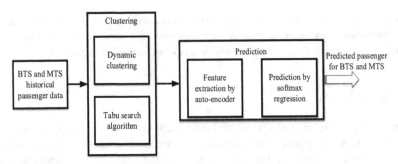

Fig. 1. Process flow for proposed (Cluster-SAE-DNN) method

Finally, SAE with a softmax regression-based model is developed for passenger flow prediction. Recently, the SAE technique is often included as a modelling process as it exhibits some advanced features like nonlinearity, capability of mapping arbitrary function, and flexibility. Moreover, it also affect the difficult non-linear issues without having any former knowledge about the relationships among the output and input variables.

3.1 Clustering

3.1.1 Dynamic Clustering

Assume we are given a set of values, $x = x_1, x_2, x_3, \ldots, x_n$. The major role of this clustering technique is to partition the given set of data into m disjoint subsets (clusters). Generally, this clustering process is accomplished by determining the squared Euclidean distance that exist between the data point x_i and the subset c_k, centroid M_k (cluster centre) which contains, x_i. The following procedures are followed to minimize the problems that occur while clustering the M clusters. Initiate the process with one cluster ($k = 1$) and determine its optimal position that matches the centroid of the dataset, X. Therefore, to solve the issue with second cluster, ($k = 2$), perform N executions within the dynamic algorithm from the succeeding initial cluster centre positions. Normally, the first cluster center for ($k = 1$) is placed at optimal location, however the second cluster having n executions are placed at the info point position i.e. $X_n (n = 1, 2, \ldots, N)$. Finally, the ordinary solution that obtained after performing N executions with this dynamic clustering algorithm is taken into account to obtain a solution for the clustering problem of ($k = 2$).

Calculate the Euclidean distance using the given Eq. (1)

$$Distance[(x, y), (a, b)] = \sqrt{(x - a)^2 + (y - b)^2} \qquad (1)$$

In the dynamic clustering the initial values are as the passenger flow. Based on the distance value of each cluster assignment and centroid calculations are done. The step is repeated until satisfactory results are obtained.

3.1.2 Tabu Search Algorithm

Many authors proposed the Tabu search algorithm using new methods to overcome the existing problems. To make the algorithm very efficient we define a precise possible solution to the problem. Given a set Z having a feasible solutions S and a function F which is assigned to each in Z a real values $f(s)$. It is essential to determine a solution S^* in Z for which $F(S^*)$ is minimum. The value of S^* cannot be obtained in a single step and so iterative process is applied to get the solution naturally. In the iterative procedure it move from a position S to the new position S' and repeat it until satisfied result or the region obtained. The move to the next location is based on the best search. Let us consider $p' = p \oplus q$ with the meaning p' is obtained by introducing a modification q into solution p.

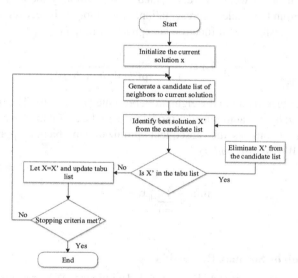

Fig. 2. Flowchart for Tabu search algorithm

Define q as the set of acceptable modification which are acceptable at solution p. The neighborhood calculation is done by using the formula

$$N(p) = \{p' | \exists q \in q_i; p' = p \oplus q\} \tag{2}$$

If we are in the current node C and then we need to move to the next node which is better than the current node (i.e. $n \leftarrow best(neighbour)$). If it is best than the current node then move to n (i.e. $c \leftarrow n$). Some Tabu conditions or the least move which is better to be identified and some of the moves are not allowed because of Tabu. In this algorithm the aspiration criteria has been identified and it represents that if the disallowed move is best then move to that position. Tabu search algorithm is used to enhance the cluster centroid.

3.2 Stacked Auto-encoder with Softmax Regression for Prediction

3.2.1 Feature Extraction by Stacked Auto-Encoder (SAE)

Two auto-encoders are stacked to form SAE [24]. With this SAE the feature extraction process is carried out for passenger flow prediction. For clarification here a single layer auto-encoder network is explained. It contains encoder and decoder. An input x_i is mapped by this encoder to its hidden representation, h_i. The non-linear mapping function is applied in this method and its common form is represented as:

$$h_i = f(x_i) = \frac{1}{1 + \exp(-(W_1 x_i + b_1))} \tag{3}$$

Where, the encoding weight is represented as W_1, similarly the bias vector is represented as b_1. From the hidden representation, h_i the input x_i is recovered by decoder. The formula for transformation function is expressed in Eq. (4),

$$x_i' = g(h_i) = \frac{1}{1 + \exp(-(W_2 h_i + b_2))} \tag{4}$$

The decoding bias vector and weight are represented as, W_2, b_2. The reconstruction error is minimized by this auto-encoder model to learn the useful hidden representation. Thus, for N training samples, the subsequent optimization problem is applied to resolve the parameters, $W_1, W_2, b_1,$ and b_2,

$$\min \frac{1}{N} \sum_{i=1}^{N} \left\| x_i - x_i' \right\|^2 \tag{5}$$

3.2.2 Prediction by Softmax Regression

The supervised learning approach that is included within the DNN as a output layer is the softmax regression (SR) model. This type of supervised learning are widely applied to

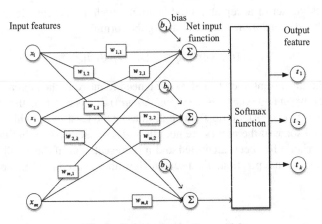

Fig. 3. Softmax regression model

predict outcome or future. The model for Softmax regression is shown in Fig. 2. **Input:** clustered data (month, week, weekend, holidays, seasons, and normal days), a_1- input of first neuron, b_1- label for a_1. **Output:** (predicted passenger flow) (Fig. 3).

It is a supervised learning approach, therefore it requires both input a and label b [25]. A training set for m sample is represented as $\{(a_1, b_1), (a_2, b_2), \ldots, (a_m, b_m)\}$, where $b_i \in \{1, 2, .., k\}$, after that determine the probability $p(b = j|a)$ for each value of $j = 1, 2, .., k$. The formula applied to evaluate $h_\theta(a)$ is given in Eq. (6),

$$h_\theta(a_i) = \begin{bmatrix} p(b_i = 1|a_i; \theta) \\ p(b_i = 2|a_i; \theta) \\ \vdots \\ p(b^i = k|a^i; \theta) \end{bmatrix} \tag{6}$$

$$= \frac{1}{\sum\limits_{i=1}^{k} e^{\theta_j^T a_i}} \begin{bmatrix} e^{\theta_1^T a_i} \\ e^{\theta_2^T a_i} \\ \vdots \\ e^{\theta_k^T a_i} \end{bmatrix} \tag{7}$$

Where, the model parameters are represented as $\theta_1, \theta_2, \ldots, \theta_k \in R^{n+1}$, then the distribution is normalized by $1 \left/ \sum\limits_{i=1}^{k} e^{\theta_j^T a_i} \right.$, so that this distribution is then sum to 1. In terms of log likelihood the cost function for Softmax regression is expressed as,

$$J(\theta) = -\frac{1}{m} \left[\sum_{i=1}^{m} (1 - b_i) \log(1 - h_\theta(a_i)) + \sum_{i=1}^{m} b_i \log h_\theta(a_i) \right] \tag{8}$$

Another form of cost function is

$$J(\theta) = -\frac{1}{m} \left[\sum_{i=1}^{m} \sum_{j=1}^{k} 1\{y_i = j\} \log \frac{e^{\theta_j^T a_i}}{\sum\limits_{l=1}^{k} e^{\theta_l^T a_i}} \right] \tag{9}$$

Then the weight decay term is added in this Eq. (9), then this model becomes more robust to various input. After adding weight decay the cost function is expressed as

$$J(\theta) = -\frac{1}{m} \left[\sum_{i=1}^{m} \sum_{j=1}^{k} 1\{b_i = j\} \log \frac{e^{\theta_j^T a_i}}{\sum\limits_{l=1}^{k} e^{\theta_l^T a_i}} \right] + \frac{\lambda}{2} \sum_{i=1}^{k} \sum_{j=0}^{n} \theta_{ij}^2 \tag{10}$$

The main aim of this SR is passenger flow prediction with less complexity but with high accuracy. By this method, the passenger flow is accurately predicted for BTS and MTS during holidays, weekends, normal days, summer, winter, one month, and for one year. This prediction is very much useful for transportation industry.

4 Simulation Analysis and Results

In this method, the passenger flow for one year is predicted. This passenger flow prediction is performed for both BTS and MTS passengers. The passenger detail for this prediction process is taken from Surat city dataset. The passenger details are taken for one year (June 2017 to June 2018) for passenger flow prediction in both BTS and MTS transportation. With this details the passenger flow during summer, winter, weekend, weekdays, and during public holidays are predicted. Two performance metrics RMSE and MAPE are evaluated in this method to illustrate the effectiveness of this proposed (Cluster-SAE-DNN) prediction approach. MAPE determines the prediction accuracy of this proposed forecasting technique. The implementation for this prediction process is carried out in Matlab environment. The equation for RMSE and MAPE are given in Eqs. (11 and 12) respectively.

$$\overline{RMSE} = \sqrt{\frac{1}{n}\sum_{i=1}^{n}|xr_i - \overline{xp_i}|^2} \tag{11}$$

$$\overline{MAPE} = \frac{1}{n}\sum_{i=1}^{n}\frac{|xr_i - \overline{xp_i}|}{xr_i} \tag{12}$$

Where, the number of actual passengers is represented as xr_i, similarly the predicted passenger is represented as xp_i. These two metrics are evaluated for both BTS and MTS passenger to depict the effectiveness of this proposed (Cluster-SAE-DNN) technique.

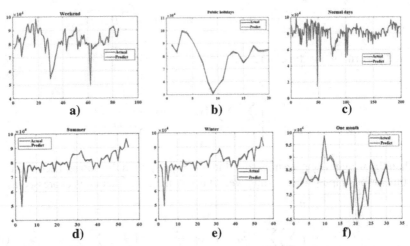

Fig. 4. Actual and predicted passenger flow for BTS (a. Weekend, b. Public holidays, c. Normal days, d. summer, e. winter, and f. One month), X axis – number of days, Y axis – Passenger availability

In Fig. 4(a), the real and predicted passenger flow in BTS for weekend (Saturday and Sunday). Similarly, the passenger flow prediction for summer, weekdays (normal days), winter, one month, and one year is also attained. The actual and predicted passengers during summer and winter are given in Fig. 4(d & e), for holidays and normal days are depicted in Fig. 4(b & c). Moreover, the actual and predicted values for one month and one year is illustrated in Fig. 4(f & g) respectively. Similarly, the MTS passenger availability for summer, weekdays (normal days), winter, one month, and one year is also attained.

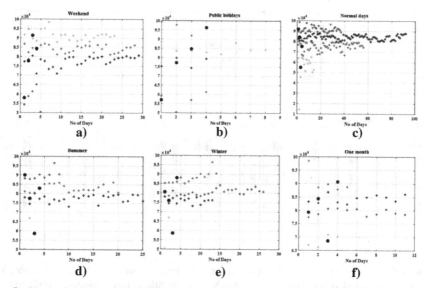

Fig. 5. Cluster formation for BTS passenger (a. Weekend, b. Public holidays, c. Normal days, d. summer, e. winter, and f. One month), X axis – number of days, Y axis – Passenger availability

Figure 5 represents the cluster formation for BTS and MTS using the historical dataset. The centroid is calculated by using the dynamic clustering algorithm and it is enhanced by Tabu search algorithm. The historical BTS passenger flow data obtained from the dataset is clustered for one month, one year, weekend, weekdays, summer, winter, and public holidays. The formed clusters are shown in Fig. 5 (a, b, c, d, e, f, and g). In similar way, the clustered data is attained by tabu search based clustering process for MTS passengers.

The passenger flow for MTS is predicted by this deep learning technique. The error values that are obtained during prediction process of BTS and MTS passenger for both proposed (Cluster-SAE-DNN) and existing (SAE-DNN) is tabulated in Table 1. An increase in accuracy minimize the presence of error in prediction process. The accuracy of BTS and MTS for proposed method is found higher than existing approach [20], which depicts that the prediction error of proposed (Cluster-SAE-DNN) approach is much lower than existing method.

Both the actual and predicted passenger flow in summer and winter seasons for BTS passengers is shown in Fig. 6(a). The actual and predicted passenger flow (one year (i.e. June 2017 to June 2018)) for both BTS transportation is shown in Fig. 6(b), which depicts that during the month of August 2017 more number of passenger flow is predicted

Table 1. RMSE and MAPE values for MTS and BTS

Parameter	RMSE and MAPE for MTS passenger				RMSE and MAPE for BTS passenger			
	RMSE (Proposed)	MAPE (Proposed)	RMSE (Existing)	MAPE (Existing)	RMSE (Proposed)	MAPE (Proposed)	RMSE (Existing)	MAPE (Existing)
Weekend	7.68	0.0096	18	0.0235	7	0.0079	21	0.0216
Holidays	7.85	0.0125	17.25	0.0201	7.6	0.0087	22	0.022
Weekdays	7	0.0098	19.89	0.022	7.542	0.0075	22.5	0.0219
Summer	7.12	0.0085	20.8	0.0219	6.9	0.007	20	0.019
Winter	7	0.0082	21	0.0246	6.4	0.0068	17.5	0.016
1 month	6.85	0.0105	21	0.033	8.5	0.009	18.2	0.0175
1 year	7.86	0.0101	19.9	0.024	7.68	0.0065	19.75	0.0182

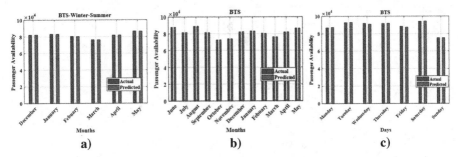

Fig. 6. BTS passenger flow (actual and predicted) [a] winter and summer (X-axis – Months, Y-axis – Passenger availability), b) for 12 months (X-axis – month, Y-axis – passenger availability), c) for weekdays (X-axis – Days, Y-axis – Passenger availability)

by this method for BTS transportation. The BTS passenger flow for a particular month (August for BTS) is predicted and depicted in Fig. 6(c). The passenger flow predicted on Saturday (August 2017) is found higher than other weekdays for BTS transportation.

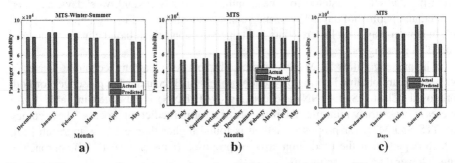

Fig. 7. MTS passenger flow (actual and predicted)[a] winter and summer (X-axis – Months, Y-axis – Passenger availability), b) for 12 months (X-axis – month, Y-axis – passenger availability), c) for weekdays (X-axis – Days, Y-axis – Passenger availability)]

The actual and predicted passenger flow for MTS transportation is shown in Fig. 7(a, b, & c). The amount of passengers predicted for MTS during summer (March, April, and May) and winter (December, January, and February) season is shown in Fig. 7(a), which depicts that during the month of January 2018 more number of passenger flow is predicted by this method. Then, the predicted and actual amount of passenger availability for the month of January 2018, is shown in Fig. 7(c). BTS experience high passenger flow in summer season, however the MTS experience high passenger flow in winter season. Similarly, the actual and predicted amount of passengers for one year (from June 2017 to May 2018) is shown in Fig. 7(b).

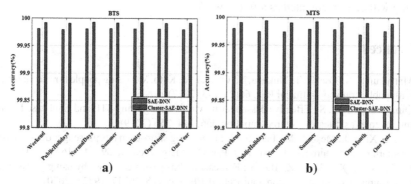

Fig. 8. Accuracy comparison for proposed prediction method

The accuracy value attained by proposed (Cluster-SAE-DNN) BTS passenger flow method for weekend, holidays, normal days, summer, winter, 1 month, and 1 year is shown in Fig. 8(a). From this result, it is clear that the accuracy attained by BTS transportation for summer season is found highest than others. Similarly, the accuracy value attained by MTS transportation for weekend, holidays, normal days, summer, winter, 1 month, and 1 year is shown in Fig. 8(b). The highest accuracy attained by MTS transportation for passenger flow prediction is during public holidays. This prediction is performed for one year, most particularly for winter, summer, weekend, weekdays, and public holidays. This prediction methods are very much useful for transportation field. With this details, an effective scheduling is performed by operators to satisfy the passenger demand. Due to this the economic condition of transportation industry is also gets improved.

5 Conclusion

Passenger flow prediction are gaining a huge demand in recent days. Accurate prediction of passenger flow has major implication in real-time bus scheduling, moreover it is also found essential to improve the reliability of bus service. The proposed method accurately predict the passenger flow for both BTS and MTS with available dataset. In this method, the passenger flow is predicted for one year. From the performance result, it is ensured that with this hybrid model the 22 passenger flow prediction is accomplished robustly and accurately than the other single prediction models. This hybrid prediction models effectively utilize the historical information to accurately provide the prediction results. Even though it attains higher accuracy, but the complexity of this prediction process is found high. Therefore, in future we will introduce an optimization based learning approaches to avoid this system complexity. In this approach, our main consideration is passenger flow detection, but an increase in passenger count causes crowding due to this the passenger comfort gets reduced. Moreover, the bus needs to be scheduled for each route based on the passenger availability or else the improper bus scheduling may lead to the wastage of transport resources. By keeping this into consideration, the bus scheduling for two different routes on the basis of passenger availability using deep learning will be implemented as a future work.

References

1. Matsukuma, N., Osawa, T., Nukaga, N., Otsuka, R., Kato, M.: Using people flow technologies with public transport. Hitachi Rev. **66**(2), 145 (2017)
2. Qin, L., Li, W., Li, S.: Effective passenger flow forecasting using STL and ESN based on two improvement strategies. Neurocomputing **356**, 244–256 (2019)
3. Ma, Z., Xing, J., Mesbah, M., Ferreira, L.: Predicting short-term bus passenger demand using a pattern hybrid approach. Transp. Res. Part C: Emerg. Technol. **39**, 148–163 (2014)
4. Li, C., Wang, X., Cheng, Z., Bai, Y.: Forecasting bus passenger flows by using a clustering-based support vector regression approach. IEEE Access **8**, 19717–19725 (2020)
5. Bai, Y., Sun, Z., Zeng, B., Deng, J., Li, C.: A multi-pattern deep fusion model for short-term bus passenger flow forecasting. Appl. Soft Comput. **58**, 669–680 (2017)
6. Zhao, S.Z., Ni, T.H., Wang, Y., Gao, X.T.: A new approach to the prediction of passenger flow in a transit system. Comput. Math Appl. **61**(8), 1968–1974 (2011)
7. Petersen, N.C., Rodrigues, F., Pereira, F.C.: Multi-output bus travel time prediction with convolutional LSTM neural network. Expert Syst. Appl. **120**, 426–435 (2019)
8. Zheng, X., et al.: Big data for social transportation. IEEE Trans. Intell. Transp. Syst. **17**(3), 620–630 (2015)
9. Amita, J., Jain, S.S., Garg, P.K.: Prediction of bus travel time using ANN: a case study in Delhi. Transp. Res. Procedia **17**, 263–272 (2016)
10. Wang, D.-L., Yao, E.-J., Yang, Y., Zhang, Y.-S.: Modeling passenger flow distribution based on disaggregate model for urban rail transit. In: Sun, F., Hu, D., Liu, H. (eds.) Foundations and Practical Applications of Cognitive Systems and Information Processing. AISC, vol. 215, pp. 715–723. Springer, Heidelberg (2014). https://doi.org/10.1007/978-3-642-37835-5_62
11. Li, Y.-H., Han, H.-Y., Liu, X., Li, C.: Passenger flow forecast of sanya airport based on ARIMA model. In: Zhou, Q., Miao, Q., Wang, H., Xie, W., Wang, Y., Lu, Z. (eds.) ICPCSEE 2018. CCIS, vol. 902, pp. 442–454. Springer, Singapore (2018). https://doi.org/10.1007/978-981-13-2206-8_36
12. Shiao, Y.C., Liu, L., Zhao, Q., Chen, R.C.: Predicting passenger flow using different influence factors for Taipei MRT system. In: 2017 IEEE 8th International Conference on Awareness Science and Technology (iCAST), pp. 447–451, November 2017
13. Zhang, J., Shen, D., Tu, L., Zhang, F., Xu, C., Wang, Y., Li, Z.: A real-time passenger flow estimation and prediction method for urban bus transit systems. IEEE Trans. Intell. Transp. Syst. **18**(11), 3168–3178 (2017)
14. Liu, Y., Liu, Z., Jia, R.: DeepPF: a deep learning based architecture for metro passenger flow prediction. Transp. Res. Part C: Emerg. Technol. **101**, 18–34 (2019)

15. Huang, Z., Li, Q., Li, F., Xia, J.: A novel bus-dispatching model based on passenger flow and arrival time prediction. IEEE Access **7**, 106453–106465 (2019)

16. Chen, S., Lan, X., Hu, Y., Liu, Q., Deng, Y.: The time series forecasting: from the aspect of network. arXiv preprint arXiv:1403.1713 (2014)

17. Ladha, A., Bhattacharya, P., Chaubey, N., Bodkhe, U.: *IIGPTS*: IoT-based framework for intelligent green public transportation system. In: Singh, P.K., Pawłowski, W., Tanwar, S., Kumar, N., Rodrigues, J.J.P.C., Obaidat, M.S. (eds.) Proceedings of First International Conference on Computing, Communications, and Cyber-Security (IC4S 2019). LNNS, vol. 121, pp. 183–195. Springer, Singapore (2020). https://doi.org/10.1007/978-981-15-3369-3_14

18. Chaubey, N.K.: Security analysis of vehicular ad hoc networks (VANETs): a comprehensive study. Int. J. Secur. Appl. **10**(5), 261–274 (2016)

19. Chaubey, N.K., Yadav, D.: A taxonomy of Sybil attacks in vehicular ad-hoc network (VANET). In: IoT and Cloud Computing Advancements in Vehicular Ad-Hoc Networks, pp. 174–190. IGI Global (2020)

20. Yu, H.T., Jiang, C.J., Xiao, R.D., Liu, H.O., Lv, W.: Passenger flow prediction for new line using region dividing and fuzzy boundary processing. IEEE Trans. Fuzzy Syst. **27**(5), 994–1007 (2018)

21. Li, L., Wang, Y., Zhong, G., Zhang, J., Ran, B.: Short-to-medium term passenger flow forecasting for metro stations using a hybrid model. KSCE J. Civ. Eng. **22**(5), 1937–1945 (2018)

22. Hu, R., et al.: Mass rapid transit system passenger traffic forecast using a re-sample recurrent neural network. J. Adv. Transp. **2019** (2019)

23. Liu, L., Chen, R.C.: A novel passenger flow prediction model using deep learning methods. Transp. Res. Part C: Emerg. Technol. **84**, 74–91 (2017)

24. Song, C., Huang, Y., Liu, F., Wang, Z., Wang, L.: Deep auto-encoder based clustering. Intell. Data Anal. **18**(6S), S65–S76 (2014)

25. Tao, S., Zhang, T., Yang, J., Wang, X., Lu, W.: Bearing fault diagnosis method based on stacked autoencoder and softmax regression. In: 2015 34th Chinese Control Conference (CCC), pp. 6331–6335. IEEE, July 2015

Deep Recurrent Neural Network with Tanimoto Similarity and MKSIFT Features for Medical Image Search and Retrieval

Hardik H. Bhatt[1]([⊠]) [iD] and Anand P. Mankodia[2] [iD]

[1] Research Scholar, Ganpat University, Gujarat, India
hbhatt992@gmail.com

[2] Department of Electronics and Communication, Ganpat University, Gujarat, India

Abstract. The innovation of digital medical images has led to the requirement of rich descriptors and efficient retrieval tool. Thus, the Content Based Image Retrieval (CBIR) technique is essential in the domain of image retrieval. Due to the growing medical image data, the searching or retrieving a relevant image from the dataset is a major problem. To address this problem, this paper propose a new medical image retrieval technique, namely Multiple Kernel Scale Invariant Feature Transform-based Deep Recurrent Neural Network (MKSIFT-Deep RNN) using the image contents. The goal is to present an effective tool that can be utilized for effective retrieval of image from huge medical image database. Here, MKSIFT is adapted for extracting the relevant features obtained from acquired input image. Moreover, MKSIFT evaluates the key point descriptor using kernels functions, wherein the weights are allocated to kernels. The feature vectors are employed in the Deep RNN for classifying the images by training the classifier, which is considered as training phase. In testing phase, a set of query images is given to the classifier which adapts Tanimoto similarity for retrieving the images. The proposed MKSIFT-Deep RNN outperformed other methods with maximal precision of 93.723%, maximal recall of 93.652% and maximal F-measure of 93.687%.

Keywords: Computer vision · Medical images · Multiple Kernel Scale Invariant Feature Transform (MKSIFT) · Deep recurrent neural network · Image retrieval

1 Introduction

The information retrieval is a trending domain due to medical imaging systems as it deal with audio, image and video which provide huge information that changes the world of medicines. In recent times, the huge-scaled medical image search acquired more consideration in the retrieval of images from big sized image datasets [5]. The innovation in medical imaging technologies increased due to the use of Internet, digital cameras, and smart-phone. The stored medical image data are increasing and for searching and retrieving the relevant medical image from an archive is challenging issue. The need of any medical image retrieval model is to assemble and search the medical images that are

© Springer Nature Singapore Pte Ltd. 2020
N. Chaubey et al. (Eds.): COMS2 2020, CCIS 1235, pp. 42–54, 2020.
https://doi.org/10.1007/978-981-15-6648-6_4

visual semantic relation using the query provided by the user [6]. There is also a need to search images from the dataset which is handled by model for effectual recovery of medical images [7].

The CBIR is adapted on existing techniques and gained interest in the retrieval of medical images. Different feature extraction methods are adapted on the basis of boundary contour, spatial layout, color, and texture. In [8], CBIR technique is devised using the features like histograms of oriented gradients (HOG), SIFT, and local binary pattern (LBP), for attaining improved results in image retrieval. In [9], improved CBIR technique is developed using certain attributes like wavelet-based histogram approaches that utilize relevance feedback for retrieving the images. An optimized technique is devised in [10] for pattern retrieval on the basis of quantized histograms. In [11], a technique is devised for training deep convolutional neural network (DCNN) in order to enhance the CBIR.

This research presents a novel method, namely MKSIFT-Deep RNN for medical image retrieval using data set of medical images. Here, MKSIFT feature is adapted for generating the feature vector by extracting significant features from the medical image database. The purpose is to retrieve the images from the huge database. Here, MKSIFT is adapted for extracting the relevant features using acquired input image. Moreover, MKSIFT evaluates the key point descriptor using kernel function, wherein the weights are allocated to the kernels. The feature vectors are employed in the Deep RNN for classifying the images by training the classifier, which is considered as training phase. In testing phase, a set of query images is given to the classifier which adapts Tanimoto similarity for retrieving the images.

The major contribution of the research is:

- **Proposed MKSIFT-Deep RNN for Medical Image Retrieval**: Develop a novel medical image retrieval model, namely Multiple Kernel Scale Invariant Feature Transform-based deep recurrent neural network (MKSIFT-Deep RNN) for effective medical image retrieval.

2 Motivation

From the literary works, the CBIR models are devised and modified using deep learning approaches. However, there are still some issues which are not addressed. Firstly, the semantic gap is unsolved that still exist between low level feature representation of medical images. Moreover, the issues confronted by the existing methods stood as the motivation for devising a novel medical image retrieval method.

2.1 Literature Review

The eight existing techniques based on medical image retrieval is deliberated below: Mathan Kumar, B. and Pushpa Lakshmi, R [1] devised a method for effective retrieval of image. Here, MKSIFT was adapted for extracting the features from the pre-processed image. The MKSIFT computed key point descriptor with kernel functions for selecting the weights using Particle Swarm-Fractional Bacterial foraging optimization (PS-FBFO). The method adapted cross-indexed image search by transforming the feature points to binary codes. However, the method failed to use advanced optimization techniques like lion optimization for choosing the weight coefficients to enhance performance. Sharif, U *et al.* [2] developed a technique by hybridizing visual words with SIFT. The local feature descriptors were selected that adds harmonizing upgrading to CBIR. The SIFT descriptor was able to detect the objects vigorously under cluttering because of rotation, noise, and illumination variance. The method enhanced the performance of CBIR, but failed to use deep learning model for huge scale Image Retrieval. Saritha, R.R. *et al.* [3] developed deep belief network (DBN) technique for CBIR. The method extracted the features and the classification was initiated using DBN for classifying the images. The DBN was trained using effective feature representations for retrieving the relevant images. However, the method failed to provide real time feature extraction. Xia, Z *et al.* [4] devised an outsourced CBIR method using bag-of-encrypted-words (BOEW) model for retrieving images. Here, the method utilized permutation, and color value substitution. Moreover, the BOEW model was designed for representing each image using feature vector. The similarity between the images was computed using Manhattan distance. However, the method failed to utilize local descriptors for BOEW model.

2.2 Challenges

The challenges confronted by the existing methodologies are deliberated below:

- Even though, different methods are devised for medical image retrieval [20] semantic gap remains a challenging issue in current CBIR methods. The semantic gap existsamid low-level image pixels obtained via machine and high-level semantic concept obtained via humans [3].
- In [1], outsourced CBIR scheme is devised using bag-of-encrypted-words (BOEW) model for retrieving the images from massive datasets. The method is effective for faster retrieval, but confronted issues like complex computations and heavy storage.
- The proficient recovery of images using massive image datasets is major issue. In recent days, the images are retrieved using visual information and CBIT techniques.

3   Proposed MK-SIFT-Based Deep RNN for Image Retrieval

Figure 1 illustrates the schematic view of medical image retrieval model using proposed MK-SIFT-based Deep-RNN. Initially, the medical images are fed to feature extraction module. The extraction of features is done using MK-SIFT [1]. Once the significant features are obtained, then the group retrieval is performed using the generated features and Deep RNN [12]. The training of Deep RNN is performed using the MKSIFT features for tuning the optimal weights in order to perform group retrieval. Here, query image is given as an input, which is further matched with the classified images using Tanimoto similarity measure [13]. Thus, the image retrieval is performed using Tanimoto similarity measure. By computing the similarity between query image and classified image set using Tanimoto similarity measure, the retrieval of relevant instances is done. The briefer illustration of each steps is illustrated in the below section.

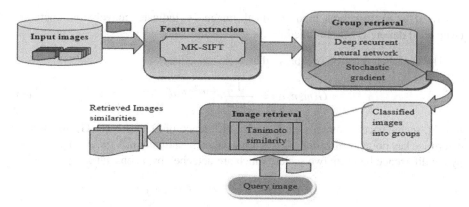

Fig. 1. Schematic view of CBIR using proposed MK-SIFT-based Deep RNN

Assume a database D with d number of medical images and is represented as,

$$D = \{I_1, I_2, \ldots, I_k, \ldots, I_l\} \tag{1}$$

where, I_k represent k^{th} input image, and l indicate total number of images.

Each image I_k is processed for extracting the significant features using MKSIFT approach which is elaborated in the below subsection.

3.1 Extraction of Significant Feature Using MK-SIFT

The noteworthy features obtained from input image and the connotation of feature extraction is to produce highly relevant features which facilitate improved retrieval of medical images. Meanwhile, the complexity of analyzing the medical image is reduced as the image is modelled as the reduced set of features. In addition, the precision allied with the classification is guaranteed with efficient feature extraction for which the MKSIFT [1] approach is employed. The MKSIFT is a feature extraction technique which is devised by modifying the SIFT feature with different weightage method in key point descriptor for extracting features from input medical image. The MKSIFT-based feature extraction is classified into different steps which involve extremadetection, key point's removal, assignment of orientation, and calculation of descriptors. Moreover, the Gaussian function present in the key point descriptor is restored with exponential kernel and tangential kernel functions.

SIFT [14] is a method which transforms the image into different scale invariants on the basis of local features. The method devises vast features which covers the complete variety of images. For matching images, the SIFT features are mined from images. The four steps considered for the generating the feature set which are described below:

(i) Discovery of Scale-Space Extrema: The first phase for extracting feature is to determine the location and image scales by detecting steady features over scales considering Gaussian function, that can be modelled as,

$$S(m, n, \alpha) = G(m, n, \alpha) * I(m, n) \tag{2}$$

Where, $I(m, n)$ represent input medical image, $*$ indicate convolution operator, $G(m, n, \alpha)$ denote Gaussian function.

The Gaussian function is expressed as,

$$G(m, n, \alpha) = \frac{1}{2\pi\alpha^2}e^{-(m^2+n^2)/2\alpha^2} \tag{3}$$

In [15], scale-space extrema is employed in difference-of-Gaussian (DoG) function to determine key point localization. This is represented by a function, $X(m, n, \alpha)$ generated by the difference between two scales, which are detached by a constant as,

$$X(m, n, \alpha) = G(m, n, v\alpha) - G(m, n, \alpha) \tag{4}$$

$$X(m, n, \alpha) = S(m, n, v\alpha) - S(m, n, \alpha) \tag{5}$$

where, v indicate constant.

In addition, the DoG function provides an approximation based on the Laplacian of Gaussian $\alpha^2\nabla^2 G$. From the equation, the relation between $\alpha^2\nabla^2 G$ is,

$$\frac{\partial G}{\partial \alpha} = \alpha^2\nabla^2 G \tag{6}$$

The extrema are determined using each sample point, which is further compared to its neighbours and other nine neighbours that reside in scale. The point is chosen if result is either larger or smaller.

(ii) Localization of Key Point: After detecting key points, the subsequent steps are followed which is elimination of key points with low contrast by carrying a data fit for determining the scale and location. This is computed on the basis of expansion of scale-space function using Taylor series by,

$$X(g) = X + \frac{\partial X}{\partial g}g + \frac{1}{2}g^T\frac{\partial^2 X}{\partial g^2}g \tag{7}$$

where, g indicate offset given by $g = (m, n, \alpha)^T$

The location is expressed as,

$$g = -\frac{\partial^2 X^{-1}\partial X}{\partial g^2\partial g} \tag{8}$$

While the offset is instituted to be larger than value of threshold, then the extremum is at the diverse sample point, which holds low contrast. Hence, by this assessment, the low contrast key point is eliminated. The unstable extrema with low contrast are eliminated using function $K(\hat{d})$ expressed as:

$$X(\hat{g}) = X + \frac{1}{2}\frac{\partial X^T}{\partial g}\hat{g} \tag{9}$$

In DoG, an anomalous peak poses a outsized principal curvature, which is removed. The principal curvatures isevaluated considering Hessian matrix as,

$$K = \begin{bmatrix} X_{mm} & X_{mn} \\ X_{mn} & X_{nn} \end{bmatrix} \tag{10}$$

where, K represent Hessian matrix.

(iii) Assignment of Orientation: The key point descriptor is expressed using proper orientation assignment considering key points based on local images. For evaluating the scale invariant, the Gaussian smoothed image is chosen considering scale of the key point. The magnitude and orientation is computed using pixel differences as follows:

$$M(m, n) = \sqrt{(S(m+1, n) - S(m-1, n))^2 + (S(m, n+1))^2} \tag{11}$$

$$\varphi(m, n) = \tan^{-1}((S(m, n+1) - M(m, n-1)))/((m(m+1, n) - M(m-1, n))) \tag{12}$$

where $M(m, n)$ indicate magnitude, $w(m, n)$ represent orientation, and S indicate scale space. Based on magnitude and orientations of the key point, a histogram based on the orientation is designed.

(iv) Computation of Descriptor Using Multi-kernel Function: The last phase is computation of key point descriptor using image gradients considering region of key point. On the basis of scale of key point, the orientation and the magnitude are computed to choose the Gaussian blur level of image. The coordinate of descriptor are rotated on the basis of orientation of key point to determine the orientation invariance. However, Gaussian function could not protect image brightness, offering less emphasis to gradients. Thus, MKSIFT method devises two kernel functions, namely tangential and exponential kernels which help to augment variance, thereby minimizing relics of image. Thus, the weight function of MKSIFT is expressed as,

$$W = M(m, n) * w(m, n) \tag{13}$$

The kernel function is represented by,

$$w(m, n) = \eta * \exp(f(m, n)) + \rho * \tanh f(m, n) \tag{14}$$

where, η and ρ represent weight coefficients that ranges between $[0, 1]$.

The obtained features is accumulated in the feature vector denoted as F; $(1 \leq a \leq e)$. The feature vector F is fed to the Deep RNN for classifying the images into groups.

3.2 Classifying the Medical Images for Group Retrieval Using Deep RNN

The Deep RNN is employed to retrieve the groups considering the MKSIFT features. The architecture of Deep RNN is portrayed below.

3.2.1 Architecture of Deep RNN

The features F extracted from the input images are given as the input to the Deep RNN classifier. Deep RNN [12] is the network architecture that contains multiple recurrent hidden layers in network hierarchy layer. In Deep RNN the recurrent connection exists at the hidden layer. The Deep RNN classifier operates effectively under the varying input feature length based on the sequence of information. It uses the knowledge of previous state as input in the current prediction and process the iteration using the hidden state information. The recurrent feature makes the Deep RNN to be highly effective in working with the features. Due to the sequential pattern of information, Deep RNN is considered as the best classifier among traditional deep learning approaches. The architecture of Deep RNN is represented in Fig. 2.

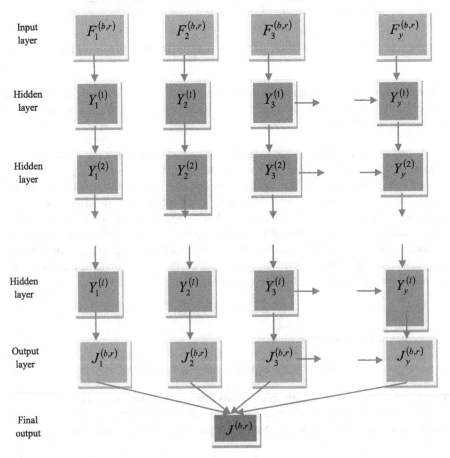

Fig. 2. Architecture of Deep RNN classifier

The structure of Deep RNN is made by considering the input vector of bth layer at r^{th} time as $F^{(b,r)} = \left\{ F_1^{(b,r)}, F_2^{(b,r)}, \ldots F_i^{(b,r)}, \ldots F_y^{(b,r)} \right\}$ and the output vector of bth

layer at r^{th} time as, $J^{(b,r)} = \left\{ J_1^{(b,r)}, J_2^{(b,r)}, \ldots J_i^{(b,r)}, \ldots J_y^{(b,r)} \right\}$, respectively. The pair of each elements of input and the output vectors is termed as the unit. Here, i denotes the arbitrary unit number of bth layer, and y represents the total number of units of bth layer. In addition to this, the arbitrary unit number and the total number of units of $(b-1)^{th}$ layer is denoted as j and E, respectively. At this time, the input propagation weight from $(b-1)^{th}$ layer to b^{th} layer is expressed as, $W^{(b)} \in H^{y \times E}$, and the recurrent weight of bth layer is modelled as $w^{(b)} \in H^{y \times y}$. Here, H denotes the set of weights. However, the components of the input vector is expressed as,

$$F_i^{(b,r)} = \sum_{z=1}^{E} p_{iz}^{(b)} J_z^{(b-1,r)} + \sum_{i'}^{y} x_{ii'}^{(b)} J_{i'}^{(b,r-1)} \tag{15}$$

where, $p_{iz}^{(b)}$ and $x_{ii'}^{(b)}$ are the elements of $W^{(b)}$ and $w^{(b)}$. i' denotes the arbitrary unit number of bth layer. The elements of the output vector of bth layer is represented as,

$$J_i^{(b,r)} = \beta^{(b)} \left(F_i^{(b,r)} \right) \tag{16}$$

where, $\beta^{(b)}$ denotes the activation function. However, the activation functions, like sigmoid function as $\beta(F) = \tanh(F)$, rectified linear unit function (ReLU) as $\beta(F) = \max(F, 0)$, and the logistic sigmoid function as $\beta(F) = \frac{1}{(1+e^{-F})}$ are the frequently used activation function.

To simplify the process, 0th weight as $p_{i0}^{(b)}$ and 0th unit as $J_0^{(b-1,r)}$ are introduced and hence the bias is represented as,

$$J^{(b,r)} = \beta^{(b)} \cdot \left(W^{(b)} J^{(b-1,r)} + w^{(b)} \cdot J^{(b,r-1)} \right) \tag{17}$$

Here, $J^{(b,r)}$ denotes the output of classifier.

3.3 Image Retrieval Using Tanimoto Measure Based Similarity

For effective image retrieval, a query image Q is fed to the feature extractor and is described for producing its new feature vector F'; $(1 \le a \le e)$. The searching is done by matching training feature vector F against new feature F' using Tanimoto similarity measure. The feature fetches the matching images as the result of search output. The Tanimoto metric is represented as,

$$\frac{\sum\limits_{a=1}^{e} h_a c_a}{\sum\limits_{a=1}^{e} h_a^2 + \sum\limits_{a=1}^{e} c_a^2 - \sum\limits_{a=1}^{e} h_a c_a} \tag{18}$$

where, h_a represent a^{th} feature residing in feature vector F, and c_a indicate the ath feature residing in feature vector F'.

Thus, the Tanimoto similarity is employed for retrieving the relevant images from the classified database.

4 Results and Discussion

This comparison of proposed method with conventional methods using precision, F-measure and recall is illustrated. In addition, the effectiveness of proposed MKSIFT-Deep RNN method is analyzed by varying number of query.

4.1 Experimental Setup

The execution of proposed MKSIFT-Deep RNN is done in PYTHON using PC having Windows 10 OS, 4 GB RAM, and Intel i5 core processor.

4.2 Dataset Description

The medical image dataset employed for the experimentation to describe the analysis of performance using each medical image retrieval method is described below. Here, the database is designed by considering prostate cancer images, retinal images, iris images, breast cancer images, skin cancer images, bacilli images, and BRATS dataset images [17–19].

4.3 Evaluation Metrics

The effectiveness of proposed MKSIFT-Deep RNN is employed for analyzing methods includes the precision, recall and F-measure.

4.3.1 Precision

The precision parameter defines the ratio of relevant images from the retrieved images considering a query and is given as,

$$precision = \frac{|\{rel \cap ret\}|}{|ret|} \tag{19}$$

where, *rel* denote relevant images, *ret* represent retrieved images.

4.3.2 Recall

The ratio of total relevant images that are actually retrieved is given as,

$$recall = \frac{|\{rel \cap ret\}|}{|rel|} \tag{20}$$

4.3.3 F-measure

The harmonic mean of recall and precision is termed as F-measure and is represented as,

$$F - measure = 2 * \frac{precison * recall}{precison + recall} \tag{21}$$

4.4 Comparative Methods

The methods employed for the analysis include: SIFT [14], HOG + MKSIFT (Applied HOG [16] in MKSIFT), MKSIFT [1], and proposed MKSIFT-Deep RNN algorithm.

4.4.1 Analysis Based on Query Set-1

Figure 3 portrays the analysis of methods considering query set-1 using precision, recall and F-measure parameter. Each query set poses 15 images from the acquired database. The analysis based on precision parameter is described in Fig. 3a. When the number of query is 4, the precision values computed by SIFT, HOG + MKSIFT, MKSIFT, and proposed MKSIFT-Deep RNN are 85.706%, 89.043%, 89.584%, and 90.124%. Likewise, when the number of query is 18, the precision values computed by SIFT, HOG + MKSIFT, MKSIFT, and proposed MKSIFT-Deep RNN are 91.384%, 92.103%, 93.183%, and 93.723%. The analysis based on recall parameter is portrayed in Fig. 3b. When the number of query is 4, the recall values computed by SIFT, HOG + MKSIFT, MKSIFT, and proposed MKSIFT-Deep RNN are 75.884%, 77.246, 77.446, and 83.693%. Similarly, when the number of query is 18, the recall values computed by SIFT, HOG + MKSIFT, MKSIFT, and proposed MKSIFT-Deep RNN are 78.301%, 80.859%, 81.159%, and 86.415%. The analysis based on F-measure parameter is portrayed in Fig. 3c. When the number of query is 4, the recall values computed by SIFT,

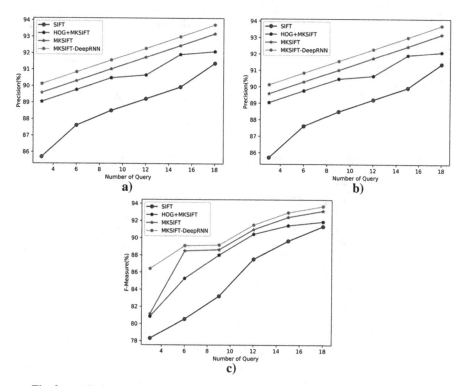

Fig. 3. Analysis based on query set-1 considering a) Precision b) Recall c) F-measure

HOG + MKSIFT, MKSIFT, and proposed MKSIFT-Deep RNN are 91.347%, 91.887%, 93.147%, and 93.687%. Similarly, when the number of query is 18, the recall values computed by SIFT, HOG + MKSIFT, MKSIFT, and proposed MKSIFT-Deep RNN are 91.42%, 91.959%, 93.219% and 93.76%.

4.4.2 Analysis Based on Query Set-2

Figure 4 portrays the analysis of methods considering query set-2 using precision, F-measure and recall parameter. The analysis using precision parameter is described in Fig. 3a. When the number of query is 4, the precision values computed by SIFT, HOG + MKSIFT, MKSIFT, and proposed MKSIFT-Deep RNN are 85.785%, 88.989%, 89.53%, and 90.07%. Likewise, when the number of query is 18, the precision values computed by SIFT, HOG + MKSIFT, MKSIFT, and proposed MKSIFT-Deep RNN are 92.049%, 92.589%, 93.129%, and 93.67%. The analysis based on recall parameter is portrayed in Fig. 4b. When the number of query is 4, the recall values computed by SIFT, HOG + MKSIFT, MKSIFT, and proposed MKSIFT-Deep RNN are 79.711%, 82.266%, 84.046%, and 84.396%. Similarly, when the number of query is 18, the recall values computed by SIFT, HOG + MKSIFT, MKSIFT, and proposed MKSIFT-Deep RNN are 92.031%, 92.572%, 93.111%, and 93.652%. The analysis based on F-measure parameter is portrayed in Fig. 4c. When the number of query is 4, the recall values computed

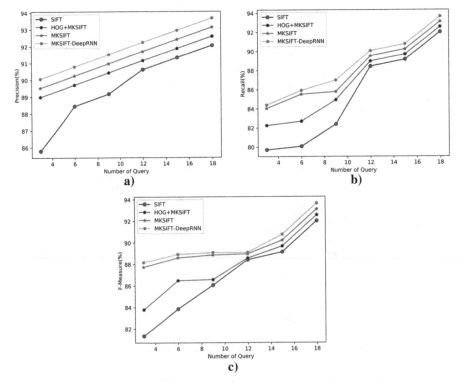

Fig. 4. Analysis based on query set-2 considering a) Precision b) Recall c) F-measure

by SIFT, HOG + MKSIFT, MKSIFT, and proposed MKSIFT-Deep RNN are 81.329%, 83.787%, 87.728%, and 88.170%. Similarly, when the number of query is 18, the recall values computed by SIFT, HOG + MKSIFT, MKSIFT, and proposed MKSIFT-Deep RNN are 92.013%, 92.553%, 93.093%, and 93.634%.

5 Conclusion

This research proposes an image retrieval model, namely MKSIFT-Deep RNN for retrieving the relevant image from the medical image database. Here, MKSIFT approach is employed for selecting the relevant feature from the database. The MKSIFT utilizes the SIFT wherein key point descriptor is computed based on different kernel functions. In MKSIFT, the weight is assumed to be stable for classifying the input images. In addition, Deep RNN is employed for classifying the images into groups using generated feature vector. Whenever the query set is given to the proposed MKSIFT-Deep RNN, the medical image is processed to extract the features in order to devise the image contents. These features adapt Tanimoto similarity measure for comparing the images of the classified database for effective image retrieval. The proposed MKSIFT-Deep RNN outperformed other methods with maximal precision of 93.723%, maximal recall of 93.652% and maximal F-measure of 93.687%. For future works, some advanced optimization techniques can be employed to train the deep classifier in order to improve performance by accomplishing better image retrieval.

References

1. Mathan Kumar, B., Pushpa Lakshmi, R.: Multiple kernel scale invariant feature transform and cross indexing for image search and retrieval. Imaging Sci. J. **66**(2), 84–97 (2018)
2. Sharif, U., Mehmood, Z., Mahmood, T., Javid, M.A., Rehman, A., Saba, T.: Scene analysis and search using local features and support vector machine for effective content-based image retrieval. Artif. Intell. Rev. **52**(2), 901–925 (2018). https://doi.org/10.1007/s10462-018-9636-0
3. Saritha, R.R., Paul, V., Kumar, P.G.: Content based image retrieval using deep learning process. Cluster Computing **22**(2), 4187–4200 (2018). https://doi.org/10.1007/s10586-018-1731-0
4. Xia, Z., Jiang, L., Liu, D., Lu, L. and Jeon, B., "BOEW: A content-based image retrieval scheme using bag-of-encrypted-words in cloud computing," IEEE Transactions on Services Computing, 2019
5. Zhou, W., Li, H., Hong, R., et al.: BSIFT: toward data-independent codebook for large scale image search. IEEE Trans. Image Process. **24**(3), 967–979 (2015)
6. Latif, A., et al.: Content-based image retrieval and feature extraction: a comprehensive review. Math. Problems Eng. (2019)
7. Munjal, M.N. and Bhatia, S.: A novel technique for effective image gallery search using content based image retrieval system. In: Proceedings of International Conference on Machine Learning, Big Data, Cloud and Parallel Computing, pp. 25–29. IEEE (2019)
8. Yu, J., Qin, Z., Wan, T., Zhang, X.: Feature integration analysis of bag-of-features model for image retrieval. Neuro Comput. **120**, 355–364 (2013)
9. Raja, N.M.K., Bhanu, K.S.: Content bases image search and retrieval using indexing by k means clustering technique. Int. J. Adv. Res. Comput. Commun. Eng. **2**(5), 2181–2189 (2013)

10. Zhong, D., Defée, I.: DCT histogram optimization for image database retrieval. Pattern Recogn. Lett. **26**(14), 2272–2281 (2005)
11. Tzelepi, M., Tefas, A.: Deep convolutional learning for content based image retrieval. Neurocomputing **275**, 2467–2478 (2018)
12. Inoue, M., Inoue, S., Nishida, T.: Deep recurrent neural network for mobile human activity recognition with high throughput. Artif. Life Robot. **23**(2), 173–185 (2017). https://doi.org/10.1007/s10015-017-0422-x
13. Sergyan, S.: Color histogram features based image classification in content-based image retrieval systems. In: Proceedings of 6th International Symposium on Applied Machine Intelligence and Informatics, pp. 221–224 (2008)
14. Lowe, D.G.: Distinctive image features from scale-invariant keypoints. Int. J. Comput. Vis. **60**(2), 91–110 (2004)
15. Lowe, D.G.: Object recognition from local scale-invariant features. In: Proceedings of the Seventh IEEE International Conference on Computer Vision, Kerkyra, vol. 2, pp. 1150–1157 (1999)
16. Vijendran, A.S., Kumar, S.V.: A new content based image retrieval system by HOG of wavelet sub bands. Int. J. Sig. Process. Image Process. Pattern Recogn. **8**(4), 297–306 (2015)
17. Menze, B.H., Jakab, A., Bauer, S., Kalpathy-Cramer, J., Farahani, K., Kirby, J., et al.: The multimodal brain tumor image segmentation benchmark (BRATS). IEEE Trans. Med. Imaging **34**(10), 1993–2024 (2015). https://doi.org/10.1109/TMI.2014.2377694
18. Bakas, S., Akbari, H., Sotiras, A., Bilello, M., Rozycki, M., Kirby, J.S., et al.: Advancing The Cancer Genome Atlas glioma MRI collections with expert segmentation labels and radiomic features. Nat. Sci. Data **4**, 170117 (2017). https://doi.org/10.1038/sdata.2017.117
19. S. Bakas, et al.: Identifying the best machine learning algorithms for brain tumor segmentation, progression assessment, and overall survival prediction in the BRATS challenge. arXiv preprint arXiv:1811.02629 (2018)
20. Chaubey, N.K., Jayanthi, P.: Disease diagnosis and treatment using deep learning algorithms for the healthcare system. In: Wason, R., Goyal, D., Jain, V., Balamurugan, S., Baliyan, A. (eds.), Applications of Deep Learning and Big IoT on Personalized Healthcare Services, pp. 99–114. IGI Global, Hershey (2020). https://doi.org/10.4018/978-1-7998-2101-4.ch007

Demystifying Computational Techniques Used to Diagnose Tuberculosis

Dhruvi J. Ka Patel$^{(\boxtimes)}$ (iD), Mosin I. Hasan (iD), and Narendar M. Patel (iD)

Birla Vishvakaram Mahavidyalaya, Engineering College, Vallabh Vidyanagar, Gujarat, India
dhruvi0502@gmail.com, mosin83@gmail.com,
nmpatel@bvmengineering.ac.in

Abstract. Tuberculosis is one of the most deathful diseases in the entire world and remains a major reason for death worldwide. In 2017, around 10.0 million people infected with tuberculosis. For detecting disease in the medical field using the computational technique, MRCNN & UNET Model has achieved impressive accuracy across multiple datasets like brain tumor (Multimodal Brain Tumor Image Segmentation (BRATS 2015) datasets), glaucoma and other based on data collected. This Research is based on the detection of WBC (White Blood Cell) form the stained Microscopy image, by collecting past data form patients. In India, medical patient data is not stored anywhere systematically, we made extra effort to find hidden patterns from data. The article deeply discusses the various approaches to diagnose tuberculosis. It summarizes the advantages and disadvantages of the existing techniques and why deep learning technology use in the various medical diagnosis process. In this study, we propose a fully automatic method for WBC segmentation, which is developed using MRCNN based deep convolutional networks. Proposed technique was evaluated on a dataset that contains 2500 stained microscopy images are used to train the system and 540 images are used to test the system. We have achieved nearly 92% accuracy with a low false-positive type error.

Keywords: Tuberculosis · UNET · Mycobacterium · Deep learning · Medical · Microscopy images · MRCNN

1 Introduction

Tuberculosis is caused by mycobacterium bacteria. The world health organization published a tuberculosis report every year. Diagnosis of tuberculosis is done in various ways like staining technique, X-Ray and etc. and its purpose is to provide information about diagnosis technique and Tuberculosis epidemic.

1.1 Tuberculosis

Tuberculosis is a deathful disease which is caused by mycobacterium bacteria [1]. Tuberculosis mostly damages the lungs but can also damage other parts of the body like eyes,

© Springer Nature Singapore Pte Ltd. 2020
N. Chaubey et al. (Eds.): COMS2 2020, CCIS 1235, pp. 55–69, 2020.
https://doi.org/10.1007/978-981-15-6648-6_5

brain & lags. According to the study of human skeletons, human affected by this diseases from thousands of years and this disease is remained unknown until Dr. Robert Koch discovered the Tuberculosis bacteria called mycobacterium [2]. Tuberculosis is of two types 1) Latent 2) Active. Most of the infections do not have any symptoms called latent tuberculosis. About 10% of latent tuberculosis is called active tuberculosis. Tuberculosis diseases are spread through the air from one person to another. Active tuberculosis is visible more in people who smoke and who affected by HIV/AIDS [3]. Classical symptoms are fever, cough with blood-containing mucus, Chest pain, weight loss, Chills and etc. [4, 5]. World health organization (WHO) publishing a report on tuberculosis since 1997 and its purpose is to provide information about the diagnosis technique and Tuberculosis epidemic. In 2017 report WHO discusses that 10.0 million cases of Tuberculosis registered worldwide and from that 1.3 million people deaths [6].

Mycobacterium is a family of Mycobacteriaceae [7]. Tuberculosis is caused by bacteria called mycobacterium bacteria. The size of mycobacterium is 2 to 4 μm in length and 0.2 to 0.5 μm in width [8]. Mycobacterium growing in road shape. Mycobacterium takes 15 to 20 h to spreading [9, 10]. Figure 1 and 2 show how the mycobacterium visible in different technique.

Fig. 1. Tuberculosis bactria in ZN staining technique [11] (Color figure online)

1.2 Diagnosis Techniques

Microscopy technique is the technical field of microscopes, its way to identify bacteria with the help of a microscope by staining them using gram stain [13]. Gram stain is a technique to classify the bacteria into two class gram-positive type and gram-negative type [14]. A microscopy image is a technique to view the microscopy world [15]. We have prepared the dataset by collecting the stained microscopy images, the system is trained using a prepared dataset and this system will help to diagnosis the various diseases having microscopic analysis based on images.

Fig. 2. Tuberculosis bactria in fluorescent staining technique [12] (Color figure online)

Tuberculosis diagnosis is done in a various way:

1. **Staining Technique**

The staining technique is the oldest technique and one of the most popular. This technique is cost-effective (Only RS. 300) but it is time-consuming because the result of the diagnosis process takes more than 4 h.

Type of Staining:
A. ZN Staining: In this technique background is visible in blue color and the object is visible in pink color. Figure 1 shows mycobacterium in this technique.
B. Fluorescent Staining: In this technique background is visible in black color and the object is visible in golden color. Figure 2 shows mycobacterium in this technique.

Staining Process:
Figure 3 shows the fluorescent staining process, it is a process of diagnosis of tuberculosis by the sputum Checking. For this process, two samples of sputum are collected and prepare the 2 × 3 slide and for diagnosis of tuberculosis, it needs to count mycobacterium bacteria. Size of mycobacterium is too small so for counting them zooming is perform (10 × 10 zoom so it is a matrix of 100 fields and at a time only one field is visible).

2. **X-Ray**

X-Ray technique is the process of diagnosis tuberculosis by checking the lungs. And it is a process of finding the whole in the lungs. Figure 4 shows the lung's image. Usual X-Ray based tuberculosis detection is done by an expert in the field of medical science by looking at x-Ray reports.

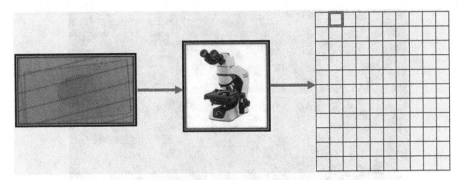

Fig. 3. Staining process

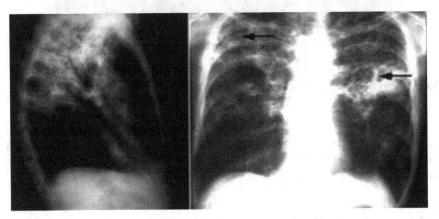

Fig. 4. Lung's X-Ray image [16]

3. GeneXpert Machine

GeneXpert Machine technique is a process of diagnosis tuberculosis by sputum checking. For this process, four samples of sputum are collected and directly put the sample into a machine and the final printed result is product. This technique is costly (US $17) but time saving. This process is based on the cartridge and the lifetime of a cartridge is only 18 months which is too short. The entire process is shown in Fig. 5.

1.3 Why Deep Learning

The previous topic describes information about different tuberculosis diagnosis techniques like staining, X-ray and GeneXpert Machine. A staining technique is a complex diagnosis process and the result of the process is dependences on the technical person who carried out the diagnosis process and also a technical person can also suffer from the eye problem due to the manual counting of this tine mycobacterium. A GeneXpert Machine and X-Ray techniques are costly and due to its cost, this technique is not prescribed by a doctor every time.

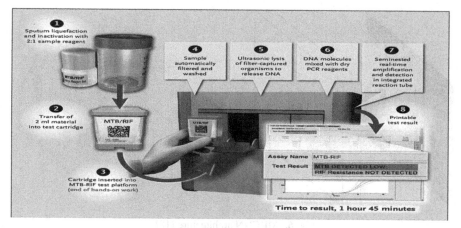

Fig. 5. GeneXpert machine [17]

There will be an error in the existing technology that is

1 False_positive type – means that Tuberculosis affected by a person but the report says that Tuberculosis is not affected. This means a normal report.
2 False_negative type – means that Tuberculosis not affected by a person but the report says that Tuberculosis is affected. This means a major report.

The Solution of the above address problem is given by the deep learning Technique (MRCNN, UNET model) used to diagnosis the process. In this diagnosis process human intervention is not there so there is no chicness of errors.

1.4 MRCNN

Masked Region-Based Convolution Neural Network (MRCNN) is an Image segmentation technique that is a combination of Faster RNCC and Fully Convolution Neural Network. Figure 6 Shown the MRCNN Architecture and it does the following steps.

1. It takes an image as input and extracts features from an image using ResNet 101 architecture.
2. The feature is passed to Region proposal network (RPM) which is used to predict that the object is present in given region?
3. With the help of ROI Align property of MRCNN, it finds out labels and bounding boxes of the fully connected networks.
4. All-Region IoU is calculated [IoU = Area of the intersection/Area of the union].
5. Output pass to convolution layer for pixel-wise Segmentation Mask.

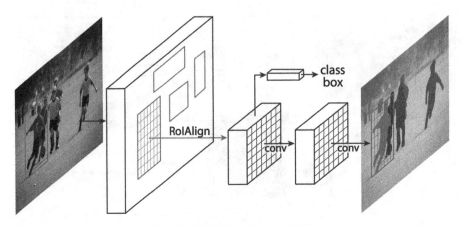

Fig. 6. MRCNN architecture [18]

1.5 UNET Model

UNET module is one of the most popular deep learning technique developed by Olaf Ronneberger, Philipp Fischer, and Thomas Brox in 2015. UNET model is based on convolution neural network and its special developed for biomedical image processing. UNET model is also called as a 'U-shape' Architecture. Architecture is combination of Down-Sampling part and Up-Sampling part. The down-sampling part aim is to collect the information and the Up-Sampling part aim is to expanding path and provide a precise location [19].

2 Existing Research in Diagnosis of Tuberculosis and Medical Diagnosis

Tuberculosis is caused by mycobacterium bacteria. The manual process of diagnosis of tuberculosis (Staining Technique, X-ray, GeneXept Machine) some are complex and time-consuming and some are costly, so for giving the solution of existing manual process data mining, deep learning is used.

2.1 Tuberculosis

Mosin I. Hasan et al. (2011) discussed that tuberculosis is an infectious disease in India. The main objective is to develop the technique which categorizes tuberculosis in two categories as yes and no using naïve Bayesian classification and its aim is to extract the hidden patterns of Tuberculosis from the past patient data. Dataset contains detail of 154 cases by considering the 19 symptoms. 154 cases of tuberculosis is consider for processing by dividing the cases into two equal part of training and testing. The result is given in two ways using the weka tool and c program [20]. The advantages and limitations are discussed in the research finding section.

Yu Cao et al. (2016) discussed that tuberculosis is a deathful disease worldwide. The main aim of this research is to create large scale, real-world and freely available datasets of chest images and also provide well annotation and create a mobile phone based computing system to diagnosis tuberculosis effectively. Dataset is a collection of 4701 images from that 453 is normal images and 4248 abnormal images. The system is the train in two way Binary classification and multiple classification based level of infection [21]. Advantages and limitations are discussed in the research finding section.

Paras Lakhani et al. (2017) discussed that tuberculosis is danger disease worldwide. The main objective of this research is to show that how deep convolution neural network (DCNN) is used to diagnose tuberculosis is there or not. Dataset is a collection of cheat images of 150 cases and getting the accuracy of 97.3%. The author used two most popular DCNNs techniques called AlexNet and GoogLeNet for the diagnosis of tuberculosis. Process identify the hole in the chest [22].

2.2 Microscopy

John A. Quinn et al. (2016) discussed that microscopy is the standard method for diagnosing various diseases. Microscopy is one of the well adapted to low-resource, high disease burden areas. Microscopy based technique result of the process is dependent on the Technical person who carried out the diagnosis process. The main aim of this research is to show how microscopy is giving the best result for tuberculosis, malaria and Intestinal parasites. For the tuberculosis diagnosis process, stained sputum microscopy images are taken and using the CNN algorithm to train the system and find the mycobacterium and getting 0.99 area under the cove. For the malaria diagnosis process, stained blood sample microscopy images are taken and using the CNN system are train and find thick blood cell and getting 1.00 area under the cove [23].

Sonaal Kant et al. (2018) discussed that tuberculosis is danger disease worldwide. The author used deep learning techniques to diagnosis tuberculosis using CNN and SVM techniques. Accuracy is calculated using precision and recall factor and getting 83.78% and 67.55% respectively. The author used Dataset 3 of ZiehlNeelsen Sputum smear Microscopy image Database (ZNSM-iDB) which contain 6 set and each set have 50 field sputum images [24].

2.3 Medical Imaging Computation

Medical Image computation is done in many ways like data mining, image processing, and etc. one of the most popular fields for doing the processing of medical images called Deep learning (UNET). UNET model of deep learning is specially developed for biomedical image segmentation. The concept is introduced by Olaf Ronneberger, Thomas Brox, and Philipp Fischer in 2015 at the University of Freiburg, Germany. Figure 7 shows the architecture of the UNET model. Overall architecture UNET model has divided into two parts 1) Down Sampling and 2) Up Sampling.

UNET model is based on a convolution neural network. Architecture is work from left to right. Downsampling part is a collection of five convolution block and each block contains another three convolutions at the end of each convolution block max-pooling operation is performed. Upsampling part is a collection of four convolution block and

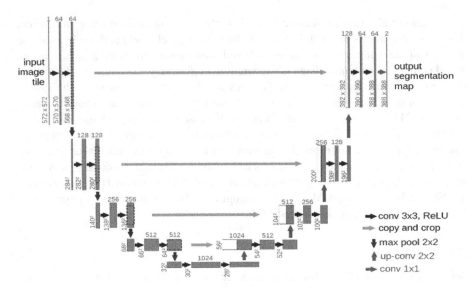

Fig. 7. UNET model architecture [19]

each block contains another three convolution blocks, the main purpose of Upsampling is to extract the content. The main purpose of downsampling is to capture context. The last step is the 1×1 convolution for classification of facture map into two class foregrounds and background [19].

Dong Hao et al. (2017) discussed that Detecting Brain Tumor Using MIR Technique is a very time-consuming process and the performance of the system is depended on the technical person who does this test, so automatic fully convolution network is used for efficient tumor segmentation based on UNET module of deep learning. For this technique multimodal brain tumor image segmentation BRATS dataset is used, the dataset has 220 high-grade brain tumor images and 54 low-grade brain tumor images. The primary effect of Brain Tumor is a dreadful type of cancer [25].

Artem Sevastopolsky et al. (2017) discussed that Glaucoma is a condition of eyes. A person can blind also due to this condition, so it is important to detect it in the early stages. One of the main symptoms of Glaucoma disease is a cup-to-disc ratio (CDR) is a ratio between heights of cup and disc. People are affected by Glaucoma or not, this decision is based on CIDR Parameter. CDR is at least 0.65 is considered Glaucoma positive [26].

Zhou Zongwei et al. (2018) discussed that UNet++ model is a more powerful architecture for medical image segmentation. The architecture of UNET++ is combination of encoder and decoder, this encoder and decoder are known as sub-network, this sub-network are combination of nested dense skip layers path called pathways. The main aim of using pathways is to reduce the semantic gap between encoding network and decoding network. Using this concept of path getting 92.52% of accuracy for detecting cell nuclei. UNet++ architecture is combination of nested and dense skip connection which is used to find fine-grained details of an object. In UNET model the feature maps of the encoder are directly expected in the decoder; however, in UNet++ model the feature maps of the encoder sub network first passed to the dense convolution level and then feature maps passed to the decoder [27].

Weng Yu et al. (2019) discussed that NAS (Neural Architecture Search) is a subtopic of auto-machine learning that has significant overlap on two parameter 1) hyper parameter optimization and 2) meta-learning. Current research on Neural Architecture Search based on three topics: search strategy, search space and different performance estimation strategy. Search space give the information about which architecture represented in given principle. The combine architecture of NSA and UNET is based on DownSC and UpSC, this DownSC and UpSC is called cell architecture. With the help of combine technique 98% of accuracy is obtain [28].

Zyuzin Vasily et al. (2018) discussed that modern cardiology of heart is done using ultrasound technique also known as echocardiography (EchoCG). Manual technique of cardiology is time consuming process and result is depends on technical person, so author used to train the system using UNET model. Health of heart is check by segmenting left ventricular (LV) border of the EchoCG. This LV image are represent in 2D manner, for training system 94 patients data is used and using this proposed technique author obtain 92% of accuracy [29].

3   Research Findings

Mosin I. Hasan et al. [20] discussed that the manual tuberculosis test process is complex and the result is dependent on the technical person. Using a naïve Bayesian algorithm author achieved 78% accuracy. Dataset content only 154 cases and its symptoms. The efficiency of naïve Bayesian by selecting weighted features. Dataset is of very small size and the author has not discussed False-negative results as in disease diagnosis false negative has a crucial impact on the efficiency of the algorithm. This technique can be used as a supplementary method to further strengthen the result of other systems. Apart from this more data should be collected [20].

Yu Cao et al. [21] discussed that successfully creating a well-formed tuberculosis chest dataset that contains 4701 images from that 453 is normal (tuberculosis not there) and 4248 abnormal (tuberculosis is there). The system is trained in two-way Binary classification and multiple classifications based levels of infection and getting 89.6% and 62% accuracy respectively. But in the binary case, it only saying that tuberculosis is there or not by only find the whole chest images form that we are not getting any information about at which stage tuberculosis is there. In the second case multiple classifications not discuss anything about the false negative, it means that the tuberculosis is caused by the person but report saying that it not there so it's a very compacted thing [21].

Paras Lakhani et al. [22] discussed that using DCNNs techniques (AlexNet & GoogLeNet) system is trained using 150 cases of tuberculosis and getting 97.3% accuracy. The ratio of misclassification is more in case of new dataset [22].

Dong Hao et al. [25] discussed that in the UNET model Soft Dice based loss function is used for making unbalanced samples uniformed. Data Augmentation technique is used to increase the number of training samples. Data augmentation methods like flipping, rotation, shift, and zoom. The limitation of this proposed method is system is evaluated using cross-validation schema using this proposed technique, getting 82% accuracy and provides an unbalance predicate [25].

Artem Sevastopolsky et al. [27] discussed that manual method of optic disc and cup requires about eight minutes per eye for technical person and this test done efficiently using UNET in less time. The author used less number of the filter then the original UNET Module have, the main aim of the author is to provide lightweight architecture and getting 89% of accuracy [26].

Each and every method have its own pros and cons. Existing work done in tuberculosis will diagnosis diseases correctly but the system is trained on a dataset that contains small sample and also that samples are not of all the type. Accuracy getting in existing system is also too less. Existing research work not force on false-negative type of prediction, false-negative means tuberculosis is caused by the person but system product result as tuberculosis is not there which major problem is. Research work done in 2017 on the chest dataset consider only 13 cases to train the system which not the correct way for diagnosis the diseases.

4 Implementation Result

In this study, we developed MRCNN model to detect and return mask of WBC cell in an image. System is train on 2500 images of WBC and 540 image are used to test the system. Using this MRCNN we get 92% of accuracy. The system take original image and its annotation file as an input at time of training. The system take original image and product output as an image which contain highlight mask of all the WBC.

Figure 9, 10, 11 and 12 show the result of Object segmentation in which it display the WBC cell mask if image have more than one WBC cell then it display in different color.

Steps to Implement Mask RCNN for Identifying WBC Cell

1. To train the system using MRCNN model annotation of an image is required to identify WBC cell. Annotation is done using VGG Image Annotation tool, Fig. 8 shows the example of Image Annotation.
2. For the implementation of MRCNN Required following Packages are need to be install which is opencv-python, numpy, keras $\geq$ 2.0.8, matplotlib, cython, scikit-image, tensorflow $\geq$ 1.3.0, h5py, imaguag, IPython, scipy, and pillow.
3. Download pre-trained weight of a COCO model called mask_rcnn_coco.h5.
4. For doing a Predicting on our image we will use the Mask R-CNN architecture and the pre-trained weights of COCO model to generate Mask of WBC cell.

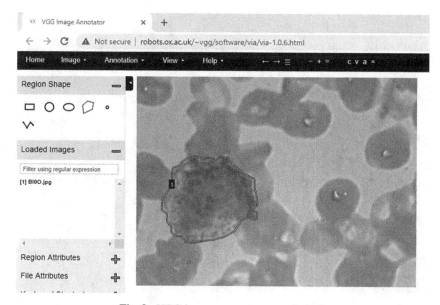

Fig. 8. VGG image annotator example [30]

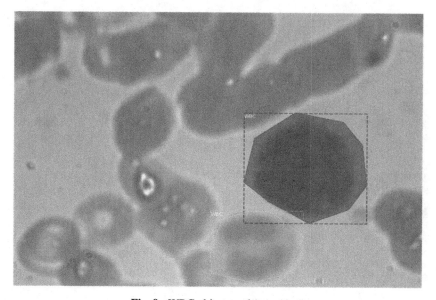

Fig. 9. WBC object mask output—1

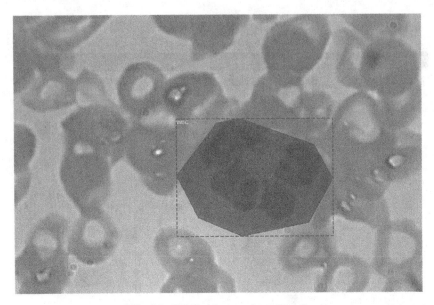

Fig. 10. WBC object mask output—2

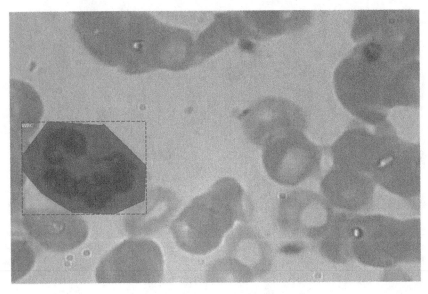

Fig. 11. WBC object mask output—3

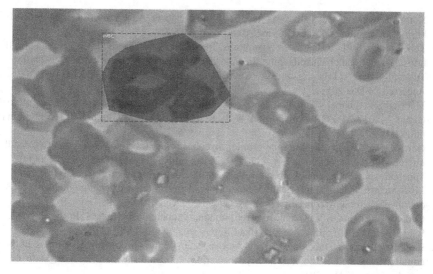

Fig. 12. WBC object mask output—4

5 Conclusion

Accounting to the world health organization tuberculosis is one of the deathful diseases worldwide. One fourth of the world population affected by tuberculosis. In 2017 10.0 million cases of tuberculosis are resisted worldwide and from that 1.3 million people deaths. Well-formed and annotated Dataset pertaining to stained slides is not available which important task is and it needs attention. X-Ray based diagnosis technique has potential but the cost of X-Ray based technique is high and the result is based on the technical person who carried out the diagnosis process and due to cost concern it is prescribe in later stage. Staining based technique for diagnosis of tuberculosis sputum checking is done by finding the mycobacterium. Size of mycobacterium is tony (0.2–0.5 μm) and manually counting of the bacteria is a complex task which is prone to error due to manual intervention of technical person., we come known that how the MRCNN model give the efficient result in medical diagnosis like brain tumor detection, Glaucoma detection and etc. MRCNN model has capability to detected tony thing and give the best result. Well-formed and well-annotated dataset (that contain sputum stained images) is not available. Furthermore, Creation of this dataset the having sputum stained images are the imported task to explored it further. UNET model is special developed for biomedical image processing. We also combine MRCNN and UNET Model to increase accuracy of diagnosis process.

References

1. WHO | What is TB? How is it treated? In: WHO. http://www.who.int/features/qa/08/en/. Accessed 22 Nov 2019
2. World Health Organization (2018) Global tuberculosis report (2018)

3. Konstantinos, A.: Diagnostic tests: testing for tuberculosis. Aust. Prescr. **33**, 12–18 (2010). https://doi.org/10.18773/austprescr.2010.005
4. Tuberculosis: PPD test, causes, symptoms, treatment & prognosis. In: eMedicineHealth. https://www.emedicinehealth.com/tuberculosis/article_em.htm. Accessed 24 Dec 2019
5. Tuberculosis   (TB).   https://www.who.int/news-room/fact-sheets/detail/tuberculosis. Accessed 24 Dec 2019
6. MacNeil, A.: Global epidemiology of tuberculosis and progress toward achieving global targets—2017. MMWR Morb. Mortal. Wkly. Rep **68** (2019). https://doi.org/10.15585/mmwr.mm6811a3
7. Gordon, S.V., Parish, T.: Microbe profile: mycobacterium tuberculosis: humanity's deadly microbial foe. Microbiology **164**, 437–439 (2018). https://doi.org/10.1099/mic.0.000601
8. Tuberculosis. http://textbookofbacteriology.net/tuberculosis.html. Accessed 20 Dec 2019
9. Mycobacteria I General information. https://www.hain-lifescience.de/en/products/microbiol ogy/mycobacteria/mycobacteria.html. Accessed 20 Dec 2019
10. Cudahy, P., Shenoi, S.V.: Diagnostics for pulmonary tuberculosis: Table 1. Postgrad. Med. J. **92**, 187–193 (2016). https://doi.org/10.1136/postgradmedj-2015-133278
11. File:Mycobacterium tuberculosis Ziehl-Neelsen stain 02.jpg - Wikimedia Commons. https://commons.wikimedia.org/wiki/File:Mycobacterium_tuberculosis_Ziehl-Neelsen_stain_02.jpg. Accessed 25 Dec 2019
12. Mycobacterium Tuberculosis I Fraen. http://www.fraen.com/optics/microscopes/case-stu dies/mycobacterium-tuberculosis/. Accessed 25 Dec 2019
13. What is Microscopy? I The University of Edinburgh. https://www.ed.ac.uk/clinical-sciences/ edinburgh-imaging/for-patients-study-participants/tell-me-more-about-my-scan/what-is-microscopy. Accessed 25 Dec 2019
14. Gram Staining - Coico - 2006 - current protocols in microbiology. Wiley Online Library. https://currentprotocols.onlinelibrary.wiley.com/doi/abs/10.1002/9780471729259.mca03cs00. Accessed 25 Dec 2019
15. Microscopy Imaging Techniques. In: MicroscopeMaster. https://www.microscopemaster.com/microscopy-imaging-techniques.html. Accessed 21 Dec 2019
16. Tuberculosis, advanced - chest x-rays: MedlinePlus medical encyclopedia image. https://med lineplus.gov/ency/imagepages/1607.htm. Accessed 25 Dec 2019
17. (48) 18 Demonstration of Xpert MTB RIF assay for diagnosis of tuberculosis from sputum specimens - YouTube. https://www.youtube.com/watch?v=VIR9gufNrBo. Accessed 25 Nov 2019
18. He, K., Gkioxari, G., Dollár, P., Girshick, R.: Mask R-CNN. In: Proceedings of the IEEE International Conference on Computer Vision, pp. 2961–2969 (2017)
19. Ronneberger, O., Fischer, P., Brox, T.: U-Net: convolutional networks for biomedical image segmentation. In: Navab, N., Hornegger, J., Wells, W.M., Frangi, A.F. (eds.) MICCAI 2015. LNCS, vol. 9351, pp. 234–241. Springer, Cham (2015). https://doi.org/10.1007/978-3-319-24574-4_28
20. Maniya, H., Hasan, M.I., Patel, K.P.: Comparative study of Naïve Bayes classifier and KNN for tuberculosis, p. 5 (2011)
21. Cao, Y., Liu, C., Liu, B., et al.: Improving tuberculosis diagnostics using deep learning and mobile health technologies among resource-poor and marginalized communities. In: 2016 IEEE First International Conference on Connected Health: Applications, Systems and Engineering Technologies (CHASE). IEEE, Washington, DC, USA, pp. 274–281 (2016)
22. Lakhani, P., Sundaram, B.: Deep learning at chest radiography: automated classification of pulmonary tuberculosis by using convolutional neural networks. Radiology **284**, 574–582 (2017). https://doi.org/10.1148/radiol.2017162326
23. Quinn, J.A.: Deep convolutional neural networks for microscopy-based point of care diagnostics, p. 12 (2016)

24. Towards automated tuberculosis detection using deep learning. IEEE Conference Publication. https://ieeexplore.ieee.org/abstract/document/8628800/. Accessed 22 Dec 2019

25. Dong, H., Yang, G., Liu, F., Mo, Y., Guo, Y.: Automatic brain tumor detection and segmentation using U-Net based fully convolutional networks. In: Valdés Hernández, M., González-Castro, V. (eds.) MIUA 2017. CCIS, vol. 723, pp. 506–517. Springer, Cham (2017). https://doi.org/10.1007/978-3-319-60964-5_44

26. Sevastopolsky, A.: Optic disc and cup segmentation methods for glaucoma detection with modification of U-Net convolutional neural network. Pattern Recognit. Image Anal. **27**, 618–624 (2017)

27. Zhou, Z., Rahman Siddiquee, M.M., Tajbakhsh, N., Liang, J.: UNet++: a nested U-Net architecture for medical image segmentation. In: Stoyanov, D., et al. (eds.) DLMIA/ML-CDS -2018. LNCS, vol. 11045, pp. 3–11. Springer, Cham (2018). https://doi.org/10.1007/978-3-030-00889-5_1

28. Weng, Y., Zhou, T., Li, Y., Qiu, X.: NAS-Unet: neural architecture search for medical image segmentation. IEEE Access **7**, 44247–44257 (2019)

29. Zyuzin, V., Sergey, P., Mukhtarov, A., et al.: Identification of the left ventricle endocardial border on two-dimensional ultrasound images using the convolutional neural network UNet. In: 2018 Ural Symposium on Biomedical Engineering, Radioelectronics and Information Technology (USBEREIT), pp. 76–78. IEEE (2018)

30. VGG Image Annotator. http://www.robots.ox.ac.uk/~vgg/software/via/via-1.0.6.html. Accessed 26 Nov 2019

Indian Currency Recognition from Live Video Using Deep Learning

Kushal Bhavsar[1] , Keyurbhai Jani[2(✉)] , and Rakeshkumar Vanzara[1]

[1] U. V. Patel College of Engineering, Ganpat University, Mehsana 384012, Gujarat, India
kushalbhavsar58@gmail.com, rakesh.vanzara@ganpatuniversity.ac.in
[2] Gujarat Technological University, Ahmedabad 382424, Gujarat, India
keyur.soft@gmail.com

Abstract. Foreign and Visually disable people in India often find difficulties in recognizing different currency notes. Even if some time it is also difficult for Indian healthy people to identify same amount of currency notes with different-new designs. Human eye has also some limitation so some time fake currency not identifiable by them. In this paper using deep learning technique, detection model trained with dataset and tested it with different Indian currency with good accuracy.

Keywords: Deep learning · Object detection · Computer vision · Currency recognition · Image processing

1 Introduction

Aim of this paper is to propose a concept of Indian currency recognition. Actually, main aim of this paper is to do this project for a blind person who cannot see anything, so this work can help blind people to recognize currency, they will have App/device for this, which can scan currency from camera image and predict the result and tell to the blind user which currency is this via voice. Authors gathered dataset of new Indian currencies as well as old Indian Currencies. This is the starting point so authors are gathering a data day by day and increasing the good amount of data with good quality images [1].

Dataset is the most important thing in this project, it should be clear and very high quality. Quality of images matters a lot on our classification result, another thing is background, it should be clear in every images of prepared dataset otherwise model can get confused with objects & noise. So data gathering is the most important thing. Now 2nd thing is training, Authors are training their machine to learn to detect & recognize object from given input, so author's machine learning is based on what it see, and it is seeing and learnt from their image dataset. Therefore, with a good amount of quality images authors can improve machine's learning ability. Before discussing implementation, first let's understand what Deep learning is, and what approach we are using for training.

© Springer Nature Singapore Pte Ltd. 2020
N. Chaubey et al. (Eds.): COMS2 2020, CCIS 1235, pp. 70–81, 2020.
https://doi.org/10.1007/978-981-15-6648-6_6

2 The Problem

In India, people are using paper currencies for daily transactions, currency have some particular format, and with the help of that format, people can recognize any currency. Every normal person can recognize any currency with eye, but what about blind people? They cannot recognize any currency with eyes, any people can do fraud with them. Second Objective is that in Indian Banking System, they are working with lots of currencies, so we want to use deep learning for currency recognition using images & video input feed. Ex In cash counter a one camera can recognize currency and it can make a total of cash. Third Objective is that now in this time robots doing work instead of humans, so authors want every robot can recognize any currency so it can do money transaction like normal human.

3 The Problem Solution

Problem can be solve with the use of Deep learning techniques to recognize any Indian Currency using Image or Video as an Input Feed. Authors developed one solution using Deep Learning, which can identify Indian Currency. Authors want to create one application, which can do this task for any blind person. Even authors want to make an API so any Robots and any other software can use our applications advantage without any work and research, they need to just use our API. Now let us understand how it is working.

4 Working Structure

In this system, we have to just feed image of currency or video, which contain currency, it can detect which currency is this. So now question is that what mechanism is running in behind of this? The answer is very simple we are using Deep learning & Image processing. However, another question is that why we are using Deep learning instead of machine learning? What is difference between Machine learning and Deep Learning? So, let's see all those answers. First, we need to understand what is Machine Learning and Deep Learning [15, 16].

5 Literature Review

Since, our existing system had limitation, example image is folded or rotated, we had another limitation, if there are many currencies in one bundle, in this condition we need to detect whole currency note one by one. So we need to open the bundle for detecting currency, so it should be not a good approach. The lightning conditions is also depending on our prediction [1].

We also done survey on Genetics Algorithm (GA) for a Currency Recognition. It has an ability to learn the patterns by self-learning. This learning or we can say information it will obtained by gene, then it will compare it with original data. It can perform the optimization in relatively short time. This optimization can help us to achieve a good accuracy in currency recognition [1].

According to [1] paper they captured video of currencies and then they converted frames into images. They have total 300 number of images in dataset. This is good dataset gathering approach. We applied another approach we captured images of currencies one by one. It is time consuming but with this technique, we can make the good dataset. In dataset, quality of images should be very clear and complete in each image. We used 1200*800 resolution for every image.

In kim [10], they experimented classification tasks of pre-training. According to them moving objects cannot recognized at a time, the reason is speed of object. Therefore, in that case they used RMI (Recurrent motion image). It is used to provide vectors for feature extraction and to calculate the target object that is repeated in motion [9].

In [11], the output of the first task was proposed as another task. This method is iterative which performs object detection between each other objects. In [1], it represents an overview of currency recognition they choose CNN model to do currency recognition, they extracts the currency features layer by layer.

We seen in almost research papers they are using neural networks for this type of object detection but in [12] they used RBFN (Radial Basic Function network). They are using correlations between images. According to them no human interaction needed in this system. Even accuracy is also good.

Authors of [13] implemented Real time fake currency detection using deep learning, in this research, they used transfer-learning approach for detecting Indian currency, even they implemented fake currency detection. They used Alexanet model as a classifier. They make pipelines in between every layer and with model; they predict the result that is recognition of currency.

Ms. Reshu Gupta, Author of [14] use MATLAB to Identify and authenticate original Rs. 2000 note by image processing steps.

6 Strategy of Research

We seen 100 Rupees old note have green color but new note have purple color, 50 rupees new note have light green color but old have dark purple, there are many differences in new & old currency so with that parameters we can classify currencies. We captured images of currency from different angles with different side objects.

We split the images in 80:20 ratio for training & testing. Every Image size is 1200*800. We seen every country have their own pattern, In India every currency notes have different colors, looks and size.

7 Machine Learning

Machine learning is the technique in which we perform a scientific analysis on different algorithm and statistical models. In this approach we use heuristic algos and approach like Linear Regression, SVM, Naïve Bayes, KNN, KMeans Clustering. These all are the different types of working algorithms of Machine Learning [15]. But the question is that how Machine learning is working?

Simple answer is that it takes data as a input, find a patterns in it using algorithms and heuristics approach and give predictions of our test data based on input training data and algorithms learning pattern. In machine learning we need to do feature extraction by self, then we need to train the model. But this approach is not best and optimal solution for our application so we choose a Deep Learning approach for it. In Machine learning it always go for a solution but that solution could be a optimal or may be not also [4] (Fig. 1).

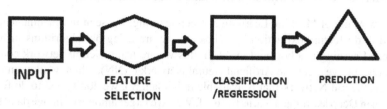

INPUT   FEATURE   CLASSIFICATION   PREDICTION
               SELECTION   /REGRESSION

Fig. 1. Machine Learning

8 Deep Learning

We mimic the human learning pattern and it create the new algorithm, we call it artificial neural network, it has same structure as biological neural network.

There are different types of neural network available; we can use it according to our work. However, most important thing is that to understand a structure of artificial neural Deep learning is the approach in that it mimic the humans learning patterns, we humans learn using Biological Neural Network(which is in-build in our body), In deep learning network. Now let see working of deep learning [7].

8.1 Working of Deep Learning

Deep learning is becoming the most evolving AI technique in 21st century. In this modern era, we have lots of data, and deep learning needs a data, that's why it becomes so popular in this modern era. We can see the usage of deep learning everywhere like social media,

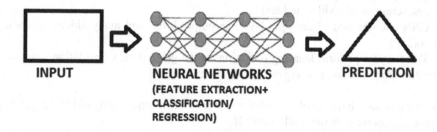

INPUT   NEURAL NETWORKS   PREDITCION
               (FEATURE EXTRACTION+
               CLASSIFICATION/
               REGRESSION)

* WORKING OF DEEP LEARNING

Fig. 2. Deep Learning

government, IT sector, Cinemas, Search engines. We humans already implemented Face recognition, self-driving car, auto drones and we are continuously evolving like we are in infinity loop of mega evolution of AI. Now let us understand some algorithms that we used in our research [7] (Fig. 2).

8.2 Difference Between Machine Learning and Deep Learning

We seen working of Machine Learning & Deep learning. We seen in Machine learning we need to do feature extraction by self, even we are using old algorithms in it, but now Deep Learning is a hot field in AI. In this we are using Neural network concept. In this concept, we create an Artificial Neural Network (ANN), which works same as a Biological Neural Network that is available in human. So, we don't need to do feature extraction in Deep learning, it learns by itself. We have larger amount of Image data. Deep learning can perform better on images rather than Machine learning. Even it provides higher accuracy than machine learning. We can tune different parameters according to our data and model. Just one requirement is that we need a good GPU power for training. Moreover, another thing is that it takes longer time to train but it is worth [4].

8.3 Convolutional Neural Network

A Convolutional Neural Network is most popular Deep learning algorithm in which it takes an input image, assign weights and biases to various aspect according to the object in the image. In other algorithms we need to do lots of image processing and hand engineering to achieve the accuracy. But in CNN have the ability to learn these all the characteristics of images [5]. So, we don't need to do a lots of hand engineering in images, CNN will do for us. And also, we can achieve a good accuracy in our work.

8.4 Working of Convolutional Neural Network (CNN)

A Convolutional Neural Network have a n numbers of layers which can learn to detect different features from an image data, and the output of each processed image is used as the input to the next layer. The filters or we can say processing like edges, increase complexity, adjust brightness. CNN can perform feature identification classification of images, sound, audio, video and text [2].

CNN is composed of an input layer, an output layer, and many hidden layers in network.

These layers perform learning operation on the given data, Convolution function, Activation function and pooling are hidden layers (Fig. 3).

- **Convolution** It have set of convolutional filters, which find features from images, so images pass through these all filters [2].
- **Rectified linear unit (ReLU)** is useful for mapping negative values into zero so it's maintaining positives values, so this is one kind of activation function, we have many more choices like Sigmoid, hyperbolic tangent, but choosing a layer for a model is a depends on your data. It affects the accuracy [2].

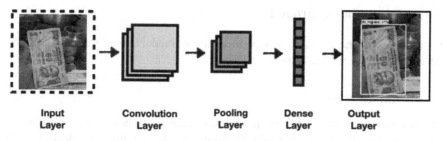

Fig. 3. Layers of CNN [8]

- **Pooling** performs the non-linear down stamping which can reduce the number of parameters then the network needs to learn and simplify the output [8].
- **Dense** layer is collections of neurons. It describes how neurons connected to the next layer of neurons (In short each neuron is connected to every neuron in the next layer). It is also known as Fully Connected layer [8].

These operations iterative on neural network layers, in which each layer learning to identify different features.

8.5 Training Time Increasing with GPU

A convolutional neural network is trained on hundreds, thousands, or even millions of images. When we have to work with lots of data then we can use GPUs for processing and computing. It can decrease the model training time and after training we can use our model in real world application.

8.6 Tools and Technology Used

Python Programming Language. Python is programming language like C, C++, C#. It is an interpreted high-level programming language. Guido van Rossum created it, and it was first released in 1991. Python coding style is so comfortable for programmer, it has indentation feature so our code structure always stays good and understandable for other. Python is dynamically type language and also, it's have garbage collection so we don't feel to worry about unnecessary garbage in programming, It supported Procedural programming, functional programming and also object oriented programming. With OOP user can write clear & logical code for small- and large-scale project.

Tensorflow. Tensorflow is a Deep learning library for implement neural network algorithms in our work. In February 2017 version 1 released. It is an open source library. In deep learning, we do lots of math and numerical calculation but with Tensorflow API we can do this thing easily. It is just like feed your data, choose your model, number of layers and activation and starts a training and wait for an outcome. It is developed by Google brain team. It runs on CPUs and GPUs, we can use it in mobile and embedded platforms, it also can process on TPUs, which is hardware to do math on tensors.

9 Experimental Approach

During this experiment, Faster_RCNN_Inception v2 model is used for training. Let us understand about it and pre-trained model.

9.1 Pre-trained Model

A pre-trained model, a name defining this term, it means model is trained on large dataset. You can use directly pre-trained model, in this just you have to feed your data and it can train on your data but it is already learnt on the large dataset, now you are re-training model so it will give you a better result. This learning approach is called Transfer learning. For example, you trained network on one lakhs images and now you are retraining it on 500 images for a classification purpose. There are some Transfer learning models like Googlenet, Imagenet, Alexanet, VGG16, VGG19, RCNN Inception and many more models you can use from tensorflow, keras and pytorch [6].

9.2 Faster RCNN

Faster RCNN has improved running time of network, it becomes so less compared to previous. In this we are using Regions Proposal Network (RPN) which shares convolutional features of images with the network, it simultaneously predicts the object and bounds with score at each position. RCNN is trained to generate high quality region proposals which is used by RCNN for faster detection, we required good enough GPU power for training. Faster RCNN is the 1st place winner in foundations [3] (Fig. 4).

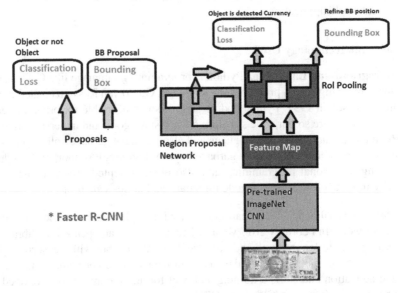

Fig. 4. Faster R-CNN working

9.3 Currency Dataset

In this part, we are discussing how we made our currency dataset, we captured images from 48 MP camera, every image has 4k*3k dimensions, let see some samples of our currency dataset. We used black marble as a background because of image clarity (Fig. 5).

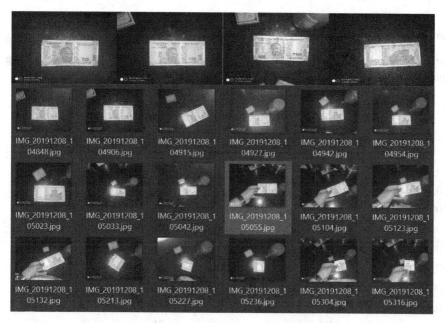

Fig. 5. Sample of dataset images

9.4 Dataset Gathering

Data gathering is the most important part of any research. We gathered number of images for every currency. So, we started gathering dataset with old currency. For a good quality images currency should be new. So, I collected currencies from ATM. Because from ATM we get a new note without any fold with clean paper. Then we make a one excel file in which we define what will be our label name & what will be our image count for particular one currency. First, I started with old currencies then click the photos from mobile, compress the images in zip. You can see structure of imaged below. After gathering of images, we converted our images into one scale of height & width (1200*800) with the help of python code. So now first step is done, now 2nd and most important step is image labelling. So, let see and understand image labelling in brief.

9.5 Dataset Labelling

Labelling is terminology or concept in which we give some particular name to a particular object. So in labelling we create a rectangle box which determines the object, then we give a name to that object. We are using labelImg tool for a image labelling. Then we give labels to every image which we gathered for our dataset.

9.6 Structure of Dataset

For Experiment below are dataset structure with Label, training images and testing images numbers (Table 1).

Table 1. Dataset structure used with model

Label	Number of training images	Number of testing images
10_new _note	201	50
10_old_note	201	52
100_new_note	204	47
100_old_note	201	50
50_new_note	202	51
50_old_note	201	54
200_note	210	55
20_new_note	201	56
20_old_note	200	51
2000_note	201	48

9.7 Workflow

After image labelling, we created training and testing subfolder in images main folder, then we spilt our images into training & testing. Our splitting ratio is 80:20.

After that, we created .csv file for both training & testing, it contains image label, name and pixels value of object, which we selected during image labelling, and we did this with our python code. After that, we have created Tensorflow record file using a python code. It created two files one is 'train.record' and 'test.record'. Now we need to define our deep learning model. So we have downloaded a faster RCNN v2 models & config file from TensorFlow's official GitHub page. It is already pre-trained model just we need to feed our images. After that, we need to edit config file of model and need to give a path of our images, record file. Then we did training using 'model_main.py' which is available in 'object_detection' repository. Our training taken almost 8 h, after the getting expected loss we stopped the training. On Tensorboard we observe the measures of loss and iteration continuously. After the training we need to generate a graph file (means model file). From that file machine can see what it is learnt. With code, we generate the inference graph of our training. Now it is time for testing. We created two programs, one for image recognition and another for a recognition from currency. Then we tested our models on different currencies. You can see the results & testing below.

9.8 Testing Procedure of Trained Model

In testing phase as per shown in Fig. 6 User have to feed currency through capturing device in application and that trained deep learning model predict currency amount with accuracy.

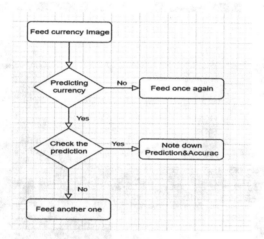

Fig. 6. Testing flowchart

9.9 Results

Resnet v2 (Pre-Trained model) gives me 0.87 accuracy and 0.201 loss. We have trained model many times on prepared dataset, even we got a lower loss of 0.115 but at that loss I got very bad prediction ratio. Means my model is overfitted.

At current scenario, we are trying Restnet_50_coco model, but it is given memory error because of less GPU power, but we are trying to implement resnet50 for a better accuracy. Figure 7 shows output of our trained model for different amount notes.

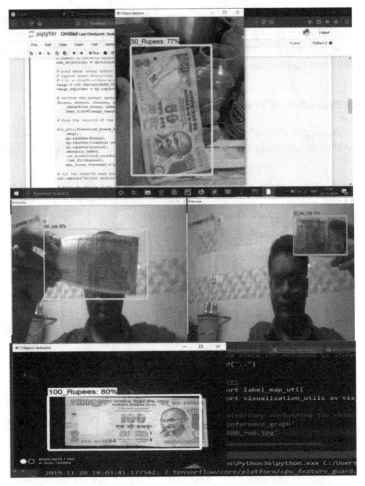

Fig. 7. Detection of few Indian currency notes with their confident

10   Conclusion

By studied various research papers on currency detection and Deep learning, Authors in this paper choose Faster RCNN to train model and recognize Indian currency very well, which will help a lot to visual disable, foreign and old age people.

In future work planning to increase accuracy of currency recognition and make an API for this system. Authors will also try this on different pre-trained model and will make it more efficient with very less loss and higher accuracy.

References

1. Zhang, Q., Yan, W.Q., Kankanhalli, M.: Overview of currency recognition using deep learning. J. Banking Financ. Technol. **3**(1), 59–69 (2019)

2. Xu, L., Ren, J.S., Liu, C., Jia, J.L.: Deep convolutional neural network for image deconvolution. In: Advances in Neural Information Processing Systems, vol. 2, pp. 1790–1798 (2014)
3. Ren, S., He, K., Girshick, R., Sun, J.: Faster R-CNN: towards real-time object detection with region proposal networks. In: Neural Information Processing Systems, pp. 91–99 (2015)
4. Kurkova, V., Manolopoulos, Y., Hammer, B., Iliadis, L., Maglogiannis, I.: Artificial neural networks and machine learning—ICANN 2018. In: Proceedings of 27th International Conference on Artificial Neural Networks (part II), vol. 11141, pp. 4–7 (2018)
5. Saha, S.: A comprehensive guide to convolutional neural networks — the ELI5 way, 15 December 2018. https://towardsdatascience.com/a-comprehensive-guide-to-convolutional-neural-networks-the-eli5-way-3bd2b1164a53. Accessed 2 Feb 2020
6. Xu, Y.: Faster R-CNN (object detection) implemented by Keras for custom data from Google's Open Images Dataset V4 (2018). https://towardsdatascience.com/faster-r-cnn-object-detection-implemented-by-keras-for-custom-data-from-googles-open-images-125f62b9141a. Accessed 2 Feb 2020
7. Goodfellow, I., Bengio, Y., Courville, A.: Deep Learning. MIT Press, Cambridge (2016)
8. Convolutional neural network. https://www.mathworks.com/solutions/deep-learning/convolutional-neural-network.html#howitworks. Accessed 2 Feb 2020
9. Javed, O., Shah, M.: tracking and object classification for automated surveillance. In: Heyden, A., Sparr, G., Nielsen, M., Johansen, P. (eds.) ECCV 2002. LNCS, vol. 2353, pp. 343–357. Springer, Heidelberg (2002). https://doi.org/10.1007/3-540-47979-1_23
10. Kim, Y.: Convolutional neural networks for sentence classification. In: Proceedings of the 2014 Conference on Empirical Methods in Natural Language Processing (2014). https://doi.org/10.3115/v1/d14-1181
11. Song, Z., Chen, Q., Huang, Z., Hua, Y., Yan, S.: Contextualizing object detection and classification. Pattern Anal. Mach. Intell. IEEE Trans. 37, 1585–1592 (2011). https://doi.org/10.1109/cvpr.2011.5995330
12. Sarfraz, M.: An intelligent paper currency recognition system. Procedia Comput. Sci. 65, 538–545 (2015). https://doi.org/10.1016/j.procs.2015.09.128
13. Lavanya, M., Vijayraghvan, V.: Real time fake currency detetcion using deep learninng. Int. J. Eng. Adv. Technol. (IJEAT) 9(1S5) (2019). ISSN: 2249–8958
14. Gupta, M.R.: Indian currency recognition and authentication using image processing. J. Gujarat Res. Soc. 21(15) (2019)
15. Zhang, Q., Yan, W.Q., Kankanhalli, M.: Overview of currency recognition using deep learning. J. Bank Financ. Technol. 3, 59–69 (2019). https://doi.org/10.1007/s42786-018-00007-1
16. Chaubey, N.K., Jayanthi, P.: Disease diagnosis and treatment using deep learning algorithms for the healthcare system. In: Wason, R., Goyal, D., Jain, V., Balamurugan, S., Baliyan. A. (eds.) Applications of Deep Learning and Big IoT on Personalized Healthcare Services, pp. 99–114. IGI Global, Hershey (2020). https://doi.org/10.4018/978-1-7998-2101-4.ch007

RETRACTED CHAPTER: Optimization of Driving Efficiency for Pre-determined Routes: Proactive Vehicle Traffic Control

Amelec Viloria[1](✉) , Omar Bonerge Pineda Lezama[2] , Noel Varela[1] ,
and Jorge Luis Diaz Martínez[1]

[1] Universidad de la Costa, Barranquilla, Colombia
{aviloria7,nvarela2,jdiaz5}@cuc.edu.co
[2] Universidad Tecnológica Centroamericana (UNITEC), San Pedro Sula, Honduras
omarpineda@unitec.edu

Abstract. With the excessive growth of modern cities, great problems are generated in citizen administration. One of these problems is the control of vehicle flow during peak hours. This paper proposes a solution to the problem of vehicle control through a proactive approach based on Machine Learning. Through this solution, a traffic control system learns about traffic flow in order to prevent future problems of long queues at traffic lights. The architecture of the traffic system is based on the principles of Autonomous Computing with the aim of changing the traffic light timers automatically. A simulation of the roads in an intelligent city and a Weka-based tool were created to validate this approach.

Keywords: Machine Learning · Proactive control · Traffic · Smart cities · Autonomous Computing

1 Introduction

The potential benefits of IoT are becoming increasingly apparent, including apps that are changing lifestyle current. The IoT paradigm proposes a scheme where many objects that surround us will be in the same network in one way or another using sensors to monitor physical or environmental conditions [1]. With the increasing presence of new technologies with internet access, the evolution towards ubiquitous information networks is evident. However, for this to be possible, the informatics paradigm must go beyond the traditional mobile network scenarios, which use smartphones and laptops; evolving into an environment surrounded by smart objects interconnected with each other.

IoT is a vital instrument in which the interconnection of devices; which will have great potential to optimize all kinds of mobile systems. IoT will allow the vehicle networks of the future to replace their current traffic control systems, thus evolving into a system that will use the available information from the medium provided by the sensors; which will

---

The original version of this chapter was retracted: The retraction note to this chapter is available at https://doi.org/10.1007/978-981-15-6648-6_28

N. Chaubey et al. (Eds.): COMS2 2020, CCIS 1235, pp. 82–94, 2020.
https://doi.org/10.1007/978-981-15-6648-6_7

be interconnected with each other. IoV (Vehicle Internet), is the inevitable convergence between the mobile Internet for vehicles and IoT. When in a vehicular network human control is removed by autonomous vehicles; they cooperate efficiently thus controlling the flow of traffic on the roads [2]. Visionaries predict that autonomous vehicles behave much better than human drivers, which will allow controlling more traffic in less time, producing less pollution and generating greater comfort for passengers [3]. However, the complexity of communicating hundreds of cars and their need to communicate with each other brings multiple challenges for communication networks.

There is an exponential growth in the population of cities turning them into mega cities. This phenomenon generates many problems, one of which is traffic congestion [4]. This problem negatively affects the quality of life of citizens by the increasing of travel time, generating stress and economic losses, and producing an increase in environmental pollution.

Currently, fixed time strategies and traffic sensitive strategies have been implemented to manage vehicle flow. These strategies are presented below.

Fixed time strategies are adjusted for long periods of time where these parameters are constant. This may therefore be different in contexts with demands of high variability or with the usual presence of unconventional conditions (e.g. accidents, disturbances, or unexpected events) [5].

Within this category is SIGSET, which calculates the time of the traffic light in each cycle, based on the vehicle flow patterns at a crossing. This system is a well-known by traffic engineers [6]. SIGSET works in isolation at each crossing and assigns fixed times to the traffic lights.

Traffic-sensitive control strategies execute their logic based on real-time traffic measurements taken at intersection entrances. To carry out these measurements, it is necessary to have some kind of traffic detectors.

Within the traffic-sensitive methods there are two reactive methods that solve problems when they are already evident. On the one hand, there are approaches that detect the presence of a lot of traffic at an intersection and modify the times of the traffic lights to give preference to the direction with the most traffic. On the other hand, other solutions are adaptive. In these solutions, traffic light networks are implemented with action plans for the optimization of vehicle flow [7].

This approach depends on a central control module. This study proposes that a more decentralized approach could be used to distribute the calculations where the traffic passes by [8–10]. In this way, the costs and complexity related to the communication infrastructure could be reduced.

1.1 Underlying Concepts

The solution proposed in this research is intelligent, autonomous, and proactive. These underlying concepts are described below.

1) Machine Learning

Machine Learning is a term used to encompass a wide variety of techniques applied to discover patterns and relationships in data sets. The primary objective of any Machine Learning algorithm is to discover significant relationships in training data sets and to produce a generalization of these relationships that can be used to interpret new unknown data [11].

Within the Machine Learning methods are forecasts. Forecasting is the process of making statements about events whose results have not yet been observed [12].

2) Autonomous Computing [13].
3) Proactive Adaptations.

On the one hand, reactive adaptations are made in response to an incident. On the other hand, proactive adaptations are carried out beforehand (i.e. before an incident negatively affects the system) [14]. Reactive adapting mechanisms can cause increased run time and financial loss, which can lead to user dissatisfaction [15]. Proactive approaches seek to address these problems by identifying the need for adaptation before the problem becomes apparent.

1.2 The Problem

This section presents the problem statement and justification.

1) Statement of the problem
The common denominator of the solutions currently implemented for traffic control in intelligent cities is that they wait for an event to happen (e.g. a long queue at a traffic light) to generate a solution to that event.

2) Justification
This section presents a simulation of the roads in a city that justifies the traffic problem. This simulation consists of a unidirectional two-way vehicular crossing. In order to simplify the simulation, the traffic lights only change between green and red lights.

On a road, the speed of vehicle flow is determined both by the regulations in force and by the existing intersection. Congestion at a traffic light occurs when the traffic light allows fewer vehicles to pass than the number of vehicles that reach the queue. In the simulation, each traffic light was assigned a time value "x" for each stage (red or green). It was also determined the average time it takes for vehicles to cross the intersection ("y"). Based on this data, the number of cars that cross the traffic light when it is green was calculated. A random value for the incoming flow was also assigned to the queue at the "y" traffic light.

As shown in Fig. 1, the number of vehicles tends to increase linearly over time. In this simulation, this trend was generated when "x" takes a value equal to 15 s, "i" has values between 0 and 9, and "y" is equal to 3 s.

1.3 Objective

This paper presents a proactive solution for vehicle traffic control using Machine Learning and Autonomous Computing. Firstly, the proposal analyses traffic level data using Machine Learning. Using this artificial intelligence technique, the system makes proactive decisions regarding historical traffic data. In order to make autonomous adjustments to traffic lights, the system adapts itself using IBM's autonomous computing principles [16]. The efficiency of this solution is demonstrated by a traffic simulation in a smart city. To predict the problems that may occur, the tool relies on the Weka API [17].

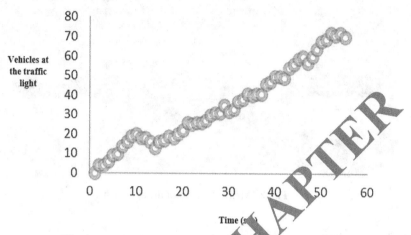

Fig. 1. Results of the traffic simulation in a smart city.

1.4 Questions and Hypotheses

Can Machine Learning help make proactive decisions to avoid traffic flow problems?

Can a system based on the principles of Autonomous Computing be used to automatically change the timers of the traffic lights?

Is it possible to test an automatic and proactive traffic management approach using a computer simulation?

The following hypothesis arises: The use of Machine Learning and Autonomous computing can proactively solve problems in vehicle traffic control.

2   The Method

The solution is based on the ASM-K cycle (see Fig. 2). In the Monitor component, a training period is considered for collecting the traffic data by means of sensors. The task of traffic observation is carried out by the Traffic Observer. The Traffic Watcher is also in charge of detecting times when there is a violation of any expected Service Level Agreement (SLA) of traffic in queue. Then, after the training is completed, Weka's prediction plug-in analyzes the data collected in the Analysis component and predicts possible traffic problems [18]. The Adaptive Planner in the Planning component then calculates the necessary changes to traffic light timers in order to proactively prevent traffic problems. After planning, in the Execution component, the Timer Modifier makes the necessary changes to the traffic light timers using actuators. This solution is described below, based on the components of the ASM-K cycle and the traffic simulation described above.

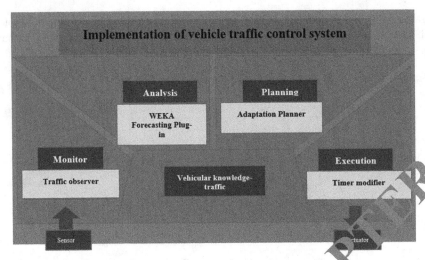

Fig. 2. MAPE-K cycle of the approach

2.1 The Monitor

Monitoring involves capturing properties of the environment that are important to the system's self-properties. In this case, it is interested in traffic observation. For this purpose, the Traffic Observer is proposed, which is a tool that observes the traffic through sensors.

When the simulation starts, two traffic lights are created, and each of them is assigned a status (Green or Red) and a random number of vehicles. The preventive stage (yellow) of a traffic light was included in the crossing phase (green). This is for simplifying the simulation.

Files with the .arff extension have the format necessary to be able to run forecasts on this data according to the Weka libraries. Specifically, the .arff file format requires the data to have a special header, as in the following example [19]:

```
@relation A
@attribute second numeric
@attribute cars numeric
@data 5,14
```

First, there is a data relationship (@relation A), and this relationship has two attributes, both of a numerical type: seconds (@attribute seconds numeric) and cars (@attribute cars numeric). After this, the data of the problem event (i.e., an SLA violation) is recorded (@data). In the example above, there is a violation of the SLA in the second 60th execution of the simulation where there are 7 cars in the queue, when the SLA indicates that no more than 3 cars should be in the queue.

2.2 Analysis

From the methods to make predictions [20], the Multilayer Perceptron was chosen in this study due to the lower percentage of error shown after testing with the different methods present in Weka (Gaussian Process, Kernel Regression, Linear Regression, Multilayer Perceptron, and SMOreg).

For the Forecaster to work, the following parameters are provided: type of data to predict, time measurement of training data, and the number of times to predict. In this case, the Forecaster predicts the number of cars that will arrive at the traffic light after training by following the time measurement of the training data. The data that the Forecaster generates is stored in a text file.

For example, a possible training (i.e., observing the traffic in the simulation for a certain time) was completed in the 1,800th second of the execution. During this time, 25 SLA violations were found. This data is used to make the prediction. Specifically, Forecaster predicts that if the current timer value of any traffic light continues, a greater number of cars than specified in the SLA will arrive at the 1,800th second. By means of the forecasting, it is possible to predict a problem that has not yet happened, based on historical data.

2.3 Planning

During this phase, after the previous training, the planning of automatic solution of traffic problems predicted in the previous phase is carried out. Specifically, in this phase, the times that traffic lights must take to prevent the predicted problems are calculated.

During the planning phase, the file created in the Analysis component is read. Every entry in this file is a problem to be solved (e.g. any SLA violation). In this phase, the Adapting Planner is proposed as a tool that executes the following steps to plan a change in the traffic light timer:

1) The Adapting Planner saves, in a variable, the text retrieved from the previous phase file.
2) The Adapting Planner performs the following operation [21–25]:

$$timeR = (int)(d * tCross) \tag{1}$$

"d" is the value read in step 1. "tCross" is the average time a vehicle takes to pass the crossing. "timeR" is the new traffic light time. The result of the operation is transformed into integer data type.

3) The value of "timeR" corresponding to the solution to a problem (i.e., any SLA violation) is saved. For example, when applying the previous formula, if a vehicle takes 3 s to pass the intersection (tCross) and 35 cars are expected to reach the traffic light (d), then 105 s (timeR) are needed for the 35 cars to pass the intersection.

Each of the values calculated in this phase corresponds to the solution of each of the problems foreseen in the Analysis phase [26–29].

2.4 Execution

In it, the purpose is to ensure that the predicted problems do not occur. In order to make these changes, the operation of actuators was simulated, whose objective is to take the new traffic light time from the data generated in the previous stage, and modify the traffic light timer.

For example, in the Planning phase it was obtained that 105 s are needed for 35 cars to pass the intersection. Therefore, at this stage our Timer Modifier assigns a time of 105 s to the traffic light timer. This way, when 35 cars reach the traffic light, it gives enough time to allow all of them to pass.

3 Results

This section describes the prototype that was created to demonstrate the approach. The prototype was created in Java and the Weka API can be used via Java [30]. The source code is presented in the Appendix at the end of this document.

The prototype GUI is divided into three areas (see Fig. 3). Area 1 shows the conditions under which traffic control is performed. Specifically, the time of the red lights, the time of the traffic simulation, the time of the crossing, and the expected SLA are determined. The text fields in Area 2 show the events where the SLA was violated at each of the traffic lights. The first column is the time in seconds that the event occurred (i.e., the SLA violation) and the second column is the number of cars with which the SLA was violated. Area 3 shows the number of times the SLA was exceeded at each traffic light before and after the implementation of Machine Learning.

The prototype is trained with the values set out in Sect. 1 of Fig. 3. In the execution, it was noted that, during the data capture for training, the number of times the SLA was violated is quite high at each traffic light (e.g. 59 violations for traffic light A and 57 for B). Then, by implementing Machine Learning with forecasts, the number of SLA violations drops dramatically (17 violations in A and 26 in B). Figure 4 shows that, with the implementation of Machine Learning, the trend of increasing number of vehicles waiting at a traffic light decreases abruptly. The implementation of Machine Learning

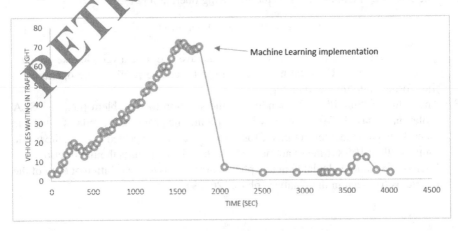

Fig. 3. Prototype execution

occurs at the 1,800th s. From this moment on, it is possible to see that the number of incidents in the SLA keeps at a quite low level [31].

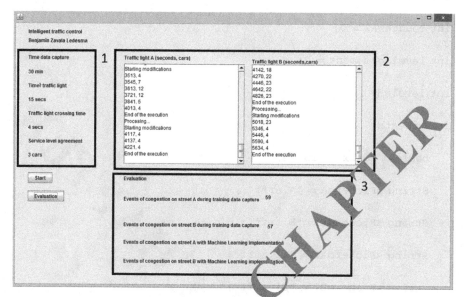

Fig. 4. Complete execution of the tool

Proactive solutions to the problem of traffic can help improve the quality of life for the inhabitants of large cities.

The source code is shown below.

```java
ArrayList incidentsA = new ArrayList ();

ArrayList incidentsB = new ArrayList ();

boolean repp = true;

boolean ea11 = false; //Red

boolean ea22 = true; // green

boolean traffi = false;

boolean statee = true;

boolean training = false;

boolean time = false;
```

```
boolean time2 = false;

int counterA1 = 0;

int counterA2 = 0;

int levelAgreement = 0;

int levelsd;

int repeats;

    boolean slaExc = false;

    String sFicheroA = "A.arff";

    String sFicheroB = "B.arff";

    String sFicheroA1 = "A1.arff";

    String sFicheroB1 = "B1.arff";

    String sPredA = "predA.txt";

    String sPredB = "predB.txt";

    String backingAB = "backinggenA.csv";

    String backingB1 = "backinggenB.csv";

    String backupAxis = "backupgenAxis.csv";

    String backupBeje = "backupgenBeje.csv";

    String sPredResp = "predRespA.txt";

    String sPredRespB = "predRespB.txt";

    String modResp = "modResp.txt";

    String stdr;

    String strdB;

    String hd;
```

```
int dif1 = 1;

int dif2 = 1;

int t Cross = 1;

int timerr = 1;

int timerrB = 1;

int cont = 1;

int repe = 1;

int t Red Ori;

int t Red A;

int t Red B;

int cars = 0;

int carsB = 1;

int cars A =
```

4 Conclusions

Quite promising results were obtained by using Machine Learning and Autonomous Computing through the MAPE-K cycle in a tool for vehicle traffic control. The use of these approaches could alleviate congestion in cities in a proactive way, i.e. even before the problem becomes apparent.

A proactive solution to traffic control was proposed in this study through the use of Machine Learning and the principles of Autonomous Computing. Since this solution is completely autonomous, it can minimize the factor of human error when controlling events on the traffic. So, the objectives proposed in the research were fully covered.

The proposal offers the following benefits for the development of mega-cities: 1) avoid economic losses by allowing a shipment or a worker to arrive in the shortest possible time at its destination. In a traffic jam, vehicles must move very slowly and be braking continuously. This means an increase in the change of worn parts and a greater expenditure of gasoline; 2) reach a more constant vehicle flow thus decreasing the time a vehicle is on the road; 3) increase the work performance of the citizen by improving punctuality in their daily commitments by moving faster; 4) decrease the emission of environmental pollutants (CO_2) by keeping a vehicle running for less time; and 5) decrease the number of vehicle accidents at peak hours. These accidents can be caused by the stress caused by traffic jams [32–35].

The solution proposed must be extended to control more than one crossing. At the moment, it only works at one crossing. In addition, in order to validate the solution, it is necessary to have real environments for testing purposes. This aspect will lead to seeking partnerships with the government to test the real-world approach. In order to extend this research, links should be built with European projects focused on smart cities.

Future studies will include the implementation of computer vision module for live traffic control through traffic cameras. It will also seek to develop a mobile application through which the user can make queries about the traffic status and find the most optimal route between the starting point and the destination point obtaining real-time data directly from the central vehicle control system.

References

1. Mittal, A., Ostojic, M., Mahmassani, H.S.: Active traffic signal control for mixed vehicular traffic in connected environments: self-identifying platoon strategy. (No. 19-05931 (2019)
2. Fang, J., Ye, H., Easa, S.M.: Modified traffic flow model with connected vehicle microscopic data for proactive variable speed limit control. J. Adv. Transp. **2019**, 18 (2019)
3. Xie, H., Tu, L., Fang, J., Easa, S.M.: Proactive highway traffic control with intelligent multi-objective optimisation algorithm. In: Proceedings of the Institution of Civil Engineers-Transport, pp. 1–11. Thomas Telford Ltd. (2019)
4. Lum, C., Koper, C.S., Wu, X., Johnson, W., Stoltz, M.: Examining the empirical realities of proactive policing through systematic observations and computer-aided dispatch data. Police Q. (2020). https://doi.org/10.1177/1098611119896081
5. Ferenchak, N.N., Marshall, W.E.: Equity analysis of proactively-vs. reactively-identified traffic safety issues. Transp. Res. Record **2673**(7), 596–606 (2019)
6. Xie, K., Ozbay, K., Yang, H., Li, C.: Mining automatically extracted vehicle trajectory data for proactive safety analytics. Transp. Res. Part C: Emerg. Technol. **106**, 61–72 (2019)
7. Azari, A., Papapetrou, P., Denic, S., Peters, G.: User traffic prediction for proactive resource management: learning-powered approaches. arXiv preprint arXiv:1906.00951 (2019)
8. Gillani, R., Nasir, A.: Proactive control of hybrid electric vehicles for maximum fuel efficiency. In: 2019 16th International Bhurban Conference on Applied Sciences and Technology (IBCAST), pp. 396–401. IEEE (2019)
9. Bui, D.P., et al.: The use of proactive risk management to reduce emergency service vehicle crashes among firefighters. J. Saf. Res. **71**, 103–109 (2019)
10. Batkovic, I., Zanon, M., Ali, M., & Falcone, P. Real-time constrained trajectory planning and vehicle control for proactive autonomous driving with road users. In: 2019 18th European Control Conference (ECC), pp. 256–262. IEEE (2019)
11. Lee, D., Tak, S., Choi, S., Yeo, H.: Development of risk predictive collision avoidance system and its impact on traffic and vehicular safety. Transp. Res. Record **2673**(7), 454–465 (2019)
12. Fuentes, A.: Proactive decision support tools for national park and non-traditional agencies in solving traffic-related problems. Doctoral dissertation, Virginia Tech (2019)
13. Kathuria, A., Vedagiri, P.: Evaluating pedestrian vehicle interaction dynamics at un-signalized intersections: a proactive approach for safety analysis. Accid. Anal. Prev. **134**, 105316 (2020)
14. Hu, Y., Chen, C., He, T., He, J., Guan, X., Yang, B.: Proactive power management scheme for hybrid electric storage system in EVs: an MPC method. IEEE Trans. Intell. Transp. Syst. (2019)

15. Silva, R., Couturier, C., Ernst, T., Bonnin, J.M.: Proactive decision making for ITS communication. In: Global Advancements in Connected and Intelligent Mobility: Emerging Research and Opportunities, pp. 197–226. IGI Global (2020)
16. Formosa, N., Quddus, M., Ison, S., Abdel-Aty, M., Yuan, J.: Predicting real-time traffic conflicts using deep learning. Accid. Anal. Prev. **136**, 105429 (2020)
17. Zahid, M., Chen, Y., Jamal, A., Memon, M.Q.: Short term traffic state prediction via hyperparameter optimization based classifiers. Sensors **20**(3), 685 (2020)
18. Viloria, A., Acuña, G.C., Franco, D.J.A., Hernández-Palma, H., Fuentes, J.P., Rambal, E.P.: Integration of data mining techniques to PostgreSQL database manager system. Procedia Comput. Sci. **155**, 575–580 (2019)
19. Paranjothi, A., Khan, M.S., Patan, R., Parizi, R.M., Atiquzzaman, M.: VANETomo: a congestion identification and control scheme in connected vehicles using network tomography. Comput. Commun. **151**, 275–289 (2020)
20. Zahed, M.I.A., Ahmad, I., Habibi, D., Phung, Q.V., Mowla, M.M.: Proactive content caching using surplus renewable energy: a win–win solution for both network service and energy providers. Future Gener. Comput. Syst. **105**, 210–221 (2020)
21. Perez, R., Vásquez, C., Viloria, A.: An intelligent strategy for faults location in distribution networks with distributed generation. J. Intell. Fuzzy Syst. **36**(2), 1627–1637 (2019)
22. Viloria, A., Robayo, P.V.: Virtual network level of application composed IP networks connected with systems-(NETS Peer-to-Peer). Indian J. Sci. Technol. **9**, 46 (2016)
23. Liu, J., Khattak, A.: Informed decision-making by integrating historical on-road driving performance data in high-resolution maps for connected and automated vehicles. J. Intell. Transp. Syst. **24**(1), 11–23 (2020)
24. Rivoirard, L., Wahl, M., Sondi, P.: Multipoint relaying versus chain-branch-leaf clustering performance in optimized link state routing-based vehicular ad hoc networks. IEEE Trans. Intell. Transp. Syst. **21**, 1034–1043 (2019)
25. Ramezani, M., Ye, E.: Lane density optimisation of automated vehicles for highway congestion control. Transportmetrica B: Transp. Dyn. **7**(1), 1096–1116 (2019)
26. Rahman, M., et al.: A review of sensing and communication, human factors, and controller aspects for information-aware connected and automated vehicles. IEEE Trans. Intell. Transp. Syst. **21**(1), 7–29 (2020)
27. de Souza, A.M., Braun, T., Botega, L.C., Cabral, R., Garcia, I.C., Villas, L.A.: Better safe than sorry: a vehicular traffic re-routing based on traffic conditions and public safety issues. J. Internet Serv. Appl. **10**(1), 17 (2019)
28. Vijayaraghavan, V., Rian Leevinson, J.: Intelligent traffic management systems for next generation IoV in smart city scenario. In: Mahmood, Z. (ed.) Connected Vehicles in the Internet of Things, pp. 123–141. Springer, Cham (2020). https://doi.org/10.1007/978-3-030-36167-9_6
29. Wu, Y., Tan, H., Peng, J., Zhang, H., He, H.: Deep reinforcement learning of energy management with continuous control strategy and traffic information for a series-parallel plug-in hybrid electric bus. Appl. Energy **247**, 454–466 (2019)
30. Chen, X., He, X., Xiong, C., Zhu, Z., Zhang, L.: A bayesian stochastic kriging optimization model dealing with heteroscedastic simulation noise for freeway traffic management. Transp. Sci. **53**(2), 545–565 (2019)
31. Boucetta, C., Baala, O., Ali, K.A., Caminada, A.: Performance of topology-based data routing with regard to radio connectivity in VANET. In: 2019 15th International Wireless Communications & Mobile Computing Conference (IWCMC), pp. 609–614. IEEE (2019)
32. Balouchzahi, N.M., Rajaei, M.: Efficient traffic information dissemination and vehicle navigation for lower travel time in urban scenario using vehicular networks. Wirel. Personal Commun. **106**(2), 633–649 (2019)
33. Xu, H., Liu, J., Qian, C., Huang, H., Qiao, C.: Reducing controller response time with hybrid routing in software defined networks. Comput. Netw. **164**, 106891 (2019)

34. Chaubey, N.: Security analysis of Vehicular Ad Hoc Networks (VANETs): a comprehensive study. Int. J. Secur. Appl. **10**, 261–274 (2016)
35. Chaubey, N.K., Yadav, D.: A taxonomy of sybil attacks in Vehicular Ad-Hoc Network (VANET). In: Rao, R., Jain, V., Kaiwartya, O., Singh, N. (eds.) IoT and Cloud Computing Advancements in Vehicular Ad-Hoc Networks, pp. 174–190. IGI Global, Hershey (2020). https://doi.org/10.4018/978-1-7998-2570-8.ch009

Emotion Classification with Reduced Feature Set SGDClassifier, Random Forest and Performance Tuning

Kaushika Pal[1]([⊠]) [iD] and Biraj V. Patel[2] [iD]

[1] Sarvajanik College of Engineering & Technology, Surat, Gujarat, India
Kaushika.pal@scet.ac.in
[2] G. H. Patel P. G. Department of Computer and Technology Science, Sardar Patel University,
V. V. Nagar, Gujarat, India

Abstract. Text Classification is vital and challenging due to varied kinds of data generated these days; emotions classification represented in form of text is more challenging due to diverse kind of emotional content and such content is growing on web these days. This research work is classifying emotions written in Hindi in form of poem with 4 categories namely Karuna, Shanta, Shringar and Veera. POS tagging is used on all the poem and then features are extracted by observing certain poetic features, two types of features are extracted and the results in terms of accuracy is measured to test the model. 180 Poetries were tagged and features were extracted with 8 different keywords, and 7 different keywords. The model is build with Random Forest, SGDClassifier and was trained with 134 poetries and tested with 46 Poetries for both types of features. The results with 7 keyword feature is comparatively better than 8 keyword feature by 7.27% for Random Forest and 10% better for SGDClassifier. Various combinations of hyper parameters are used to get the best results for statistical measure precision and recall for performance tuning of the model. The model is also tested with k – fold cross validation with average result 62.53% for 4 folds and 60.45% for 8 folds with Random Forest and 54.42% for 4 folds and 48.28% for 8 folds with SGDClassifier, the experimentation result of Random Forest is better than SGDClassifier on the given dataset.

Keywords: Emotions · Poetry · Feature extraction · Machine learning · POS tagging · SGDClassifier

1 Introduction

Feelings, emotions, sentiments are beautiful substance which human being cannot get rid of, we feel we express, the emotions either by crying, laughing, singing, dancing, jumping or by writing. The cyberspace has given every individual an opportunity to freely express by various means, videos on YouTube with poetry and story telling episodes, or using any short videos featuring applications. Some sing, some speak and some write, applications like YouQuote, allows individual to express by writing statements, quotes or poetries, there are many such applications. When it comes to express, anyone

© Springer Nature Singapore Pte Ltd. 2020
N. Chaubey et al. (Eds.): COMS2 2020, CCIS 1235, pp. 95–108, 2020.
https://doi.org/10.1007/978-981-15-6648-6_8

prefer in the language they are comfortable, India with 22 major languages expressed using 13 different scripts with approximately 720 dialects give options to everyone to express in the language they know, they understand and can write. This huge literature in multiple languages in India, gives the researcher a challenge to provide computerized and automated solutions for almost all problems.

Hindi known to be an official language of India, with nearly 420 million speakers needs special attention from researchers of this country. There are many researchers who are consistently trying to contribute for enriching the web with all options to get the things we need. Poetries are written emotions, which are expressed and measured in Navrasas in Hindi, Ras means sentient, which also implies to sensation, sensation of feelings. This research work is classifying those sensations in 4 categories Karuna, Shanta, Shringar and Veera. The details of the data set used along with meaning and associated emotions are shown in Table 1.

Table 1. Data set class and it's meaning and associated emotions

Class	Karuna	Shanta	Shringar	Veera
Meaning	Pity, sadness	Peace	Romance, love	Heroic, courage
Associated emotions	Compassion, sympathy	Calmness, relaxation	Devotion, beauty	Confidence, pride

2 Study of Related Work and Motivation

The feasibility to implement current work needed exploration of work done in Indic Language and Hindi Language, The work done in Hindi is focused to get insight, and image processing which are representing characters by some researchers is also studied. M. Shalini [1] used neural network to recognize Hindi words from image, the researcher used line segmentation, word segmentation techniques to extract word from the image. Shalini Puria [2] introduced tri-layered segmentation and bi-leveled-classifier-based classification system for Hindi printed documents using Support Vector Machine and Fuzzy. Jasleen [3] classified Punjabi poetry using linguistic features and weighing, she found 72.04% accuracy with TF weighing and 66.43% with TF-IDF weighing using Support Vector Machine with dataset of 2034 Poetries. Mandal AK [4] explored machine learning and used Decision Tree (C4.5), Naïve Bayes, K-Nearest Neighbor, and Support Vector Machine for Bangla corpus, the author performed classification of corpus into business, sports, health, technology, and education classes. Vandana Jha [5] proposed a method for opinion about Hindi movie review and used lexicon based classification techniques using Naïve Bayes, Support Vector Machine. Jasleen [6] analyzed performance comparison of different Techniques used in Formal and Informal Text Classification for sentiment classification. Noraini Jamal [7] classified Malay poetry into different genre using Support Vector Machine with 'rbf' and 'linear' kernel and found maximum accuracy of 58.44% with dataset of 1500 Poetries. The author also experimented to identify poetry and non-poetry contents and the accuracy found was 99.9%, the author claims Support Vector

Machine with 'linear' kernel is giving better results than with 'rbf' kernel. Hamid R [8] proposes novel poetic features and classified poem from normal text with 5 different approaches namely Text Classification, Shape features, combining Rhyme and shape, combining Rhyme, meter and Shape, combining rhyme and shape with word frequency. He concludes that using all approaches very efficient classifier is build to classify Normal Text from Poetry. Shalini Puria [11] proposed a model for devanagari character classification using Support Vector Machine for printed and handwritten image based characters and claiming to have accuracy of 99.54% for printed characters and 98.35% for handwritten characters by using dataset of 60 Documents, there accuracy is high as they are only categorizing into characters. K Pal [21] surveyed on research done in Indic Languages and found that the research needs more attention from feature extraction, feature selection, Classification, Text Summarization aspects using Artificial Intelligence. Ishaan [12] used Naïve Bayes to build spam filter for Hindi language. C Anne [14] developed multiclass document Classification using ML and NLP techniques. Experiments by Noraini Jamal [7], evidently shows classifying poetries into poetic genre is very challenging and achieved accuracy of 58.44% using Support Vector Machine with 1500 Poetries. Yu Meng [15] proposed weakly Supervised Neural Text Classification, which addresses the lack of training data for text classification using Neural Networks by using pseudo document generator for generating pseudo training data. Qiancheng Liang [16] has combined word meaning and semantic features for text classification using neural networks and machine learning. Tu Cam Thi Tran [17] proposed a model, which uses keywords with different thresholds for Text Classification. Md Zahidul Islam [18] claims random Forest is good to deal with noisy data in Text Classification and proposes semantic aware random forest for text classification. Wanwan Zheng [19] claims that feature selection helps to have 66.67% less training samples. Rui Yao [20] proposed a model, which identifies false promotions by webpages using sensitive word filtering method. Cannannore Nidhi Kamath [9] compared performance of many machine learning algorithms and CNN for text classification and found that Logistic regression is performing better than other machine learning algorithms but CNN is performing better than all. Mariem Bounabi [10] have raised issues in TF-IDF for text classification and proposes extended form of it called as FTF-IDF which uses fuzzy to increase the performance of classification. Anna Surkova [13] uses cognitive approach and linguistic approach for text classification and claims that linguistic approach does not improve classification.

Studying all the work carried out by diverse researchers motivated to experiment the capabilities of machine learning techniques for emotion classification represented in Hindi, which is yet to be explored.

Human beings can understand emotions but training machines to understand "emotions" is challenging due to words order, rhythm, Shape, different way of expressing emotions by different writer; so much information is fused in short sentences; writing style of each poet is very different from another poet of same genre poetry; special characters used to end or express certain emotions is also used by some writers but same special characters are used by different writers in other way.

3 System Architecture

The System comprises of **POS tagging Module, Feature Extraction, Training the Classifier**, and **Testing of the Classifier** with new unseen test data. The System Architecture for the classifier using Part-of-the-speech tagging for feature extraction is shown in Fig. 1.

The System is implemented in Python 3.6 using PyCharm Community Edition on macOS High Sierra version 10.13.1 with 1.8 GHz Intel Core i5 Processor.

The Data Set comprises of 180 Poems of 4 Categories namely Shringar, Karuna, Veera and Shanta Ras and represents emotions of Love, Pity, Heroic and Peace respectively.

Bulk POS tagging Module is developed which perform part of the speech tagging and tagged 48 Shringar, 49 Karuna, 43 Veera and 40 Shanta Ras Poems. This module generates tagged poem files, which are stored and used for Feature Extraction.

POS tags which are used for tagging are 'PRP Pronoun, 'NNP' Proper noun, 'NN' Noun, 'JJ' Adjective, 'VAUX' auxiliary Verb, 'RP' Particle, 'RB' Adverb, 'CC' Conjunction, 'QF' Quantifiers, 'PREP' Postposition, 'VFM' Verb Finite main, 'INTF' Intensifier, 'NLOC' Noun Location, 'NNC' Compound, 'NEG' Negative, noun 'QFNUM' Quantifiers number, 'QW' Question words, 'PUNC' punctuation, 'NNPC' Compound proper nouns, 'VNN' Verb non-finite nominal, 'NVB' Noun in Kriyamula, 'VJJ' Verb non-finite adjectival and 'Unk' Unknown. Figure 2 shows a Sample of one-tagged poetry.

Feature Extraction is crucial for efficient classification; predicting feature set for classification without experimenting on given data set is not possible, starting experiment using large Feature set and carefully observing the results the features can be reduced

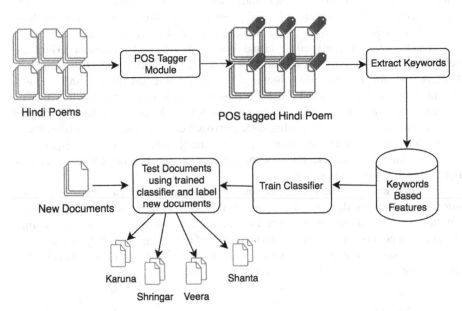

Fig. 1. System architecture for the classifier using part-of-the-speech tagging for feature extraction

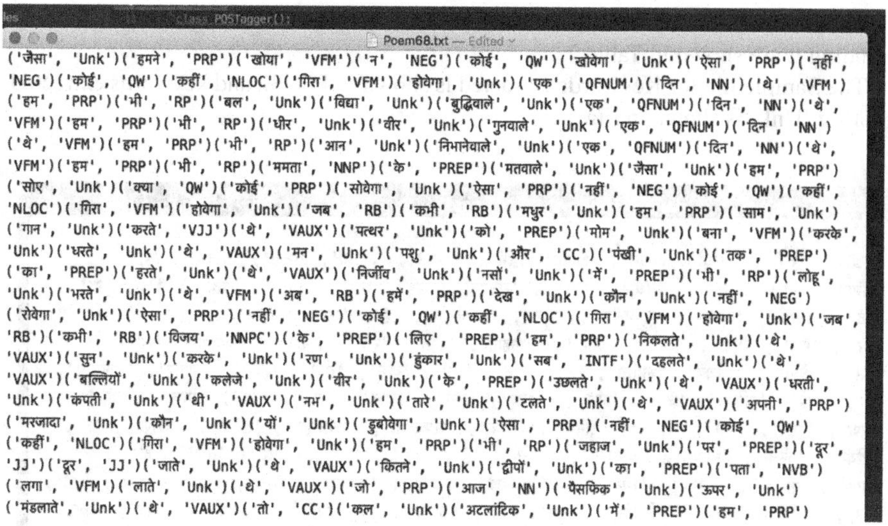

Fig. 2. Sample file showing tagging of each word of the poetry

using feature selection. For this research work the POS tagged poems were used to extract features by monitoring the tagged poem document. There were two ways the features were extracted using this experiment. Since the poetry express emotions, the words tagged with 'Unk' was ignored for one experiment but was considered for the second experiment. The words, which were given more importance for this classification, were Adverbs, Adjectives as they have higher chance to represent emotions. The feature Set that used 'Unk' meaning unknown words was challenging as it was having certain important features but were also loaded with lot of garbage values including printed and non-printed characters, this characters were removed by observing keywords extracted with 'Unk' tag and writing script in python to remove unwanted characters from the Feature Set.

Table 2. Statistics of POS tagging and Keywords Extracted

Poem class	No. of documents	No. of words tagged	No. of keywords extracted	Duration of process (HH:MM:SS)	No. of keywords ignoring 'Unk' tag	Duration of process (HH:MM:SS)
Karuna	49	7400	5246	00:01:33	1405	00:01:25
Shanta	40	5144	3818	00:00:51	926	00:00:47
Shringar	48	6875	5066	00:01:11	1002	00:01:05
Veera	43	10537	7966	00:03:10	2022	00:02:59
Total	180	29,956	22,096	00:06:45	5,352	00:06:16

The Statistics of number of words tagged and feature extracted ignoring 'Unk' and including it are shown in Table 2.

The Sample file for Keywords extracted is shown in Fig. 3., and keywords extracted ignoring 'Unk' is shown in Fig. 4.

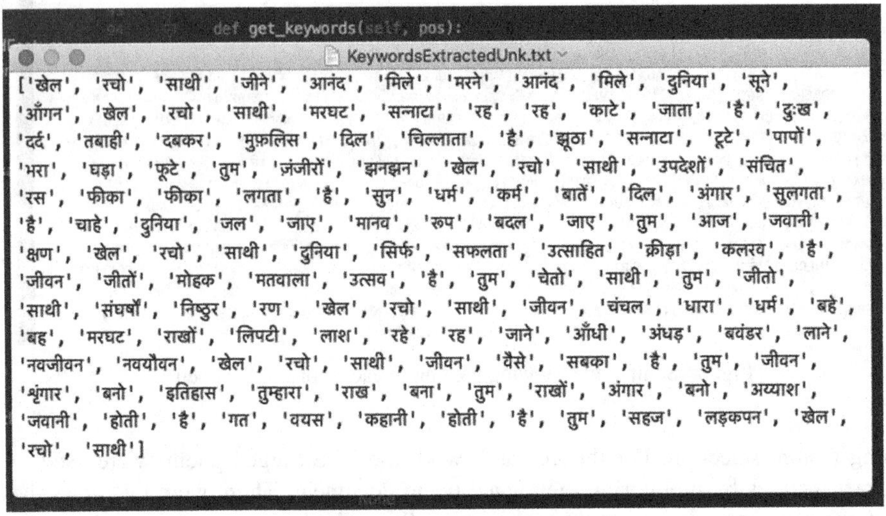

Fig. 3. Sample extracted keywords

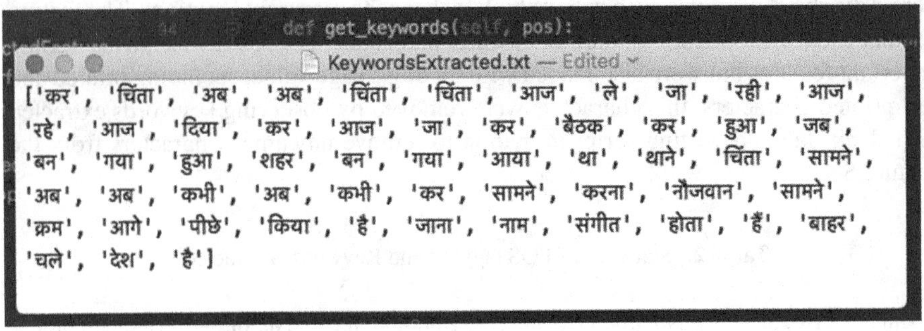

Fig. 4. Sample extracted keywords ignoring 'Unk' tagged words

The extracted keywords were having certain very common words, which was removed by creating stop word list. After removing stop words the features were converted into their numeric representation, a sample features along with their numeric form is shown in Fig. 5.

```
{'कर': 327, 'शत': 1079, 'गय': 392, 'आन': 158, 'नमन': 695, 'बर': 815, 'पह': 766, 'अभय': 105, 'भग': 840, 'दह': 638,
'अहर': 135, 'बड': 797, 'आग': 148, 'अभ': 104, 'आज': 150, 'इत': 191, 'गव': 400, 'रत': 969, 'जय': 497, 'अलग': 115,
'पत': 739, 'धर': 628, 'सम': 1147, 'शह': 1098, 'वतन': 1057, 'आरत': 170, 'उठ': 225, 'लपट': 1034, 'सद': 1130, 'फक':
773, 'लगत': 1018, 'इत': 1193, 'अस': 126, 'शस': 1097, 'गय': 468, 'बल': 820, 'पहर': 770, 'यथ': 1059, 'अचल': 46,
'पख': 715, 'रथम': 975, 'चरण': 442, 'नए': 681, 'जन': 479, 'मन': 895, 'आई': 139, 'पहल': 771, 'यन': 1060, 'गत': 384,
'यल': 1069, 'पतय': 745, 'अम': 106, 'मह': 916, 'बम': 1107, 'खल': 366, 'समस': 1155, 'रम': 986, 'बन': 809, 'चलत': 448,
'हय': 1218, 'रश': 995, 'u200dनच': 14, 'खड': 357, 'गई': 371, 'मट': 881, 'सन': 1135, 'रह': 1002, 'उठत': 227, 'इन':
195, 'मश': 913, 'डगर': 551, 'हट': 1189, 'उसफ': 262, 'डर': 555, 'षण': 1102, 'कमज': 323, 'हम': 1199, 'घर': 415, 'अमर':
107, 'लहर': 1049, 'सवहम': 994, 'bud1': 0, 'उन': 237, 'वसन': 1074, 'जय': 507, 'बचपन': 791, 'इर': 524, 'नयन': 698,
'घट': 407, 'सक': 1113, 'पहच': 767, 'कब': 349, 'तन': 589, 'चल': 447, 'जत': 475, 'इसर': 528, 'नन': 690, 'कम': 321,
'लक': 1010, 'परछ': 754, 'रज': 959, 'सदन': 1131, 'सपन': 1138, 'अपन': 93, 'पन': 749, 'अयग': 118, 'ठठन': 568, 'अपलक':
95, 'आनन': 159, 'नख': 682, 'धपन': 671, 'भरत': 857, 'उर': 255, 'उपवन': 245, 'तर': 602, 'बह': 830, 'नयन': 706, 'मय':
901, 'दन': 641, 'लकन': 1012, 'खर': 363, 'लन': 1031, 'जग': 469, 'गन': 386, 'दर': 650, 'अभर': 73, 'इनक': 511, 'लग':
1017, 'बड': 796, 'धर': 675, 'खत': 359, 'उनक': 238, 'चढ': 424, 'पर': 753, 'कय': 344, 'भर': 855, 'रहकर': 1004, 'झकड':
512, 'यत': 1056, 'लय': 1041, 'बदलन': 806, 'बदलकर': 805, 'छल': 464, 'ओछ': 284, 'मक': 865, 'जयच': 498,
'गद': 385, 'धमक': 674, 'यरत': 936, 'गम': 391, 'सय': 1156, 'मजहब': 879, 'बदन': 800, 'सकत': 1114, 'सरद': 1161, 'इसल':
205, 'जब': 491, 'बदल': 804, 'यम': 933, 'जलन': 506, 'गल': 396, 'वर': 1064, 'तब': 596, 'मर': 902, 'समझ': 1149, 'कड':
301, 'अब': 100, 'तसर': 620, 'भरकर': 856, 'यरत': 676, 'अभ': 68, 'कमर': 351, 'रग': 951, 'एग': 278, 'टय': 541, 'हमस':
1202, 'पड': 734, 'यलप': 1070, 'आलम': 172, 'दबलन': 635, 'पछत': 728, 'कहल': 352, 'जह': 509, 'जभवन': 494, 'आश': 176,
'दसत': 652, 'लत': 1027, 'उम': 251, 'भटकन': 848, 'लस': 1046, 'मटम': 883, 'रच': 955, 'तरह': 611, 'जल': 501, 'कट': 298,
'बरसन': 819, 'उत': 230, 'उड': 229, 'गए': 372, 'सतर': 1128, 'फट': 774, 'षह': 1075, 'बरस': 817, 'तह': 585, 'मछल': 875,
'तरस': 609, 'सकर': 1115, 'हर': 1205, 'सतप': 1127, 'घन': 411, 'घत': 410, 'अनमन': 85, 'खड': 370, 'चल': 759, 'सह':
1184, 'पथ': 746, 'दल': 657, 'इनक': 196, 'अटपट': 56, 'उलझ': 257, 'पकड': 719, 'अच': 44, 'कप': 313, 'पकड': 867, 'सर':
1157, 'मच': 872, 'छर': 463, 'झन': 519, 'यहन': 1076, 'इतन': 192, 'सहन': 1180, 'कष': 345, 'अजगर': 50, 'अगम': 41, 'बड':
837, 'गरज': 394, 'दह': 661, 'कनकन': 311, 'जनवन': 487, 'तगड': 579, 'आत': 152, 'ससर': 1168, 'लपकत': 1033, 'मत': 885,
'करत': 330, 'गह': 406, 'इय': 199, 'मथ': 888, 'जहर': 510, 'शम': 1086, 'गर': 393, 'नत': 688, 'कलग': 341, 'तलय': 615,
'शक': 1077, 'अप': 90, 'कक': 294, 'पकड': 716, 'जलत': 504, 'कम': 320, 'भय': 851, 'नर': 699, 'उगलत': 215, 'अक': 33,
'भर': 1109, 'बनत': 811, 'हरदम': 1207, 'लझ': 1048, 'इल': 1214, 'महल': 922, 'रहत': 1006, 'चमकल': 434, 'दरव': 655, 'बत':
798, 'बजत': 793, 'सय': 1174, 'चत': 426, 'यल': 937, 'मध': 894, 'रस': 997, 'कण': 304, 'कमल': 326, 'रछ': 958, 'चमक':
```

Fig. 5. Sample extracted features converted to numeric representation

4 Performance Tuning

SGDClassifier and Random Forest classification algorithms were used for this experiment, for better results of precision and recall along with accuracy as measure of performance for classification, Hyper parameter tuning was done for each of the algorithm and the model was Grid searched to find the best parameters for precision and recall.

The SGDClassifier used parameters loss, alpha, random_state, and shuffle. The loss parameter was set to 'hinge' rest of the parameter was changed; alpha was set to 2 values $1e-3$ and $1e-4$, random_state was set to "1", "10", "100", "500", "1000" and shuffle was set to "True", "False" values. 20 combinations of parameters were used to search the best parameter for precision and 20 combinations for best parameters for recall. Duration of performance tuning with 20 Plus 20 combinations was 0:00:01.310747 h, i.e. 1:31 s.

The best parameter set for precision and recall was found to be same and is { 'alpha': 0.001, 'loss': 'hinge', 'random_state': 1, 'shuffle': False}. A Subset of combinations of parameters along with accuracy is represented in Table 3 for precision and recall.

The random Forest algorithm used parameters n_estimators, which decides number of decision tree to create the forest, random_state with 4 different values and bootstrap to "True" and "False", there were 50 combinations of parameters for searching the best parameters for good precision and 50 combinations for recall. Duration of performance tuning with 50 Plus 50 combinations was 0:04:43.029051 h, i.e. 4 min and 43 s. The experiment shows that the best parameter combination found for precision score

Table 3. Subset of parameters used for parameter tuning for precision and recall

Parameters for SGDClassifier with loss = 'hinge'			
Alpha	Shuffle	Random state	Accuracy
0.001	False	1	56.06%
		10	56.06%
	True	100	56.03%
		10	52.38%
0.0001	False	1	55.30%
		1000	55.30%
	True	10	53.99%
		100	54.42%

is {'bootstrap': False, 'n_estimators': 500, 'random_state': None} and best parameter combination for recall score is {'bootstrap': False, 'n_estimators': 500, 'random_state': 42}. A subset of parameters combinations for precision along with accuracy achieved is shown in Table 4 and a subset of all the combinations of parameters used for recall is shown in Table 5.

Table 4. Subset of Parameters used for parameter tuning for precision

Parameters for Random Forest			
Bootstrap	Estimator	Random state	Accuracy
True	50	42	64.81%
		20	65.16%
	100	None	65.32%
		21	62.23%
True	250	21	64.52%
		20	62.89%
	500	None	63.61%
		42	62.13%

Random Forest is taking longer time for performance tuning than SGDClassifier.

Table 5. Subset of parameters used for parameter tuning for recall

Parameters for Random Forest			
Bootstrap	Estimator	Random state	Accuracy
True	500	42	57.02%
		None	56.51%
	1000	42	57.02%
		20	55.68%
False	50	21	59.25%
		20	59.16%
	500	None	59.49%
		42	60.03%

5   Experimentation Results

The performance tuning provided us with best parameters combinations, which can be used to train the classifier. The model was trained with 134 Poems and tested with 46 poems using SGDClassifier and Random Forest algorithms. Model was trained and tested using both the feature Set; the results were better when reduced feature set was used. The Feature Set used along with its statistics and results of the model in terms of accuracy in shown in Table 6.

Table 6. Results in accuracy

Classifier	Feature set with 8 keywords Unk	Accuracy	Feature set with 7 keywords	Accuracy
Random Forest	22,096	51.42	5,352	58.69%
SGDClassifier	22,096	40.00	5,352	50.00%

The results of classification is measured in terms of accuracy, but to know the details about how each class was classified precision and recall of each of the class is monitored. The Classification Report is shown in Table 7 for Random Forest and SGDClassifier in Table 8. Shringar and Shanta are having most overlapping features; bringing accuracy of the entire model down. In future fuzzy logic can be used to deal with the problem of overlapping. Karuna poems are the most correctly classified class of Poetries.

The model is trained with set of 134 poetries, and tested with 46 poetries, for a robust classifier it is better to train them with different set of data and test the performance, k – fold cross validation is done with k = 4 and k = 8 for both the classifiers, the results of each fold is shown in Table 9 for 4 folds and results are shown in Table 10 for 8 folds. In k –fold cross validation the data is divided into k equal portions called folds, 1 fold

Table 7. Classification report of Random Forest with reduced feature set

Class	Precision	Recall	F1 - score	Support
Karuna	0.92	0.85	0.88	13
Shanta	0.55	0.50	0.52	12
Shringar	0.37	0.64	0.47	11
Veera	0.75	0.30	0.43	10
Accuracy			0.59	46
Macro avg.	0.65	0.57	0.57	46
Weighted avg.	0.65	0.59	0.59	46

Table 8. Classification report of SGDClassifier with reduced feature set

Class	Precision	Recall	F1 - score	Support
Karuna	1.00	0.77	0.87	13
Shanta	0.42	0.42	0.42	12
Shringar	0.42	0.45	0.43	11
Veera	0.25	0.30	0.27	10
Accuracy			0.50	46
Macro avg.	0.52	0.49	0.50	46
Weighted avg.	0.55	0.50	0.52	46

is used for testing and rest portions are used for training, the model is trained and tested for k times. Visualization of how k-fold works is shown in Fig. 6.

Table 9. Results of k - folds cross validation with k = 4

Classifier/folds	Fold 1	Fold 2	Fold 3	Fold 4	Average accuracy
Random Forest	70.27%	64.86%	59.45%	55.55%	62.53%
SGDClassifier	62.16%	43.24%	56.75%	55.55%	54.42%

Table 10. Results of k - folds cross validation with k = 8

Classifier/folds	Fold 1	Fold 2	Fold 3	Fold 4	Fold 5	Fold 6	Fold 7	Fold 8	Average Accuracy
Random Forest	63.15%	68.42%	63.15%	61.11%	50.00%	61.11%	66.66%	50.00%	60.45%
SGDClassifier	57.89%	47.36%	42.10%	27.77%	55.55%	61.11%	55.55%	38.88%	48.28%

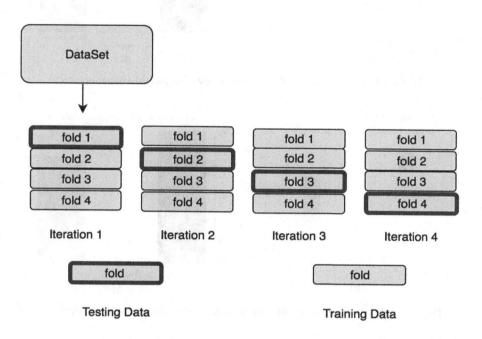

Fig. 6. K-fold cross validation data set division

The results of k – fold cross validation consistently shows good results, except 1 or 2 fold with poor accuracy. The range of results in accuracy using box plot is shown in Fig. 7 (a) and average accuracy using bar plot is shown in Fig. 7 (b) for k = 4. For k = 8 the results are visualized using box plot for showing range in Fig. 8 (a) and average results are shown in Fig. 8 (b) using bar plot.

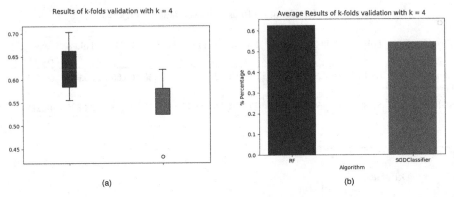

Fig. 7. K-fold cross validation with 4 folds (a) range of results (b) average accuracy

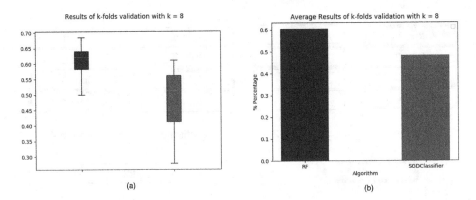

Fig. 8. K-fold cross validation with 8 folds (a) range of results (b) average accuracy

6 Conclusion

Emotion Classification in any form is challenging, this research work used 180 poetries and tagged using part-of-the-Speech tagging, and the data set was then partitioned into 134 poetries for training and 46 poetries for testing. The feature was extracted on keywords basis by manually monitoring the tagged files, two set of Feature set was prepared one using 8- keywords with 22,096 features and another reduced the feature set using 7 keywords with 5352 features. The experiment used Grid Search for performance tuning and experimented with 50 combinations of parameters using Random Forest for score precision and 50 combinations for score recall, to find the best parameter set for the dataset using Random Forest. To find best parameters set for SGDClassifier 20 combinations for precision and 20 combinations for recall were used. Both the algorithms trained the model one at a time using their best parameters found using performance tuning. The accuracy achieved with 8-keyword feature set was found to be 51.42% for Random Forest and 40% for SGDClassifier. Using reduced Feature set to train classifier; the classification accuracy was better with 58.69% accuracy for random forest and 50:00% accuracy for SGDClassifier. The results were also validated using k – fold cross validation giving average results of 62.53% for 4 folds and 60.45% for 8 folds using Random Forest and 54.42% for 4 folds and 48.28% for 8 folds using SGDClassifier. The results of Random Forest are better compared to SGDClassifier in all scenarios.

7 Limitation and Future Work

The Classes Shanta and Shringar is having overlapping features which is troubling the performance of the model developed in this research work. In future fuzzy logic will be used to solve the overlapping feature problem.

Secondly POS tagger available for Hindi language available in NLTK is used which is tagging a lot of words in the poetry as 'Unk' meaning unknown, but observing the tagged poems shows that there are important words related to Hindi poetry which are tagged as 'Unk' but certain garbage values are also tagged as 'Unk'. Currently all those visible and not visible garbage values are cleaned with script in python. In future algorithm will be developed to extract important features from 'Unk' keywords extracted from tagged poems to make feature set rich for better emotion Classification.

References

1. Shalini, M., Indira, B.: Implementation of Hindi word recognition and classification of system using artificial neural network. Int. J. Pure Appl. Math. **117**(15), 557–564 (2017)
2. Shalini, P., Satya Prakash, S.: A hybrid Hindi printed document classification system using SVM an Fuzzy: an advancement. J. Inf. Technol. Res. **12**(4), 107–131 (2019)
3. Jasleen, K., JatinderKumar, S.: PuPoCl: development of Punjabi poetry classifier using linguistic features and weighting. INFOCOMP J. Comput. Sci. **16**(1–2), 1–7 (2017)
4. Mandal, A.K.: Supervised learning method for bangla web document categorization. Int. J. Artif. Intell. Appl. **5**(5), 93–105 (2014)
5. Vandana, J., Manjunath, N.: Sentiment analysis in a resource scarce language: Hindi. Int. J. Sci. Eng. Res. **7**(6), 968–980 (2016)
6. Jasleen, K., JatinderKumar, S.: Emotion detection and sentiment analysis in text corpus: a differential study with informal and formal writing styles. Int. J. Comput. Appl. **101**(9), 1–9 (2014)
7. Noraini, J., Masnizah, M., Shahrul, A.: Poetry classification using support vector machines. Int. J. Comput. Sci. **8**(9), 1441–1446 (2012)
8. Hamid, R.: Poetic features for poem recognition: a comparative study. J. Pattern Recognit. Res. **3**, 24–39 (2008)
9. Kamath, C.N., Bukhari, S.S., Dengel, A.: Comparative study between traditional machine learning and deep learning approaches for text classification. In: Proceedings of the ACM Symposium on Document Engineering 2018 DocEng 2018, pp. 1–11 (2018). Article No.: 14
10. Bounabi, M., El Moutaouakil, K., Satori, K.: Text classification using fuzzy TF-IDF and machine learning models In: BDIoT 2019: Proceedings of the 4th International Conference on Big Data and Internet of Things, pp. 1–6 (2019). Article No.: 18
11. Puri, S., Singh, S.P.: An efficient Devanagari character classification in printed and handwritten documents using SVM. Procedia Comput. Sci. **152**, 111–121 (2019). https://doi.org/10.1016/j.procs.2019.05.033
12. Ishaan, T., Ashyush, C.: Classification of spam categorization on Hindi documents using Bayesian Classifier. IOSR J. Comput. Eng. **20**(6), 53–58 (2018)

13. Surkova, A., Skorynin, S., Chernobaev, I.: Word embedding and cognitive linguistic models in text classification tasks. In: Proceedings of the XI International Scientific Conference Communicative Strategies of the Information Society CSIS 2019, pp. 1–6 (2019). Article No.: 12

14. Anne, C., Mishra, A., Hoque, M.T., Tu, S.: Multiclass patent document classification. Artif. Intell. Res. 7(1), 1–14 (2018)

15. Meng, Y., Shen, J., Zhang, C., Han, J.: Weakly-supervised neural text classification In: Proceedings of the 27th ACM International Conference on Information and Knowledge Management CIKM 2018, pp. 983–992 (2018)

16. Liang, Q., Wu, P., Huang, C.: An efficient method for text classification task In: BDE 2019: Proceedings of the 2019 International Conference on Big Data Engineering pp. 92–97 (2019)

17. Tran, T.C.T., Huynh, H.X., Tran, P.Q., Truong, D.Q.: Text classification based on keywords with different thresholds In: ICIIT 2019: Proceedings of the 2019 4th International Conference on Intelligent Information Technology, pp. 101–106 (2019)

18. Islam, M.Z., Liu, J., Li, J., Liu, L., Kang, W.: A semantics aware random forest for text classification In: Proceedings of the 28th ACM International Conference on Information and Knowledge Management CIKM 2019, pp. 1061–1070 (2019)

19. Zheng, W., Jin, M.: Do we need more training samples for text classification? In: Proceedings of the 2018 Artificial Intelligence and Cloud Computing Conference AICCC 2018, pp. 121–128 (2018)

20. Yao, R., Cao, Y., Ding, Z., Guo, L.: A sensitive words filtering model based on web text features In: Proceedings of the 2018 2nd International Conference on Computer Science and Artificial Intelligence CSAI 2018, pp. 516–520 (2018)

21. Pal, K., Patel, B.V.: A study of current state of work done for classification in Indian languages. Int. J. Sci. Res. Sci. Technol. 3(7), 403–407 (2017)

Melanoma Detection Using HSV with SVM Classifier and De-duplication Technique to Increase Efficiency

Mayura Patil$^{(\boxtimes)}$ and Nilima Dongre

Ramrao Adik Institute of Technology, Nerul, Navi Mumbai, India
mayurapatil.b4u@gmail.com, nilima.dongre@rait.ac.in

Abstract. Around one third of all recorded cancers account worldwide for skin cancer, according to the World Health Organization. Every year in the USA there are over 5 million non-melanoma, although about 13,000 cases of melanoma are reported in the UK and Australia. Over the last few decades, occurrences of skin cancer have also risen by 119%, from 1990 to 91270, from 27,600 in 2018. Melanoma has risen 119 million in nations such as the United Kingdom. Not only has the ozone layer reduced ultraviolet radiation safety but the misuse of the atmosphere and heat and tanning [2] has explained this trend. The medical fraternity has spent enormous time and energy on sensitizing people by awareness initiatives. Human skin cancer is the most dangerous variety, with its effects growing rapidly. Early detection of melanoma in dermoscopic photos is extremely important as they are useful for early diagnosis and treatment of ailment. Computer-aided diagnostic tools may promote the detection of cancer early for dermatologists. In this method pre-processing shall take place by applying a list of filters for removing hair, spots and assorted noises from pictures and the methodology of photographs painting shall then be used to fill unspecified areas. In this paper system uses PH2 dataset for evaluation. Also proposed de-duplication method will help in image preprocessing time which will also help in detection of melanoma. KNN, Naïve Bayes and SVM classifier are used for training and testing purpose also SVM shows the highest accuracy of classifier with de-duplication techniques.

Keywords: Melanoma · SVM · Image processing · Data de duplication

1 Introduction

Around one third of all recorded cancers account worldwide for skin cancer, according to the World Health Organization. Every year in the USA there are over 5 million non-melanoma, although about 13,000 cases of melanoma are reported in the UK and Australia. Over the last few decades, occurrences of skin cancer have also risen by 119%, from 1990 to 91270, from 27,600 in 2018. Melanoma has risen 119 million in nations such as the United Kingdom. Not only has the ozone layer reduced ultraviolet radiation safety but the misuse of the atmosphere and heat and tanning [2] has explained this trend. The medical fraternity has spent time and energy on sensitizing people by

N. Chaubey et al. (Eds.): COMS2 2020, CCIS 1235, pp. 109–120, 2020.
https://doi.org/10.1007/978-981-15-6648-6_9

awareness initiatives. Nevertheless, irresponsible behavior may not guarantee safety, as there is also a possibility that the number of people with sunburns will develop skin cancer over their lives. Hence there is need to invest in development of technologies for the early diagnosis of skin cancer. Two more popular methods to obtain color images of skin wounds are the numerous, non-invasive dermatologist techniques. The images under observation can be of two types namely macroscopic or dermoscopic based on the collection system. Macroscopic images or clinical image that are taken by regular or smart phone cameras, while dermoscopic images are collected by means of a special lens system with an oil/gel interface (disposal touch dermoscopy). In this article [9], the images are not just dermoscopic, they allow the visualization of additional colors and patterns that make skin injuries more accurate.

Another problem to address is the principle of photo repetition, which is useful for performance. From a visible angle, however, completely different codes can be observed from images with consistent visual perceptions. Therefore, the successful removal of duplicate photo copies by large data center storages and data clouds would increase the processing usage. The optimization of storage may have a critical sensitivity. Manual process extracted redundant objects. The downside was that the de-duplication method was totally dependent on human intervention. In the immense knowledge, tons of human resources would be necessary and vulnerable in order to produce subjective judgment errors. For backup systems and database schemes, replication has been commonly used to significantly improve space usage. Nevertheless, the standard de-duplication software just removes exactly the same things, but is out of inventory for replicate pictures which nevertheless have completely different codes with a constant visual perception. This paper provides a high-precision duplicate de-duplication method to tackle the higher than problem. Duplicate photos are eliminated as the most plan in the proposed approach.

2 Litreature Survey

During the last decade many research have been undertaken in the area of the detection of melanoma, covering a large array of computer vision and patterns. The most widely used techniques found in literature are the segmentation and classification of images. Techniques for segmentation include assignment to the affected region and the non-affected region of threshold binary values. The technique proposed provides a good outcome, but the exactness is near the border of skin color and color of the affected area overlaps. The technique proposed provides good results. N. The hybrid or mix of functional extraction methods used by Moura et al. [5] were the ABCD rule (A is for asymmetry, B is for borderline, C is for color and D is for the diameter of affected area or diameter of mole) and textural characteristics. A classification system with a support vector machine was set and SVM was implemented after a Hybrid feature, which results in a performance rate of 75%. In various classification schemes proposed by many authors, ABCD rule features key role. Shape, colour, edge and texture characteristics are mostly used. The majority of works found in the literature are also based on computer vision and techniques of segmentation. Whereas pattern recognition algorithms are used for the detection of skin lesions due to melanoma with different characteristics. In contrast to the proposed methods, this method is focused on the extraction and use of SVM classifier for classifying Melanoma Images from all the dermoscopic images of new statistical colors and texture characteristics.

In its planned model, Mogensen, Jemec [3] uses background neural networks. The methodology envisaged, however, has some disadvantages. Slow convergence rates and native minimum trapping are the major disadvantages of this method.

Whereas Rehman, Mobeen [6] has projected that CNN does not need any additional classifier, KNN is used for classification model training since three fully connected layers have been used. Specific advantages of such a classification are its own, as a back propagation algorithm can be used to adjust neuron parameters entirely in layers so as to achieve higher classification patterns. In the approach proposed for TS also Pennisi [7] is very appropriate once benign lesions are handled, whereas when malignant melanoma pictures are divided the detection accuracy significantly decreases. Moreover, this rule is extremely sensitive to images which contain irregular boundaries, a variety of recalls and a range structure, and therefore has a space for a lesion that is less than that of the specific area.

Jacob and Rekha [18] explored double recognition algorithms to identify objects in a series of visually duplicated images. In many applications for large image collections it is important to find visually identical objects. For each image, the Kbits hash code is calculated first, i.e. each picture is converted to a k-bit hash code based on its contents and then only the hash codes can be used to detect the double image.

Prathilothamai and Nair [14] provided a method for almost duplicated object detection and recovery. The issue of near-duplicate detection and image recovery is solved by rigorous interest point detection (DoG detector), local layout (PCA-SIFT) and an active similitude analysis (LSH) of high dimensional images. The photograph representation focuses on sections which use local descriptors and offer high-quality matches under various transformations. Sensitive locality hazard used for local descriptors indexing. A limited solution is a technology vulnerability and a potential drawback that the system requires hundreds or thousands of apps at a time that can be inefficient.

Majumdar and Ullah [16] provided an approach to hierarchical object matching centered on an area. The two pictures are given to identify the largest part of Fig. 1 and the match for Fig. 2 with the most similarity of areas (e.g., surfaces, boundary shapes and colors) defined. The authors [15] suggest sorting criteria to classify the latter into two sets: a collection of edges probable to be in the same category and a sets of edges that are highly likely in different groups to be statistically significant. Any particular edge name as l is selected as a background element when the ratio of a particular group edge to no group edge is higher than a certain threshold. This procedure will lead to asymmetric labeling procedure in which the figure is separated from background discrimination. The main elements are considered edges with highly prominent features, and separated from the background elements. We are not uniquely different if there is overlap in it.

Table 1. Comparative analysis

Paper Name	Author	Technique
Combining ABCD Rule, Texture Features and Transfer Learning in Automatic Diagnosis of Melanoma	N. Moura et al. [5]	ABCD rule of dermoscopy is used for extraction of skin lesion. Feature extraction is utilised on the pre-processed image inorder to find – Area (A), Border (B), Colour(C), and D (Diameter) square measure extraction
Diagnosis of non melanoma skin cancer karatirocyte melanoma: A review of diagnosis and its accuracy of non melanoma skin cancer diagnostic tests and technologies	Mogensen M, Jemec GBE [3]	In this project, model is making use of Backpropagation neural networks. The major drawbacks of this methodology is square measure slow convergence rates and trapping in native minima
Convolution Neural Network based identification	Rehman, Mobeen [17]	The proposed system is advantageous as it does not need extra classifiers as SVM, KNN since three full-connected layers are used for training purpose of classification. This classification is feasible to use back-propagation method which can adjusts various parameters of neurons for further classification
Detection using Delaunay Triangulation	A. Pennisi [7]	The proposed approach is handling benign lesions efficiently, whereas the detection of melanoma accuracy considerably decreases once malignant melanoma pictures are divided. This rule is sensitive to images with irregular shapes and borders, multiple layer of pigmentation, and structure and so, it presents a lesion space that's smaller compared to particular space

3   Proposed Method

Early detection in dermoscopic pictures of malignant melanoma is very important and critical as they can be useful for early treatment. Diagnostic code machine assisted can be valuable to support dermatologists in early detection of cancers. Cancer is the most deadly disease in the world today and the detection and diagnosis are an important area for image processing science. An efficient machine-learning method for the identification

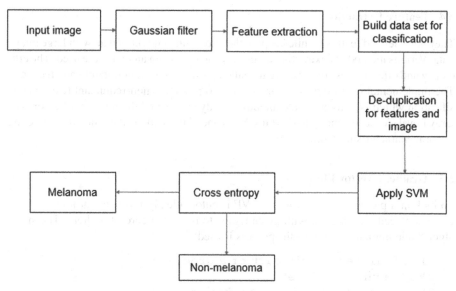

Fig. 1. System Architecture

of dermoscopic objects of melanoma that identifies lesions based on skin melanoma, e.g. different types of color and texture. For the elimination of the same object and function during the train/test phase, software replication definition is used to improve reliability and performance. Several steps are listed below (Fig. 1).

3.1 Pre-processing

It is very important and necessary to rescale the lesion images in order to perform deep learning network. As directly resizing image may distort the shape and size of skin lesion, it requires cropping the center area of lesion image and then needs to proportionally resize the area to a lower resolution.

3.2 Dermoscopic Images

The skin specialist uses optical enlargement and polarized light to magnify the photos and make out the segmented portion. The photos are not easy to identify the segmented part as feathers, nuclei, objects and replacement are part of the photograph. For the purpose of implementation we use ABCDE, the array of 7 points to identify artefacts accurately.

3.3 Gaussian Filter

Gaussian noise is statistical noise, the normal density function probability. Instead of noise patterns, the filter is used to remove noise over edges. The black and white image usually has a natural appearance called the sounds of salt popper.

3.4 Feature Extraction

They have deleted features while keeping the maximum amount of data with large image data. Various methods of extracting color, text and type from an image are used. The efficiency and effectiveness of the current challenges to achieve functionality and recovery. The implementations use gray color matrices to provide a non-redundant texture classification which is immune to the alteration of dynamics and the removal of color. The Gray Level Co-occurrence Matrix (GLCM) is one of the statistical method for extracting textural characteristics from images.

3.5 Gradient Vector Flow

To look in a picture for smoothness. GVF is automatically formatted at low levels. A cycle is placed on a picture with given radius to reach the core of a photo. The snake algorithmic implementation of the process is used:

```
1) Calculate max-min part of a group
2) Take union of 2 set
3) Increase/decrease parts during a set
4) Decrease the key value of an element
```

$$(x + a)^n = \sum_{k=0}^{n} \binom{n}{k} x^k a^{n-k} \tag{1}$$

3.6 Classification

The serial move is to separate the malignant structures from their equivalents after an important stage in an appropriate set of choices. During this step, at least one in each class of cancerous, benign, or healthy is assigned a region of interest to the lesion image. The malignancy level of the tissue (i.e. grading) can be classified as a field of diagnosis. The groups are the potential degrees of cancer of interest in this case. For nomination, a research cluster takes a look at the options. To investigate whether or not a massive difference occurs for several groups at the cost of a minimum of 1 value element. For the photos, however, it is important, for the following reason, to understand the results of the set tests with additional caution. Unit evaluations conclude that the specimens are independent and therefore result in assumptions.

On the other side, the data set consisted of separate cloth footage taken from the same, non-freelancing client, which could contribute to misleading and ambiguous tests. Another research cluster uses algorithms for computer teaching to be informed (from data) by discriminating between different categories.

3.7 Image De-duplication

The client has to calculate the value (hash and feature) of the image I, and upload stands to the server. Then D-phash will list "Duplicate Check" (key part).

```
Phase-I: Duplicate Check
    Input Image;
    1) Read imageI
    imgbgr = inread(I);
    2) Convert the image in greyscale
    Imgray = cvtColor(imgbgr);
    3) Resize the image
    imgdst = resize(imgray);
    4) Compute the DCT matrix F
    F = dct(imgdsr);
    5) Select low frequency DCT matrix keep the loop 8x8ofF
    6) Compute the mean value of F
    mean = (ΣF(i,j) − F(0,0))/63 Where0 ≤ i≤7,0 ≤ j≤7
    F (0,0)is DCT Coefficient
    7) Normalize into Binary form
    8) Construct the Features value p = p(i,j)
    9) Return P;
```

Phase-II (Proof of Ownership): Challenge:

1: The server S randomly select an auxiliary image Ia, it send id of Aa to the client and request the client C to provide the proof.

2: The server S reads the auxiliary image Ia and the image I', where I' is the image saved on the server which will be similar to the image I.

3: The server S resize the auxiliary image Ia: size (width Ia, Height Ia) = size(width Ia,Height Ia).

4: Let the blending parameter α = 0.5, the server S generates the blended image I = Blend (I,Iα,α),which means the server S computes the feature value.

Response:

1: After receiving id of the auxiliary image Ia, the client C creates the auxiliary image Ia, corresponding to the id and reads the image I.

2: The client C resize the size of Ia.

3: Let α = 0.5, the client C generates the blended image, which means, the client C computes the feature value, then it send feature value to the server.

Mathematical system

$S = \{I, O, F\}$
Where,
S = the system for device specific image processing.
I is set of inputs.
O is set of outputs.
F is set of functions

$I = \{M1, M2\}$

Where, M1 = Input Images for Test. M2 = Input Images for Training

$O = \{O1, O2\}$

Where, O1 = Melanoma detected Images. O2 = Non-Melanoma Images.

$F = \{F1, F2, F3\}$
Where,
F1 = rgb (RGB) To HSV
F2 = de-duplication(set(I))
F3 = feature vector ()

The evaluation of system uses metrics such as accuracy, sensitivity, specificity. Here several terms are commonly used to calculate Specificity, Sensitivity and Accuracy. These terms are True positive (TP), True negative (TN), False negative (FP), False positive (FP). These metrics are given mathematically as follows.
Accuracy - $((T N + T P)/(T N + T P + F N + F P))$

4   Results and Dataset

We also mentioned a prototype that is applied in a high specification machine using the Help Vector. Intel Core i5 with 4 GB of RAM was the system setup. For project execution, we used the java open source platform and cv repository.

In a public PH2 database are included 437 image studies consisting of 80 standard nevi, eighty atypical nevi and 40 melanomas. Depending on their picture type, the PH2 data set was split into two groups. There were 160 general cases: 152 with healthy photos were detected and 8 melanoma images recorded a whole skin region.

Table 1 for time required for execution has shown below. Which clearly shows the required time for two method which are system with de-duplication and without de-duplication. As de-duplication system neglect duplicate image and features so it requires less time for final execution. Figure 2 graph shows a comparison without the DE reproduction method of the existing system. This finding shows the time needed for the image test. Clearly, we can say that using image processing duplication technology results better.

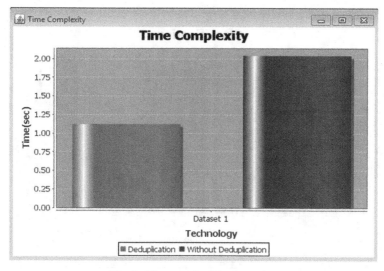

Fig. 2. Time required for execution

Table 2. Time required for execution

Method Used	Required time
De-duplication	1.12 s
Without De-duplication	2.04 s

As system provides better result in respect of accuracy and time by using duplication techniques. So classification also works better in such scenario. System has evaluated three classifier SVM, KNN and Naïve Bayes. So The better result we get through SVM classification. Table 2 contains the accuracy in percent for these three classifier. Also in Fig. 3 shows the graph of the increasing classifiers. The system is assessed by three different KNN, Naive Bayes and SVM classifier classifiers. Between these data sets, SVM gives the best results. Accuracy of classifiers given in table above (Table 4).

Table 3. Classification accuracy

Classifier	Accuracy (in %)
KNN	90
Naïve Bayes	94
SVM	96

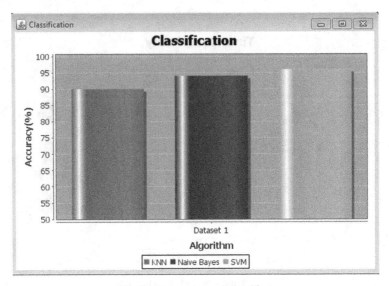

Fig. 3. Comparison of classifiers

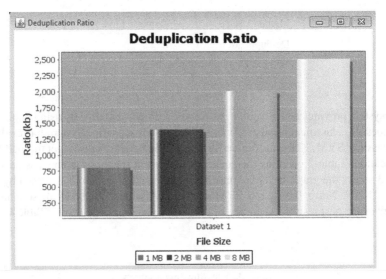

Fig. 4. Deduplication ratio graph

Third evaluation is checked on de-duplication ratio graph. As Table 3 and Fig. 4 shows ratio graph and changing size of image. After this approach has been used a deduction graph shows that some objects are smaller and have decreased their volume by almost 50% once implementation of techniques. Objects have various sizes in PH2 dataset. Upon implementing replication technique, the table displayed certain objects with their original size.

Table 4. Change in size of image before and after duplication

Before duplication	After duplication
1 MB	750 kb
2 MB	1.4 MB
4 MB	2 MB
8 MB	2.5 MB

5 Conclusion

The system has presented an effective machine-based method for the early detection of melanoma with dermoscopic images based on distinctive effects of skin lesions on melanoma. First, the dermoscopic images will extract new characteristics of color and texture. The vector feature is stored to display all objects. Use of SVM classifier to clinch melanoma images from a set of dermoscopic images of PH2, with the feature vectors stored in the database has worked efficiently. System has evaluated and gave the accuracy of 96% with less time. There is huge scope of further development in this project. This includes detection of various other types of melanoma as we have only focused on visible skin moles, complexity of diagnosis can vary as per the melanoma types, preprocessing time can further be reduced with new techniques, more work can be done towards the security of data.

References

1. Auxilia, L.A.: Accuracy prediction using machine learning techniques for indian patient liver disease. In: 2018 2nd International Conference on Trends in Electronics and Informatics (ICOEI), Tirunelveli, pp. 45–50 (2018)
2. Zhang, W., Gao, L., Tang, Z., Ran, M., Lin, Z.: A benchmark for automatic acral melanoma preliminary screening. In: 2018 IEEE International Conference on Bioinformatics and Biomedicine (BIBM), Madrid, Spain, pp. 2829–2831 (2018)
3. Mogensen, M., Jemec, G.B.E.: Diagnosis of non melanoma skin cancer karatirocyte melanoma: A review of diagnosis accuracy of non melanoma skin cancer diagnostic tests anud technologies. Dermatol. Surg. **33**, 115874 (2007)
4. Roy, S.S., Haque, A.U., Neubert, J.: Automatic diagnosis of melanoma from dermoscopic image using real-time object detection. In: 2018 52nd Annual Conference on Information Sciences and Systems (CISS), Princeton, NJ, pp. 1–5 (2018)
5. Moura, N., et al.: Combining ABCD rule, texture features and transfer learning in automatic diagnosis of Melanoma. In: 2018 IEEE Symposium on Computers and Communications (ISCC), Natal, pp. 00508–00513 (2018)
6. Rehman, M., et al.: Classification of skin lesion by interference of segmentation and convolution neural network. In: 2018 2nd International Conference on Engineering Innovation (ICEI). IEEE (2018)
7. Pennisi, A., et al.: Melanoma detection using delaunay triangulation. In: 2015 IEEE 27th International Conference on Tools with Artificial Intelligence (ICTAI), IEEE (2015)

8. Sabbaghi, S., Aldeen, M., Garnavi, R.: A deep bag-of-features model for the classification of melanomas in dermoscopy images. In: 2016 38th Annual International Conference of the IEEE Engineering in Medicine and Biology Society (EMBC), Orlando, FL, pp. 1369–1372 (2016)

9. Adjed, F., Gardezi, S.J.S.: Fusion of structural and textural features formelanoma recognition, March 2018. https://doi.org/10.1049/iet-cvi.2017.0193

10. Dhinagar, N.J., Wilson, M., Celenk, M.: Standardizing pre-processing for digital skin-lesion image analysis. In: 2017 2nd International Conference on Bio-engineering for SmartTechnologies (BioSMART), Paris, pp. 1–4 (2017)

11. Joseph, S., Panicker, J.R.: Skin lesion analysis system for melanoma detection with an effective hair segmentation method. In: 2016 International Conference on Information Science (ICIS), Kochi, pp. 91–96 (2016)

12. Thaiyalnayaki, S., Sasikala, J., Ponraj, R.: Indexing near-duplicate images in web searchusing minhash algorithm. Mater. Today: Proc. **5**(1), 1 (2018)

13. Jacob, C., Rekha, V.R.: Secured and reliable file sharing system with de-duplication using erasure correction code. In: 2017 International Conference on Networks & Advancesin Computational Technologies (NetACT), Thiruvanthapuram, pp. 221–228 (2017)

14. Prathilothamai, M., Nair, P.S.: De-duplication of passports using Aadhaar. In: 2017 International Conference on Computer Communication and Informatics (ICCCI), Coimbatore, pp. 1–5 (2017). https://doi.org/10.1109/iccci.2017.8117744

15. Guo, Y., Liu, Y.: CNN-RNN: a large-scale hierarchical image classification framework. Multimedia Tools Appl. **77**(8), 1025110271 (2018)

16. Majumder, S., Ullah, M.A.: Feature extraction from dermoscopy images for an effective diagnosis of melanoma skin cancer. In: 2018 10th International Conference on Electrical and Computer Engineering (ICECE), Dhaka, Bangladesh, pp. 185–188 (2018)

17. Rehman, M., et al.: Classification of skin lesion by interference of segmentation and convolution neural network. In: 2nd International Conference on Engineering Innovation (ICEI). IEEE (2018)

18. Jacob, C., Rekha, V.R.: Secured and reliable file sharing system with de-duplication using erasure correction code. In: 2017 International Conference on Networks & Advances in Computational Technologies (NetACT), Thiruvanthapuram, pp. 221–228 (2017)

Cyber Intrusion Detection Using Machine Learning Classification Techniques

Hamed Alqahtani[1,7], Iqbal H. Sarker[2(✉)], Asra Kalim[3], Syed Md. Minhaz Hossain[2,4], Sheikh Ikhlaq[5], and Sohrab Hossain[2,6(✉)]

[1] King Khalid University, Abha, Saudi Arabia
[2] Chittagong University of Engineering and Technology, Chittagong, Bangladesh
iqbal@cuet.ac.bd
[3] Jazan University, Jizan, Saudi Arabia
[4] Premier University, Chittagong, Bangladesh
[5] Accenture Solutions Private Limited, Mumbai, India
[6] East Delta University, Chittagong, Bangladesh
sohrab.h@eastdelta.edu.bd
[7] Macquarie University, Sydney 2109, Australia

Abstract. As the alarming growth of connectivity of computers and the significant number of computer-related applications increase in recent years, the challenge of fulfilling cyber-security is increasing consistently. It also needs a proper protection system for numerous *cyberattacks*. Thus, detecting inconsistency and attacks in a computer network and developing *intrusion detection system* (IDS) that performs a potential role for cyber-security. Artificial intelligence, particularly *machine learning techniques*, has been used to develop a useful data-driven intrusion detection system. In this paper, we employ various popular machine learning classification algorithms, namely Bayesian Network, Naive Bayes classifier, Decision Tree, Random Decision Forest, Random Tree, Decision Table, and Artificial Neural Network, to detect intrusions due to provide intelligent services in the domain of cyber-security. Finally, we test the effectiveness of various experiments on cyber-security datasets having several categories of cyber-attacks and evaluate the effectiveness of the performance metrics, precision, recall, f1-score, and accuracy.

Keywords: Cybersecurity · Cyber-attacks · Intrusions · Intrusion detection system · Machine learning · Classification · Cyber-attack prediction · Artificial intelligence · Cybersecurity analytics

1 Introduction

In recent days, cyber-security and protection against numerous *cyber-attacks* are becoming a burning question. The main reason behind that is the tremendous growth of computer networks and the vast number of relevant applications used by individuals or groups for either personal or commercial use, specially after the acceptance of Internet-of-Things (IoT). The cyber-attacks cause severe damage and severe financial losses in

© Springer Nature Singapore Pte Ltd. 2020
N. Chaubey et al. (Eds.): COMS2 2020, CCIS 1235, pp. 121–131, 2020.
https://doi.org/10.1007/978-981-15-6648-6_10

large-scale networks [25]. The existing solutions like hardware and software firewalls, user's authentication, and data encryption method are not sufficient to meet the challenge of upcoming demand, and unfortunately, not able to protect the computer network's several cyber-threats. These conventional security structures are not sufficient as safeguard due to the faster rigorous evolution of intrusion systems [13, 26, 27]. Firewall only controls every accesses from network to network, which means prevent access between networks. But it does not provide any signal in case of an internal attack. So, it is obvious to develop accurate defense techniques such as *machine learning-based intrusion detection system (IDS)* for the system's security.

In general, an intrusion detection system (IDS) is a system or software that detects infectious activities and violations of policy in a network or system. An IDS identifies the inconsistencies and abnormal behavior on a network during the functioning of daily activities in a network or system used to detect risks or attacks related to network security, like denial-of-service (DoS). An intrusion detection system also helps to locate, decide, and control unauthorized system behavior such as unauthorized access, or modification and destruction [12, 31]. There are different types of intrusion detection systems based on the user perspective. For instance, they are host-based and network-based IDS [25].

These are in the scope of single computers to large networks some extend. In a host-based intrusion detection system (HIDS), it lies on an individual system and keeps track of operating system files for inconsistency and abnormalities in the activity. In contrast, the network intrusion detection system (NIDS) investigates and scans connections in the network for unwanted traffic. On the other hand, there are two approaches based on detection, one is signature-based, and another one is anomaly-based detection [25, 18]. Signature-based IDS explores the byte patterns in the path of the network. One can treat it as malicious instruction sequences used by malware. It arises from antivirus software referred to the groups or patterns as signatures detected in it. Signature-based IDS cannot detect attacks, for which there is no pattern available before. An anomaly-based IDS, it examines the behavior of the network and finds patterns, automatically creates a data-driven model for profiling the expected behavior, and thus detects deviations in the case of any anomalies [18]. The merit of this anomaly-based IDS is to trace current, latest, and unseen inconsistencies or cyber-attacks like denial-of-services.

For developing computational methods to identify various cyber-attacks, it needs to analyze different incident patterns, and eventually predict the threats utilizing cyber-security data. It is known as a data-driven intelligent intrusion detection system [25]. To build a data-driven intrusion detection model, the knowledge of artificial intelligence, particularly *machine learning* techniques, is essential. However, the prediction of cyber-attacks using machine learning algorithms is problematic due to the several identifications of multiple classifiers results in different contexts depending on data characteristics [23]. For this reason, we analyze several machine learning algorithms on intrusion detection systems for utilizing cyber-security data. For this purpose, we employ various popular machine learning classification techniques, such as Bayesian Network (BN), Naive Bayes (NB), Random Forest (RF), Decision Tree (DT), Random Tree (RT), Decision Table (DTb), and Artificial Neural Network (ANN), for providing intelligent services in the domain of cyber-security, particularly for intrusion detection. Finally, the effectiveness is tested by conducting numerous experiments on cyber-security datasets consisting of several categories of cyberattacks, and evaluates the effectiveness by measuring the performance metrics precision, recall, f1-score, and accuracy for these machine learning-based IDS models.

The remaining part of the paper arranges as follows. Section 2 depicts background and related works. Data-driven intrusion detection modeling is incorporated in Sect. 3. Section 4 presents experimental analysis and results followed by the conclusion in Sect. 5.

2 Background and Related Work

In this section, we first define cyber-security, represents the systems or software of protection of data, program, connections among computers from several unwanted attacks such as unauthorized attacks, modification, fabrication [2]. As conventional security systems are not enough for detecting network security [13, 26, 27], we focus on developing an *intrusion detection system (IDS)* to explore and detect the system's security.

Intrusion defines as an unauthorized activity that causes damage to an information system [10]. That means any attack that could pose a possible threat to information confidentiality, integrity, or availability is considered an intrusion. Presently firewalls, access control, and cryptography are the main defensive mechanisms deployed against intrusions used for detecting internal attacks [5]. However, intrusion detection systems are used for detecting internal as well as external attacks. Despite detecting known attacks on signature-based IDS discussed above, in this work, we aim to focus on an anomaly-based intrusion detection model [10].

An anomaly is a state of deviation from familiarized behavior. Profiles are the general or wanted behaviors extracted from tracking activities of users, network connections, and hosts during a fixed time [11]. Anomaly-based intrusion detection model is also called the behavior-based model and represented as a dynamic approach [11]. The fundamental merit of an anomaly-based intrusion detection model is to detect zero-day attacks because it is not reliable to acknowledge the unwanted users' activity in the signature database [3]. Further, another technique exists, and it is a hybrid detection [28] technique or protocol analysis [11] detection techniques. The hybrid technique has the advantage of a high detection rate in the misuse detection and high potentiality of inconsistency detectors in recognizing the latest attacks. It expands the rate of detection of previously known intrusions and to decrease the false-positive rate of undefined attacks [31]. This work focuses on an intrusion detection model constructed in machine learning techniques utilizing cyber-security data.

Machine learning uses to make decision using computers [8, 29]. It is a part of artificial intelligence and further related to computational statistics. Classification refers to supervised learning that predicts the cyber-attack class labels of samples from training security data [8, 23]. Thus, we analyze various popular classification techniques that include Bayesian approach [17, 22], Tree-based model [14, 20, 24, 18], Artificial Neural Network based model [23] that are used frequently in predictive analytics [8, 16, 29, 30], to develop a fruitful data-driven IDS predictive model for providing intelligent services of cyber security.

In this paper, we employ various popular machine learning classification techniques, such as Bayesian Network (BN), Naive Bayes (NB), Random Forest (RF), Decision Tree

(DT), Random Tree (RT), Decision Table (DTb), and Artificial Neural Network (ANN) for classifying cyber-attacks and make a comparative analysis with experiments.

3 Data-Driven IDS Modeling

This section presents our data-driven IDS model of numerous machine learning techniques. It incorporates several steps: dataset exploration, data processing, and machine learning-based security modeling. It has been discussed these steps chronologically, as below.

3.1 Dataset Exploration and Preprocessing

Datasets represent a collection of information records that consist of several attributes or features and related facts related to the cyber-security model [25]. So, it is essential to realize the nature of cyber-security data containing various types of cyber-attacks and relevant features. The reason is that raw security data collected from relevant cyber sources could be used to analyze the various patterns of security incidents or malicious behavior, to build a data-driven security model to achieve our goal. In this work, KDD'99 cup data has been used [1] to develop predictive models for differentiating the relationship between intrusions or several attacks. This dataset contains 4898431 instances with 41 attributes. In Table 1, we have shown the features of KDD'99 cup datasets [1]. In this dataset, attacks are classified into four main groups:

- DoS: Denial of service (DoS) is a kind of attack in which a legitimate user does not have access to the system and network resources. Online banking services, email may be affected. DoS attacks comprise of the SYN flood attack and the Smurf attack.
- R2L: Remote to Local (R2L) is an attack where an attacker tries to gain access to the victim machine without having an account in it.
- U2R: User to Root (U2R) is an attack where an attacker tries to gain privileges having local access in the victim machine.
- PROBE: In Probe, the attacker targets the host and tries to get information about the host.

We first prepare the dataset, including these attack categories and available attributes for developing machine learning-based IDS models. There are four types of features used in this dataset; they are Basic features, Content Features, Time-based Traffic Features, and Host-based Traffic Features. Feature-based attributes are extracted from TCP/IP connections. Traffic features are computed by window interval. It divides into two groups; one is 'same host features' and another one is 'same service features.' They are both called time-based features. Sometimes, in the case of probing, there is a slower scan than 2 s. To solve this problem, 'same host features' and 'same service features' are recomputed by the connection window. Then it is called connection based features. DoS and probing may have several connections to a host/s during a period. In Table 2, we have summarized these categories of attacks. In contrast to that, Root to Local (R2L) and User to Root (U2R) attacks generally require a single connection. Content-based features have been used to detect these attacks. Then process these features according to the requirements and design the target machine learning-based IDS model. This data-driven pattern-based decision analysis plays a useful role in providing data-driven intelligent cyber-security services.

3.2 Machine Learning Classification Based Modeling

Classification is a supervised learning technique and popularly used to model cyber intrusions based on multi-category of attacks. In supervised learning, data is always labeled previously. In the training phase, the classifier learns the labels so that in the test phase, it can predict correctly for unseen data. In our analysis, we implement the popular machine learning techniques used for various purposes. Several techniques summarize as below:

- *Bayesian Network and Naive Bayes:* A Bayesian Network, breaks up a probability distribution based on the conditional independencies, while Bayesian inference is used to infer a marginal distribution given some observed evidence [29]. Bayesian Network is used to detect, diagnose, and reasoning. Naive Bayes is a kind of Bayesian network and is a commonly used machine learning algorithm. [9]. It is a basic probabilistic based technique that calculates the probability to classify or predict the cyber-attack class in a given dataset. This method assumes each feature's value as independent and considers the correlation or relationship between the features [8]. Naive Bayes includes two probabilities; one is the conditional probability, and another one is class probability. Class probability is determined by dividing the frequency of each class instance by total instances. Conditional probability is the ratio of the occurrence of each attribute for a given class, and the occurrence of samples for that class. Naive Bayes is faster than other classifiers.
- *Decision Tree and Decision Table:* Decision tree is one of the most popular classification and prediction algorithms in machine learning [14, 23]. ID3 proposed by J. R. Quinlan [14] is a common top-down approach for building decision trees. Based on this, the C4.5 algorithm [15], and later BehavDT approach [20], IntruDTree model [18] have been constructed to generate the decision trees. Decision Tree is a tree-like structure, in which an internal node represents attributes, and branches represent the outcome, and leaf represents a class label. These algorithms generate decision rules to predict the outcome for unseen test cases. These algorithms provide high accuracy and better interpretation. The Decision Tree can work with both continuous and discrete data. A Decision Table illustrates the complex decision rules representing a tabular form consists of rows and columns [8, 29].
- *Random Forest and Random Tree:* Random Forest is a classifier comprising of decision trees operated as an ensemble learning [7]. Breiman et al. propose it. The reason is that it combines both the different set of data called bootstrap aggregation [6] and also numerous features selection [4], to predict the outcome. Similarly, Random Trees are essentially the combination of single model trees with Random Forest ideas, where each node contains k randomly chosen attributes in tree [29]. So, it increases the accuracy of Random Forest than that of a single tree.

Table 1. An example of features of KDD'99 cup dataset.

No.	Features	Types	No.	Features	Types
1	duration	Continuous	22	is_guest_login	Symbolic
2	protocal_type	Symbolic	23	count	Continuous
3	service	Symbolic	24	srv_count	Continuous
4	flag	Symbolic	25	serror_rate	Continuous
5	stc_bytes	Continuous	26	srv_serror_rate	Continuous
6	dst_bytes	Continuous	27	rerror_rate	Continuous
7	Land	Symbolic	28	srv_rerror_rate	Continuous
8	wrong_fragment	Continuous	29	same_srv_rate	Continuous
9	urgent	Continuous	30	diff_srv_rate	Continuous
10	hot	Continuous	31	drv_diff_host_rate	Continuous
11	num_failed_logins	Continuous	32	dst_host_count	Continuous
12	logged_in	Symbolic	33	dst_host_srv_count	Continuous
13	num_compromised	Continuous	34	dst_host_same_srv_rate	Continuous
14	root_shell	Continuous	35	dst_host_diff_srv_rate	Continuous
15	su_attempted	Continuous	36	dst_host_same_src_port_rate	Continuous
16	num_root	Continuous	37	dct_host_srv_diff_host_rate	Continuous
17	num_file_creations	Continuous	38	dst_host_serror_rate	Continuous
18	num_shells	Continuous	39	dst_host_srv_serror_rate	Continuous
19	num_access_files	Continuous	40	dst_host_rerror_rate	Continuous
20	num_outbound_cmds	Continuous	41	dst_bost_srv_rerror_rate	Continuous
21	is_host_login	Symbolic			

– *Artificial Neural Network:* In addition to the above classical machine learning techniques, we also take into account a neural network learning model. The most commonly used form of neural network architecture is the Multilayer Perceptron that has an input layer consisting of several inputs, one or more hidden layers that typically use sigmoid activation functions and one output layer to predict the attack. This approach uses backpropagation to build the network [8, 29].

We discuss our machine learning-based intrusion detection model that carries out on four main components:

– *Attack Class Label:* All the diverse threats have been counted as different distinct class labels to put them into model intrusion detection systems. For instance, different types of attacks such as DoS, U2R, R2L, PROBE shown in Table 2 are represented as distinct classes; Class 1, Class 2, Class 3, and Class 4 respectively.

Table 2. Various types of attacks in KDD'99 cup dataset.

Categories of attack	Attack name	Number of instances
DOS	SMURF	2807886
	NEPTUNE	1072017
	Back	2203
	POD	264
	Teardrop	979
U2R	Buffer Overflow	30
	Load Module	9
	PERL	3
	Rootkit	10
R2L	FTP Write	8
	Guess Password	53
	IMAP	12
	MultiHop	7
	PHF	4
	SPY	2
	Warez client	1020
	Warez Master	20
PROBE	IPSWEEP	12481
	NMAP	2316
	PORTSWEEP	10413
	SATAN	15892
normal		972781

- *Security Features or Attributes:* These are used independently to predict the above cyber threats. These are also known as features such as protocol type, service, duration, and error-rate. shown in Table 1, on which the cyberattacks class levels are dependent.
- *Training and Testing Dataset:* The dataset is categorized into two; one is a training dataset, and another one is the test dataset. The training data set is used to train the IDS model, and the testing dataset is used to evaluate the generalization of that IDS model. We use a large amount of the cybersecurity data mentioned above for developing the IDS model and the rest for testing purposes.

4   Experimental Evaluation

This section defines the performance metrics in terms of intrusion detection and discusses the outcome by conducting experiments on cybersecurity datasets with different categories of attacks. If TP denotes true positives, FP denotes false positives, TN denotes true negative, and FN denotes false negatives, then the formal definition of below metrics are [30]:

$$Precision = \frac{TP}{TP + FP} \qquad (1)$$

$$Recall = \frac{TP}{TP + FN} \qquad (2)$$

$$Fscore = 2 * \frac{Precision * Recall}{Precision + Recall} \qquad (3)$$

$$Accuracy = \frac{TP + TN}{TP + TN + FP + FN} \qquad (4)$$

4.1 Experimental Results and Discussion

In the section, we show the effectiveness of machine learning classification techniques for detecting intrusions. For this, we analyze various popular classification techniques that include the Bayesian approach, tree-based model, Artificial Neural Network in our IDS model. Notably, we have compared the effectiveness of several popular classification techniques, such as Bayesian Network (BN), Naive Bayes (NB), Random Forest (RF), Decision Tree (DT), Random Tree (RT), Decision Table (DTb), and Artificial Neural Network (ANN), to evaluate the intrusion detection model. To test the IDS model, we use the 10-fold cross-validation on the dataset. 10-fold cross-validation evaluates models by breaking the data into ten different sets of samples. From them, nine partitioned sets are trained, and the remaining one is tested. It continues ten times and then takes the average accuracy. To compare the potentiality of models, precision, recall, f1-score, and accuracy, are calculated as defined above.

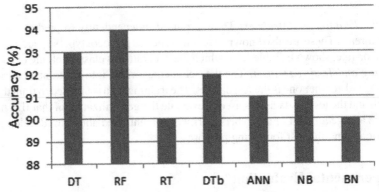

Fig. 1. Performance comparison results with respect to accuracy for numerous machine learning based IDS model.

To evaluate the performances of each classifier based IDS model, Fig. 1 and Fig. 2 show the comparison of accuracy, precision, recall, and f1-score, respectively. For evaluation, we use the same set of train and testing data in each classification based IDS model.

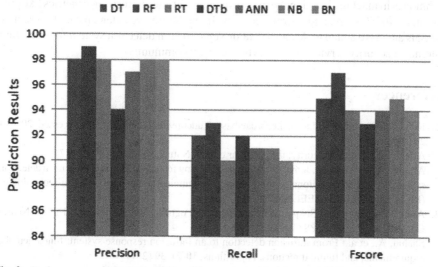

Fig. 2. Performance comparison results with respect to precision, recall, f1-score for numerous machine learning classification based IDS model.

From Fig. 1 and Fig. 2, we find that Random Forest classifier based IDS model consistently performs better than other classifiers for detecting intrusions. In particular, the Random Decision Forest gives the best results concerning the accuracy, precision, recall, f1-score. The reason behind it is that the Random Forest classifier at first originates several decision trees and thus deduces a set of rules in the forest. Every tree in a Random Forest Model behaves as a different machine learning classification technique, and thus it generates more logic rules by taking into account the majority voting of these trees while producing the outcome. For this reason, the Random Forest Model performs better in precision, recall, f1-score, and accuracy. Overall, the machine learning classifier based IDS model discussed above is fully data-oriented that reflects the behavioral patterns of various cyber-attacks. Although we consider data-driven prediction according to the patterns available in a given dataset using machine learning techniques, a recency-based model [19] could be more effective in developing a data-driven intrusion detection system. Moreover, incorporating contextual information and their analysis [21, 16] could play an important role to build smart intrusion detection system.

5   Conclusion and Future Work

The potentiality and fruitfulness of a machine learning-based intrusion detection modeling is a great concern for IT personals, e-commerce, and application developers for security purposes. Generally, a cyber-security data set consists of different categories of cyber attacks with relevant features. Hence, some classifiers may not perform well in terms of accuracy and their actual prediction rate based on diverse categories of attacks and a variety of features. In this paper, we have discussed the effectiveness of the data-driven intrusion detection model by taking into account popular classification techniques in machine learning. We have evaluated various performance metrics like precision, recall, f1-score, and overall accuracy. In the future, we extend the cyber-security datasets and have a plan to design a data-driven intrusion detection system for providing automated security services for the cyber-security community.

References

1. Kdd cup 99. http://kdd.ics.uci.edu/databases/kddcup99/kddcup99.html. Accessed 20 Oct 2019
2. Aftergood, S.: Cybersecurity: the cold war online. Nature **547**(7661), 30 (2017)
3. Ammar, A., Michael, H., Jemal, A., Moutaz, A.: Using feature selection for intrusion detection system. In: 2012 International Symposium on Communications and Information Technologies (ISCIT), pp. 296–301. IEEE (2012)
4. Amit, Y., Geman, D.: Shape quantization and recognition with randomized trees. Neural Comput. **9**(7), 1545–1588 (1997)
5. Shahid, A., et al.: From intrusion detection to an intrusion response system: fundamentals, requirements, and future directions. Algorithms, **10**(2), 39 (2017)
6. Breiman, L.: Bagging predictors. Mach. Learn. **24**(2), 123–140 (1996)
7. Breiman, L.: Random forests. Mach. Learn. **45**(1), 5–32 (2001)
8. Han, J., Pei, J., Kamber, M.: Data Mining: Concepts and Techniques. Elsevier, Amsterdam (2011)
9. John, G.H., Langley, P.: Estimating continuous distributions in bayesian classifiers. In: Proceedings of the Eleventh Conference on Uncertainty in Artificial Intelligence, pp. 338–345. Morgan Kaufmann Publishers Inc. (1995)
10. Khraisat, A., Gondal, I., Vamplew, P., Kamruzzaman, J.: Survey of intrusion detection systems: techniques, datasets and challenges. Cybersecurity **2**(1), 20 (2019)
11. Liao, H.-J., Lin, C.-H.R., Lin, Y.-C., Tung, K.-Y.: Intrusion detection system: a comprehensive review. J. Netw. Comput. Appl. **36**(1), 16–24 (2013)
12. Milenkoski, A., Vieira, M., Kounev, S., Avritzer, A., Payne, B.D.: Evaluating computer intrusion detection systems: a survey of common practices. ACM Comput. Surv. (CSUR) **48**(1), 1–41 (2015)
13. Mohammadi, S., Mirvaziri, H., Ghazizadeh-Ahsaee, M., Karimipour, H.: Cyber intrusion detection by combined feature selection algorithm. J. Inf. Secur. Appl. **44**, 80–88 (2019)
14. Quinlan, J.R.: Induction of decision trees. Mach. Learn. **1**(1), 81–106 (1986)
15. Quinlan, J.R.: C4.5: programs for machine learning. Machine Learning (1993)
16. Sarker, I.H.: Context-aware rule learning from smartphone data: survey, challenges and future directions. J. Big Data **6**(1), 1–25 (2019). https://doi.org/10.1186/s40537-019-0258-4
17. Sarker, I.H.: A machine learning based robust prediction model for real-life mobile phone data. Internet of Things **5**, 180–193 (2019)
18. Sarker, I.H., Abushark, Y.B., Alsolami, F., Khan, A.I.: Intrudtree: a machine learning-based cyber security intrusion detection model. Symmetry **12**, 754 (2020)
19. Sarker, I.H., Colman, A., Han, J.: Recencyminer: mining recency-based personalized behavior from contextual smartphone data. J. Big Data **6**(1), 49 (2019)

20. Sarker, I.H., Colman, A., Han, J., Khan, A.I., Abushark, Y.B., Salah, K.: Behavdt: a behavioral decision tree learning to build user-centric context-aware predictive model. Mobile Netw. Appl. **1**, 1–11 (2019)

21. Sarker, I.H., Colman, A., Kabir, M.A., Han, J.: Individualized time-series segmentation for mining mobile phone user behavior. The Comput. J., **61**(3), 349–368 (2018). Oxford University, UK

22. Sarker, I.H., Kabir, M.A., Colman, A., Han, J.: An improved naive bayes classifier-based noise detection technique for classifying user phone call behavior (2017)

23. Sarker, I.H., Kayes, A., Watters, P.: Effectiveness analysis of machine learning classification models for predicting personalized context-aware smartphone usage. Journal of Big Data (2019)

24. Sarker, I.H., Salim, F.D.: Mining user behavioral rules from smartphone data through association analysis. In: Phung, D., Tseng, V.S., Webb, G.I., Ho, B., Ganji, M., Rashidi, L. (eds.) PAKDD 2018. LNCS (LNAI), vol. 10937, pp. 450–461. Springer, Cham (2018). https://doi.org/10.1007/978-3-319-93034-3_36

25. Sarker, I.H., et al.: Cybersecurity data science: an overview from machine learning perspective (2020)

26. Tapiador, J.E., Orfila, A., Ribagorda, A., Ramos, B.: Key recovery attacks on kids, a keyed anomaly detection system. IEEE Trans. Dependable Sec. Comput. **12**(3), 312–325 (2013)

27. Tavallaee, M., Stakhanova, N., Ghorbani, A.A.: Toward credible evaluation of anomaly-based intrusion-detection methods. IEEE Trans. Syst. Man Cybern. Part C (Applications and Reviews), **40**(5), 516–524 (2010)

28. Viegas, E., Santin, A.O., Franca, A., Jasinski, R., Pedroni, V.A., Oliveira, L.S.: Towards an energy-efficient anomaly-based intrusion detection engine for embedded systems. IEEE Trans. Comput. **66**(1), 163–177 (2016)

29. Witten, I.H., Frank, E.: Data Mining: Practical Machine Learning Tools and Techniques. Morgan Kaufmann, Burlington (2005)

30. Witten, I.H., Frank, E., Trigg, L.E., Hall, M.A., Holmes, G., Cunningham, S.J.: Weka: practical machine learning tools and techniques with java implementations (1999)

31. Xin, Y., et al.: Machine learning and deep learning methods for cybersecurity. IEEE Access **6**, 35365–35381 (2018)

Prediction of Lung Cancer Using Machine Learning Classifier

Radhanath Patra$^{(\boxtimes)}$ ⓘ

Electronics Science, Berhampur University, Berhampur, Odisha, India
radhanath.patra@gmail.com

Abstract. Lung cancer generally occurs in both male and female due to uncontrollable growth of cells in the lungs. This causes a serious breathing problem in both inhale and exhale part of chest. Cigarette smoking and passive smoking are the principal contributor for the cause of lung cancer as per world health organization. The mortality rate due to lung cancer is increasing day by day in youths as well as in old persons as compared to other cancers. Even though the availability of high tech Medical facility for careful diagnosis and effective medical treatment, the mortality rate is not yet controlled up to a good extent. Therefore it is highly necessary to take early precautions at the initial stage such that it's symptoms and effect can be found at early stage for better diagnosis. Machine learning now days has a great influence to health care sector because of its high computational capability for early prediction of the diseases with accurate data analysis. In our paper we have analyzed various machine learning classifiers techniques to classify available lung cancer data in UCI machine learning repository in to benign and malignant. The input data is prepossessed and converted in to binary form followed by use of some well known classifier technique in Weka tool to classify the data set in to cancerous and non cancerous. The comparison technique reveals that the proposed RBF classifier has resulted with a great accuracy of 81.25% and considered as the effective classifier technique for Lung cancer data prediction.

Keywords: KNN · ML · RBF · Lung cancer · ANN

1 Introduction

Lung cancer considers as the deadlier disease and a primary concern of high mortality in present world. Lung cancer affects human being at a greater extent and as per prediction it now takes 7th position in mortality rate index causing 1.5% of total mortality rate of the world [2]. Lung cancer originates from lung and spreads up to brain and spreads Lung cancer is categorized in to two major group. One is non-small cell lung cancer and another is small cell lung cancer. Some of the symptoms which are associated with the patients like severe chest pain, dry cough, breathlessness, weight loss etc. Looking in to the cultivation of cancer and its causes doctors give stress more on smoking and second-hand smoking as if the primary causes of lung cancer. Treatment of lung cancer involves surgery, chemotherapy, radiation therapy, Immune therapy etc. In-spite of this

© Springer Nature Singapore Pte Ltd. 2020
N. Chaubey et al. (Eds.): COMS2 2020, CCIS 1235, pp. 132–142, 2020.
https://doi.org/10.1007/978-981-15-6648-6_11

lung cancer diagnosis process is very weak because doctor will able to know the disease only at the advanced stage [18]. Therefore early prediction before final stage is highly important so that the mortality rate can be easily prevented with effective control. Even after the proper medication and diagnosis survival rate of lung cancer is very promising. Survival rate of lung cancer differs from person to person. It depends on age, sex and race as well as health condition. Machine learning now days plays a crucial role for detection and prediction of medical diseases at early stages of safe human life. Machine Learning makes diagnosis process easier and deterministic. Machine learning now a day's have already dominated medical field. Every county is now adopting machine learning techniques in their health care sector. With the application of machine learning the actual detection of diseases can be explored. Some of the crucial application of machine learning is described as Feature Extraction: In any disease attributes are the real information container of the diseases. Machine learning (ML) helps for easy of data analysis and process the real attributes or information and finds the actual problem creator of diseases. It helps medical expert to find the root cause of diseases. Image processing: Using various process of machine learning the image analysis has been found accurate and valuable. That helps the concerned doctors to have a better diagnosis of the diseases such that money and time can be saved and value proportion can also be increased. Drug manufacturing: Depending up on the increase of various diseases, drug should be multi functional and quantity should be known. So ML has solved the problem and helps the drug industry to use of ML application for manufacturing. Better Prediction of diseases: ML helps to predict the severity of diseases and its outcome. ML controls disease outbreak through early prediction such that appropriate measures can be taken. Still machine learning application needs to be refined such that it can be more standardized and more reliable. Thus the need of more improvement in machine learning algorithm would help the physicians, health catalyst for accurate clinical decision making with high efficiency as well as good accuracy.

Machine learning makes the system to find the solution of problem with own learning strategies. ML classifies in to three categories such as unsupervised learning, supervised learning, Reinforcement learning. Supervised learning identifies two processes under its umbrella, one is classification and another is regression. Classification is process in which input data is processed and categorized in to certain group. The proposed work was carried out in Weka tool. Algorithm like j48, KNN, Naive Bias and RBF are used in Weka tool and a comparative analysis was derived finally.

2 Related Work

Z. Zubi et al. (2014) extracted features from chest x ray images and used concept of back propagation neural network method to improve the accuracy [31]. Rashmee Kohad et al. (2015) used ant colony optimization with ANN and SVM to predict the accuracy of 98% and 93.2% respectively on 250 lung cancer CT images [16]. Kourou et al. (2015) outlined a review of various machine learning approach on several cancer data and concluded that application of integration of feature selection and classifier will provide a promising result in analysis of cancer data [17]. Hosseinzadeh et al. (2013). Proposed SVM model on selection of protein attributes and concluded that the result is having 88% accuracy in compared to other classifier technique for prediction of lung cancer tumors [11].

Naveen and Pradeep (2018) proposed that among SVM, Naive Bayes and C4.5 classifier, C4.5 performs better on North central cancer treatment group (NCCTG) lung cancer data with better accuracy and also predicted that C4.5 is better classifier with the increase of lung cancer training data [25]. Gur Amrit Pal singh and P.K Gupta (2018) proposed new algorithm for feature extraction on image data and applied machine learning classifier to improve the accuracy [29]. Hussein et al. (2019) proposed supervised learning using 3D Convolutional neural network(3D CNN)on lung nodules data set as well as unsupervised learning SVM approach to classify benign and malignant data with a accuracy of 91% [12]. Monkam et al. (2019) provided survey on importance of Convolutional neural network for predicting lung module with almost greater than 90% accuracy [21]. Asuntha and Andy Srinivasan (2019) proposed fuzzy particle swarm optimization with deep neural network on lung cancer images to achieve an accuracy of 99.2% [5]. Ganggayah et al. (2019) used various classifiers on breast cancer data having 8066 record with 23 predictor and concluded that random forest classifier gives 82% better accuracy [9]. Gibbons et al. (2019) used supervised learning such as linear regression model, support vector machine, ANN etc. and predicted that SVM results an better accuracy of 96% as compared to other methods [28]. Shakeel et al. (2019) used feature selection process and a novel hybrid approach of ANN on lung cancer data available from ELVIRA biomedical data to predict an accuracy of 99.6% [26]. Bhuvaneswari et al. (2015) used gabor filter for feature extraction and G-knn approach to classify lung cancer images with an accuracy of 90% [7]. Xin Li, Bin Hu, Hui Li Bin (2019) used 3D dense sharp network and IBM SPSS25.0 statistical analysis software on 53 patients to obtain an accuracy of 88% in finding malignant and benign [19]. Shanti and raj Kumar (2020) used wrapper feature selection method as well as stochastic diffusion research algorithm on lung cancer image and concluded that this is one of the best performing algorithm for classification [27]. Rezaei Hachesu P et al. (2017) proposed a different approach for analysis of survival rate and the method find a correlation between various attributes and their survival rate and this process is carried out with 470 records having 17 features [10]. Kadir et al. (2018) provided an overview approach of various deep learning strategies used for accuracy prediction of lung cancer CT images [15]. Paing et al. (2019) used computer aided diagnosis process in which in three phases segmentation, detecting and staging process are followed for classification of CT lung cancer images with a greater accuracy [23].

3 Dataset Description

Dataset was available in UCI machine learning repository. Data consists of 32 instances and it has 57 features (1 class attribute and 56 input data), all predictive attributes are nominal range between 0–3 while class attribute level of 3 types [1]. Nominal attribute and class label data are converted in to binary form such that data analysis process becomes easier. Nominal to binary form is the most standardization process for data analysis. Data set comprises of some missing values which degrades the algorithm performances so care full execution before analysis on data is required. Label is described as high, low, medium. In the paper we categorized high to 2, medium to 1 and low to 0.

4 Classification Techniques

Classification comes under supervised learning process in order to predict given input data to a certain class label. The novelty in classification relies on mapping input function to a certain output level. Various learning classifiers are described as Perceptron, Naïve Bayes, Decision Tree, Logistic Regression, K nearest neighbour, Artificial Network, Support Vector Machine. Classification in machine learning is one of prior decision making techniques used for data analysis. Various classifier techniques are too used to classify data samples [20, 22]. The concept of our paper focuses on novel approach of Machine Learning for analysis of lung cancer data set to achieve a good accuracy. Some of the mostly used classifier techniques are described as.

4.1 Neural Network

Neural network are the basic block of machine learning approach in which the learning process is carried in between neuron. Artificial neural network (ANN) comprises of input layer, intermediate layer having hidden neurons and output layer. Every input neuron is connected to hidden neuron through appropriate weight and similarly weight is connected between hidden unit to output unit. Neuron presented in hidden neuron and output neuron are processed with some known threshold functional value. Depending on the requirement the activation will be used to process the neuron. The synaptic weight gets multiplied with the corresponding neuron presented in hidden layer and output layer for classification process. The desired target is adjusted through the weight adjustment technique either in feed forward approach or feed back approach to get the required target. Feed forward network approaches are simpler process for classification approaches.

4.2 Radial Basis Function Network

Radial basis function network comes under neural network that uses radial basis function as its threshold function.RBF network has advantage of easy of design and strong tolerance to input noises. Radial basis Function is characterized by feed forward architecture

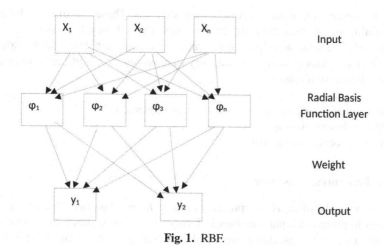

Fig. 1. RBF.

which comprises of an one middle layer between input and output layer. It uses a series of basis function that are centered at each sampling point. Formally for a given input x the network output can be written as (Fig. 1).

Where

$$y = \prod_{i=1}^{N} w_i R_i(x) + w_0 \tag{1}$$

w_i: *weight*, w_0: *biasterm*, R: *Activation function*

$$R_i(x) = \varphi[\|x_i - c_i\|] \tag{2}$$

φ: *radial function*, c_i: *RBF centre*

In RBF architecture the weight that connects to input unit and middle layer represents the centre of the corresponding neuron where as weights connecting to middle layer and output layer are used to train the network.

4.3 Support Vector Classifter

One of the simple and useful approaches in supervised learning is support vector classification. Support vector classifier (SVC) is usually preferred for data analysis because of its computational capability with in very less time frame. This classifier works on the decision boundary concept Recognized as hyper plane. The hyper plane is used to classify the input data in to required target group. But in order to fit the decision boundary in a plane maximize distance margin is chosen from data points for classification. User defined support vector classifier can be framed using various kernel function to improve the accuracy. Support vector classifier is well suited for both structured and unstructured data. Support vector classifier is not affected with over fitting problem and makes it more reliable.

4.4 Logistic Regression Classifter

Logistic Regression classifier is brought from statistics. These classifiers is based on the probability of outcome from the input process data. Binary logistic regression is generally preferred in machine learning technique for dealing with binary input variables. To categorize the class in to specific category sigmoid function is utilized. Advantages of Logistic Regression classifier.

- Logistic regression classifier is very flexible to implement
- Suitable for binary classification
- Depend on probabilistic model

4.5 Random Forest Classifter

Combination of classifier trees represents random forest classifier. One of the finest approaches to represent input variables in form of trees that makes a forest like structure. Input Data are represented in trees and each tree specifies a class label. Random forest depends on its error rate. Error rate signifies in to two directions. First one is the correlation between trees and second one is the strength of the tree. Advantages of random forest.

- Proper method for noisy and Imbalanced data representation.
- Data can be represented without any data reduction.
- Best approach for analysis of large data set.
- Finest approach in machine learning platform for improvement of accuracy.
- It handles the over fitting problem which mostly occurs in different Machine learning algorithm.
- one of the best reliable algorithm

4.6 J48 Classifter

J48 is representation of c4.5 in weka tool developed from java. Decision tree implements tree concepts to find the solution of the problem. class label is represented by leaf node where as attributed are defined with internal node of tree. In decision tree attribute selection process is done by Information gain and gain index. Depending on the concept of information gain and depending on the importance of information gain Decision tree classifier performs the classification. The information gain for a particular attribute X at a node is calculated as

$$\text{Information Gain (N, X)} = \text{Entropy (N)} - \sum_{value\ at\ x} \frac{|N|}{|N_i|} Entropy(N) \qquad (3)$$

Where N is the set of instance at that particular node and

$$|N| : cardinality$$

Entropy of N is found as:

$$Entropy\ (N) = \sum_{i=1}^{N} -p_i \log_2 p_i \qquad (4)$$

4.7 Naïve Bayes Classifter

Naive Bayes classifier is one of the probabilistic classifier with strong indepenent assumption between features. Naive Bayes is based on bayes Theorem where Naive Bayes classifier uses bayesian network model p using the maximum a posteriori decision rule in Bayesian Setting. The feature which are classified in naive Bayes are always independent to each other. If y is class variable and x is dependent feature vector then.

$$y = argmax_y\ p(y) \prod_{i=1}^{n} p\left(\frac{x_i}{y}\right) \qquad (5)$$

P (y) is called class probability and

$$p\left(\frac{x_i}{y}\right) \qquad (6)$$

is conditional probability. Bayesian probability says

$$Posterior = \frac{Prior * Likelihood}{Evidence}$$

4.8 Knn Classifter

Knn classifier comes under lazy learning process in which training and testing can be realized on same data or as per the programmer's choice. In the process, the data of interest is retrieved and analyzed depending upon the majority value of class label assigned as per k, where k is an integer. The value of k is based on distance calculation process. The choice of k depends on data. Larger value of k minimizes the noise on classification. Similarly Parameter selection is also a prominent technique to improve the accuracy in classification. Weighted Knn classifier: A mechanism in which a suitable weight can be assigned to the neighbor's value so that its contribution has great impact to neighbors than distant ones. In the weighted knn approach the weight has a significant value in evaluating the nearest optimistic value. Generally the weight is based on reciprocal of distance approach. The weight value of attribute is multiplied with distance to obtain the required value.

Pseudo code for Knn

- Take the input data
- Consider initial value of k
- Divide the train and test data
- For achieving required target iteration for all training data points
- Find the distance between test data and each row of training data. (Euclidean Distance is the best Choice approach)
- Arrange the calculated distance in ascending order based on distance values.
- Consider the Top k value from sorted value.
- Find the Majority class label
- Obtain the target class.

5 Proposed Model

Data analysis process was carried using both weka tool of version 3.6 and Jupiter platform in python tool [13, 24]. Weka is an open source tool used for classification, clustering, regression and data visualization. Weka generally supports input file either in .csv or .arff extension format. Weka explore has various tabs for data analysis such as prepossess, classify, cluster, association, select attribute and visualize. When data prepossessing is selected it enables to upload the input data in weka tool [3, 30]. Weka tool clearly understands and represents the data for easy of data analysis. Before running any classification algorithm, Weka tool asks various option like splitting percentage, used training set, supplied test set, Cross validation option etc. Classificationn mostly occurs with splitting of 80% trainning and 20% testing [6]. But In Weka tool our analysis process was carried out with 10 fold cross validation with selected classifier technique to obtain an output of interest [8]. Weka is a user friendly visualization tool with we have tested various classifier technique and its output performance.

6 Result Analysis

The Input data consists of missing values. So it is required to prepossess the data such that the missing values have been replaced with the most occurrence value of the corresponding column. Then the processed data is applied in Weka data mining tool for analysis. The prepossessed data is converted in to suitable form for classification using different classifier approach. The classifier approach is executed with 10 cross validation method. The cross validation is a powerful data analysis process where 10 folds can be done with the available data and an accurate decision can be made on the provided data with good prediction. With the classify tab of Weka tool different classifier approaches are verified. After careful analysis results of proposed classifiers are compared. J48 and Naive Bayes algorithm classifies 32 instances in to 25 correctly classified instances and 7 incorrectly classified instances. Like wise 24 correctly classified instances and 8 incorrectly classified instances are obtained from 32 instances using knn with 5 nearest neighbour. As per our analysis the RBF classifier is mostly preferred among various classifiers. This is due to its highest classification accuracy which is obtained from its 26 correctly classified instances and 6 incorrectly classified instances from 32 instances. Similarly False

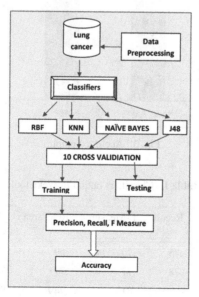

Fig. 2. Process flow of various classifiers in Weka tool.

Positive and False Negative both have a value of 3 each. The output result of various classifiers used in Weka tool on lung cancer data is represented in below table. Generally in confusion matrix Accuracy, Recall, Precision and F-Measure are the key process parameter for classification [4, 14]. Classification accuracy is the measure of number of correct prediction made out from total number of prediction. These parameters depend on some specific outcome. Those are 'TP (True Positive) which is the correctly predicted event values and 'TN (True Negative) is correctly predicted no event values. Similarly 'FP (False Positive) is incorrectly predicted event values and 'FN (False Negative) for incorrectly predicted no event values. Relationship are derived as below (Figs. 2, 3) and (Table 1).

$$Accuracy = \frac{^J TP + {}^J TN}{^J TP + {}^J TN + {}^J FP + {}^J FN} \tag{7}$$

$$Recall = \frac{^J TP}{^J TP + {}^J FN} \tag{8}$$

$$Precision = \frac{^J TP}{^J TP + {}^J FP} \tag{9}$$

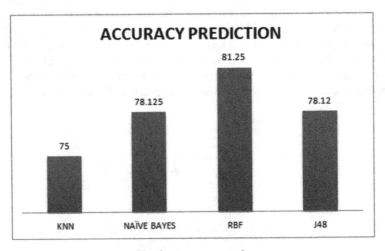

Fig. 3. Accuracy graph.

Table 1. Classifiers output in Weka tool.

Classifier	Precision	Recall	F-Measure	ROC area	Correctly. classified	Incorrectly classified
KNN(5)	.73	.75	.70	.69	75%	25%
Naïve Bayes	.775	.78	.77	.77	78.125%	21.87%
RBF	.813	.813	.813	.749	81.25%	18.75%
J48	.768	.781	.766	.708	78.12%	21.87%

$$F\_Measure = \frac{2 * Recall * Precision}{Recall + Precision} \tag{10}$$

7 Conclusion

In this paper we have shown that with RBF classifier the accuracy is found to be 81.25% on lung cancer data. So In the analysis it can be predicted that with suitable feature selection method and integrated approach with other supervised learning process and modified functional approach in RBF, accuracy will be further improved.

References

1. https://archive.ics.uci.edu/ml/dataset/Lung+cancer. Accessed 12 Feb 2020
2. WHO Deaths by cause, sex and mortality stratum, World Health Organization. https://www.who.int/news-room/fact-sheets/detail/the-top-10-causes-of-death. Accessed 25 Jan 2020
3. Ada, R.K.: Early detection and prediction of lung cancer survival using neural network classifier (2013)
4. Alcantud, J.C.R., Varela, G., Santos-Buitrago, B., Santos-Garcia, G., Jimenez, M.F.: Analysis of survival for lung cancer resections cases with fuzzy and soft set theory in surgical decision making. PLoS ONE **14**(6), e0218283 (2019)
5. Asuntha, A., Srinivasan, A.: Deep learning for lung cancer detection and classification. Multimedia Tools Appl. **79**, 1–32 (2020)
6. Bhatia, S., Sinha, Y., Goel, L.: Lung cancer detection: a deep learning approach. In: Bansal, J.C., Das, K.N., Nagar, A., Deep, K., Ojha, A.K. (eds.) Soft Computing for Problem Solving. AISC, vol. 817, pp. 699–705. Springer, Singapore (2019). https://doi.org/10.1007/978-981-13-1595-4_55
7. Bhuvaneswari, P., Therese, A.B.: Detection of cancer in lung with k- nn classification using genetic algorithm. Procedia Mater. Sci. **10**, 433–440 (2015)
8. Chaubey, N.K., Jayanthi, P.: Disease diagnosis and treatment using deep learning algorithms for the healthcare system. In: Applications of Deep Learning and Big IoT on Personalized Healthcare Services, pp. 99–114. IGI Global (2020)
9. Ganggayah, M.D., Taib, N.A., Har, Y.C., Lio, P., Dhillon, S.K.: Predicting factors for survival of breast cancer patients using machine learning techniques. BMC Med. Inform. Decision Making **19**(1), 48 (2019)
10. Hachesu, P.R., Moftian, N., Dehghani, M., Soltani, T.S.: Analyzing a lung cancer patient dataset with the focus on predicting survival rate one year after thoracic surgery. Asian Pacific J. Cancer Prevention: APJCP **18**(6), 1531 (2017)
11. Hosseinzadeh, F., KayvanJoo, A.H., Ebrahimi, M., Goliaei, B.: Prediction of lung tumor types based on protein attributes by machine learning algorithms. SpringerPlus **2**(1), 238 (2013)
12. Hussein, S., Kandel, P., Bolan, C.W., Wallace, M.B., Bagci, U.: Lung and pancreatic tumor characterization in the deep learning era: novel supervised and unsupervised learning approaches. IEEE Trans. Med. Imag. **38**(8), 1777–1787 (2019)
13. Jacob, D.S., Viswan, R., Manju, V., PadmaSuresh, L., Raj, S.: A survey on breast cancer prediction using data mining techniques. In: 2018 Conference on Emerging Devices and Smart Systems (ICEDSS), pp. 256–258. IEEE (2018)
14. Jakimovski, G., Davcev, D.: Using double convolution neural network for lung cancer stage detection. Appl. Sci. **9**(3), 427 (2019)

15. Kadir, T., Gleeson, F.: Lung cancer prediction using machine learning and advanced imaging techniques. Transl. Lung Cancer Res. **7**(3), 304 (2018)
16. Kohad, R., Ahire, V.: Application of machine learning techniques for the diagnosis of lung cancer with ant colony optimization. Int. J. Comput. Appl. **113**(18), 34–41 (2015)
17. Kourou, K., Exarchos, T.P., Exarchos, K.P., Karamouzis, M.V., Fotiadis, D.I.: Machine learning applications in cancer prognosis and prediction. Comput. Struc. Biotechnol. J. **13**, 8–17 (2015)
18. Krishnaiah, V., Narsimha, G., Chandra, D.N.S.: Diagnosis of lung cancer prediction system using data mining classification techniques. Int. J. Comput. Sci. Inf. Technol. **4**(1), 39–45 (2013)
19. Li, X., Hu, B., Li, H., You, B.: Application of artificial intelligence in the diagnosis of multiple primary lung cancer. Thoracic Cancer **10**(11), 2168–2174 (2019)
20. Lynch, C.M., et al.: Prediction of lung cancer patient survival via supervised machine learning classification techniques. Int. J. Med. Inform. **108**, 1–8 (2017)
21. Monkam, P., Qi, S., Ma, H., Gao, W., Yao, Y., Qian, W.: Detection and classification of pulmonary nodules using convolutional neural networks: a survey. IEEE Access **7**, 78075–78091 (2019)
22. Murty, N.R., Babu, M.P.: A critical study of classification algorithms for lungcancer disease detection and diagnosis. Int. J. Comput. Intell. Res. **13**(5), 1041–1048 (2017)
23. Paing, M.P., Hamamoto, K., Tungjitkusolmun, S., Pintavirooj, C.: Automatic detection and staging of lung tumors using locational features and double-staged classifications. Appl. Sci. **9**(11), 2329 (2019)
24. Patel, D., Shah, Y., Thakkar, N., Shah, K., Shah, M.: Implementation of artificial intelligence techniques for cancer detection. Augmented Human Res. **5**(1), 6 (2020)
25. Pradeep, K., Naveen, N.: Lung cancer survivability prediction based on performance using classification techniques of support vector machines, c4. 5 and naive bayes algorithms for healthcare analytics. Procedia computer science **132**, 412–420 (2018)
26. Shakeel, P.M., Tolba, A., Al-Makhadmeh, Z., Jaber, M.M.: Automatic detection of lung cancer from biomedical data set using discrete adaboost optimized ensemble learning generalized neural networks. Neural Comput. Appl. **32**(3), 777–790 (2020)
27. Shanthi, S., Rajkumar, N.: Lung cancer prediction using stochastic diffusion search (sds) based feature selection and machine learning methods. Neural Process. Lett. **1**, 1–14 (2020)
28. Sidey-Gibbons, J.A., Sidey-Gibbons, C.J.: Machine learning in medicine: a practical introduction. BMC Med. Res. Methodol. **19**(1), 64 (2019)
29. Singh, G.A.P., Gupta, P.K.: Performance analysis of various machine learning-based approaches for detection and classification of lung cancer in humans. Neural Comput. Appl. **31**(10), 6863–6877 (2018). https://doi.org/10.1007/s00521-018-3518-x
30. Varadharajan, R., Priyan, M., Panchatcharam, P., Vivekanandan, S., Gunasekaran, M.: A new approach for prediction of lung carcinoma using back propogation neural network with decision tree classifiers. J. Ambient Intell. Human. Comput. **1**, 1–12 (2018)
31. Zubi, Z.S., Saad, R.A.: Improves treatment programs of lung cancer using data mining techniques. Journal of Software Engineering and Applications **2014**, 69–77 (2014)

A Rule-Based Expert System to Assess Coronary Artery Disease Under Uncertainty

Sohrab Hossain[1](✉), Dhiman Sarma[2], Rana Joyti Chakma[2], Wahidul Alam[3], Mohammed Moshiul Hoque[4], and Iqbal H. Sarker[4]

[1] Department of Computer Science and Engineering, East Delta University, Chittagong, Bangladesh
sohrab.h@eastdelta.edu.bd
[2] Department of Computer Science and Engineering, Rangamati Science and Technology University, Rangamati, Bangladesh
[3] Department of Computer Science and Engineering, University of Science and Technology Chittagong, Chittagong, Bangladesh
[4] Department of Computer Science and Engineering, Chittagong University of Engineering and Technology, Chittagong, Bangladesh
iqbal@cuet.ac.bd

Abstract. The coronary artery disease (CAD) occurs from the narrowing and damaging of major blood vessels or arteries. It has become the most life-threatening disease in the world, especially in the South Asian region. Its detection and treatment involve expensive medical facilities. The early detection of CAD, which is a major challenge, can minimize the patients' suffering and expenses. The major challenge for CAD detection is incorporating numerous factors for detailed analysis. The goal of this study is to propose a new Clinical Decision Support System (CDSS) which may assist doctors in analyzing numerous factors more accurately than the existing CDSSs. In this paper, a Rule-Based Expert System (RBES) is proposed which involves five different Belief Rules, and can predict five different stages of CAD. The final output is produced by combining all BRBs and by using the Evidential Reasoning (ER). Performance evaluation is measured by calculating the success rate, error rate, failure rate and false omission rate. The proposed RBES has higher a success rate and false omission rate than other existing CDSSs.

Keywords: Rule based system · Expert system · Prediction · Uncertainty · Coronary artery disease · Clinical decision support systems · Health analytics

1 Introduction

Coronary artery disease (CAD) is a condition when the coronary arteries become narrow or blocked. It is developed when bad cholesterols and plaques (fatty droplets) deposit inside the wall of arteries. The process is termed as atherosclerosis which means clogging of arteries, and reduces blood flow inside the heart muscle. Blood carries oxygen and essential nutrients to the heart [1]. Lack of sufficient blood supply can cause angina

© Springer Nature Singapore Pte Ltd. 2020
N. Chaubey et al. (Eds.): COMS2 2020, CCIS 1235, pp. 143–159, 2020.
https://doi.org/10.1007/978-981-15-6648-6_12

(chest pain), and lead to a heart attack by injuring heart muscle. The death toll due to heart disease is 16.3 million in America each year which has made it the leading cause of death in the United States. According to the American Heart Association (AHA), one person is suffered from a heart attack in every 40 s. Having zero risk factors of heart disease, any male has 3.6% and any female has less than 1% chance of getting cardio-vascular disease in his/her lifetime. Moreover, the chances are 37.5% and 18.3 respec-tively [2] for having 2 risk factors. In Bangladesh, CAD is responsible for a 17% mortal-ity rate [3]. The regular diagnostic approach of CAD relies on coronary angiogram test [4], echo-cardiogram ram (ECG) [5, 6], nuclear scan test and exercise stress test. ECG and exercise stress do not produce sustainable results for CAD prediction due to their non-invasiveness properties and numerous biases. Moreover, walking on a trade mill in a stress test makes the patient discomfort heart function than normal condition. Nowa-days, support vector machine (SVM) [7, 8] and artificial neural network (ANN) [5, 8–17] based Clinical Decision Support Systems (CDSS) [18–20] are developed for CAD pre-diction. Unfortunately, SVM and ANN have no direct impact on the reasoning process due to their black-box- type modeling approaches. As a result, the degree of significance of individual factors cannot be resolved. So, human judgment and clinical data are both two essential factors for CAD diagnosis. For this purpose, CDSS combines both histori-cal data and doctors' domain specific knowledge. But clinical data, like clinical domain knowledge, signs, and symptom, contain various uncertainties [21–23], and pose chal-lenges for selecting domain knowledge to construct knowledge base. Moreover finding the reasoning under uncertainty requires an excellent computational algorithm. To mit-igate the challenges, researches introduced different CDSSs, based on the fuzzy inter-face system and Bayesian interface system, which also has limitations [10, 24–26]. In this paper, the proposed expert system can predict CAD by five classifications according to the severity. They are as follows:

Class A: (Normal or zero sign of heart disease).

Class B: (Unstable angina) - when new symptoms are introduced beside regular stable angina, and appears frequently (mostly when at rest), last long with more severity, and can lead to a heart attack. It can be treated with oral medications (such as nitroglycerine).

Class C: (Non-ST segment elevation myocardial infarction) - echocardiogram does not indicate the symptom of this type of myocardial infarction (MI) but chemical markers in the blood show the damage of heart muscles. The damage may not be significant and artery blockages are usually partial or temporary.

Class D: (ST-segment elevation myocardial infarction) - this type of MI is occurred quickly due to sudden blockage by blood clogging. It can be detected by ECG and chemical markers in the blood, and causes damage to vast heart muscles.

Class E: (Silent ischemia)- Patient with heart disease can be suffered from a sudden heart attack (called silent ischemia) without any prior or early warning, and diabetic patients are common victims of this type [1].

2 Related Research

Researchers recently worked on machine learning and rule-based systems for different purposes [30–33]. Many researchers developed belief-rule-based interference method-ology by using evidential reasoning (RIMER) for CAD diagnosis [18, 27]. The RIMER process uses belief-rule-base for modeling clinical domain knowledge, and applies an evidential reasoning approach for implementing reasoning. Studies show that RIMER based clinical decision support systems are highly efficient in supporting and interacting with clinical domain knowledge under uncertainty. In [28], Multi-Criteria Decision Making Methods were presented for accessing CAD under uncertainty where presence and absence of CAD is predicted through using symptom and signs of CAD. But these approaches report neither the number of blocked arteries nor the significance of severity of the disease [8, 16, 26, 28, 29]. Weak parameters, like signs and symptoms, are used for predicting CAD as well as for predicting the similar types of diseases like mitral regurgitation, dilated cardiomyopathy, congenital heart disease, hyper-tropic cardiomyopathy, myocardial infarction etc. Some researchers developed the Medical Decision Support System (MDSS) to predict CAD. Other proposer polygenic risk scores (PRS), a nonlinear, for CAD prediction with accuracy an 0.92 under the receiver operating curve (AUC) [8].

Experimental analysis reveals that CAD diagnosis and its severity can be predicted significantly through clinical features along with pathological and demographic features [23, 25, 26, 28]. In this paper, we consider all these parameters, and proposed a cooperative-belief-rule based prototype (CDSS) to assist doctors for CAD analysis under uncertainty.

3 Methodology

3.1 Proposed Rule Based Expert System for CAD

In this paper, five separate BRBs are developed based on five distinct feature sets of patients such as i) patients' pathological features, ii) patients' physiological features, iii) patients' demographic features, iv) patients' behavioral features, and v) patients' non-modifiable risk factors. The BRBs are as follows:

$$D_A = f_A(S, P_A) \tag{1}$$

$$D_B = f_B(T, P_B) \tag{2}$$

$$D_C = f_C(X, P_C) \tag{3}$$

$$D_D = f_D(Y, P_D) \tag{4}$$

$$D_E = f_E(Z, P_E) \tag{5}$$

Here, $S = \{a_1, a_2, \ldots . a_l \}$, $T = \{b_1, b_2, \ldots . b_m \}$, $X = \{c_1, c_2, \ldots . c_n \}$, $Y = \{d_1, d_2, \ldots . d_o \}$, $Z = \{e_1, e_2, \ldots . e_p \}$ represent the demographic, physiological, clinical, behavioral, and Non-modifiable features respectively (where l, m, n, o, and p indicate attributes' number for factors).

Suppose that P_A, P_B, P_C, P_D and P_E are the corresponding vectors for the five BRBs, and $\omega = [\omega_1, \omega_2, \omega_3, \omega_4, \omega_5]$ represent the weight coefficients to the relative BRB where

f_A, f_B, f_C, f_D and f_E functions are for demographic, physiological, clinical, behavioral, and non-modifiable factors. To calculate the individual matching degree for each rule, the following equation is used:

$$\alpha_{i,j} = \frac{u(A_{i,j+1}) - x_i}{u(A_{i,j+1}) - u(A_{i,j})} \tag{6}$$

Where u is utility value, a_{ij} is individual matching degree, A_{ij} is j^{th} referential value for i^{th} attribute, and x_i is the input for i^{th} antecedent (Fig. 1).

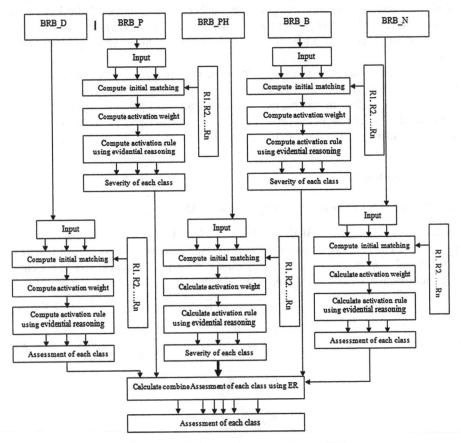

Fig. 1. Rule Based Expert System to assess CAD

To calculate activated weight to each rule the following equation is used:

$$w_k = \frac{\theta_k \alpha_k}{\sum_{i=1}^{L} \theta_i \alpha_i} \tag{7}$$

Where w_k is the kth rule's activation weight and a_k is the interrelation between attributes. To calculate a_k, the following equations is used:

$$\alpha_k = \prod_{i=1}^{M} \left(\alpha_i^k \right)^{\bar{\delta}_i^k} \tag{8}$$

$$\bar{\delta}_i = \frac{\delta_i}{max_{i=1,...,M}(\delta_i)} \tag{9}$$

Where $\bar{\delta}_i$ is the antecedent weight and α_i^k represents individual matching degrees for i^{th} attribute. Five separate BRBs to predict CAD are BRB_P, BRB_PH, BRB_D, BRB_B, and BRB_N. BRB_PH considers physiological factors like blood pressure and stress. BRB_P considers pathological factors like blood sugar level, low density lipoprotein, and triglyceride level. BRB_D considers factors like age and body mass index. BRB_B considers behavior factors like diet, smoking, and physical activities. BRB_N considers non-modifiable risk factors like gender, family history, and residential Area.

3.2 Uncertainties in the Attribute

Attributes like blood pressure, stress, blood sugar, lipoprotein, triglyceride, age, body mass index, unhealthy diet, smoking, family history, and race are categorized into five classes, namely Physiological, Pathological, Demographical, Behavioral, and Non-modifiable risk factors. All the attributes have uncertainties at some level except gender attribute (Table 1).

Table 1. Uncertainties in the attributes

Attributes	Types of uncertainty	Description
Blood Pressure, Stress, Blood sugar, Triglyceride, Lipoprotein	Impression	Information on the attributes is collected through medical instrumentations. The chances are high for storing wrong data in patient profile due to instrumental malfunctioning or operators' wrong procedural approaches. Moreover, the data for the same patient may vary in different conditions. For example, blood pressure rises after some physical activities, blood sugar level falls after fasting and rises after a meal. So, uncertainty in data may exist due to dataset in different physical conditions or instrumental malfunctions

(*continued*)

Table 1. (*continued*)

Attributes	Types of uncertainty	Description
Age	Inconsistency	Old people may face hurdles of remembering their actual age. In underdeveloped countries, the young generation tends to hide actual the age to apply for the Government job
Body mass index	Inconsistency	Patients' weight varies due to clothes, shoes, and after having meals. In this case, wrist measurement is more accurate which are maximum 35 in. for female and 40 in. for male
Unhealthy diet	Vagueness, Incompleteness	Standard calorie demand varies from 1800 to 3000 calories and depends on height, weight, age, and physical activities. The exact amount of food consumption is very hard to measure, and an accurate amount of calorie consumption may be unknown to patients
Smoking	Incompleteness	Patients try to hide their smoking habit as they feel uncomfortable disclosing it in front of their family members
Family history	Vagueness, Incompleteness	Most of the time, parents' heart disease information is not available. Even if some information available, the age, at which they got the disease, cannot be determined
Race	Imprecision, Incompleteness	Usually patients use two or more addresses like present address, mailing address, and permanent address

3.3 Explanation of Antecedent Attributes

Five different types of attributes have been considered in this research. Explanations of the numerical values of each attribute are as follows:

Physiological Factor

Blood Pressure (BP)
The blood pressure which creates heartbeats is known as BP. For BP, several numerical points namely Usual, Elevated, Hypertension Stage 1, Hypertension Stage 2, Hypertension Stage 3 are reflected and shown in Table 2.

Table 2. Numerical values for blood pressure

Terms	Numerical values mm Hg (upper/lower)
Usual (U)	Less than 120/80
Elevated (E)	120/80–129/80
Hypertension Stage 1(H1)	130/89–139/89
Hypertension Stage 2 (H2)	140/90 or higher
Hypertensive Stage 3(H3)	Higher than 180/120

Here, the referential numerical points are presented as in the Eq. (10).

$$PH1 \in \{U,\ E,\ H1,\ H2,\ H3\} \tag{10}$$

Stress Score (SS)
Intermediate risk of heart problems can be expressed in the SS score. It can be distributed into several referential numerical points, namely regular, mildly irregular, moderately irregular and severely irregular are shown in Table 3.

Table 3. Numerical value for stress score

Terms	Numerical points
Regular (R)	below 4
Insignificantly Irregular (M)	4–8
Significantly Irregular (SI)	9–13
Extremely Irregular (ES)	Higher than 13

The referential numerical values can be presented as in Eq. (11).

$$PH2 \in \{R, M,\ MI,\ S\} \tag{11}$$

Pathological Factor

Blood Sugar Level. It is the amount of sugar in the blood. Five referential points are shown in Table 4 and expressed by the Eq. (12).

Table 4. Numerical points for blood sugar

Terms	Amount shown (mg/dL)
Fasting (FA)	Less than 100
Before Meal (BM)	70–130
After meal (1–2 h) (A)	Less than 180
Before Exercise (B)	If taking insulin, at least 100
Bed Time (BT)	100–140

$$P1 \in \{FA, \ BM, \ A, \ B, \ BT\} \tag{12}$$

Its measures triglycerides amount in blood. Four referential points are described in Table 5 and Eq. (13).

Table 5. Numerical point for triglyceride

Terms	Triglyceride level (mg/dL)
Healthy (H)	Up to 150
Marginal high (BH)	151–200
High (H)	201–500
Extremely high (EH)	above 500

$$P2 \in \{H, \ BH, \ H, \ EH\} \tag{13}$$

Low Density Lipoprotein (LDL)
It contains both lipid and protein, and carries cholesterol to body tissues. Five referential values related to LDL are shown in Table 6 and Eq. (14).

$$P3 \in \{D, \ NO, \ BH, \ H, \ VH\} \tag{14}$$

Table 6. Numerical point for LDL

Terms	Numerical points (mg/dL)
Good (D)	Less than 100; below 70 if CAD is present
Moderately elevated (NO)	100–140
Near to high (BH)	141–160
High (H)	161–190
Extremely high (VH)	Above 190

Demographic Factor

Age

Older people are more likely to be victims of coronary artery disease, especially, after the age of 65 years. Usually, aged people have higher chance of getting CAD (Table 7).

Table 7. Numerical values for age

Terms	Numerical values (age)
Young (Y)	<35
Middle age (M)	35–49
Old (O)	50–65
Extreme (E)	>65

Four referential values, namely, young (< 35 years), mature (35–49 years), old (50–65), and extremely old (E), have been considered in the following equation from the above table.

$$D1 \in \{Y, M, O, E\} \tag{15}$$

Body Mass Index (BMI)

It indicates the amount of fat ratio. It is applicable for the age range from 18 to 65. It is the ratio of weight to height (Table 8).

Four referential values, namely, healthy weight (18.5–24.9), overweight (25–29.9), obese (30–39.9), and morbidly obese (>=40), have been considered in the following equation from the above table.

$$D2 \in \{H, O, OB, MO\} \tag{16}$$

Table 8. Numerical points for BMI

Terms	Numerical points (BMI)
Healthy weight (H)	18.5–24.9
Overweight (O)	25–29.9
Obese (OB)	30–39.9
Morbid Obese (MO)	> = 40

Behavior

Unhealthy Diet
Mediterranean diet can reduce the risk of CAD by 30%. It is mainly plant based food and categorized into four sections shown in Table 10 and expressed by Eq. (17) (Table 9).

Table 9. Numerical values of diet

Terms	Numerical points (Calories/ day)
Low (L)	<1800
Healthy (H)	1800–2200
Moderate (M)	2200–2800
Eating Disorder (ED)	>2800

$$B1 \in \{L, \ H, \ M, \ ED\} \tag{17}$$

Smoking
Smokers or exposers to smoke have a high risk of CAD. Smoking is categorized into four sections, and shown in Table 10 and expressed by Eq. (18).

Table 10. Numerical values for smoking

Terms	Numerical points (Cigarettes/ day)
Non-Smoker (NS)	0
Smoker (S)	1–5
Moderate Smoker (MS)	6–20
Chain Smoker (CS)	>20

$$B2 \in \{NS, \ S, \ MS, \ CS\} \tag{18}$$

Physical Activities

Inactive and less active people are at high risk to develop CAD. Physical activities are categorized into four sections which are shown in Table 11 and expressed by Eq. (19).

Table 11. Numerical values for physical activities

Terms	Numerical points (Minutes/ day)
Inactive (I)	0–10
Less Active (LA)	11–20
Active (A)	21–30
Very Active (VA)	>30

$$B3 \in \{I, \ LA, \ A, \ VA\} \tag{19}$$

Non-modifiable risk Factors

Gender

Male has higher risk of CAD than female. Besides, male suffers from CAD in earlier age than female. But after the age of 70 years, both males and females have similar chances of getting heart disease (Table 12).

Table 12. Numerical values for gender

Terms	Numerical points
Male (M)	0
Female (F)	1
Other (O)	2

$$N1 \in \{M, \ F, \ O\} \tag{20}$$

Family History

If parents have histories of heart disease, children have a high risk of developing CAD. The risk is even higher if parents have suffered before early 50 years of age. The numerical points for the family history are represented by 0 (No history of parent's heart disease), 1 (History of parent's heart disease), and 2 (History of parent's heart disease before age of 50), and expressed in Table 13 and by Eq. (21).

$$N2 \in \{L, \ M, \ H\} \tag{21}$$

Table 13. Numerical values for family history

Terms	Numerical points
Low (L)	0
Medium (M)	1
High (H)	2

Residential Area

People from mega-cities are more prone to CAD. This is because of a higher rate of diabetes and obesity. On the other hand, people from hill track areas are less likely to develop heart disease. The numerical points for the residential areas are 0(Mega City), (Rural Area), and 2 (Hill track area), and expressed in Table 14 and by Eq. (22).

Table 14. Numerical values for residential area

Terms	Numerical points
Low (L)	0
Medium (M)	1
High (H)	2

$$N3 \in \{L, \ M, \ H\} \tag{22}$$

3.4 Rule Base

All attributes from Eqs. (10) to (22) are applied as input variables to predict the CAD class. Sub rules 1 to 20 are expressed in Table 15 for the two Physiological factors from Eqs. (10) and (11).

A sub rule of the CAD can be shown as:

R3: IF blood pressure is usual AND stress score is significantly irregular
THEN Overall Prediction is
{(Stage 1, 0.6), (Stage 2, 0.3), (Stage 3, 0.1), (Stage 4, 0.0), (Stage 5, 0.0)}

In the R3, the antecedent attributes are and the consequence attributes are. The rule shows that patient with usual blood pressure and significantly irregular stress score has the probability of developing CAD are (Stage 1 is 60%), (Stage 2 is 30%), (Stage 3 is 10%), (Stage 4 is 0%), (Stage 5 is 0%). The summation of all referential values for R3 is (0.6 + 0.3 + 0.1 + 0.0 + 0.0 =) 1. If the summation of all referential values for a particular rule is 1, we can say that the rule is competed. For some missing attributes or ignorance, the summation may be less than 1 and the rule is incomplete [34].

Table 15. Attributes' sub rule-base for physiological factors

Rule no.	IF		THEN				
	PH1	PH2	Stage 1	Stage 2	Stage 3	Stage 4	Stage 5
R1	U	R	1.0	0.0	0.0	0.0	0.0
R2	U	M	0.9	0.1	0.0	0.0	0.0
R3	U	SI	0.6	0.3	0.1	0.0	0.0
R4	U	ES	0.5	0.3	0.2	0.1	0.0
R5	E	R	0.8	0.2	0.0	0.0	0.0
.....	.....	.....	....	.....	....	.....	......
R18	H3	M				0.2	0.8
R19	H3	SI	0.0	0.0	0.0	0.1	0.9
R20	H3	EI	0.0	0.0	0.0	0.0	1.0

3.5 Data Set Description

Dataset was collected from the National Heart Foundation, Bangladesh with proper authorization. The data set description is shown in Table 16.

Table 16. Summary of patients' data

Patient information	Number
Total patients	1100
Age interval in year	30–95
Average age	59
Ratio (Male: Female)	711:389
Class A (Normal)	450
Class B (Unstable angina)	300
Class C (Non-ST segment)	287
Class D (ST segment)	43
Class E (silent Ischemia)	20

4   Result and Discussion

In the binary diagnostic test, a positive or negative diagnosis is made for each patient. When the result of diagnosis is compared to the true condition, we find four possible outcomes: true positive, true negative, false positive, false negative.

4.1   Success Rate

It is the ratio of correctly identified patient' numbers and total patients. Equation (23) is used to calculate the success rate and average success rate.

$$Success\ Rate = \frac{Number\ of\ correctly\ identified\ patients}{Total\ patients}\ X\ 100\% \qquad (23)$$

4.2   Error Rate

It is the ratio of incorrectly identified patients' numbers and total patients. Equation (24) is used to calculate the error rate and average error rate.

$$Error\ Rate = \frac{Number\ of\ patients'\ incorrectly\ identified}{Total\ number\ of\ patients}\ *\ 100\% \qquad (24)$$

4.3   Failure Rate

It is the ratio of the number of non-recognized patients to total patients. Equation (25) is used to calculate the failure rate and average failure rate.

$$Failure\ Rate = \frac{Number\ of\ non\ recognised\ patients}{Total\ patients}\ X\ 100\% \qquad (25)$$

4.4   False Omission Rate (fOR)

False omission rate is the ratio the of number of patients identified to a class A to the total number of patients belongs to a particular class except for class A. Eq. (26) is used to calculate the false omission rate and average false omission rate.

$$FOR = \frac{Number\ of\ patients'\ identified\ to\ a\ class\ A}{Total\ number\ of\ patients\ belong\ to\ a\ particular\ class\ except\ class\ A}\ X\ 100\% \qquad (26)$$

Table 17 explains the results obtained by the equation number (23), (24), (25), and (26). Class A is considered as CAD negative patients and the remaining classes are CAD positive patients. It is observed that the success rate of predicting class C type heart disease is the highest (94.08%) among five classes. On the other hand, the success rate of class E prediction is the lowest (50% only). Class E is very hard to predict as most of the time it does show any symptoms.

Table 17. Success rate, failure rate, error rate, false omission rate by expert system

Class	Total No. of Patients (True Condition)	Total No. of Patients (Test Condition)					Total Non-Recognized Patients	False Omission Rate (%)	Error rate (%)	Failure Rate (%)	Success Rate (%)
		A	B	C	D	E					
A	450	405	7	3	0	25	10	–	07.78	10.00	90.00
B	300	15	268	10	0	07	10	05.00	08.33	10.67	89.33
C	287	1	07	270	10	0	6	00.35	03.83	05.92	94.08
D	43	2	03	02	36	0	0	04.65	16.27	16.27	83.72
E	20	05	0	0	0	10	05	25.00	25.00	50.00	50.00
Average Rate (%)								03.54	08.81	11.10	89.90

5 Conclusion

Heart disease is one of the major threats to public health and the reason for the main cause of death worldwide. Although numerous researches are carried out in this area, still there are challenges to diagnose CAD for treatment. In this paper, the proposed expert system results in an average accuracy rate of 89.90% which is the highest among other existing CDSS. The average false omission rate (3.54%) is also the lowest in this system than that of other CDSS. Our test results satisfy one of the main goals of this research. The average failure rate (11.10%) and average error rate (8.81%) also remain as marginal. Class E (silent Ischemia) success rate is the lowest among all classes. The reason is that Class E occurs suddenly without showing any warning signs of heart problems. It was noted that Class E is common to people with diabetes. It requires further research work to investigate whether or not diabetes influences the success rate in Class E type patients. Apart from this, our research concludes that RBES has a higher success rate and false omission rate than other existing CDSS.

References

1. Coronary Artery Disease. https://my.clevelandclinic.org/health/diseases. Accessed 21 Nov 2016
2. Benjamin, E.J., et al.: Heart disease and stroke statistics-2017 update: a report from the American Heart Association. Circulation **135**, e146–e603 (2017)
3. Islam, A.M., Mohibullah, A., Paul, T.J.B.H.J.: Cardiovascular disease in Bangladesh: a review. Heart Journal, **31**, 80–99 (2016)
4. Perez Ruiz De Garibay, A., Kellum, J., Honigschnabel, J., Kreymann, B.: Respiratory and metabolic acidosis correction with the advanced organ Support system. Intensive Care Medicine Experimental **7**, 56 (2019)
5. Shadmi, R., Mazo, V., Bregman-Amitai, O., Elnekave, E.: IEEE: Fully-convolutional deep-learning based system for coronary calcium score prediction from non-contrast chest ct. In: 2018 IEEE 15th International Symposium on Biomedical Imaging, pp. 24–28 (2018)

6. Kirsch, J., Buitrago, I., Mohammed, T.L.H., Gao, T.M., Asher, C.R., Novaro, G.M.: Detection of coronary calcium during standard chest computed tomography correlates with multidetector computed tomography coronary artery calcium score. Int. J. Cardiovascular Imag. **28**, 1249–1256 (2012)

7. De Vijver, R.V., et el.: In-field detection of Altemaria solani in potato crops using hyperspectral imaging. Comput. Electron. Agric. **168**, 105106 (2020)

8. Gola, D., Erdmann, J., Muller-Myhsok, B., Schunkert, H., Konig, I.R.: Polygenic risk scores outperform machine learning methods in predicting coronary artery disease status. Genetic Epidemiol. **44**, 125–138 (2020)

9. Weber, M., et al.: Automatic identification of crossovers in cryo-EM images of murine amyloid protein A fibrils with machine learning. J. Microscopy **277**, 12–22 (2020)

10. Tang, X.L., Xiao, M.Q., Liang, Y.J., Zhu, H.Z., Li, J.F.: Online updating belief-rule-base using Bayesian estimation. Knowledge-Based Syst. **171**, 93–105 (2019)

11. Penson, A., et al.: Development of genome-derived tumor type prediction to inform clinical cancer care. JAMA Oncol. **6**, 84–91 (2020)

12. Penafiel, S., et al.: IEEE: Associating risks of getting strokes with data from health checkup records using dempster-shafer theory. In: 2018 20th International Conference on Advanced Communication Technology, pp. 239–246 (2018)

13. Khanna, N.N., et al.: Nonlinear model for the carotid artery disease 10-year risk prediction by fusing conventional cardiovascular factors to carotid ultrasound image phenotypes: A Japanese diabetes cohort study. Echocardiography-A J. Cardiovascular Ultrasound Allied Techniques **36**, 345–361 (2019)

14. Hyer, J.M., et al.: Can we improve prediction of adverse surgical outcomes? development of a surgical complexity score using a novel machine learning technique. J. Am. College Surgeons, pp. 43–52 (2020)

15. Chicco, D., Jurman, G.: Machine learning can predict survival of patients with heart failure from serum creatinine and ejection fraction alone. BMC Med. Inform. Decis. Mak. **20**, 16 (2020)

16. Apostolopoulos, I.D., Groumpos, P.P., Apostolopoulos, D.I.: A medical decision support system for The Prediction Of The Coronary Artery Disease Using Fuzzy Cognitive Maps. In: Kravets, A., Shcherbakov, M., Kultsova, M., Groumpos, P. (eds.) Creativity in Intelligent Technologies and Data Science, vol. 754, pp. 269–283 (2017)

17. Aggarwal, S., Azad, V., Bhattacharyya, S., De, S., Pan, I., Dutta, P.: A Hybrid System Based on FMM and MLP to Diagnose Heart Disease (2017)

18. Zhou, Z.-G., et al.: A cooperative belief rule based decision support system for lymph node metastasis diagnosis in gastric cancer. Knowledge-Based Syst. **85**, 62–70 (2015)

19. Zhou, Z.-G., et al.: A bi-level belief rule based decision support system for diagnosis of lymph node metastasis in gastric cancer. Knowledge-Based Syst. **54**, 128–136 (2013)

20. Christo, V.R.E., Nehemiah, H.K., Brighty, J., Kannan, A.: Feature selection and instance selection from clinical datasets using co-operative co-evolution and classification using random forest. IETE Journal of Research

21. Long, N.C., Meesad, P., Unger, H.: A highly accurate firefly based algorithm for heart disease prediction. Expert Syst. Appl. **42**, 8221–8231 (2015)

22. Li, G.L., Zhou, Z.J., Hu, C.H., Chang, L.L., Zhang, H.T., Yu, C.Q.: An optimal safety assessment model for complex systems considering correlation and redundancy. Int. J. Approximate Reason. **104**, 38–56 (2019)

23. Hossain, M.S., Ahmed, F., Fatema Tuj, J., Andersson, K.: A belief rule based expert system to assess tuberculosis under uncertainty. J. Med. Syst. **41**, 43 (2017)

24. Sparapani, R., Logan, B.R., McCulloch, R.E., Laud, P.W.: Nonparametric competing risks analysis using bayesian additive regression trees. Stat. Methods Med. Res. **29**, 57–77 (2020)

25. Onisko, A., Druzdzel, M.J., Austin, R.M.: Application of Bayesian network modeling to pathology informatics. Diagnostic Cytopathol. **47**, 41–47 (2019)
26. Gupta, A., et al.: Probabilistic graphical modeling for estimating risk of coronary artery disease: applications of a flexible machine-learning method. Med. Decis. Mak. **39**, 1032–1044 (2019)
27. Wang, Y., et al.: Reliability assessment model for industrial control system based on belief rule base. Int. J. Comput. Commun. Control **14**, 419–436 (2019)
28. Kishore, A.H.N., Jayanthi, V.E.: Multi criteria decision making methods to predict the prevalence of coronary artery disease. J. Med. Imag. Health Inform. **8**, 719–726 (2018)
29. Sofian, H., Ming, J.T.C., Mohamad, S., Noor, N.M.: Calcification detection using deep structured learning in intravascular ultrasound image for coronary artery disease. In: 2018 2nd International Conference on BioSignal Analysis, Processing and Systems (ICBAPS), pp. 47–52 (2018)
30. Sarker, I.H.: Context-aware rule learning from smartphone data: survey, challenges and future directions. J. Big Data **6**(1), 1–25 (2019). https://doi.org/10.1186/s40537-019-0258-4
31. Sarker, I.H., Colman, A., Han, J.: RecencyMiner: mining recency-based personalized behavior from contextual smartphone data. J. Big Data **6**(1), 1–21 (2019). https://doi.org/10.1186/s40 537-019-0211-6
32. Sarker, I.H., Colman, A., Han, J., Khan, A.I., Abushark, Y.B., Salah, K.: BehavDT: a behavioral decision tree learning to build user-centric context-aware predictive model. Mobile Netw. Appl. **25**, 1–11 (2019). https://doi.org/10.1007/s11036-019-01443-z
33. Sarker, I.H., Kayes, A.S.M., Watters, P.: Effectiveness analysis of machine learning classification models for predicting personalized context-aware smartphone usage. J. Big Data **6**(1), 1–28 (2019). https://doi.org/10.1186/s40537-019-0219-y
34. Hossain, S., et al.: A belief rule based expert system to predict student performance under uncertainty. In: 2019 22nd International Conference on Computer and Information Technology (ICCIT), pp. 1–6. IEEE (2019)

Multiclass MI-Task Classification Using Logistic Regression and Filter Bank Common Spatial Patterns

Md. Mahmudul Haque Joy⬤🆔, Mohammad Hasan$^{(\boxtimes)}$🆔, Abu Saleh Musa Miah$^{(\boxtimes)}$🆔,
Abir Ahmed⬤🆔, Sadia Anwar Tohfa⬤🆔, Md. Farukul Islam Bhuaiyan⬤🆔,
Ashrafun Zannat⬤🆔, and Md Mamunur Rashid🆔

Department of CSE, Bangladesh Army University of Science and Technology (BAUST),
Saidpur, Bangladesh
hasancse.cuet13@gmail.com, abusalehcse.ru@gmail.com

Abstract. We proposed a classification technique of EEG motor imagery signals using Logistic regression and feature extraction algorithm using filter bank common spatial pattern (FBCSP). Main theme of FBCSP is that the signals decomposed into 5 sub band then calculated CSP for each sub band, this algorithm also allows automated frequency band selection. We combined each subband CSP feature vector, feed this feature vector into machine learning algorithm. In the paper Logistic regression is used to classify among multiple classes. To evaluate this method, we used here publicly available dataset namely Brain-Computer Interface competition IV-2a. Because of high accuracy and kappa that shown in accuracy table that proposed method is promising.

Keywords: Motor Imagery (MI) · Brain Computer Interface (BCI) ·
Electroencephalogram (EEG) · EEG signal classification · Logistic Regression

1 Introduction

BCI uses EEG signal to establish a direct communication path away between an enhanced or wired brain and external device based on signal processing system [1].

For the people suffering from neural disorders, motor imagery brain computer interface provides a non-muscular solution [2].

EEG based invasive BCI system is immense temporal solution, relatively high portability, low-cost and non-invasive. The raw EEG signals are noisy or corrupted with various artifacts or noises like cardiac activity, muscular activity, eye blinking etc. [3].

So, some initial steps is necessary to minimize background noise and artifacts named preprocessing. Preprocessing of high dimensional data results in noise-free and artifact less data which can be converted into commands by classifying the preprocessed data using a machine learning algorithm.

The EEG signal from motor cortex is used in this paper. Which is correlate to the environment when a subject thinking a movement like left or right-hand movement. It is called sensory-motor activity. Movement imagined or done in real-life cases increases

© Springer Nature Singapore Pte Ltd. 2020
N. Chaubey et al. (Eds.): COMS2 2020, CCIS 1235, pp. 160–170, 2020.
https://doi.org/10.1007/978-981-15-6648-6_13

or decreases in μ activity in the device of motor-cortex-sensor. The band frequencies μ (8–15 Hz) and beta β (15–25 Hz) rhythms are activated when the persons imagined motor movement and the amplitude decreases before the actual movement [4].

2 Related Works

The proposed system is dealing with the BCI competition where many numbers of the methodology used to solve the BCI competition problem since the start of the BCI competition. The success of brain signal classification in BCI competition significantly depends on feature extraction from the observed data, firstly used auto-regressive (AR) model with adaptive auto-regressive models (AAR) [5], fast Fourier analysis and windowed and cross-correlation. Then Principle Component Analysis (PCA), Common spatial patterns (CSP) are broadly used [6]. In BCI research common spatial pattern is a very popular method to obtain features from the EEG signal. LDA (Linear Discriminate Analysis), ANN (Artificial Neural Network), KNN (K-Nearest Neighbor) classification algorithm, SVM (Support Vector Machine) algorithm are used for classify into right intention [5, 7]. First developed the support vector machine (SVM) by Vapni based on statistical learning theory k in 1995, which is used for nonlinear regression and classification. The main concept of SVMs is to make samples linearly separable by calculating optimal planes from high dimensional space. Based on the high dimension, local minima, non-linear relationships, and small sample size SVMs can solve practical problems.

For the random and non-stationary nature of electro encephalography (EEG) signals is the main difficulty of SVM to choose kernel function in practical application [8]. The concept of the Naive Bayes (NB) algorithm is to find the probability of a dependent event based on occurring given the probability of another event that has already occurred, The problem of Naïve-Baise algorithm are, produced estimated probability can be inaccurate, sometimes maximum probability assigns to the correct class. In our proposed methodology for feature extraction. The method we proposed here namely filter bank common spatial pattern is the modified version of common spatial pattern and for classification we used the Logistic Regression model.

3 Methodology

For feature extraction we used in the paper Filter Bank Common Spatial Pattern (FBCSP) and Logistic regression is used for identifying right intention of human thinking. Feature selection is performed in FBCSP where as we are classifying the data directly by Logistic regression [9].

3.1 Preprocessing the Data

Cross Validation
Cross validation tests the model in training phase for the dataset in order to restrict problems like overfitting and under fitting. It's important that the validation and training set is drown from the same distribution.

Validation helps us to find out the model which will performs best on unseen data. It also evaluates the quality of the model. It mainly depends on the number of splits and fold in the datasets to produce random train validation split. With stratification when splitting data, we achieve similar target distribution over different folds. Cross validation is very useful to tackle overfitting and under fitting in addition it also determines which parameters will result in lowest test error.

Noise Removal
Obtained signal from signal acquisition steps are usually contains a lot of artifacts because of high frequency noise such as EOG's and EMG's because of electrical interference. Besides the distance between the scalp and the neurons makes it difficult to pin point the exact location of where an activation took place can also be an issue. As a result, preprocessing these signals is an import step for such experiments.

Band Pass Filtering
A band pass filter passes signals between two specific frequencies.

Most human brain activity produced within the frequency band of (2–40 Hz). For while, a band pass filter with range of frequency 2–40 Hz used here. Most of the high frequency noises can be filtered using band pass filter. The filter can have as much as sub bands as one wants. Sub band is used because alpha beta brain rhythms resides within such frequency [8].

Butterworth Filtering
It has a maximum flat frequency response with slow cut off and no gain ripple in pass and stop band. In the butterworth filter zero frequency is used as stop band and maximally in pass band.

Standard Scaling
Data have collected from multiple sources so lack of standardization can be create problem during data preprocessing. Large scale collection development is the process to test the neurological phenomenon across experiment and subject with robustness of approaches. If we use only raw data without standard preprocessing then it might create conflicts with respect to collection development. So, standardization format is very much important to progress in large scale in EEG. This kind comparison needs to start from datasets that are well documented and analysis ready. The important step for preprocessing of large scale is noise removal and inefficient channel detection.

Several criteria use standard deviation of Z-score to replace the mean by the median and the standard deviation. It also detects nan-data from the channels. So, the key step of mining EEG across large collections is to develop a standardize preprocessing pipeline that will allow as to preform various analysis with reference to the raw data [9].

Normalization
Normalization mainly is removal of mean and division by standard deviation which can be performed across the band over time. There are two types of normalization:

i)   **Temporal:** Subtraction of mean of each window and division by standard deviation.

ii) **Ensemble:** Pointwise subtraction of an ensemble means and division by ensemble standard deviation.

Temporal normalization is usually a good idea when possible and reasonable

3.2 Logistic Regression

We got a feature vector f_i from FBCSP from both training and testing EEG dataset. Now we used Logistic Regression model used to feed the training feature then evaluate this model using testing feature. Classification algorithm Logistic Regression is a statistic technique borrowed by machine learning. It is used for estimating values from parameters coefficient. It predicts the outcome based on the given parameters. Logistic Regression can be divided in to two kinds. They are:

(i)   Binary (example: cancer yes or no)
(ii) Multi-linear functions (example: Book, pencil, pen).

Based on the number of parameters, there are three kinds of logistic regression:

1. Binominal: Categorical output with two values '0' or '1'.
2. Multinomial: Categorical output with more than two values: good, better, best
3. Ordinal: If multiple categories are in orders. Like 0, 1, 2, 3, 4 or A, B, C etc.

In this paper, we are dealing with ordinal or multi-linear functions. Our feature vector can be represented as matrix M.

$$
M = \begin{bmatrix} m_{11} & m_{12} & \cdots & m_{1k} \\ m_{21} & & & \\ \vdots & & \ddots & \vdots \\ m_{n1} & & \cdots & m \end{bmatrix}
$$

Where 'k' is the feature variables. And $m_{i,j}$ represents values of features and observation. A single observation can be represented as below M.

$$
X = \begin{bmatrix} 1 \\ m_{i1} \\ m_{i2} \\ m_{i3} \\ . \\ . \\ . \\ m_{in} \end{bmatrix}
$$

The hypothesis of Logistic Regression $h(x_i)$ presents the predicted response for i^{th} observation.

The hypothesis is described in Eq. (i):

$$0 \leq h_\theta(x) \leq 1 \tag{i}$$

Where $h(x_i) = g(z) = \frac{1}{1+e^{-z}}$

Logistic function can be defined using Eq. (i). This function can take input any range's number and produced a output value between 0 and 1, making the function useful in the prediction in probabilities (Fig. 1).

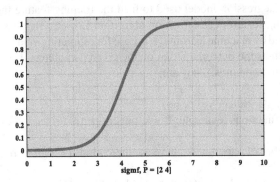

Fig. 1. Sigmoid function outcome.

The hypothesis also can be written as:

$$\sigma(z) = \sigma(\beta_0 + \beta_1 x)$$

Where, $z = \beta_0 + \beta_1 x$

The cost function of linear regression is,

If $y = 1$ $log(h_\theta(x))$

If $y = 0$ $log(1 - h_\theta(x))$.

Cost function measures the machine learning performance for the given data. This calculates the difference between the expected value and predicted value called error value. Presents it in the form of a single real number which should not be negative. To minimize the cost value gradient descent is used. A gradient descent function should be run on every parameter to minimize the cost. The equation is:

$$\theta_J := \theta_J - \alpha \frac{\partial}{\partial \theta_J} j(\theta)$$

Hence θ_J is the gradient descent and $j(\theta)$ is the cost function.

3.3 Filter Bank Common Spatial Pattern

In a task like motor imagery, FBCSP is one of the most popular features obtaining method based on a common spatial pattern. It consists of four steps which use the Common Spatial Pattern algorithm for feature selection and classification on selected feature [10].

The first multiple bandpass filter namely the Chebyshev type II filter is used to remove the artifact from EEG.

To compute the most effective feature of the EEG signal, we used spatial filtering with CSP on each frequency subband. For finding ERD and ERS from EEG, CSP is one of the powerful algorithms which is used [6, 11].

The method named common spatial pattern is used to designs spatial filters that have an ideally fixed variance between the filtered time-series data.

We have given input data denoting EEG/ECoG data from trial i for class c {1, 2, 3, 4} (e.g., left hand, right hand, tongue versus foot motor imagery). Each of the sets is an X × Y matrix, where X is the number of channel used during recording time, and Y denotes the number of sample points in time per channel [12].

Here used a Butterworth filter to scale those data. Low-pass Butterworth filter design can be defined as:

$$\frac{v_0(s)}{v_i(s)} = \frac{R}{s^3(L_1C_2L_3) + s^2(L_1C_2R) + s(L_1 + L_2) + R}$$

After scaling the data, we will perform a Common spatial pattern on it.

Our spatial filter we obtained from the CSP method can be used to linearly transform the EEG measurement in Eq. (ii) [13, 18].

$$Z = W^T E \tag{ii}$$

$W \in R^{ch*ch}$ represents CSP projected matrix, $E \in R^{ch*s}$ is the trial of EEG signal measurement, and $Z \in R^{ch*s}$ which are the filtered signals where ch represents the number of electrod and s represents the number of sample point per channel [14]. Projected matrix W also called a Transformation matrix that sums up the features whose variance is used to determine the EEG between two classes [15, 19]. Solving the equivalent decomposition problem can be useful to calculate W using Eq. (iii).

$$\Sigma_1 W = (\Sigma_1 + \Sigma_2) W D \tag{iii}$$

Σ_1 and Σ_2 are calculated from the respective motor imagery task by estimating the band pass filter EE measurement from the covariance matrix. The eigenvalue of Σ_1 is contained in a diagonal matrix D. For i^{th} trial the CSP features for the EEG measurements are calculated by Eq. (iv) by:

$$f_i = \log\left(\frac{diag(\bar{W}^T E_i E_i^T \bar{W})}{trace(\bar{W}^T E_i E_i^T \bar{W})}\right) \tag{iv}$$

Here f_i is the features which we get from the common spatial pattern. We are calculating the diag() using transposed projection matrix and with the Eigen value. The trace is similarly calculated with the same attribute. The divisor result is then passed as parameter into a logarithmic function to calculate the features.

3.4 Random Forest

To classify our CSP feature vector f_i we also used the Random Forest machine learning algorithm as a classifier [16, 17]. The concept of this algorithm is to calculate Gini index and information gain from the feature vector f_i to build up the decision tree. Multiple trees are created to classify EEG label in accordance with their attributes, each tree individually gives a classification result and saves them as for appropriate class, which has the most overall the trees is chosen for classification. For regression, the average output by different trees is taken. Pseudocode of random forest is given below:

- A number of training features set is N. then, randomly take samples for these N cases with replacement.
- For M input features or variables, m variables are selected as m < m. m is constant although growing the forest. We used the best split of m to split the given node.
- Each tree is expanded as large as possible without pruning.
- By summing up the prediction odd n trees new data is predicted.
- Maximum numbers of votes are accountable for classification.
- Average votes are used for classification.

Random Forest with two decision trees is given below:

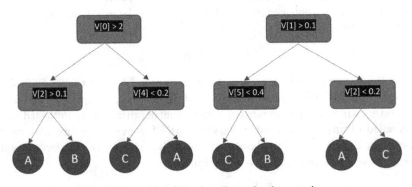

Fig. 2. Example of Random Forest implementation.

In Fig. 2, V[i] is the *i*-th value of the feature vector. The random forest depicted in figure predicts one of 3 class labels: *A*, *B*, or *C*. Many kinds of decision trees are used for classification in a random forest. It uses bagging and feature randomness to build individual trees to build an uncorrelated forest of the tree, to make predictions more accurate than individual trees. It is an ensemble machine learning algorithm, uses a divide and concurs approach.

4   Experimental Analysis and Discussion

4.1   Dataset Description

For dataset 2a of Brain Computer Interface (BCI) competition IV that is contained Electroencephalogram (EEG) data from 9 subjects. It has 4 types of motor imagery tasks, these are the thinking imagination of right-hand movement, left-hand movement, both feet movement, and tongue.

Data has recorded from individual subject over two sessions. 6 runs combined into one session and separated each run by a short gap. In front of a computer screen, we make the subjects to sit comfortably. When starting a trail (t = 0), on the black screen taxation cross was appeared.

Besides, these as a short aural warning accent was presented. Subsequently 2 s (t = 2) a pointer in the form of an indicator is goes may be to the up, down, left, or right (Fig. 3).

Fig. 3. Timing diagram of an individual session.

One session has 288 trails in total, 48 trails per run, 12 for each of the four classes. To record the EEG signal 22 Ag/AgCl electrode distance of 3.5 mm was used; the image is shown in Fig. 4 most signals were recorded as mono-polar with left and right side serving as reference and ground respectively. 250 Hz sampling rate was used on the signal during signal transformation and passes those signal whose have frequency between 0.5 Hz to 100 Hz using band pass filter. The amplifier had a sensitivity of 100 μv. To discard line noise, we used an additional notch filter of 50 Hz.

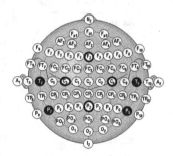

Fig. 4. International 10–20 system electrode montages.

4.2 Results

To obtain 9 band-pass filters here band pass filter is applied to cover 4–40 Hz. Later we have used CSP for extracting features for each band.

The best results appeared for subject A01T, A02T, A07T, A08T, A09T is giving the best possible results using our proposed method and the overall result is better than the results we found for Naïve Base Classifier and Random Forest classifier for the same dataset. While we are getting a comparatively less performing model for other subjects like A03T (Table 1).

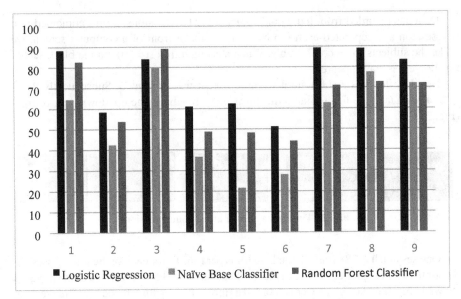

Fig. 5. Comparison result between different classifier.

Table 1. Comparison between Logistic Regression and Random Forest Classifier results.

Subject	Logistic Regression	Naïve Base Classifier	Random Forest Classifier
A01T	88.26	64.46	82.56
A02T	58.30	42.35	53.71
A03T	83.88	79.77	89.01
A04T	60.96	36.53	48.68
A05T	62.31	21.54	48.18
A06T	51.16	28.01	44.18
A07T	89.17	62.62	71.11
A08T	88.93	77.43	72.69
A09T	83.33	71.96	71.96

The best results appeared for subjects 1, 3, 7, 8, 9 using our proposed method and the overall result is better than the results we found for Random Forest classifier for the same dataset. As we can see our model is giving better results than Random Forest Classifier, there are some factors working behind it: Sometimes Logistic regression gives better results than Random Forest Classifier because of when the dataset has a higher impurity or higher Gini index. In this case, this factor is playing a major role.

Random forest is better when it predicts actual result with a lower accuracy but if the class label of a dataset is labelled correctly then logistic regression can play the role as well. In this case our model is giving accuracy because of the accurate labeling in the preprocessing step (Fig. 5).

The result can be seen from the bar chart where the black bar represents our proposed method which is significantly rising higher than the others.

5   Conclusion and Future Work

For four class EEG motor imagery classification we have used logistic regression and FBCSP is used for feature extraction. Our experiment gives a remarkable result but the accuracy doesn't remain constant. Due to subject variability we were unable to find a method that can give equally good results for every subject. FBCSP is giving a better classification rate. As future work, we are trying to create a method which is equally effective for every subject and every dataset.

References

1. Shih, J.J., Krusienski, D.J., Wolpaw, J.R.: Brain-computer interfaces in medicine. Mayo Clin. Proc. **87**, 268–279 (2012). https://doi.org/10.1016/j.mayocp.2011.12.008
2. Lazarou, I., Nikolopoulos, S., Petrantonakis, P.C., Kompatsiaris, I., Tsolaki, M.: EEG-based brain–computer interfaces for communication and rehabilitation of people with motor impairment: a novel approach of the 21st century. Front. Hum. Neurosci. **12**, 14 (2018). https://doi.org/10.3389/fnhum.2018.00014
3. Nicolas-Alonso, L.F., Gomez-Gil, J.: Brain computer interfaces, a review. Sensors **12**, 1211–1279 (2012). https://doi.org/10.3390/s120201211
4. Padfield, N., Zabalza, J., Zhao, H., Masero, V., Ren, J.: EEG-based brain-computer interfaces using motor-imagery: techniques and challenges. Sensors **19**(6), 1423 (2019). https://doi.org/10.3390/s19061423
5. Wang, T., Deng, J., He, B.: Classifying EEG-based motor imagery tasks by means of time-frequency synthesized spatial patterns. Clin. Neurophysiol. **115**, 2744–2753 (2004)
6. Blankertz, B., Tomioka, R., Lemm, S., Kawanabe, M., Müller, K.R.: Optimizing spatial filters for robust EEG single-trial analysis. IEEE Signal Process. Mag. **25**, 41–56 (2008)
7. Allison, B.Z., Pineda, J.A.: ERPs evoked by different matrix sizes: implications for a brain computer interface (BCI) system. IEEE Trans. Neural Syst. Rehabil. Eng. **11**, 110–113 (2003)
8. Bashashati, A., Fatourechi, M., Ward, R.K., Birch, G.E.: A survey of signal processing algorithms in brain-computer interfaces based on electrical brain signals. J. Neural Eng. **4**, R32–R57 (2007)
9. Ang, K.K., Chin, Z.Y., Wang, C., Guan, C., Zhang, H.: Filter bank common spatial pattern algorithm on BCI competition IV datasets 2a and 2b. Front. Neurosci. (2012). https://doi.org/10.3389/fnins.2012.00039
10. Ha, K. W. & Jeong, J. W.: Motor imagery EEG classification using capsule networks. Sensors (Switzerland) 19, (2019). https://doi.org/10.3390/s19132854
11. Djemal, R., Bazyed, A.G., Belwafi, K., Gannouni, S., Kaaniche, W.: Three-class EEG-based motor imagery classification using phase-space reconstruction technique. Brain Sci. **6**, 36 (2016). https://doi.org/10.3390/brainsci6030036
12. Wang, D., Miao, D., Blohm, G.: Multi-class motor imagery EEG decoding for brain-computer interfaces. Front. Neurosci. **6**, 151 (2012). https://doi.org/10.3389/fnins.2012.00151
13. Pfurtscheller, G., da Lopes Silva, F.: Event-related EEG/MEG synchronization and desynchronization: basic principles. Clin. Neurophysiol. **110**, 1842–1857 (1999)

14. Cheng, D., Liu, Y., Zhang, L.: Exploring motor imagery EEG patterns for stroke patients with deep neural networks. In: IEEE International Conference on Acoustics, Speech and Signal Processing – Proceedings, ICASSP, April 2018, pp. 2561–2565. Institute of Electrical and Electronics Engineers Inc. (2018)

15. Oikonomou, V.P., Georgiadis, K., Liaros, G., Nikolopoulos, S., Kompatsiaris, I.: A comparison study on EEG signal processing techniques using motor imagery EEG data. In: Proceedings - IEEE Symposium on Computer-Based Medical Systems, June 2017, pp. 781–786. Institute of Electrical and Electronics Engineers Inc. (2017)

16. Bashashati, H., Ward, R.K., Birch, G.E., Bashashati, A.: Comparing different classifiers in sensory motor brain computer interfaces. PLoS ONE 10, e0129435 (2015). https://doi.org/10.1371/journal.pone.0129435

17. Garrett, D., Peterson, D.A., Anderson, C.W., Thaut, M.H.: Comparison of linear, nonlinear, and feature selection methods for EEG signal classification. IEEE Trans. Neural Syst. Rehabil. Eng. 11, 141–144 (2003)

18. Bentlemsan, M., Zemouri, E.T., Bouchaffra, D., Yahya-Zoubir, B., Ferroudji, K.: Random forest and filter bank common spatial patterns for EEG-based motor imagery classification. In: Proceedings - International Conference on Intelligent Systems, Modelling and Simulation, ISMS (2014). https://doi.org/10.1109/ISMS.2014.46

19. Padfield, N., Zabalza, J., Zhao, H., Masero, V., Ren, J.: EEG-based brain-computer interfaces using motor-imagery: techniques and challenges. Sensors (Switzerland) (2019). https://doi.org/10.3390/s19061423

Network, Communication and Security

A New Channel-Aware Downlink Scheduling Algorithm for LTE-A and 5G HetNets

Flávio Alves Ferreira[1][(✉)] [iD] and Paulo Roberto Guardieiro[2][(✉)] [iD]

[1] Instituto Federal do Triângulo Mineiro – IFTM, Paracatu, MG 38600-000, Brazil
flavioalves@iftm.edu.br
[2] Universidade Federal de Uberlândia – UFU, Uberlândia, MG 38400-902, Brazil
prguardieiro@ufu.br

Abstract. Current and future cellular mobile networks, such as Long Term Evolution Advanced (LTE-A) and 5G, should provide wireless broadband access over radio channels for a growing number of users each day. However, in order to satisfy the service requirements of the User Equipments (UEs) applications, Radio Resource Management (RRM) mechanisms implemented in evolved NodeB (eNB) need to use efficient techniques to overcome limitations such as bandwidth scarcity, path loss, and channel fading. Therefore, this paper proposes a new channel-aware scheduling algorithm. Evaluation results show that the proposed algorithm is able to improve the cell edge throughput if compared to other algorithms. In addition, it offers better fairness performance.

Keywords: LTE-A and 5G networks · Channel-aware scheduling · Cell edge throughput

1 Introduction

The volume of data traffic generated on cellular mobile networks is continuously increasing [1]. The efficient radio resource management (RRM) schemes are necessary in order to meet this demand. The main RRM function is scheduling, which is responsible for periodically allocate the resources to User Equipments (UEs).

One of the main features of wireless mobile communications is the fast variation in channel conditions due to the phenomenon called channel fading, distance-dependent path loss and interference [2]. The Signal-to-Interference-plus-Noise Ratio (SINR) level is a parameter that enables to qualify the channel condition between the evolved NodeB (eNB) and the UE. The greater the distance between these devices, as well as the interference, the lower the SINR and, consequently, the lower UE throughput. Therefore, the UEs present at the cell edge are the most injured.

The Resource Allocation (RA) mechanisms that consider channel conditions, also known as channel-aware, have better throughput performance when compared to channel-unaware mechanisms. This is possible because channel-aware mechanisms exploit the so-called multi-user diversity gain, which means that among several UEs

© Springer Nature Singapore Pte Ltd. 2020
N. Chaubey et al. (Eds.): COMS2 2020, CCIS 1235, pp. 173–183, 2020.
https://doi.org/10.1007/978-981-15-6648-6_14

with different channel conditions, those one with more favorable conditions for transmission must use the resources. Thus, more bits can be transmitted through the allocated resources and consequently the channel is used more efficiently [3].

Therefore, this paper proposes a new scheduling algorithm that considers the channel conditions for the downlink LTE-A and 5G networks, with the objective of increasing the cell edge throughput, and at the same time to improve the fairness. The remainder of this paper is organized as follows. In Sect. 2, we present the fundamental concepts of channel-aware scheduling, after in Sect. 3 we specifies the problem and in Sect. 4 present the solution, then follows Sect. 5 with performance evaluation, and finally, in Sect. 6 the general conclusions are made.

2   Channel-Aware Scheduling

The scheduling mechanism or Packet Scheduling (PS) is responsible for defining which Resource Blocks (RBs) are allocated to the UEs. The RBs, which convey the data bits, are the elementary frequency subcarrier allocation units (12 subcarriers of 15 kHz, totaling 180 kHz per RB) used for communication between eNBs and UEs in Long-Term Evolution Advanced (LTE-A) networks, standardized by the Third-Generation Partnership Project (3GPP).

The amount of RBs and the order of served UEs over time are the result of the scheduling strategy or policy adopted. Therefore, the scheduling strategy is a decision-making process, carried out by the MAC layer in eNB, based on input parameters such as channel state, Quality of Service (QoS) requirements, among others [4], as shown in Fig. 1.

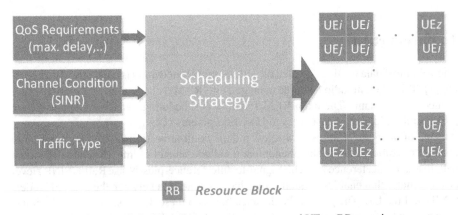

Fig. 1. Downlink scheduling: input parameters and UE-to-RB mapping.

The PS strategy in LTE-A and 5G networks is not standardized by 3GPP, therefore performance depends on the implementation designed by each mobile cellular network operator or developer. In general, most of the scheduling schemes presented in the literature can be classified according to information used for decision-making process, such as QoS requirements, and channel conditions (Channel-Aware Scheduling).

The scheduling scheme operation that consider channel conditions can be summarized as follows. At each Transmission Time Interval (TTI), UEs estimate the channel condition and report the Channel Quality Indicator (CQI) to serving eNB. This is so-called CQI feedback [5]. In eNB there is a buffer for each UE, where incoming packets are queued and has to wait for scheduling opportunity. The scheduling strategy, whose decision-making process takes channel condition into account, can allocate one or more RBs to particular UEs, and a RRM module determines the Modulation and Coding Scheme (MCS) according to CQI feedback. For instance, RBs are allocated to high SINR UEs in each cell in order to maximize system throughput because the better the channel condition, the higher the MCS order and, hence, the higher the bit rate per RB. This is an opportunistic scheduling example that is efficient for exploiting variations in channel conditions to produce significant network throughput gains.

The effectiveness of these schemes depends on the channel condition information provided by the UEs. Outdated information may result in poor performance.

In general, the PS design should consider a mathematical model, so-called utility function, to quantify system performance. The utility function result may vary with each TTI according to the UE-to-RB mapping established by the scheduling strategy. The parameterization of this function depends on the project objective. Some examples of scheduling algorithms that consider channel conditions are Maximum Throughput (MT), whose purpose is to maximize system throughput; another example is the Proportional Fairness (PF), whose objective is the balance between spectral efficiency (SE) and fairness. In the Eqs. (1) and (2) are presented utility functions of MT and PF algorithms, respectively [3].

$$p_u^k = argmax_u\left(r_k^u(t)\right) \tag{1}$$

Where $r_k^u(t)$ represents the expected data rate at time t, u is the UE index, which ranges from 1 to N, and k is the RB index. In this case, the UEs with better channel conditions has resource allocation priority and it may result in traffic starvation of UEs with low SINR.

$$p_u^k = argmax_u\left(\frac{r_k^u(t)}{R_u(t-1)}\right) \tag{2}$$

Where $R_u(t-1)$ is the achieved throughput. In this case, the UEs with lower throughput achieved could have resource allocation priority. Therefore, PF algorithm also gives the scheduling opportunity to UEs with bad channel condition.

In the literature there are several proposals based on Channel-Aware Scheduling. For example, in [6] and [7] the resource allocation decision is based on comparing one metric, per UE, which is a function of CQI; the papers presented in [8–11] and [12] take into account channel conditions and QoS parameters for resource allocation. The balance between opportunistic scheduling and fairness scheduling types is the focus of the study presented in [13] and the proposed implementation in [14, 15] and [16].

3 Problem Description

The scheduling mechanisms performance depends on the techniques employed in their implementation. The scheduling disciplines adopted in wired networks, such as Round Robin (RR), are not efficient for the wireless network scenario, where channel conditions and traffic load vary dynamically. The RR scheduling discipline aims to allocate the same amount of RBs for each UE associated with an eNB, but the UE throughput may significantly vary as the amount of bits available in each RB varies with the established MCS. The MCS is set according to the channel condition because this condition defines the SINR level and, hence, CQI value reported by UE. The amount of bits per RB allocated to UEs with low SINR, which is typical of cell edge UEs, is smaller than for UEs with high SINR. Therefore, scheduling disciplines that do not consider channel conditions to allocate resources may not to be the most efficient for improving cell edge throughput in LTE-A and 5G networks.

Even channel-aware scheduling disciplines such as MT, which optimizes system throughput at the cost of starvation of traffic flows generated by UEs with low SINR that are mainly those located at the cell edge, is not ideal algorithm for optimizing the throughput of these UEs. It is noteworthy that resource allocations projects that cannot balance spectral efficiency and fairness are not practical for real cellular mobile network scenarios. Thus, we present in the next section a new solution to improve the cell edge throughput while achieving fairer resource allocation.

4 Channel-Aware Downlink Scheduling Algorithm for LTE-A and 5G Networks

To improve the cell edge UEs average throughput, we must implement a channel-aware scheduling algorithm. Therefore, based on channel condition, we developed a novel RRM mechanism called Resource Allocation Scheme to Optimize the Throughput (RASOT). We present the RASOT operation in Fig. 2 and in the following pseudo code.

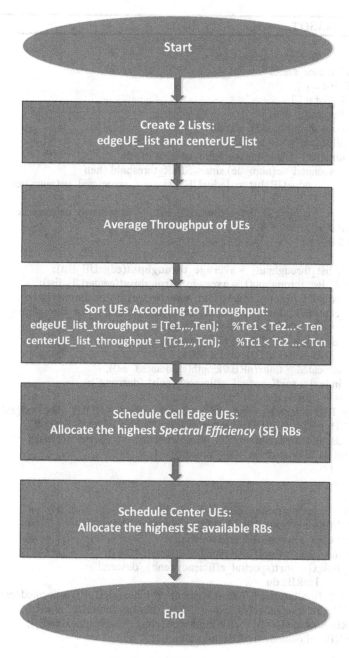

Fig. 2. RASOT basic steps.

Algorithm – RASOT

```
1   Input(s): eNB_set, associated_ue.
2   Output(s): user_alloc.
3   edgeUE_list = [ ];
4   centerUE_list = [ ];
5   nRBs_allocated = 0;
6   for eNB_i = 1:length(eNB_set) do
7      RB_allocated{eNB_i} = [ ];
8      for num_ue = 1:length(associated_ue{eNB_i}) do
9         if associated_ue(num_ue).sinr < SINR_threshold then
10              edgeUE_list = [edgeUE_list       associated_ue(num_ue)];
11        else
12              centerUE_list = [centerUE_list       associated_ue(num_ue)];
13        end if
14     end for
15  end for
16  [edgeUE_list_throughput] = average_throughput(edgeUE_list);
17  [centerUE_list_throughput] = average_throughput(centerUE_list);
18  [throug_edgeUE, throug_edgeUE_id] = sort(edgeUE_list_throughput);
19  [throug_centerUE, throug_centerUE_id] = sort(centerUE_list_throughput);
20  for eUE = 1:length(throug_edgeUE_id) do
21   enb =UE(throug_edgeUE_id(eUE)).associated_eNB.id;
22   nRBs = eNB_set(enb).RB_grid.n_RBs;
23   nRBs_allocated = floor(nRBs/length(associated_ue));
24   [se,rb_index] = sort(spectral_efficiency{enb},'descend');
25   for eRB = 1:nRBs do
26      if (n_RBs_allocated > 0)&~isMember(rb_index(eRB),RB_allocated{enb})then
27         RB_grid.user_alloc(rb_index(eRB)) = throug_edgeUE_id(eUE);
28         RB_allocated{enb} = [RB_allocated{enb}       rb_index(eRB)];
29         nRBs_allocated = n_RBs_allocated - 1;
30      end if
31   end for
32  end for
33  for cUE = 1:length(throug_centerUE_id) do
34   enb=UE(throug_centerUE_id(cUE)).associated_eNB.id;
35   nRBs = eNB_set(enb).RB_grid.n_RBs;
36   nRBs_allocated = floor(nRBs/length(associated_ue));
37   [se,rb_index] = sort(spectral_efficiency{enb},'descend');
38   for cRB = 1:nRBs do
39      if (n_RBs_allocated > 0)&~isMember(rb_index(cRB),RB_allocated{enb})then
40         RB_grid.user_alloc(rb_index(cRB)) = throug_centerUE_id(cUE);
41         RB_allocated{enb} = [RB_allocated{enb}       rb_index(cRB)];
42         nRBs_allocated = n_RBs_allocated - 1;
43      end if
44   end for
45  end for
```

First, there is a comparison, if the SINR level is less than a default value called *SINR_threshold*, then the procedure insert UEs into the *edgeUE_list* array, that forms a cell edge UEs group. However, if the SINR level is greater than *SINR_threshold*, the procedure insert UEs into the *centerUE_list* array, that forms a center UEs group. This has implemented in pseudo code between lines 6–15. Next, another procedure, between lines 16–17, calculate UEs throughput, then sort the UEs in ascending throughput order, between the lines 18–19.

We implement the procedures for allocating the highest spectral efficiency (SE) RBs for cell edge UEs between lines 20 and 32. The variable *nRBs_allocated* (line 23) represents the amount of RBs allocated to each cell edge UE, which results from the ratio between the total of RBs that eNB can allocate (*nRBs*) and the number of UEs associated with eNB (*length(associated_ue)*).

The variable *rb_index* represents the RB index and the variable *se* represents the spectral efficiency value. Line 24 defines a sequence of RBs from the highest SE value to the lowest SE value. When *eRB* and *eUE* are equal to one, the higher SE RB (*RB_grid.user_alloc (rb_index (1))*) is allocated to the first UE (*throug_edgeUE_id (1)*), i.e. the lowest throughput UE is serviced first, and so on. After to schedule cell edge UEs, RASOT algorithm schedule center UEs similarly to the previous UEs, which means to schedule first the center UE with lowest throughput, and so on. We implement this operation between the lines 33–45.

5 Performance Evaluation

To evaluate the proposed algorithm presented in Sect. 4, we used the MATLAB software with LTE-A System Level Simulator module developed by TU Wien's Institute of Telecommunications [17].

We present the values of the main parameters set in this modeling and simulation in Table 1.

Table 1. Simulation parameters values.

Parameter	Value
Simulation time	100 TTIs
Inter-site distance (MC)	500 m
Inter-site distance (SC)	250 m
Max. power transmission (MC)	46 dBm
Max. power transmission (SC)	30 dBm
Bandwidth	10 MHz
Channel model	PedA
CQI *feedback delay*	3 TTIs

The modeled scenario has 7 sites, each consisting of 3 sectors, totaling 21 Macro Cells eNBs (MCs) and 30 Small Cells eNBs (SCs), which characterize the system as a Heterogeneous Network (HetNet). This model was choose because the addition of small cells under the coverage area of traditional cells is one of the main strategies for increasing the capacity of 5G systems. In addition, the significant amount of eNBs, together with 825 UEs, that is the maximum number of UEs, as in [18], characterizes a denser network than most models presented in related works.

The average throughput and the fairness are the chosen parameters to evaluate algorithms performance. In the next figures, we present results with a 95% confidence interval.

Figure 3 shows the comparison of throughput performance for cell edge UEs among the proposed RASOT, RR, PF, and MT scheduling algorithms. RASOT outperforms the others algorithms because it gives priority to the service of cell edge UEs, as presented in Sect. 4. In addition, the proposed algorithm allocate more efficiently the RBs, which can carry more bits, since they have higher spectral efficiency. Therefore, the RASOT algorithm has better cell edge throughput for the simulated amount of UEs.

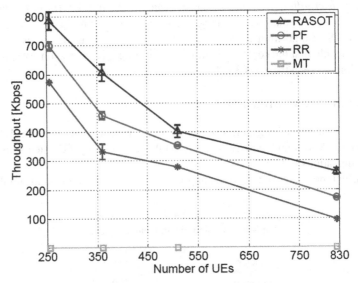

Fig. 3. Average throughput of cell edge UEs.

The results shown in Fig. 4 demonstrate that the proposed algorithm, RASOT, has a slightly lower performance than the other algorithms, except for the MT that maximizes the system throughput by sacrificing the cell edge UEs throughput. Thus, we can state about the RASOT algorithm that the improved throughput performance achieved with cell edge UEs does not occur at the expense of significant performance degradation of other UEs.

We quantify the fairness performance using the Jain's fairness index, represented in Eq. (3) by the variable J, which is a function of the throughput obtained by each of the

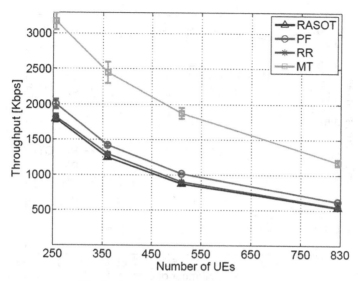

Fig. 4. Average throughput of system UEs.

n UEs, represented by the variable x_i [19]. The higher the fairness, the greater the value of this index, where 1 is the maximum value [20].

$$J = \frac{\left(\sum_{i=1}^{n} x_i\right)^2}{n. \sum_{i=1}^{n} x_i^2} \qquad (3)$$

In Fig. 5 we present the fairness index obtained by the four techniques mentioned above. The performance of the RASOT algorithm was better than the RR algorithm, which allocates the same amount of RBs for each UE regardless of channel condition, and PF, which performs the distribution of RBs relatively fairly. The MT algorithm performance was much lower than the performance of the other algorithms because it serves only the UEs with high SINR and therefore causes traffic starvation in UEs with low SINRs.

Since the objective of the RASOT algorithm is to improve the cell edge UEs throughput by first scheduling one from the lowest throughput to the highest achieved throughput, the cell edge UEs average throughput increases. However, the center UEs average throughput decreases because it has lower scheduling priority than cell edge UEs. Thus, the difference between the throughput values of the cell edge UEs and the center UEs present a significantly reduction when compared to the other algorithms. This reduction has a positive impact on the value obtained through Eq. (3), which is a function of the throughput achieved by each UE. Therefore, the proposed algorithm is the most suitable algorithm for providing the minimum throughput required by certain applications, which can be performed on both center UEs and cell edge UEs.

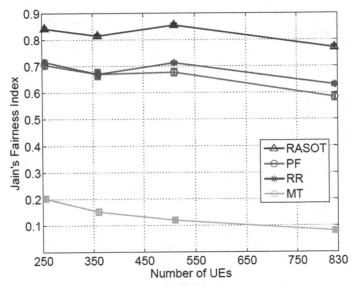

Fig. 5. Fairness.

6 Conclusion

In this paper, we present a new channel-aware scheduling algorithm, which gives priority to attend the traffic flows generated by UEs at the cell edge of LTE-A and 5G HetNets. The results obtained through modeling and simulation reveal that the proposed scheme improves the cell edge UEs throughput performance, if compared to well-known schemes such as RR, which does not consider channel conditions, and channel-aware schemes, such as MT and PF. In addition, the proposed scheme presented better fairness performance if compared to the reference schemes. Thus, we can say that it is best suited for applications with minimum throughput requirements, performed in both the center UEs and the cell edge UEs.

As future work, we aim to minimize Inter-Cell Interference (ICI), and consequently maximize the cell edge UEs throughput performance. We will design a power control module based on game theory that jointly with the proposed algorithm will meet this objective.

References

1. Hu, F.: Opportunities in 5G Networks: A Research and Development Perspective. CRC Press, Boca Raton (2016)
2. Dahlman, E., Sköld, J.: 4G, LTE-Advanced Pro and the Road to 5G, 3rd edn. Elsevier, Amsterdam (2016)
3. Sulthana, S.F., Nakkeeran, R.: Study of downlink scheduling slgorithms in LTE networks. J. Netw. **9**(12), 3381–3391 (2014)
4. Monikandan, S.B., Sivasubramanian, A., Babu, S.P.K.: A review of MAC scheduling algorithms in LTE system. Int. J. Adv. Sci. Eng. Inf. Technol. **7**(3), 1056–1068 (2017)

5. Capozzi, F., Piro, G., Grieco, L.A., Boggia, G., Camarda, P.: Downlink packet scheduling in LTE cellular networks: key design issues and a survey. IEEE Commun. Surv. Tutor. **15**(2), 678–700 (2013)
6. Escheikh, M., Jouini, H., Barkaoui, K.: Performance analysis of a novel downlink scheduling algorithm for LTE systems. In: 2014 International Conference on Advanced Networking Distributed Systems and Applications, pp. 13–18, Algeria (2014)
7. Rahman, A.A.A., Sharipp, N.M., Samingan, A.K., Yeoh, C.Y.: Improved link level LTE scheduler. In: 10th International Conference on Information, Communications and Signal Processing (ICICS), Singapore (2015)
8. Borst, S.: User-level performance of channel-aware scheduling algorithms in wireless data networks. IEEE/ACM Trans. Netw. **13**(3), 636–647 (2005)
9. Monghal, G., Pedersen, K.I., Kovacs, I.Z., Mongensen, P.E.: QoS oriented time and frequency domain packet scheduler for the UTRAN long term evolution. In: IEEE Vehicular Technology Conference, VTC Spring, vol. 1, pp. 2532–2536, Singapore (2008)
10. Fu, W., Kong, Q., Tian, W., Wang, C., Ma, L.: A QoS-aware scheduling algorithm based on service type for LTE downlink. In: 2nd International Conference on Computer Science and Electronics Engineering (ICCSEE), pp. 2201–2205 (2013)
11. Chuang, H., Hsieh, S., Wu, C.: A channel-aware downlink scheduling scheme for real-time services in long-term evolution systems. In Engineering Innovation and Design, pp. 337–343. CRC Press, London (2019)
12. Piro, G., Grieco, L.A., Boggia, G., Camarda, P.: A two-level scheduling algorithm for QoS support in the downlink of LTE cellular networks. In: European Wireless, EW2010 Italy (2010)
13. Kwan, R., Leung, C., Zhang, J.: Proportional fair multiuser scheduling in LTE. IEEE Signal Process. Lett. **16**(6), 461–464 (2009)
14. Kanagasabai, A., Nayak, A.: Channel aware scheduling algorithm for LTE uplink and downlink. Netw. Protoc. Algorithms **7**(3), 111–139 (2015)
15. Schwarz, S., Mehlführer, C., Rupp, M.: Throughput maximizing multiuser scheduling with adjustable fairness. In: 2011 IEEE International Conference on Communications (ICC), Japan (2011)
16. Chadchan, S.M., Akki, C.B.: A fair downlink scheduling algorithm for 3GPP LTE networks. Int. J. Comput. Netw. Inf. Secur. (IJCNIS) **5**(6), 34–41 (2013)
17. Mehlführer, C., Ikuno, J.C., Simko, M., Schwarz, S., Wrulich, M., Rupp, M.: The Vienna LTE simulators - enabling reproducibility in wireless communications research. EURASIP J. Adv. Signal Process. **2011**, 29 (2011)
18. Trabelsi, N., Chen, C.S., El Azouzi, R., Roullet, L., Altman, E.: User association and resource allocation optimization in LTE cellular networks. IEEE Trans. Netw. Serv. Manag. **14**(2), 429–440 (2017)
19. Jain, R.: The Art of Computer Systems Performance Analysis: Techniques for Experimental Design, Measurement, Simulation, and Modeling. Wiley, Hoboken (1991)
20. AlQahtani, S.A., Alhassany, M.: Comparing different LTE scheduling schemes. In: 2013 9th International Wireless Communications and Mobile Computing Conference (IWCMC), pp. 264–269 (2013)

Ponte Message Broker Bridge Configuration Using MQTT and CoAP Protocol for Interoperability of IoT

Madhavi Dave[1]([✉]) [iD], Mohanish Patel[1], Jyotika Doshi[2], and Harshal Arolkar[2] [iD]

[1] Indus University, Ahmedabad, India
madhvi.mca@gmail.com
[2] GLS University, Ahmedabad, India

Abstract. Internet of Things is emerging technology from few years where autonomous devices and technology communicate without human intervention. For IoT, many smart objects are interconnected and communicate through infrastructure of internet that is the base of a global network. The major challenge of IoT automation is to inter-connect heterogeneous devices, sensors and real-time application. Research has demonstrated recent development for a varied scope of solutions and devices of IoT eco-system. However, each interoperable technology provides its proprietary infrastructure and mechanism to communicate, which leads to IoT interoperability issue. Many research organizations, IoT industry and standardization institutes are working for empowering interoperability of resources between autonomous IoT devices. These efforts are categorized according to its implementation and usage considerations. The interoperable communication mechanism also depends on communication protocols and its communication models used at application layer. Major devices use MQTT, CoAP, RestAPI, AMQP and HTTP protocols at application layer for communication. This paper is intended to describe interoperability types and its impact on seamless communication. As a solution of interoperability issue, message bridge can be implemented between application layer protocols of request-response and publish-subscribe communication models. This paper demonstrate message bridge approach based on Ponte, which is open source IoT project designed by Eclipse for intercommunication between application layer protocols. The paper also demonstrates working of Ponte with the resolution of open issue related to message retention for cross protocol communication.

Keywords: Internet of Things · IoT protocol · Application layer protocol · Interoperability · MQTT · CoAP · HTTP · Message bridge · Ponte

1 Introduction

Internet of Things is a technology with connected devices to the internet having advantage of receiving and sending information over the internet and perform task depending on the information. Progressing towards recent technologies, it has become possible

N. Chaubey et al. (Eds.): COMS2 2020, CCIS 1235, pp. 184–195, 2020.
https://doi.org/10.1007/978-981-15-6648-6_15

to interconnect any device to other device using IoT [1]. This has become possible due to wireless networks and mobile devices with the help of which, we can control ample of devices from remote locations. Internet is the driving element for IoT enabled devices to have direct communication between machine-to-machine, thus coalescing digital and physical world together. Connecting each device is still a challenge to IoT as every IoT device has certain protocols and technologies upon which it is designed. It is difficult to cope with the growing requirements of humans as well as modern devices. Protocols used in majority of IoT devices which fall under Machine-to-Machine (M2M) category. With the help of these predefined protocols, IoT devices can establish seamless connection. To decide what kind of action a device should take, methods based on respective protocols are used. Majority of the event processing are based on Publish-Subscribe and Request-Response method [2], these methods are central part of MQTT and CoAP respectively. MQTT and CoAP are playing a major role in connecting devices to the internet. For achieving vision of connecting every device to the internet it must use HTTP for communication. WWW is fully based on HTTP protocol that opened a path to the internet for millions of people. The Internet of things has come so far by developing in so many areas and it has so many applications that its diversity can be an obstacle in its growth [16]. Each day many devices require seamless connection to the Internet, on the parallel side these IoT things are manufactured by different thousand manufacturers. These manufacturers are coming up with their own protocols, thus making it difficult to make devices communicate with each other. The need for Interoperability emerges due to heterogeneous devices and its manufacturer specific features.

2 IoT Interoperability

Interoperability can be defined as enabling devices and systems to communicate with each other regardless of the technical dependencies of their manufacturers. The Oxford Dictionary defines the term Interoperability as "able to operate in conjunction". The definition of IoT says that it is global platform for communication between self-configurable devices which have identities, use smart interfaces and connected to network without interruption. The devices used in IoT systems are constrained by limited memory and processing capacity. The domains using such devices and communication among them are medical, transport, business, agriculture, health care, infrastructure, etc. There are more than 300 IoT platforms for intercommunication in market and many more are coming by each passing day [17]. The well-known IoT platforms providers are AWSIoT (Amazon), HomeKit (Apple), Watson (IBM), Brillo (Google), AzureIoT (Microsoft) and Jasper (Cisco) [22].

According to McKinsey analysis, missing interoperability is threat to IoT market. It is stated by author that, 40% of potential benefits can be get by interoperability among IoT devices [3]. The case in which interoperability is not provided for communication the devices must bound to single system provided by manufacturers. It restricts the system for using the defined communication mechanism by the providers [4]. Thus it becomes difficult for users or small scale providers to take services of heterogeneous devices and integrate them to make an information network. Such issues make interoperability a biggest challenge of IoT along with standardization, scalability and security [18]. The standardization is needed for seamless communication technology among heterogeneous IoT things. Interoperability is raising day by day in IoT market due to heterogeneity of devices [21]. As it is described in Fig. 1, IoT interoperability is having four types as listed below [6],

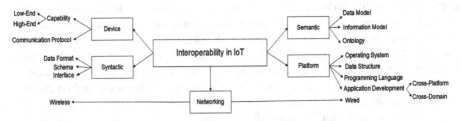

Fig. 1. Interoperability in Internet of Things [6]

Device Level Interoperability: It deals with hardware and software features of heterogeneous device which have diversity based of proprietors and thus have interconnection issues.

Network Level Interoperability: The network on which devices are performing communication are distinct in nature. There may be IoT device, mobile device or any desktop computer as "Thing" and it may use different technologies to connect to the network.

Platform Level Interoperability: It arise due to variety of platforms available for providing service and application for communication.

Protocol Level Interoperability: As there are heterogeneous devices and each may have different proprietor. The communication protocol and technology used may varies from device to device.

Data Level Interoperability: The data gathered by sensors are going to be stored either at device or at cloud for the system. The data filtration functions handle and store data in their unique formats.

Syntactical Interoperability: The message format used by communication devices to interconnect may uses different formats according to technical design of the device.

Semantic Interoperability: In case of M2M (Machine-to-Machine) communication, both intercommunicating devices must follow same units. This system will not work efficiently when communication will be obstructed by varied semantics of device.

3   IoT Interoperability Challenges

The interoperability in IoT communication can be achieved when the two devices are compatible with each other [7]. The world of Internet of Things is facing high degree of heterogeneity because of hardware, protocols and technologies used by devices. Even for one IoT system, there could be many interleaved communication technologies. Also, for one communication protocol, there could be number of communication application and design strategies. To handle such diversity in many aspects, communication within constrained devices is a big challenge. With increasing demand in future, the integration of wide variety of constrained devices will become necessary to improve [13].

The security and privacy of information and network must incorporate with basic principles like authentication, authorization, confidentiality, integrity and availability [8]. IoT covers many domains of real life and applicable to global economy. Thus, IoT security and privacy problems need most attention to be resolved. The developers and users of IoT devices and frameworks have committed for secure solution and guarantee for application used with privacy concerns. Likewise, an aggregate solution for security can also find optimal solution for scalability problem [4].

In IoT culture, many of the IoT device manufacturer are coming up with devices and services. An environment of proprietary in IoT technologies constraint growth value for users and industry. Though complete interoperability for all products and services is not possible, users may be diffident to buy IoT products and services in case of integration issues, ownership problems, and concern over proprietary for IoT device, service or platform [19].

4 Interoperability Solution

IoT has varied range of communication protocols such as MQTT, CoAP, AMQP, and HTTP at application layer [2]. Among the mentioned protocols, MQTT and AMQP use Publish-Subscribe communication model while CoAP and HTTP are based on Client-Server architecture. The intercommunication among different communication creates issues as the message format is following different patterns for fundamentally different protocols [4]. For interoperable functionality, the communication process described in Fig. 2 is followed. Thus solution for interoperability comprised of an intermediator platform who helps in converting messages from one to other format. There are many brokers, gateways and interoperable devices available for resolving the issue but most of them are having proprietary constraints [20].

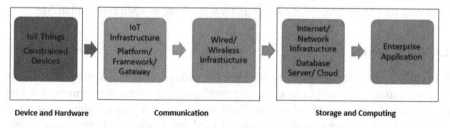

Fig. 2. Interoperable communication process

The interoperability can be achieved by various technologies of networking like virtual networking, fog computing and IP based networking solutions. It can also be implemented by open API, semantic web technology and service oriented architecture (SOA). These technologies are based on basic interoperability approaches like frameworks, platforms and open projects [21]. Each of the interoperable solution can be implemented in suitable IoT system with compatible set of protocols. The interoperability approaches are mentioned in detail as follows [22].

4.1 IoT Framework

The framework of ICT (Information and Communication Technology) system ensures to integrate necessary entities for dependency and reliability. IoT framework is expected to provide support to constrained devices having M2M inter-connectivity. IoT framework refers to the technology which is reliable and provide appropriate infrastructure for timely communication between constrained machines with proper analysis of data. Many enterprises have offered framework solutions in recent years which helps in connecting public or private network to the cloud. The key issue in success of framework is its robustness for implementing connection among devices of various manufacturers. The known IoT open source frameworks are oneM2M, HyperCat, OMA LWM2M and OpenHAB.

4.2 IoT Platform

IoT platform provides hardware and software support to build on the system. Platform follows some basic rules of implemented framework and supports the top up application features for allocated task. There are numerous IoT platforms are available in market and it's almost impossible to find out any best solutions among all available platforms. These platforms are proprietary and thus hold its communication model and data privately. User of the system need to have detailed knowledge for intercommunication among different platforms. In many cases, cross platform APIs are used for data integration of different platforms. It becomes difficult when the platform is not open source and does not allow any API to access its data without proprietary privileges. The interoperability can be achieved when data are communicated or integrated using cross-platform or cross-domain application. The examples of popular IoT platforms are Kaa and EclipseIoT, rest platforms are having proprietary rights and not available as open source platform.

4.3 IoT Project

IoT projects are the bridge, gateway or adaptor provided for communicating data, signals or specifications. The project works as the middle-ware between two or more different platforms and can be extended with the help of plugins. The major technical aspect of IoT project depends on underlying protocol used for specific communication model. Thus, the bridge or gateway can be designed for different communication protocols at sender device and receiver device. This middle-ware can be a dedicated hardware or embedded with software, which must be installed in any resource rich device. It has limited scalability based on underlying protocols used for interoperability. As the number of protocol increases in bridge or gateway, so is the complexity. For making it more usable, the standardization of protocols and its seamless integration is required. The few well-known IoT projects with open source are Ponte, OpenIoT and FiWare. Among the available open source projects for interoperability, this paper focuses on Ponte for configuration of broker bridge for widely used application layer protocols MQTT and CoAP.

5 Message Broker Bridge: Ponte

Ponte is Mobile-to-Mobile bridge framework designed under Eclipse Technology Project [10]. It can be used as bridge between devices for different communication protocol to interoperate. Ponte has reduced complexity of interoperability by bridging M2M protocols like HTTP, MQTT and CoAP together. Real power of Ponte is used, when connected devices are based on constrained protocol though it connects them to the rest of the world. Ponte has been integrated with wide number of Data Storage Engines like MongoDB, LevelDB and Redis which becomes handy for developers to analyze and store data [2]. It is a full package of many publish/subscribe brokers like RabbitMQTT, Mosquitto, ZeroMQ and also AMQP including Redis and MongoDB [4]. Ponte is a build over on QEST and Mosca, yet another contribution by creator of Ponte and was rewritten in Javascript [7]. Most of IoT communication occurs in publish/subscribe communication model, thus Ponte is implemented using pub/sub model as described in Fig. 3 [10].

- RabbitMQ with implementations of the AMQP protocol
- Redis - the key/value store by antirez
- Mosquitto with implementations of the MQTT protocol
- MongoDB - documental NoSQL web apps are built.

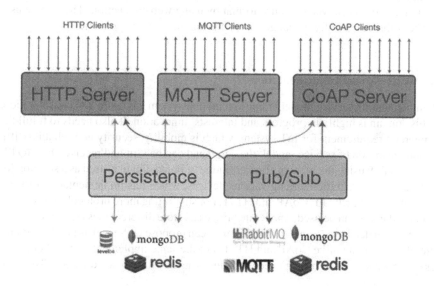

Fig. 3. Ponte architecture [10]

5.1 Case Study: Home Automation

For the explanation of the system, the home automation system is taken as example. In this case study, the communication is explained in both the ways, i.e. CoAP to MQTT and MQTT to CoAP by considering a scenario as described below.

Accessing Light from Remote Location: In the case of accessing lights from remote location, the services of web are used. The data can be sent over internet/web with the help of HTTP or REST resources. The web request can be made by application, which sends signal for accessing resource at home. The application can be considered as CoAP client, which is sending request from remote location for switching the light on at home. The request would reach CoAP server via medium of internet/web, which resides locally. The received datagram is in CoAP format and it cannot be understood by local devices (light). Here, Ponte receives the datagram sent by CoAP server and convert in MQTT packet format so the local devices can act upon it. The MQTT packet would be sent to MQTT broker, which is responsible for publishing the messages. The MQTT broker creates queue and distribute the message topic wise. The subscribed node (light) will be forwarded the message. Thus the message received by final MQTT node, which is light, in this case, is switched on/off as per the given message by remote user.

Check Lights Status from Remote Location: For checking the light's status from remote location, the event for light on/off can be driven from local source. In this scenario when the light will be on/off, the application of remote user can inform about the change in light's status. Here when the local user send command for changing state of light, the MQTT broker receives the command. The broker publishes the command to the connected devices which have subscribed on the topic "light". Thus, the devices which have light may change its state. Along with giving command to subscribed device, the broker also sends message to Ponte bridge. The message would be received in MQTT format and convert into URI format for CoAP server. The CoAP server forwards message to remote user in web response format by using web connection. The remote user can check the status of light change (on/off) using the mobile application.

5.2 Service Model Implementation

For implementing service model, home automation system has taken into consideration. As this domain is highly in progress and interests' innovation. It also needs to fulfill the commercial requirement for IoT system, which is mobility, security and reliability [9]. For demonstration of service model, the command can be sent and received by MQTT, CoAP or HTTP using the message broker bridge of Ponte. Ponte is used as a solution for the problem of integration among various devices, which has implementation of standard protocols like MQTT, CoAP and HTTP. For supporting more protocols, the specific protocol adapters can be used. The Ponte bridge can store different message semantics in non-relational database format. In MQTT, user can propose QoS level as per the requirement of the system unlike CoAP and HTTP. For the same implementation in Ponte, the message persistence can be achieved with clustering and distributed database. Thus, the user subscribes and receive high volume of data with proper availability as per configures QoS. The system using multiprotocol tends to use API for remote operations using CoAP and HTTP. Ponte message broker bridge integrate such characteristics of various protocols and make the communication possible with MQTT's publish-subscribe model and CoAP/HTTP's request-response model. The service model for communication using Ponte Bridge is shown in Fig. 4.

Ponte is an application based on node manager, thus it requires node.js to implement as a base. Node manager can be installed by NVM (Node Version Manager) as it allows user to install recommended version from available multiple versions of node.js and NPM. Installing Node will automatically install NPM on the computer using any operating system. Ponte works on node version 0.12, 4.3.1, 5.0 to any latest node version till 12.4.0. It is stated in [10] that Ponte is not working with node version 5.7 but it is implemented to communicate with all the three protocols. For installing Ponte, the two options are available as follow,

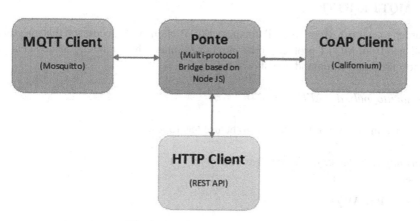

Fig. 4. Ponte bridge service model

$ npm install ponte -g or
$ npm install ponte bunyan -g

First command will install Ponte with default configuration settings, while second command demonstrates that bunyan is a functionality which outputs log messages and provides an easy logger interface for reading ongoing process in Ponte. To start Ponte in terminal,

$ ponte -v or $ ponte -v | bunyan

After Ponte will be started and terminal will show following logger,

[2019-11-25T07:28:24.485Z] INFO:ponte/30351 on mak: server started red‹→(service=MQTT, mqtt=1883)
[2019-11-25T07:28:24.491Z] INFO:ponte/30351 on mak: server started red‹→(service=MQTT, mqtt=3001)
[2019-11-25T07:28:24.492Z] INFO:ponte/30351 on mak: server started red‹→(service=MQTT, mqtt=5681)

Default port for MQTT will remain same every time as Ponte is a direct implementation of MQTT. Port number for CoAP and HTTP can be changed as shown in the logger information, default port number for CoAP and HTTP defined in Ponte is 3000 and 5683 by default. It can be done by changing port number in server.js file found at/usr/lib/node modules/ponte/lib location.

5.3 MQTT to HTTP

In order to publish from MQTT client to HTTP client it is necessary that messages published from MQTT protocol to be in retained mode, thus -r should be added at last of mosquitto pub command like shown below,

$ mosquitto_pub -d -t LED -m ON –r

To receive in HTTP GET method is to be used as follow,

$ curl http:/localhost:3001/resources/LED

5.4 CoAP to MQTT

Same as HTTP in order to receive message in CoAP retain flag should be set true by adding -r at last while publishing message from MQTT client (Fig. 5).
To receive in CoAP observe switch should be turned on.

$ mosquitto_pub -d -t LED -m ON –r
$ coap -o coap:/localhost/r/LED

5.5 CoAP to HTTP

Ponte can use PUT method to send messages from CoAP to MQTT or HTTP. CoAP client named, CoAP-CLI can be used with PUT method for the communication.

$ echo -n OFF | coap put coap:/localhost/r/LED

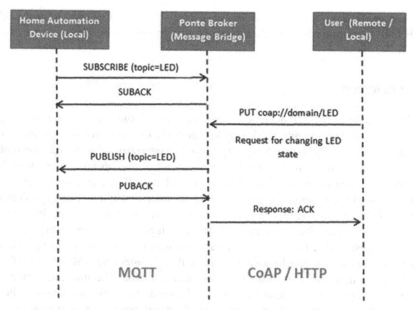

Fig. 5. MQTT-CoAP/HTTP communication in home automation system

To receive messages in MQTT client mosquitto sub can be used.

$ mosquitto_sub -d -t LED

6   Research Findings

The Ponte message bridge is lacking in the areas of IP addressing, message retention, Host Identity protocol and such other 235 issues [14]. Due to open issues, the use of Ponte has shrunk though it has least overheads for communication. The issue of IP addressing and message retention is solved as demonstrated in service model section. Ponte is also having less delay and failure compare to other interoperability solution. The payload size for Ponte depends on the sender and receiver technology, i.e. the supported packet size of CoAP and MQTT.

6.1   Open Issue Resolution: Message Retention

In Open project of Ponte, user of Ponte bridge has pointed that the message send by any protocol is not preserved for view [11]. The issue can be resolved by making changes in configuration file through set of commands. A retain flag is set to true so broker can store last received message on a particular topic. As a broker it will only store one message per topic that is last received. Broker will publish last receive message as soon as client subscribes to that particular topic. When retained flag is set to false or -r is not added to the end of the command then protocols which are working on GET/PUT method such as CoAP and HTTP will not receive messages published from MQTT client unless until first message received is from CoAP and HTTP i.e. if retained flag is set to false CoAP and HTTP clients have to send their message first in order to receive messages from MQTT.

7 Conclusion

The interoperability of IoT devices is been the major issue since inception of technology and with the growing market of IoT devices, the issue needs more attention. Although there are many researches going on for IoT interoperability, no solution is able to provide justified result for the issue. The categories of interoperability are described with available open source solutions. All categories have different approaches and techniques based on implementation domain. It is concluded that among existing solutions, IoT frameworks are having high overload for any M2M constrained device. In addition, the IoT platforms described are having proprietary rights reserved by the organization, which have designed it. Ponte is most suitable among described IoT projects, which is open source Eclipse project for IoT interoperability. It works with MQTT, CoAP and HTTP (application layer) protocols for intercommunication. The implementation and working of Eclipse Ponte is described which is based on Node Version Manager. Ponte is an open source solution with few open issues for development. An open issue of message retention is resolved by adding elements in configuration file, which can help in achieving interoperability among application layer communication protocols. For future work, the issue of security and Host Identifier Protocol is required to resolve for better interoperability among IoT devices.

References

1. Ashton, K.: Internet of Things. RFiD J. **22**, 97–114 (2009)
2. Salman, T., Jain, R.: Networking protocols and standards for Internet of Things. CSE (November 2015)
3. Manyika, J., et al.: The Internet of Things: Mapping the Value Beyond the Hype. McKinsey Global Institute, New York (2015)
4. Macaulay, T.: RIoT Control: Understanding and Managing Risks and the Internet of Things. Morgan Kaufmann, Burlington (2016)
5. Gubbi, J., Buyya, R., Marusic, S., Palaniswami, M.: Internet of Things (IoT): a vision, architectural elements, and future directions. Future Gener. Comput. Syst. **29**, 1645–1660 (2013)
6. Gaedke, M.: Interoperability in Internet of Things: taxonomies and open challenges. Mob. Netw. Appl. **24**(3), 796–809 (2019)
7. Ding, L., Shi, P., Liu, B.: The clustering of internet, Internet of Things and social network. In: 3rd International Symposium on Knowledge Acquisition and Modeling (KAM10), pp. 417–420, Wuhan, China (November 2010)
8. Suo, H., Wan, J., Zou, C., Liu, J.: Security in the Internet of Things: a review. In: International Conference on Computer Science and Electronics Engineering, ICCSEE, pp. 648–651 (2012)
9. Zamfir, S., Balan, T., Sandu, F., Costache, C.: Mobile communication solutions for the services in the Internet of Things. In: Borangiu, T., Drăgoicea, M., Nóvoa, H. (eds.) IESS 2016. LNBIP, vol. 247, pp. 619–632. Springer, Cham (2016). https://doi.org/10.1007/978-3-319-32689-4_47

10. Ponte - Connecting Things to Developers. https://www.eclipse.org/ponte/
11. Eclipse Technology Project. https://projects.eclipse.org/projects/technology/ponte/
12. Ponte - M2M Bridge Framework for REST Developers. https://www.eclipse.org/proposals/technology.ponte
13. Konduru, V.R., Bharamagoudra, M.R.: Challenges and solutions of interoperability on IoT. In: International Conference on Smart Technologies for Smart Nation. IEEE (2017). ISBN: 978-1-5386-0569-1
14. Open Issues of Ponte Message Broker. https://bugs.eclipse.org/bugs/show_bug.cgi?id=536595
15. Stallings, W.: Fundamentals of Modern Networking: SDN, NFV, QoE, IoT and Cloud. Pearson Publication, London (2016)
16. Suresh, P., Daniel, J., Aswathy, R., Parthasarathy, V.: A state of the art review on the Internet of Things (IoT) history, technology and fields of deployment. IEEE (March 2014). ISBN: 978-1-4799-7613-3/14
17. IoT-From Research and Innovation to Market Deployment. RiverPublisher (2014). ISBN: 978-87-93102-4-1
18. Vermesan, O., Friess, P.: Internet of Things-Converging Technologies for Smart Environment and Integrated Ecosystem. IEEE, Piscataway (2016)
19. Al-Fuqaha, A., Aledhari, K., Mohsen, G., Ammar, R., Mehdi, M.: Toward better horizontal integration among IoT services. IEEE Commun. Mag. 53(9), 7279 (2015)
20. Bellavista, P., Zanni, A.: Towards better scalability for IoT-cloud interactions via combined exploitation of MQTT and CoAP. In: IEEE 2nd International Forum on Research and Technologies for Society and Industry Leveraging a Better Tomorrow (RTSI) (September 2016). ISBN: 978-1-5090-1131-5/16
21. Noura, M., Atiquzzaman, M., Gaedke, M.: Interoperability in Internet of Things: taxonomies and open challenges. Mob. Netw. Appl. 24, 796–809 (2018)
22. Paolo, B., Zanni, A.: Scalability of kura-extended gateways via MQTT-CoAP integration and hierarchical optimizations. Internet of Things. IEEE (October 2016)

ITS Based OBU: A Fallback Mechanism in Vehicular Ad-Hoc Network

Bhavin A. Kayasth[1,2]([☒]) [ID] and Rachna M. Patel[1,2]([☒]) [ID]

[1] Pacific School of Engineering, Surat, Gujarat, India
bhavinkayasth24@gmail.com, rachu.cuty@gmail.com
[2] C. G. Patel Institute of Technology, Uka Tarsadia University, Bardoli, Gujarat, India

Abstract. Vehicular Ad-Hoc Network (VANET) is the largest growing sector for research in wireless communication. Advancing the research in VANET overcomes major issues present in current in wireless technology related to vanet. Major challenges include network reliability, security and safety. This paper discusses some current technologies related to ITS and sensor which are based on VANET which are used in the dissemination of information in vehicular environment. This research also proposes a phase 2 mechanism, which compliance of hardware in On Board Unit (OBU) which works as an alternative medium providing safety and an independent vehicular traffic flow which do not rely on network connectivity.

Keywords: Ad-Hoc · VANET · OBU · Sensors · Wireless · ITS · RSU

1 Introduction

VANET a concept which is a mainstream in today's researches in wireless communication. The advancement in this field is recognized all over the nations. VANET which aware us about several network related confronts like reliability, security and passenger safety. To resolve these challenges a model of Intelligent Transport System (ITS) in VANET is introduced. ITS model interchanges information among vehicles. ITS do examined as a ascending case of Mobile Ad-hoc Network (MANET) [2], here the system's facilities are assign to vehicle which generates a impulsive network tracking the motion of vehicles along road side flawless during unreliable network connection with Road Side Units (RSU) of base station. MANET do authorize the probability of direct wireless communication from Vehicle-to-Vehicle (V2V) as shown in Fig. 1. In other hands ITS too is the prime technology which intensify traffic establishments and road safety. It abets to carry signal with hotspot and also with other nearby entities through Direct Short Range Communication (DSRC).

1.1 Architecture

This section outlines the system architecture of vehicular Ad-hoc networks. According to the author in [6] of the architecture standard guidelines, one is capable to attain the VANETs system which can be summarized into three domains: (1) The Mobile Domain, (2) The Infrastructure Domain, and (3) The Generic Domain.

© Springer Nature Singapore Pte Ltd. 2020
N. Chaubey et al. (Eds.): COMS2 2020, CCIS 1235, pp. 196–209, 2020.
https://doi.org/10.1007/978-981-15-6648-6_16

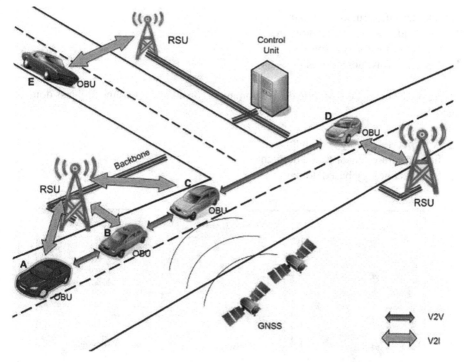

Fig. 1. VANET architecture [6]

1.2 Intelligent Transport System

In present view of Vehicular Network, the world now is at a brink of digital revolution and Internet of Things (IoT) which indicates the forthcoming frontier [1]. The attention after this development is based on two main principles i.e. (1) "Adaptive Security architecture" and (2) "Internet of Things", both are listed in Gartner's strategic technology trends which was published in 2016 [1]. IoT also reserves a position in Vehicular Network which alters vehicles into excellent sense-and-move policy and assist in secure driving, increases energy efficiency, decreases delay and gains control in congestion management for proper flow of traffic [1]. ITS vehicles uses sensors with lower in range and are able to sense, communicate and process data by accumulating information of vehicles velocity and position. The statistics are exchanged with nearby vehicle after performing computation using DSRC having range of 300 m and authorizing vehicles to communicate [1]. It relates to the mobile domain which consists of two parts: (1) The Vehicle Domain and (2) The Mobile Device Domain. Vehicles such as cars and buses are comprises in Vehicle domain and portable devices like personal navigation devices and smart phones are comprises in mobile device domain. The methods like connection oriented and connection less, which reveals some parts of the domain like vehicle domain which is connection oriented, that includes:

1. Internet infrastructure domain
2. Road side infrastructure domain
3. Private infrastructure domain
4. Central infrastructure domain.

Where on the other side, Mobile device domain is considered, as connectionless domain that includes:

1. A raspberry prototype domain
2. Infrastructure sensor based domain
3. Li-Fi technology based domain.

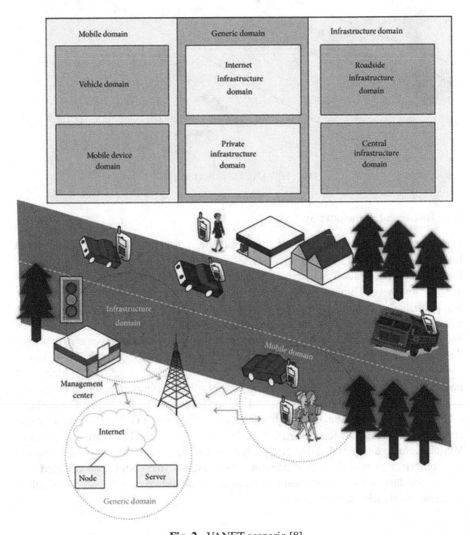

Fig. 2. VANET scenario [8]

OBU is one of the major sections in vehicular domain followed by application units (AU's), which combines and form a wired as well as wireless connections, however a ad-hoc domain comprises of OBU's and RSU's as described in Fig. 2 [8].

1.3 Connection-Oriented

An OBU can be seen as a mobile node of an ad-hoc network and RSU is a static node likewise.

An RSU can be connected to the Internet via the gateway; RSUs can communicate with each other directly or via multihop as well. According to the author Shrestha R. [7], a special case of mobile ad-hoc network (MANET) is described in which the vehicles are itself the mobile nodes, here vehicles not only communicate with the vehicles but it also communicate with the (RSU).

The two infrastructure domain access, Hot spots (HSs) and RSU's. OBUs may interact with Internet via RSUs or HSs. If one of those two are absent which is RSUs and HSs, OBUs can also interact by using cellular radio networks (GSM, GPRS, UMTS, WiMAX, and 4G) as there is merely researches done for no network coverage or unreliable network connection as shown in Fig. 3.

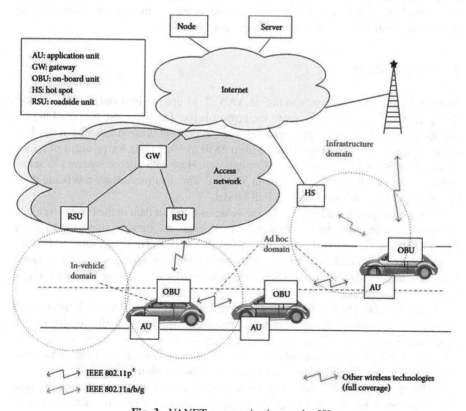

Fig. 3. VANET communication modes [8]

The greatest challenge apart from many in VANET is Quality of Service (QoS). A good QoS is tough to attain in VANET because of various topologies in networks and also due to the unavailability of information for routing [2].

1.4 Connection-Less

The backbone of all the technologies can be referred as Signal connections. If the connection is loses its connectivity from, base station unit (BSU) to targeted vehicles then, a terrible scenario can be seen. To prevent this scenario, author Truong in [3] proposed a prototype using raspberry-Pi which detects nearby vehicles with the help of Infrared sensor.

Similarly in [6] a data dissemination model is shown where Light Fidelity (Li-Fi) technology is used where data is disseminated in vehicular environment using (Li-Fi). Thus, mechanism must be introduce to handle the situations in terms of unreliable network connection in ITS. Thus, to overcome the certain issues related to connection oriented scenario a proposed block diagram named as "ITS based OBU" is proposed in this paper as a fall back mechanism which consist of two phases. Phase 1 of the block diagram with the algorithm described in [10], here the network continuously tracks the connection with making decision on commencement of phase 2. Phase 2 possesses the actual mechanism here when network is disconnected the mechanism takes over the vehicle and controls until the connection is reestablished.

2 Related Work

Number of technologies are working on VANET to get the best out of ITS, such as Wi-Max, WAVE and GSM. Some of the protocols like DSRC is also proposed in [13] that works on low latency high speed v2v and v2i communication establishment. This technology consists of a range of band from 5850 to 5925 GHz for protocol of public allocated by Federal Communication Commission. Here data interchange and its sensitivity is the main challenge encounter in VANET. The data transmission is being done in two ways (1) Push Model and (2) Pull Model.

Here for the proper understanding, the vehicles transmit data in the form of velocity and location with each other in Push model. Whereas the transmission of emergency signal to all the vehicle is done in pull model in VANET. Thus, it results in network crowding, as it floods the network with the broadcast messages. As a result of failed broadcast messages transmitted for 5000 nodes obtained when simulated using a VANET simulator is shown in the paper.

Figure 4, shows the graph of average travel time observed as 900 s in Boston which increased in non-successful of transmitted messages which eventually resulted in the expansion in travel time. Thus when, traffic congestion increases it ultimately increase the ratio of failure in broadcasted messages, therefore as a result an unstable network layout is formed. This emphasize that better broadcast medium is required.

In this paper [8] author has proposed a three levels autonomous vehicle prototype using Raspberry Pi, this system is detects the close ranged vehicles with the use of Infrared sensor. Here the main goal is to analyze the vehicles at autonomous foam from

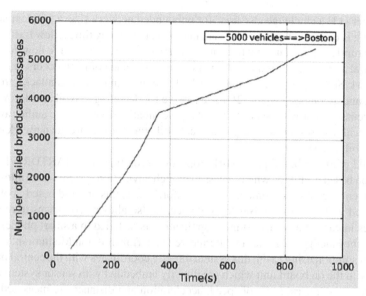

Fig. 4. VANET failed broadcasted messages [2]

at microscopic level, having focus on every vehicle with their data transmission from nearby vehicles and RSU. In this prototype a set of passive and active experiments were run, for demonstration of the interconnectivity of the developed prototype. The emulation based system on chip were incorporated with several sensors.

Moreover there are two systems which controls traffic that is centralized or decentralized in [2], although in hybrid systems which are also termed as centralized systems possess high computation and communication cost, whereas Artificial Intelligence (AI) is required in the decentralized system which is a lot more expensive than other. Thus, a white paper proposed in 2012, where autonomous vehicle uses a sensor and communication based technologies is used in which cameras and software assist driver and the computer to handle the situation in response of any problem arises.

In a paper proposed by [3] a Speed Based Lane Changing System (SBSL) is proposed. This system enables the cars to changes lanes when a desired gap distance meets the defined requirement in the algorithm at a certain speed. Here a vital role is played by OBU and it notifies the vehicle driver to change its lane. If for so called reasons the driver does not follow instructions then, the nearby vehicle and RSU convey this information to control center which looks over the traffic surveillance and the vehicle driver is punished.

A new method in [4] presented, does the vehicle detection and speed estimation task. Here the computer computes the velocity of the vehicle based on its position. An algorithm is derived as a self-locating mechanism of every vehicle on assumption basis. Thus, it is concluded that it maintains a proper speed limit also warns the driver to change velocity as well as lanes.

A framework of smart city in [5], is given where VANET is attracting research community and industry at a same time as it contains the information dissemination for both of them.

In paper [11] a challenge also arise for unbounded network size, a frequent network partitioning is occurred during rush hours in urban areas at day time as low traffic load is formed in rural areas and at night time in urban areas, this frequent traffic flow during day time in rural areas creates frequent network congestion and collision occurs in network.

Network Security is as essential as vehicle security thus various attacks are being analyzed, and among all Paper [12] made a move for detecting a Sybil attacks in vanets, which discusses to provide security in data dissemination in vanet, the author aware us with a critical review on techniques to detect Sybil attacks to secure the network by such kind of Sybil attacks.

A OBU platform based paper [14] proposes a prototype as SMARTDRIVE, it is a application based prototype which accessed though navigation system which allows road maps, current locations of vehicle and rout information, this android based application is integrated with OBU via a Bluetooth device. It also allows pedestrians to report the authorities in case of any misfortune if application is installed in a smart phone.

A "Light Fidelity (Li-Fi) as an Alternative Data Transmission Medium in VANET" provides a solution using Li-Fi, this system directly coordinates with the central processing unit with the on board unit which are directly embedded with sensor system present in it. Here, certain parameters of speed, acceleration and distance are measured by the Sensors functions from the neighboring vehicle [6]. The comparative literature review of VANET is as shown below in Table 1.

Table 1. Comparative literature review of VANET

Sr. no.	Paper	Year of pub.	Controller	Simulator	Remarks
1	"VANET routing on city roads using real-time vehicular traffic information", "IEEE Transactions on Vehicular technology" [1]	2009	–	–	This paper aims to design and implement a reactive protocol RBVT-R and a proactive protocol RBVT-P and compared them with protocols representative of mobile Ad-hoc networks and VANETs
2	"Software-defined networking for RSU clouds in support of the internet of vehicles", "IEEE Internet of Things Journal" [2]	2015	–	–	This paper aims the use of reinforcement learning to select configurations that minimize reconfiguration costs in the network over the long term

(*continued*)

Table 1. (*continued*)

Sr. no.	Paper	Year of pub.	Controller	Simulator	Remarks
3	"Software defined networking based vehicular Ad-hoc network with fog computing", "IFIP/IEEE International Symposium on Integrated Network Management" [3]	2012	SDN	Ns2	This paper aims to propose a solution to ensure the fog computing ensuring less response time
4	"DASITS: driver assistance system in "intelligent transport system", "30th International Conference on Advanced Information Networking and Applications Workshops" [4]	2016	Ns2, Sumo	Ns2	This paper aims to propose a solution to ensure the quality of service and assistance for lane changing
5	"A raspberry-pi prototype of smart transportation", "IEEE 25th International Conference on Systems Engineering" [5]	2017	Raspberry pi	Real test bed	System is focusing on each vehicle and their communications with the nearby vehicles and road-side units using several IR sensors
6	"Light Fidelity (Li-Fi) as an alternative data transmission medium in VANET", "IEEE European Modelling symposium" [6]	2017	Li-Fi	VANET simulator [15]	Optimized latency and introduce Li-Fi technology but it need to maintain a straight position

3   Implementation and Proposed Work

Here in the proposed system it is assumed that it is the driverless and autonomous vehicle scenario where, the OBU consist of two phase, where phase one is already derived in [10] where the phase two consist of all the rights to take over the vehicle in control whenever a unreliable network or signal disconnection is from with RSU is encountered.

The proposed block diagram named as "ITS based OBU" for the mechanism is shown below in Fig. 5 named as "Block Diagram of ITS based OBU" is separated into two parts, phase1 and 2, here we shall observe the operation for phase 2, if the connectivity from RSU with OBU is lost then, the activation signal from phase 1 to the mechanism in phase 2 is send. Where, possibility of the connection reestablishment is found then, the deactivation signal from phase 1 to the mechanism in phase 2 is send. Here in this scenario, phase 1 consist of global system for mobile communication board which acts as a RSU, aarduino nano micro controller board for decision making and network service is used as a RSU signal broadcaster. A dedicated and controlled closed environment is used to perform this test which will vary from real life and day-to-day environment.

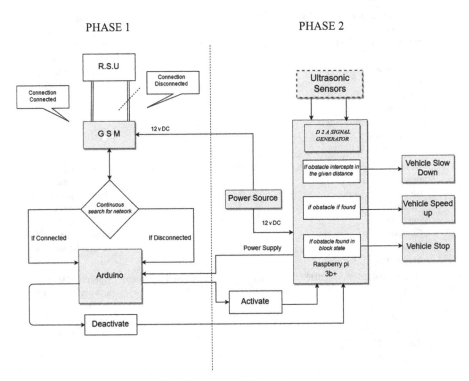

Fig. 5. Proposed block diagram

When phase 1 conveys the signal, operation of phase 2 starts. When phase 1 disconnects from the network the phase 2 activates and the mechanism starts. Phase 2 consists of ultrasonic sensors as an input of data sensors is located on the front, back and both sides of the vehicle. The sensors takes data and the mechanism starts an action to slow down the car or speed up as described in the algorithm and parameters in Sect. 3.1. The test bed is limited to 15 cm distance for a controlled atmosphere, where ultrasonic sensors have 3000 cm as working range in real terms.

Below we will have a look at the algorithm for the phase 1 followed by phase 2 which is used for the operation of this proposed work.

3.1 Proposed Algorithm

The algorithm 1 for ITS based OBU was derived for phase 1 in [10], where signal state was given as (i), 0 is the connected state and 1 is disconnected state. There, the system will continuously check for the signal whether it is connected or not. If the signal state is disconnected from the road side unit then, the phase 1 will send a request to phase 2 to activate the mechanism. If the vehicle is connected with the road side unit then, the phase 1 will send request to phase 2 to stand by the system in the on board unit placed in vehicles.

Therefore focusing further to this paper the below given algorithm consist of phase 2 where, the input is received from phase 1. The system will be activated and will start performing accordingly. Here, the system state is denoted as i (where, i = 0, 1) i.e. 1 = ON and 0 = OFF. The algorithm works in three phases denoted as F = Front, S = Sides (left and right) and B = Back, where all three of the phases works simultaneously. In the proposed block diagram when the GSM board stops receiving signal from network provider which acts as a RSU then, the arduinonano will follow the instructions provided in the form as shown in algorithm 2.

This algorithm is divided into 3 phases, 1st phase is front side which is denoted as (F), 2nd is both sides which is denoted as (S) which includes left (L) and right (R) both sides and 3rd is back side which is denoted as (B). In 1st phase the system will check for the signal state, if the system state is off then no action will be taken but, if the system state is on then, the mechanism will be activated.

When the mechanism is activated it will simultaneously takes readings from all the three phases. Here, the first phase will take readings from the ultrasonic sensor which is located in the front side of the vehicle, this readings will be send to system i.e. if the front side sensor will detect obstacle which is having distance more than 15 cm then, no action will be taken to the actuators. Else, the condition will apply where if the distance will be lesser than 15 cm then, the vehicle will reduce the speed with the help of the actuators, and if the distance will reduce the distance to 10 cm then the vehicle will stop. Thus, this process will be carried out with all the three phases at the same time to avoid vehicle collision.

Algorithm for ITS based OBU Phase 2

1. i ←System_ State
2. ▷ Where, i is used to check the system state whether it is on or off i.e. 1 = on and 0 = off
3. for F← d [vary from1 to n where F→ front, and d → distance]
4. do if i = = 1 [Front Phase(F)]
5.   then, send " System On "signal
6.   Initiate sensor reading from a and b
7.   ▷ Where, a and b are the sensors for F.
8.   n ← Sensor_ Range
9.   n1← Threshold_ Value for slow down vehicle
10.   if d >n1
11.   then, send "Do Not Stop" signal
12.   else if d <n1
13.   then send " slow Down Vehicle" signal until d ≥ n1
14.   Activate Actuator until d ≥ n1
15.   n2← Threshold_ Value to stop the vehicle for F
16.   else d < n2
17.   send "Stop Vehicle " signal for F
18.   Release Actuator after d ≥ n2
19. do if i= =1 [Side Phase (S)]
20.   then, send "System On " signal
21.   Initiate sensor reading from c & d and e & f
22.   ▷ Where, c & d are left side (L) sensors and e & f are right side (R) sensors
23.   do if d ≥ n2
24.   then, send "Do Not Stop" signal
25.   else if d <n2
26.   then, send "Slow Down Vehicle " signal until d ≥ n2
27.   Activate Actuator until d ≥ n2
28.   n3 ← Threshold_ Value to stop the vehicle for S
29.   else d <n3
30.   send "Stop Vehicle "signal for S
31.   Release Actuator after d ≥ n2
32. do if i = = 1 [Back Phase(B)]
33.   then, send "System On "signal
34.   Initiate sensor reading from g and h
35.   ▷ Where, g and h are the sensors for B
36.   do if d ≥ n1
37.   then, send "Do Not Stop " signal
38.   else if d <n1
39.   then, send "Slow Down Vehicle" signal until d ≥ n1
40.   Activate Actuator until d ≥ n1
41.   else d <n2
42.   send "Stop Vehicle " signal for B
43.   Release Actuator after d ≥ n1
44.   else i = =0
45.   do "Stand by" Signal to the system
46. Repeat Step - 3 until i = =1
47. End

4 Comparative Analysis

The comparative analysis of the ITS based OBU had been analyzed and reading between ultrasonic sensor and infrared sensor are obtained which are given as below in Table 2.

Table 2. Comparative analysis of US-IR sensor in VANET

Sr. no.	Objects	Ultrasonic sensor (ms)	Infrared sensor (ms)	Infrared sensor [9]
1	Cardboard	8.6	9	10.6
2	Paper sheet	40	20	20.2
3	Sponge	5	20	21.6
4	Wood	9	35	36.6
5	Plastic	4.3	24	25.1
6	Rubber	4.4	57	58.3
7	Tile	11	23	23.8
8	Aluminum	11	13.2	NA
9	Glass	10	NA	NA
10	Smoke	4	15	NA
11	Fog	6	17	NA
12	Water	19	22	NA

The above given results are obtained under a closed and dedicated environment which may differ from real life environment which has to be adjust accordingly when performed in real environment. The result itself denotes the clear indication that the ultra sonic sensor in any circumstances gives better results against infrared sensors.

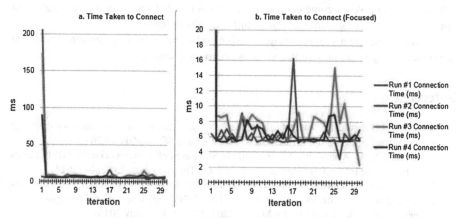

Fig. 6. Comparative of IR sensor in terms of connection

The above given Fig. 6 describes the comparative graph of response time in milliseconds and in Fig. 7 the graph of the comparative results using no connection is obtained.

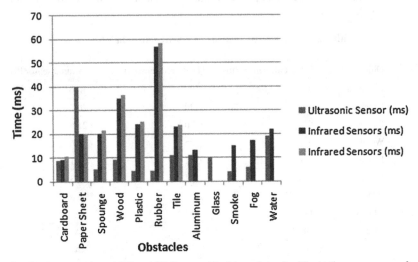

Fig. 7. Comparative of US and IR *Source:* Fictitious data, for illustration purposes only.

5 Conclusion and Future Work

There is a lot of work done in VANET but are dependent on certain connectivity with RSU thus, during the implementation of this proposed work a successful outcome of phase 1 in [10] and phase 2 with interconnection of boards and sensors with low response time with the comparative outcome is obtained. It is believed that a more optimized algorithm can be obtained and can achieve more fruitful results in future.

In future, one can also work on new design and architecture to gain more optimized response time by using new sensor such as microwave sensor.

References

1. Nzouonta, J., Rajgure, N., Wang, G., Borcea, C.: VANET routing on city roads using real-time vehicular traffic information. IEEE Trans. Veh. Technol. **58**(7), 3609–3626 (2009)
2. Salahuddin, M.A., Al-Fuqaha, A., Guizani, M.: Software-defined networking for RSU clouds in support of the internet of vehicles. IEEE Internet Things J. **2**(2), 133–144 (2014)
3. Truong, N.B., Lee, G.M., Ghamri-Doudane, Y.: Software defined networking-based vehicular adhoc network with fog computing. In: 2015 IFIP/IEEE International Symposium on Integrated Network Management (IM), pp. 1202–1207. IEEE (May 2015)
4. Joshi, J., Singh, A., Moitra, L.G., Deka, M.J.: DASITS: driver assistance system in intelligent transport system. In: 2016 30th International Conference on Advanced Information Networking and Applications Workshops (WAINA), pp. 545–550. IEEE (March 2016)

5. Tayeb, S., Pirouz, M., Latifi, S.: A raspberry-pi prototype of smart transportation. In: 2017 25th International Conference on Systems Engineering (ICSEng), pp. 176–182. IEEE (August 2017)

6. Agyemang, J.O., Kponyo, J.J., Mouzna, J.: Light Fidelity (LiFi) as an alternative data transmission medium in VANET. In: 2017 European Modelling Symposium (EMS), pp. 213–217. IEEE (November 2017)

7. Shrestha, R., Bajracharya, R., Nam, S.Y.: Challenges of future VANET and cloud-based approaches. Wirel. Commun. Mob. Comput. **2018** (2018)

8. Liang, W., Li, Z., Zhang, H., Wang, S., Bie, R.: Vehicular ad hoc networks: architectures, research issues, methodologies, challenges, and trends. Int. J. Distrib. Sens. Netw. **11**(8), 745303 (2015)

9. Adarsh, S., Kaleemuddin, S.M., Bose, D., Ramachandran, K.I.: Performance comparison of Infrared and ultrasonic sensors for obstacles of different materials in vehicle/robot navigation applications. In IOP Conference Series: Materials Science and Engineering, vol. 149, no. 1, p. 012141. IOP Publishing (September 2016)

10. Kayasth, B.A., Patel, R.M., Patel, J.R.: Intelligent transport system based fall-back mechanism-an alternative for safety approach in VANET. In: 2019 IEEE 5th International Conference for Convergence in Technology (I2CT), pp. 1–4. IEEE (March 2019)

11. Chaubey, N.: Security analysis of vehicular ad hoc networks (VANETs): a comprehensive study. Int. J. Secur. Appl. **10**, 261–274 (2016)

12. Chaubey, N.K., Yadav, D.: A taxonomy of Sybil attacks in vehicular ad-hoc network (VANET). In: Rao, R., Jain, V., Kaiwartya, O., Singh, N. (eds.) IoT and Cloud Computing Advancements in Vehicular Ad-Hoc Networks, pp. 174–190. IGI Global, Hershey (2020). https://doi.org/10.4018/978-1-7998-2570-8.ch009

13. Mejri, M.N., Ben-Othman, J., Hamdi, M.: Survey on VANET security challenges and possible cryptographic solutions. Veh. Commun. **1**(2), 53–66 (2014)

14. Sumayya, P.A., Shefeena, P.S.: Vanet based vehicle tracking module for safe and efficient road transportation system. Procedia Comput. Sci. **46**, 1173–1180 (2015)

15. VANET Simulation Tool. www.vanet-simulator.org/. Accessed 21 Oct 2018

RETRACTED CHAPTER: Design of a Network with VANET Sporadic Cloud Computing Applied to Traffic Accident Prevention

Amelec Viloria[1]([envelope]) [iD], Omar Bonerge Pineda Lezama[2] [iD], Noel Varela[1] [iD], and Jorge Luis Diaz Martínez[1] [iD]

[1] Universidad de la Costa, Barranquilla, Colombia
{aviloria7,nvarela2,jdiaz5}@cuc.edu.co
[2] Universidad Tecnológica Centroamericana (UNITEC), San Pedro Sula, Honduras
omarpineda@unitec.edu

Abstract. The study analyzes the bandwidth available in a segment of route in the VANET network, since this value directly affects sporadic cloud computing. For this purpose, the bandwidth was tested on a highly complex urban scenario, where a number of mobile nodes were used with random conditions both in mobility and in resources of transmission. The results of the tests show that the stability of the bandwidth available in each region is proportional to the number of real mobile nodes in the region. However, a considerable bandwidth is also reached with a smaller number of mobile nodes, but there is no stability in the region, thus causing the network to collapse. The VANET network simulation tool was NS-3, since it is currently one of the most commonly used free software that allows configure the simulation parameters in a vehicular environment. The urban simulation scenario is the historic center of the City of Bogotá, Colombia, which was created with SUMO for obtaining the mobility traces.

Keywords: Machine learning · Proactive control · Traffic · Smart cities · Autonomous computing · VANET

1 Introduction

In the last decade there has been a marked increase in the communication, storage and processing capabilities of mobile devices. These new capabilities, together with the development of wireless communications and the Internet, are driving the development of new and innovative applications, leading the user to have information and entertainment at any time and place [1, 2].

Taking advantage of these technological capabilities, Mobile Ad-hoc Networks (MANET) and Vehicular Ad-hoc Networks (VANET) were created, and can be used in areas of difficult access or without infrastructure. The research focuses on the design,

The original version of this chapter was retracted: The retraction note to this chapter is available at https://doi.org/10.1007/978-981-15-6648-6_28

evaluation and implementation of new protocols, in scenarios where the main challenge is the continuous changes in the network, due to the variability of the position in the nodes. These advances improve access to new communication services on the roads [2, 3].

Consistent with the above, it is possible to look forward to the future, since these types of networks will be very useful in Smart Cities, due to Intelligent Transportation Systems (ITS), which need robust communication environments to offer access in a high range of multimedia services, upload and download of information, access to social networks, etc. [4, 5]. Deploying these services requires storage and computing capabilities of the nodes outside the communication devices, therefore, a solution would be mobile cloud computing, due to its ability to provide all services by moving the storage and computing capabilities of the nodes to the cloud [6].

At present, the technological properties of portable devices allow to think about the implementation of sporadic Ad-hoc networks among a certain group of users [7, 8].

In this way, vehicles can be provided with a range of communication and storage services in a large territorial space where the coverage of networks such as GSM, 3G and LTE does not exist or is insufficient [9]. This application goes from the network link with users for the provision of vehicular intercommunication requests to the deployment of smart cities through the sporadic cloud protocols and states [10].

This study focuses on the programming and simulation of state machine for the creation of sporadic clouds, in order to illustrate and demonstrate how the system works with the different states that could occur in a given scenario with cars.

The general objective of this research is program and simulate the concept of sporadic clouds in Ad-hoc vehicle networks through the use of free software. The specific objectives are:

1) Analyze the behavior of the state machine for the creation of sporadic clouds according to the type of requirement.
2) Install and configure the simulation program (NS3), which allows its execution.
3) Program and simulate the state machine in NS3 for a given scenario in the city of Bogotá in Colombia.

1.1 Underlying Concepts

This chapter studies the operation of the Cloud-Based Mobile (CBM) state machine, developed in [11].

The project implementation is about the deployment of computer services through a sporadic cloud, applied within a VANET network. This is done to solve the limitations in the processing and storage capacity produced by the mobile nodes within a VANET network. Due to the limitations of mobile nodes when executing a service, it cannot perform its functions normally. For that reason, external resources are needed and the concept of vehicular cloud is used and, in this case, the state machine of the CBM.

The CBM state machine is composed of 5 states (see Fig. 1), for which it allows analyzing the requirements of the real mobile nodes and obtaining these resources within a VANET network. For the routing process it was decided to use the VNIBR protocol, mounted on a virtual layer, improving the performance of the services required by the nodes in mobile environments.

The operation of the CBM is based on several types of events, causing Physical Nodes (PN) to be in some states: Initial, Request for resources, Distribution, Reception and Collaboration [11, 12].

It all starts with the application layer (see Fig. 1), when the node sends a message requesting an increase in resources (M_AugmentationRequest) and activates the CBM process. As a first step, it verifies if this node is in a region of the road segment (note the state in Fig. 2, using Intersection-Flag = 0).

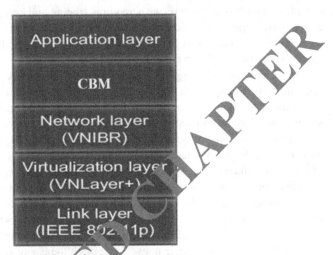

Fig. 1. Chain on communication protocols in mobile nodes [11].

When the L1VN node receives the request, it reviews the possibility of increasing resources with the help of the Collaborator Nodes (CN) that are in the cloud, and due to this, the following scenarios can be presented [13]:

- If there are no CN in the cloud, L1VN communicates to the requesting node the M_WithoutCollaborators message, and this node returns to the initial state. The application layer receives the M_UnavailableAugmentationService message.
- On the contrary, when there are CNs in the cloud, L1VN informs the amount of resources available through the M_CloudResourceInfo message.
- If resources are sufficient, the distribution of tasks continues. This process takes into account the distribution of the VNs along the segment of the road that is the cloud and the amount of resources available.

Then, the following scenarios [14] can be presented [14]:

- In the first scenario, the requesting node enters a junction before finishing the assignment of tasks.
- If the T_TaskDistribution timer ends its route three times before the task assignment is completed, the node returns to the request state and sends the M_ResourceRequest message back to the nearest L1VN, this is due to the availability of resources change because the CNs are moving.

- However, if the distribution was made before the time is up and the node is in the region, the latter sends the task to the sporadic cloud VN through the M_SendTaskToVN message. The VN presents these tasks to its collaborators through the M_SendTaskToCN message. Finally, the node changes to the task reception mode, only if the VN confirms if it accepts to carry out the assigned tasks [15].

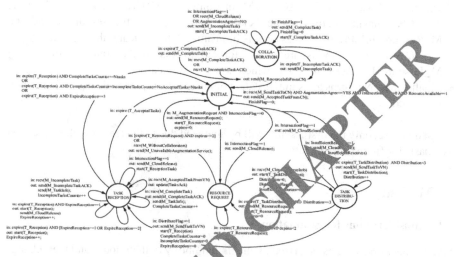

Fig. 2. Approximation of the CBM state machine [11].

The resource requesting node is notified if the CN's have completed the task, if it is incomplete, or did not agree to do it. Then, it sends that information to the application layer through the M_TaskInfo message. If more resources are needed to complete the unfinished and rejected tasks, the steps already mentioned throughout this section are performed. Finally, the requesting node changes to the initial state upon receiving notification of all tasks.

However, if this message is not received the following actions [16, 17] are performed:

- First the requesting node transmits the M_CloudRelease message to the cloud, with the objective that the collaborators immediately present the progress of the tasks assigned to the collaborators.
- Next, the node waits for incomplete tasks for a period of the T_Reception timer.

With respect to the collaborating nodes that participate in the augmentation task, they move from the initial state to the collaborative state upon receiving the M_SendTaskToCN message sent by the leader of the region and the process is constituted as follows [18–20]:

- If the collaborator completes the requested task, it sends the results directly to the petitioner node because it knows its MAC address, and thus avoids overloading the leader of the region.
- When the collaborator has an incomplete task, as explained above, it must present the progress upon receiving the M_CloudRelease message. To make this request, the CN sends the M_IncompleteTask message to the requesting node. This message contains very relevant information. The CN waits until the confirmation message is received, which are M_CompleteTaskACK or M_IncompleteTaskACK depending on the case.
- The CNs, having delivered the pending tasks, release the resources and the M_ResourceInfoFromCN message is transmitted to indicate the new availability of resources. L1VNs are also informed thanks to the transmission of the M_ResourceDiscovery message, which is sent periodically.
- Finally, the CN returns to its initial state, hoping to return to provide its services when requested.

In this case, only the first 2 states will be analyzed due to the length of the topic, and as a basis for future implementations.

2   Method

2.1   Considerations for Simulation

VANET networks are characterized by the high mobility of their nodes and their changing topology. These features produce failures in communications and communication devices within the network. These deficiencies are mostly due to the processing and storage capacities of the devices that make up that network, since they are less than the required capacities. For this reason, sporadic cloud computing was used as a solution, since it is made up of the CBL in conjunction with the VNIBR routing protocol, which improves the communication and mobility capabilities of VANET networks [21, 22].

In this case, only the following states will be evaluated: Initial and Requirement in sporadic cloud computing because these states are critical for the process of communication and allocation of resources between nodes, since the VANET network manages and organizes its components (virtual nodes), in order to meet the requirements requested by the mobile nodes (users) of VANET networks.

In order to verify the aforementioned, the experimentation will be carried out on a topology similar to the historic center of Bogota. This was designed with 7 rows and 7 columns (7 × 7 streets), within which are 400 fixed virtual nodes (regions) evenly distributed. The distribution was carried out as follows:

3 fixed virtual nodes are in the track segments, while 1 fixed virtual node is located at each intersection, as shown in Fig. 3.

In addition to these fixed virtual nodes (regions), mobile nodes will be placed within the fixed virtual nodes, so that they emulate the physical users of the network, generating communications and resource requests from one region to another. SUMO 0.23 software was used to generate traffic in the chosen scenario. The generated files containing the movement patterns of the cars were linked to NS-3 (version 3.25) by using NS2 Mobility Helper. In the simulation it is assumed that, initially, all the nodes are already within the scenario and each node performs its route generated in SUMO [23].

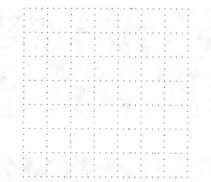

Fig. 3. Simulation scenario: historic center of Bogota.

2.2 Selection of Regions and Intersections for Simulation

Once the stage parameters are defined, the selection of a specific street where there are regions and intersections for the simulation will continue. To do this, first, a track segment and two joint intersections are chosen within the scenario. The regions of the chosen road segment are: 597–598–599, while the regions of the joint intersections are: 596–600, and are physically represented by virtual nodes with identification (ID: 292–296).

After this, a number of mobile nodes are assigned to these regions, and they will randomly request information or processing requirements. With all this, the available bandwidth capacity in each region can be evaluated when a requirement is made. For the simulation, the data rate was configured with 3G–4G technology for the different mobile physical nodes.

The simulation will be carried out 3 times, increasing the number of mobile nodes (10.50 and 100) within a track segment, with the purpose of contrasting the 3 measurements of bandwidth, and thus determining if a higher density of mobile nodes improves resources within the network.

2.3 Simulation of the CBM State Machine

The VNBR protocol assigns the corresponding level to each virtual node of the topology: the level 1 VNs, which are located at the intersections of the roads; the level 2 VNs, which appear next to the level 1 nodes (they are next to the intersections); and finally, the virtual nodes of level 3, which are among the nodes of level 2. As can be seen in Fig. 4, 5 nodes are assigned for each Way Number (WN), with their respective level. A particularity is that level 1 nodes are repeated for each WN because these nodes are shared for the road sections that are around it [24].

Before starting the program display, a scan of the mobile and virtual nodes of the simulation area is performed. As shown in Fig. 5, the virtual fixed nodes are 400 while the actual mobile nodes can be adjusted in the parameters of the simulation. In this case, 3 tests were performed, the first one with 10 mobile nodes (Fig. 5), the second test was performed with 50 mobile nodes (Fig. 6) and finally, it was performed with 100 mobile nodes (Fig. 7).

The following chapter presents the results obtained from the simulations with the aforementioned considerations, and an analysis of the obtained data is carried out.

```
WN: 38   Region: 592    RegionLevel: 1   Neig.Prev: -1    Neig.Next: 593
WN: 38   Region: 593    RegionLevel: 2   Neig.Prev: 592   Neig.Next: 594
WN: 38   Region: 594    RegionLevel: 3   Neig.Prev: 593   Neig.Next: 595
WN: 38   Region: 595    RegionLevel: 2   Neig.Prev: 594   Neig.Next: 596
WN: 38   Region: 596    RegionLevel: 1   Neig.Prev: 595   Neig.Next: -1
WN: 39   Region: 596    RegionLevel: 1   Neig.Prev: -1    Neig.Next: 597
WN: 39   Region: 597    RegionLevel: 2   Neig.Prev: 596   Neig.Next: 598
WN: 39   Region: 598    RegionLevel: 3   Neig.Prev: 597   Neig.Next: 599
WN: 39   Region: 599    RegionLevel: 2   Neig.Prev: 598   Neig.Next: 600
WN: 39   Region: 600    RegionLevel: 1   Neig.Prev: 599   Neig.Next: -1
WN: 40   Region: 600    RegionLevel: 1   Neig.Prev: -1    Neig.Next: 601
```

Fig. 4. Assignment of levels to virtual nodes.

```
scanning topology: 410 nodes...
scan topology... 99 nodes visited (24.1%)
scan topology... 199 nodes visited (48.5%)
scan topology... 299 nodes visited (72.9%)
scan topology... 399 nodes visited (97.3%)
scanning topology: calling graphviz layout
scanning topology: all done.
```

Fig. 5. Scanning of virtual and mobile nodes (10 assigned mobile nodes).

```
scanning topology: 450 nodes...
scan topology... 99 nodes visited (22.0%)
scan topology... 199 nodes visited (44.2%)
scan topology... 299 nodes visited (66.4%)
scan topology... 399 nodes visited (88.7%)
scanning topology: calling graphviz layout
scanning topology: all done.
```

Fig. 6. Scanning of virtual and mobile nodes (50 mobile nodes assigned).

```
scanning topology: 500 nodes...
scan topology... 99 nodes visited (19.8%)
scan topology... 199 nodes visited (39.8%)
scan topology... 299 nodes visited (59.8%)
scan topology... 399 nodes visited (79.8%)
scan topology... 499 nodes visited (99.8%)
scanning topology: calling graphviz layout
scanning topology: all done.
```

Fig. 7. Scanning of virtual and mobile nodes (100 mobile nodes assigned).

3   Analysis and Results

This section will detail the results obtained from the bandwidth capabilities for sporadic cloud computing within a VANET scenario. All these values were extracted from the simulation.

The main objective of the simulation is to determine the capacity of the bandwidth during some requirement of a mobile node within a region. To obtain these values, certain conditions were established in the virtual nodes such as user density, random bandwidth, and the network in which users operate (3G–4G). All this to check the operation of sporadic cloud computing within a VANET scenario and determine if the established proposal is viable.

To obtain realistic results of simulated bandwidths, simulator conditions were maintained for all experiments.

3.1 Bandwidth Assessment (BW) in Each Region of a Road and Intersection

In VANET networks, the speed in the transmission of information (data, images, videos, apps, etc.) is of great importance, since certain values must meet minimum requirements to establish vehicular communications.

Depending on the range of these values, it is possible to determine whether the proposal for sporadic cloud computing for the transmission and processing of information in VANET networks is viable. For this research, the fundamental value used to determine the viability of this implementation is bandwidth.

3.2 Bandwidth

Bandwidth is the amount of information that can be transmitted in a second by means of communication. It depends on the bit handling capacity, the speed of information handling by electronic circuits [25].

the parameters were established in the previous chapter, the graphs of the available bandwidth in a track segment were obtained. Different values were obtained for each metric depending on the transmission rate, range and density of mobile nodes in each virtual node [26, 27].

Figures 8, 9 and 10 show that the implementation of the CBM state machine and the VNIBR routing protocol in a track segment of a VANET network is efficient, because the bandwidth available as a collaboration resource is constant throughout the road segment, but only when there is a large number of real mobile physical nodes within the region of operation. This is understandable since having a greater number of users within a region can provide more resources on it. In addition, these resources are equitable and prolonged in each region of the analyzed road segment.

Another case is when there is a small number of real mobile nodes, since the available bandwidth is not constant and is limited to the mobility of the nodes. This occurs due

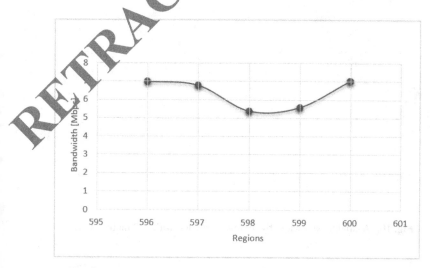

Fig. 8. Available bandwidth by region, simulated with 10 mobile nodes.

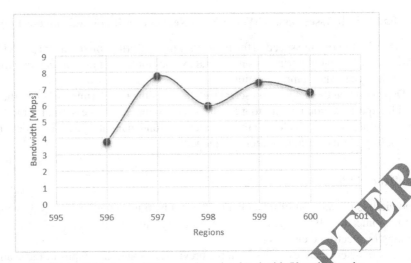

Fig. 9. Available bandwidth per region, simulated with 50 mobile nodes.

to the small number of mobile nodes, since these nodes can change region quickly and the available resources will vary according to the position of the node within the road segment. Although, it would be convenient only in the collaboration of resources since with a small number of users there is less load on the network. Therefore, the implementation shown is efficient in communication tasks in locations similar to the presented topology, but its main deficiency is the stability in the delivery of resources.

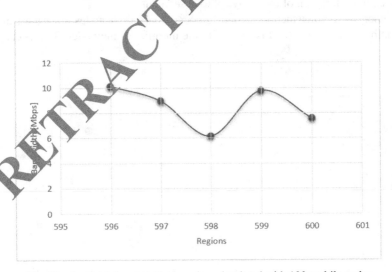

Fig. 10. Available bandwidth by region, simulated with 100 mobile nodes

4   Conclusions

VANET networks are in a position of great expectation, especially due to the scenarios that have several intersections, in which there is lack of coverage, or loss of it due to existing obstacles (buildings, geography, etc.). A fundamental characteristic for the proper functioning of a VANET network is sporadic cloud computing. In this study, the implementation of the sporadic cloud in the VNIBR protocol has begun, simulating a real environment made up of intersections and road segments [28, 29].

In the study, the programming and simulation of a sporadic cloud over VANET networks was projected for a given scenario in the city of Bogotá. This could be achieved through the use of NS-3 and SUMO, which are free software. SUMO was used to obtain the traces that simulate the historic center, which are distributed as grids emulating roads and intersections, and to implement vehicular traffic (mobile nodes) on th. These traces were then used in the NS-3 program to implement the VNIBR protocol and sporadic cloud computing. These programs are widely accepted by Ad-Hoc network researchers due to their high reliability.

VNIBR protocol was used because it is the one that has the greatest adjustment for the proposed scenario, since it is developed to work in environments composed of roads and intersections, and also because it is used in conjunction with the CBM state machine, in which, for its implementation, the first two states (initial and requirement) were used because of their importance, since they serve for the management, location and allocation of resources to users within the network. Between these two states, an analysis was made on the amount of bandwidth available within a region for an urban scenario.

The bandwidth available in the communication is indispensable, since it determines the speed in the transmission of information. In this case, it can be mentioned that the implementation of the 2 states in sporadic cloud computing works optimally due to the stability of the available bandwidth only with a large number of users within a track segment. When there is a number of mobile nodes, there is the availability of the resource, but this is unstable because it depends on the mobility of the collaborating nodes.

In addition, can be mentioned that cars work with 3G and LTE (4G) networks which allow better access to the Internet, making it possible for vehicles to handle large bandwidths in scenarios where traffic is slow and bulky. Therefore, the available bandwidth per region is limited by the number of mobile nodes, causing the scalability of the CBM to have restrictions due to the aforementioned characteristic.

Based on the objectives achieved in this study, research lines are generated to continue the development of the entire sporadic cloud, and the implementation could be achieved in a real scenario in future research or projects.

References

1. Mittal, A., Ostojic, M., Mahmassani, H.S.: Active traffic signal control for mixed vehicular traffic in connected environments: self-identifying platoon strategy (No. 19-05931) (2019)
2. Cheikhrouhou, O., Koubaa, A., Zarrad, A.: A cloud based disaster management system. J. Sens. Actuator Netw. **9**(1), 6 (2020)

3. Alam, K.M., El Saddik, A.: C2PS: a digital twin architecture reference model for the cloud-based cyber-physical systems. IEEE Access **5**, 2050–2062 (2017)

4. Lum, C., Koper, C.S., Wu, X., Johnson, W., Stoltz, M.: Examining the empirical realities of proactive policing through systematic observations and computer-aided dispatch data. Police Q. (2020). https://doi.org/10.1177/1098611119896081

5. Ferenchak, N.N., Marshall, W.E.: Equity analysis of proactively-vs. reactively-identified traffic safety issues. Transp. Res. Rec. **2673**(7), 596–606 (2019)

6. Tucker, C., Nelson, H.T., Sarbora, R.S.: U.S. Patent No. 10,534,337. Washington, DC: U.S. Patent and Trademark Office (2020)

7. Azari, A., Papapetrou, P., Denic, S., Peters, G.: User traffic prediction for proactive resource management: learning-powered approaches. arXiv preprint arXiv:1906.00951 (2019)

8. Gillani, R., Nasir, A.: Proactive control of hybrid electric vehicles for maximum fuel efficiency. In: 2019 16th International Bhurban Conference on Applied Sciences and Technology (IBCAST), pp. 396–401. IEEE (2019)

9. Rai, A., Kannan, R.J.: Co-simulation based finite state machine for telematic and data compression microservices in IoT. Wirel. Pers. Commun. **105**(3), 1069–1082 (2019)

10. Batkovic, I., Zanon, M., Ali, M., Falcone, P.: Real-time constrained trajectory planning and vehicle control for proactive autonomous driving with road users. In: 2019 18th European Control Conference (ECC), pp. 256–262. IEEE (2019)

11. Zhao, W.: Performance optimization for state machine replication based on application semantics: a review. J. Syst. Softw. **112**, 96–109 (2016)

12. Bortnikov, V., Cahana, Z., Ifergan-Shachor, S., Shnayderman, I.: U.S. Patent No. 10,083,217. Washington, DC: U.S. Patent and Trademark Office (2018)

13. Viloria, A., Robayo, P.V.: Virtual network level of application composed IP networks connected with systems-(NETS peer-to-peer). Indian J. Sci. Technol. **9**, 46 (2016)

14. Hu, Y., Chen, C., He, T., He, J., Guan, X., Yang, B.: Proactive power management scheme for hybrid electric storage system in EV via MPC method. IEEE Trans. Intell. Transp. Syst. (2019)

15. Al Shehri, A., et al.: U.S. Patent No. 10,533,937. Washington, DC: U.S. Patent and Trademark Office (2020)

16. Formosa, N., Quddus, M., Man, S., Abdel-Aty, M., Yuan, J.: Predicting real-time traffic conflicts using deep learning. Accid. Anal. Prev. **136**, 105429 (2020)

17. Zahid, M., Chen, Y., Jamal, A., Memon, M.Q.: Short term traffic state prediction via hyperparameter optimization based classifiers. Sensors **20**(3), 685 (2020)

18. Lu, Z., Xia, J., Wang, M., Nie, Q., Ou, J.: Short-term traffic flow forecasting via multi-regime modeling and ensemble learning. Appl. Sci. **10**(1), 356 (2020)

19. Paranjothi, A., Khan, M.S., Patan, R., Parizi, R.M., Atiquzzaman, M.: VANETomo: a congestion identification and control scheme in connected vehicles using network tomography. Comput. Commun. **151**, 275–289 (2020)

20. Ramanathan, R., et al.: U.S. Patent No. 10,268,467. Washington, DC: U.S. Patent and Trademark Office (2019)

21. Ma, C., Zhou, J., Xu, X.D., Xu, J.: Evolution regularity mining and gating control method of urban recurrent traffic congestion: a literature review. J. Adv. Transp. (2020)

22. Jha, S., et al.: Derecho: fast state machine replication for cloud services. ACM Trans. Comput. Syst. (TOCS) **36**(2), 1–49 (2019)

23. Liu, J., Khattak, A.: Informed decision-making by integrating historical on-road driving performance data in high-resolution maps for connected and automated vehicles. J. Intell. Transp. Syst. **24**(1), 11–23 (2020)

24. Martinov, G.M., Ljubimov, A.B., Martinova, L.I.: From classic CNC systems to cloud-based technology and back. Robot. Comput.-Integr. Manuf. **63**, 101927 (2020)

25. Chen, X., Wang, H., Ma, Y., Zheng, X., Guo, L.: Self-adaptive resource allocation for cloud-based software services based on iterative QoS prediction model. Future Gener. Comput. Syst. **105**, 287–296 (2020)

26. Viloria, A., Acuña, G.C., Franco, D.J.A., Hernández-Palma, H., Fuentes, J.P., Rambal, E.P.: Integration of data mining techniques to PostgreSQL database manager system. Procedia Comput. Sci. **155**, 575–580 (2019)

27. Perez, R., Vásquez, C., Viloria, A.: An intelligent strategy for faults location in distribution networks with distributed generation. J. Intell. Fuzzy Syst. **36**(2), 1627–1637 (2019)

28. Chaubey, N.: Security analysis of vehicular ad hoc networks (VANETs): a comprehensive study. Int. J. Secur. Appl. **10**, 261–274 (2016)

29. Chaubey, N.K., Yadav, D.: A taxonomy of Sybil attacks in vehicular ad-hoc network (VANET). In: Rao, R., Jain, V., Kaiwartya, O., Singh, N. (eds.) IoT and Cloud Computing Advancements in Vehicular Ad-Hoc Networks, pp. 174–190. IGI Global, Hershey (2020). https://doi.org/10.4018/978-1-7998-2570-8.ch009

RETRACTED CHAPTER: Management System for Optimizing Public Transport Networks: GPS Record

Jesús Silva[1]([✉]) [iD], Noel Varela[1] [iD], Erick Guerra Alemán[1] [iD], and Omar Bonerge Pineda Lezama[2] [iD]

[1] Universidad de la Costa, Barranquilla, Colombia
{aviloria7,nvarela2,eguerra4}@cuc.edu.co
[2] Universidad Tecnológica Centroamericana (UNITEC), San Pedro Sula, Honduras
omarpineda@unitec.edu

Abstract. As cities continue to grow in size and population, the design of public transport networks becomes complicated, given the wide diversity in the origins and destinations of users [1], as well as the saturation of vehicle infrastructure in large cities despite their attempts to adapt it according to population distribution. This indicates that, in order to reduce users' travel time, it is necessary to implement alternative road solutions to the use of cars, increasing investment in public transportation [2, 3] by conducting a comprehensive analysis of the state of transportation. This situation has made appear the solutions and development oriented to transportation based on Internet of Things (IoT) which allows, in a first stage, monitoring of public transport systems, in order to optimize the deployment of transport units and thus reduce the time of transfer of users through the cities [4]. These solution proposals are focused on information collected from user resources (data collected through smart phones) to create a common database [5]. The present study proposes the development of an intelligent monitoring and management system for public transportation networks using a hybrid communication architecture based on wireless node networks using IPv6 and cellular networks (LTE, LTE-M).

Keywords: Machine learning · Proactive control · Traffic · Smart cities · Public transport networks

1 Introduction

This paper presents the first part of a scalable platform that allows to connect diverse sources of monitoring and information through a hybrid network, formed by different wireless networks [6]. This platform is designed to adapt to the new needs of the city of Medellin in Colombia as it is implemented, offering a way of intercommunication with

The original version of this chapter was retracted: The retraction note to this chapter is available at https://doi.org/10.1007/978-981-15-6648-6_28

new and existing systems which allows to start the conversion to an intelligent city, by first facing one of the most important problems at this time: Public transportation [7].

Public transport is a determining factor in mobility. This statement offers a perspective of individuals in their socioeconomic and spatial reality (age, gender, social and labor category) broader than the term transport, which is limited to a relation of supply and demand expressed schematically, on the one hand, in the amount of infrastructures and means of transport and, on the other hand, in the number of trips per day, mode, itinerary, time [8–11].

Public transport and traffic are associated with the economic and technical factors that determine the movement of people, while mobility is focused on individuals and their environment. Although they are different dimensions, it is clear that proper transport planning has a positive impact on mobility. This new conception of public transport materializes in the recent policies, plans and projects in Medellin—at least in discourse— under the concept of comprehensiveness or integration: comprehensive or integrated transportation in which various means of transportation are articulated, according with the territorial ordering in the area of the city-region. Thus, an attempt has been made to overcome the conception of public transport as simply satisfying the conditions of the supply and demand for travel, based on the delimitation of the economically active population, to recognize its importance in transforming the socioeconomic structure and the social space based on the participation of the population [12–16].

The proposal is focused on solving the challenge of knowing the status of public transport, dividing it into three essential parts: the first part deals with the general hardware and software modules required for the proper operation of the system [17], then briefly describes the network architecture that will be used and the technologies and protocols required for the operation of the network. Finally, the third part describes the general architecture of the system and defines the way to communicate the information collected from the bus network to information system for subsequent deployment to the users' devices.

2 Development

Based on the characteristics of the different types of transport systems analyzed (Metrobus, Transmilenio, etc.) and the different needs of the users, a modular, scalable and minimally invasive solution is proposed, which uses new generation and low-cost technologies. These characteristics allow the implementation of monitoring and communication devices in a simple way, making use of existing infrastructure. The following is a general description of the elements that make up the system at the hardware and software levels [18].

2.1 System Elements

The elements of the system are divided into: Monitoring modules, which include the bus and station modules; Web and mobile application; and Information system [19].

2.1.1 Bus Monitoring (A: Thread, and B: Thread+LTE)

With the purpose of informing the level of saturation in transport lines, modules will be implemented for obtaining the number of users in the unit at all times. In the same way to know the location of the units, a GPS module will be installed to operate in conjunction with a BLE transceiver to detect micro location devices "Beacons" to inform the user about the station in which he is through a web application of the system [20]. As it can be seen in Fig. 1, it is proposed to distribute this monitoring in two types of modules according to the type of transport in which the system will be implemented. For transport systems with marked stations, for example RTP, type B nodes will be used, on the other hand, for transport systems with stations with fixed structures, for example MB, type A or B nodes can be used indistinctly.

The design of the nodes is shaped as follows [21, 22]:

- Control unit.
- Ascent/descent counters with direction detection
- GPS Module
- Beacons reading module
- Thread communication module
- LTE communication module (Type B only).

Figure 2 shows the block diagram of the ascent/descent modules. The monitoring modules will be distributed at each of the unit's ascent and descent points [23], and will be responsible for obtaining the ascent and descent information at each point of the unit, and communicating it to the central bus module to calculate the current number of people within the unit.

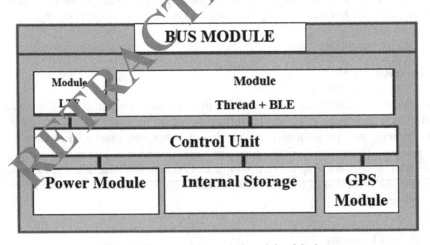

Fig. 1. Diagram of the central module of the bus.

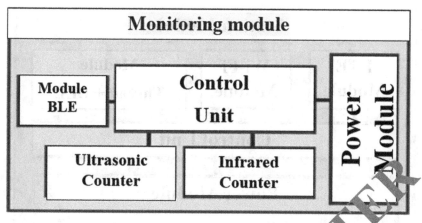

Fig. 2. Diagram of the bus ascent/descent monitoring module

2.1.2 Station Modules

As previously mentioned, this system focuses on distributing the devices on the buses, with the aim of ensuring the versatility of the solution, in other words, that any transport system is applicable to the solution with the least possible adjustments. However, it is necessary to place identification modules in the stations for a correct synchronization and deployment of user information. These modules can be completely autonomous and with minimal impact on the current infrastructure. According to the type of transport system in which the solution will be implemented, two types of modules are proposed [24, 25]:

– Signalled stations

In the case of routes that only have signposted stations, "Beacons" will be placed at each station. This device will allow to obtain the proximity of the buses to the station based on the signal intensity, that is, whether they are arriving, departing or standing at the station. The device in conjunction with the GPS module will obtain information on the location of the unit, allowing users who have the mobile application on their devices to visualize the station they are in automatically and without consuming their data packet or GPS module, as long as they are compatible with the protocol to be used in the Beacons [26–28] (Fig. 3).

– Fixed structure stations

These modules only act as repeaters and border nodes of the Thread network deployed between stations and buses. The main feature to highlight about these nodes is their capability to adapt to the communication technology at the Internet level that is available in the place, i.e. you can implement the system communication at the Internet level from a module, LTE, 3G, Wi-Fi or Ethernet, among others [29].

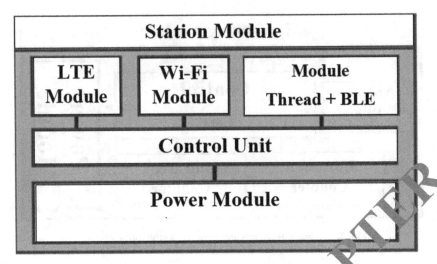

Fig. 3. Station module diagram with fixed structure.

– Web application

For the deployment of information to users, a web application will be developed for allowing access to system information from any compatible device, and adapt this web application to run on smartphones with Android and iOS operating systems.

The mobile application would allow transport users to visualize the status of the lines including: arrival time of the next bus at a specific stop, level of saturation of the bus (number of people/specified capacity, different transport routes registered in the system that stop at the same stop, as well as to automatically detect the stop it is at by detecting the "Beacon" installed in the stop [30].

2.2 Information System

The information collected from the transport systems shall be communicated through the LTE modules with the information system. This is the one in charge of processing and storing all the information of the network so that it can be displayed in an easy and understandable way by means of graphics and indicators of the different variables of the system [31].

The information system will be hosted in a private cloud platform and managed through the use of REST services. These will interconnect the different nodes of the system, as well as the mobile clients and web applications [32].

2.3 Network Architecture

For the communication of the different monitoring points, a hybrid network architecture is proposed, consisting of a network of wireless nodes that provides a first communication infrastructure between the transport units and a set of LTE links that allow all the nodes to communicate to an information system in the cloud which distributes the information to the users of the transport network (Fig. 4).

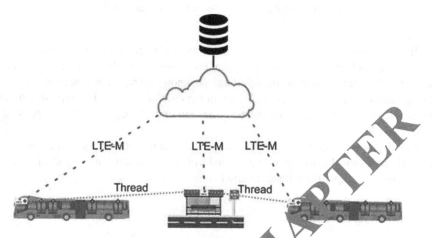

Fig. 4. Basic communication architecture.

It is necessary to place monitoring nodes at different points of the transportation unit. These points will communicate wirelessly via a Bluetooth Mesh network [2]. The information will be concentrated in the main node of the vehicle which will communicate the monitored variables with the nearby nodes using the Thread network and, in case the vehicle has a LTE modem, the information will also be sent by this means to the information system (Fig. 5).

Fig. 5. Distribution of nodes in transportation units.

In order to interconnect the different transportation units with the fixed structure stations and later communicate with the information system, Thread-based nodes will be deployed in the stations, which will allow direct communication between stations and transport units, optimizing the distribution of the variables monitored at each point in an independent way, thus helping to feed the automatic learning algorithms that will be implemented in the node network (Fig. 6), in the same way that in the transport units some specific stations will be selected (based on their geographical location) to include in their node an LTE modem for allowing the communication of the nodes with the information system [33–35].

Fig. 6. Distribution of nodes in transportation stations

In the case of stations that do not have the necessary features to operate a communication node, such as those consisting only of a sign on a road, "Beacons" micro location devices will be placed to allow transport units to know and report the location of the unit through the station identifier (Fig. 7) and, in the case of users with compatible mobile devices, to obtain information on the next transport units through the mobile application developed [36–39].

Finally, the users of the system (passengers, operators and managers of the transport network) will view the information collected from the system through a web application on any device compatible with an internet connection.

2.4   System Architecture

For the communication at a logical level of all the components of the system, a modular software architecture is proposed to allow the monitoring and notification to the modules by using REST services for the first case and PUSH notifications for the second one.

Fig. 7. Proximity detection at signaled stations.

This architecture is greatly simplified in the communication with the Thread nodes because this protocol allows redirecting the information frames directly thanks to the implementation of IPv6 within the node communication [8].

The nodes distributed in the buses communicate the information collected through the Bluetooth Mesh network deployed inside the bus, later this is communicated through the Thread network until reaching a border node from which it will communicate to the Web server using Web services [40, 41].

Once on the server, this information will be processed and stored in the information system database, and then, based on the source of the information, the nodes and users will be notified at the relevant stations through the notification channels. PUSH, which will prevent the Web application and the network nodes from constantly "pulsing" [42].

3   Implementation

Up to this moment, the analysis and design of the monitoring modules inside the bus has been carried out. These modules manage the users' account inside the transport units. Two prototypes were developed in this way, the first one using the nRF24L01+ transceiver with the objective of communicating the different nodes installed inside a unit. Due to the modularity of the system, the characteristics of the wireless sensor network can be modified, so the second prototype was chosen to use a set of different sensors and transceivers. In this second case, an infrared cut sensor was added in conjunction with the infrared distance sensors and an XBee S2C as a communication module between nodes (Fig. 8).

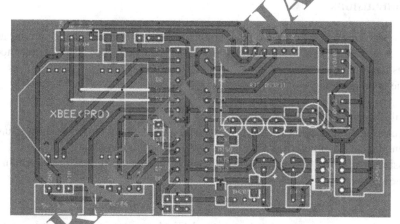

Fig. 8. Monitoring module PCB design using XBee.

Finally, an adaptable module was designed to which any of the two transceivers can be connected, as well as the different sensors analyzed. This last design was made in EAGLE and seeks to be compact and compatible with any of the transceivers tested, using ZigBee through XBee using the XB1 module or through BLE through nRF24L01+ using the JP3 connector (Fig. 9).

Likewise, the research process included the development of cards based on nRF52840 for the deployment of bus and station nodes. These modules are in charge of generating the multiprotocol Thread network with BLE for the communication of the different transport units.

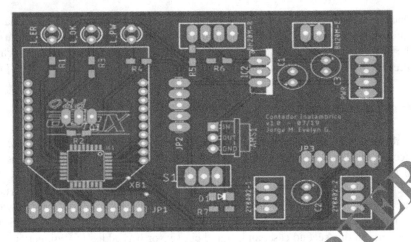

Fig. 9. Monitoring node PCB design at EAGLE

4   Conclusions

The proposed system differs from other similar implementations in the communication architecture of transport vehicles which allows the node to know the status of other nodes besides its own.

The main advantages of the proposal are

- Easily scalable architecture.
- Wireless nodes that allow high flexibility in the installation within the transport units.
- Communication of the transport units without internet connection
- Possibility of using different types of transport units and different routes within the same system.

As future work, the communication network between buses and stations based on the Thread protocol will be developed, the LTE-M communication modules will be developed, and the information system will be developed with the necessary communication technologies to verify the correct operation of the system, some nodes will also be deployed in designated vehicles which will be monitored on a defined road within the city in order to carry out operational tests in a real environment and verify the functionality of the system.

In a next stage, it is considered to visualize the possibility of integrating the payment of the transport service through the platform, as well as acting as an identification credential for access to the transport route. This can be developed through the implementation of NFC or through some dynamic two-dimensional code (QR, PDF417, etc.).

Finally, we consider that it is important to develop solutions focused on IoT, including Smart Cities that allow the integration of the diverse existing infrastructure to the new trends in information systems, so that the different services offered by cities can be optimized, reducing, in the case of public transport, transfer times and improving the efficiency of fuel consumption, gradually improving the quality of life of the inhabitants.

References

1. Handte, M., Foell, S., Wagner, S., Kortuem, G., Marron, P.J.: An Internet-of-Things enabled connected navigation system for urban bus riders. IEEE Internet Things J. **3**, 735–744 (2016). https://doi.org/10.1109/JIOT.2016.2554146
2. Cats, O., Vermeulen, A., Warnier, M., van Lint, H.: Modelling growth principles of metropolitan public transport networks. J. Transp. Geogr. **82**, 102567 (2020)
3. Tomej, K., Liburd, J.J.: Sustainable accessibility in rural destinations: a public transport network approach. J. Sustain. Tour. **28**(2), 222–239 (2020)
4. Lohokare, J., Dani, R., Sontakke, S., Adhao, R.: Scalable tracking system for public buses using IoT technologies. In: 2017 International Conference on Emerging Trends & Innovation, ICT, ICEI 2017, pp. 104–109 (2017)
5. Raj, J.T., Sankar, J.: IoT based smart school bus monitoring and notification system. In: 5th IEEE Region 10 Humanitarian Technology Conference 2017, R10-HTC 2017, pp. 89–92 (2018). https://doi.org/10.1109/R10-HTC.2017.8288913
6. Spyropoulou, I.: Impact of public transport strikes on the road network: the case of Athens. Transp. Res. Part A: Policy Pract. **132**, 651–665 (2020)
7. de Regt, R., von Ferber, C., Holovatch, Y., Lebovka, M.: Public transportation in Great Britain viewed as a complex network. Transportmetrica A: Transp. Sci. **15**(2), 722–748 (2019)
8. Lusikka, T., Kinnunen, T.K., Kostiainen, J.: Public transport innovation platform boosting intelligent transport system value chains. Util. Policy **62**, 100998 (2020)
9. Munizaga, M.A., Palma, C.: Estimation of a disaggregate multimodal public transport origin-destination matrix from passive smartcard data from Santiago, Chile. Transp. Res. Part C: Emerg. Technol. **24**, 9–18 (2012)
10. Perez, R., Vásquez, C., Viloria, A.: An intelligent strategy for faults location in distribution networks with distributed generation. J. Intell. Fuzzy Syst. **36**(2), 1627–1637 (2019)
11. Liu, Y., Cheng, T.: Understanding public transit patterns with open geodemographics to facilitate public transport planning. Transportmetrica A: Transp. Sci. **16**(1), 76–103 (2020)
12. Petersen, N.C., Rodrigues, F., Pereira, F.C.: Multi-output bus travel time prediction with convolutional LSTM neural network. Expert Syst. Appl. **120**, 426–435 (2019)
13. Viloria, A., Robayo, P.V.: Virtual network level of application composed IP networks connected with systems-(NETS peer-to-peer). Indian J. Sci. Technol. **9**, 46 (2016)
14. Viloria, A., Acuña, G.C., Franco, D.J.A., Hernández-Palma, H., Fuentes, J.P., Rambal, E.P.: Integration of data mining techniques to PostgreSQL database manager system. Procedia Comput. Sci. **155**, 575–580 (2019)
15. Tomasiello, D.B., Giannotti, M., Arbex, R., Davis, C.: Multi-temporal transport network models for accessibility studies. Trans. GIS **23**(2), 203–223 (2019)
16. Mula, F.M.: Planificación y optimización de redes ópticas en el Internet del futuro (Doctoral dissertation, Universidad Politécnica de Cartagena) (2019)
17. Saif, M.A., Zefreh, M.M., Torok, A.: Public transport accessibility: a literature review. Period. Polytech. Transp. Eng. **47**(1), 36–43 (2019)
18. Gatta, V., Marcucci, E., Nigro, M., Serafini, S.: Sustainable urban freight transport adopting public transport-based crowdshipping for B2C deliveries. Eur. Transp. Res. Rev. **11**(1), 13 (2019)
19. Cervantes, M.E.S., García, L.D.J.M.: El uso de modelos de redes y modelos de transporte para la optimización y reducción de tiempos y costos de transporte en la Comercializadora Gonac S. A de CV/The use of network models and transport models for the optimization and reduction of transport times and costs in the Comercializadora Gonac S. A de CV. RICEA Revista Iberoamericana de Contaduría, Economía y Administración **8**(15), 29–53 (2019)

20. Allulli, L., Italiano, G.F., Santaroni, F.: Exploiting GPS data in public transport journey planners. In: Gudmundsson, J., Katajainen, J. (eds.) SEA 2014. LNCS, vol. 8504, pp. 295–306. Springer, Cham (2014). https://doi.org/10.1007/978-3-319-07959-2_25

21. Shen, L., Stopher, P.R.: Review of GPS travel survey and GPS data-processing methods. Transp. Rev. **34**(3), 316–334 (2014)

22. Schüssler, N., Axhausen, K.W.: Identifying trips and activities and their characteristics from GPS raw data without further information. Arbeitsberichte Verkehrs-und Raumplanung **502**, 1–29 (2008)

23. Edwards, D., Griffin, T.: Understanding tourists' spatial behaviour: GPS tracking as an aid to sustainable destination management. J. Sustain. Tour. **21**(4), 580–595 (2013)

24. Schuessler, N., Axhausen, K.W.: Map-matching of GPS traces on high-resolution navigation networks using the multiple hypothesis technique (MHT). Arbeitsberichte Verkehrs und Raumplanung **568**, 1–22 (2009)

25. Wang, Y., Ram, S., Currim, F., Dantas, E., Sabóia, L.A.: A big data approach for smart transportation management on bus network. In: 2016 IEEE International Smart Cities Conference (ISC2), pp. 1–6. IEEE (2016)

26. Gonzalez, P., et al.: Automating mode detection using neural networks and assisted GPS data collected using GPS-enabled mobile phones. In: 15th World Congress on Intelligent Transportation Systems, pp. 16–20 (2008)

27. Ma, X., Yu, H., Wang, Y., Wang, Y.: Large-scale transportation network congestion evolution prediction using deep learning theory. PLoS ONE **10**(3), e0119044 (2015)

28. Chaix, B., et al.: Active transportation and public transportation use to achieve physical activity recommendations? A combined GPS, accelerometer, and mobility survey study. Int. J. Behav. Nutr. Phys. Act. **11**(1), 124 (2014)

29. Strutu, M., Stamatescu, G., Popescu, D.: A mobile sensor network based road surface monitoring system. In: 2013 17th International Conference on System Theory, Control and Computing (ICSTCC), pp. 630–634. IEEE (2013)

30. Dabiri, S., Heaslip, K.: Inferring transportation modes from GPS trajectories using a convolutional neural network. Transp. Res. Part C: Emerg. Technol. **86**, 360–371 (2018)

31. Harrison, F., Burgoine, T., Corder, K., van Sluijs, E.M., Jones, A.: How well do modelled routes to school record the environments children are exposed to?: a cross-sectional comparison of GIS-modelled and GPS-measured routes to school. Int. J. Health Geogr. **13**(1), 5 (2014)

32. Anderson, M.K., Rasmussen, T.K.: Matching observed public route choice data to a GIS network. In: Selected Proceedings from the Annual Transport Conference at Aalborg University, vol. 5, no. 1 (2010)

33. Badland, H., Duncan, M.J., Oliver, M., Duncan, J.S., Mavoa, S.: Examining commute routes: applications of GIS and GPS technology. Environ. Health Prev. Med. **15**(5), 327 (2010)

34. Stopher, P., FitzGerald, C., Xu, M.: Assessing the accuracy of the Sydney household travel survey with GPS. Transportation **34**(6), 723–741 (2007)

35. Gallet, M., Massier, T., Hamacher, T.: Estimation of the energy demand of electric buses based on real-world data for large-scale public transport networks. Appl. Energy **230**, 344–356 (2018)

36. Holleczek, T., Yu, L., Lee, J.K., Senn, O., Ratti, C., Jaillet, P.: Detecting weak public transport connections from cellphone and public transport data. In: Proceedings of the 2014 International Conference on Big Data Science and Computing, pp. 1–8 (2014)

37. Wang, H., Calabrese, F., Di Lorenzo, G., Ratti, C.: Transportation mode inference from anonymized and aggregated mobile phone call detail records. In: 13th International IEEE Conference on Intelligent Transportation Systems, pp. 318–323. IEEE (2010)

38. Chaix, B., et al.: GPS tracking in neighborhood and health studies: a step forward for environmental exposure assessment, a step backward for causal inference? Health Place **21**, 46–51 (2013)
39. Buys, L., Snow, S., van Megen, K., Miller, E.: Transportation behaviours of older adults: an investigation into car dependency in urban Australia. Australas. J. Ageing **31**(3), 181–186 (2012)
40. Gonzalez, P.A., et al.: Automating mode detection for travel behaviour analysis by using global positioning systems-enabled mobile phones and neural networks. IET Intell. Transp. Syst. **4**(1), 37–49 (2010)
41. Arellana, J., de Dios Ortúzar, J., Rizzi, L.I., Zuñiga, F.: Obtaining public transport level-of-service measures using in-vehicle GPS data and freely available GIS web-based ools. In: Mobile Technologies for Activity-Travel Data Collection and Analysis, pp. 2   IGI Global (2014)
42. Ladha, A., Bhattacharya, P., Chaubey, N., Bodkhe, U.: *IIGPTS*: IoT-based ram work for intelligent green public transportation system. In: Singh, P.K., Pawło ki, W. Tanwar, S., Kumar, N., Rodrigues, J.J.P.C., Obaidat, M.S. (eds.) Proceedings of First ternational Conference on Computing, Communications, and Cyber-Security (IC S 2019). LNNS, vol. 121, pp. 183–195. Springer, Singapore (2020). https://doi.org/10.1007/9   981-15-3369-3_14

Coordinator Controller Election Algorithm to Provide Failsafe Through Load Balancing in Distributed SDN Control Plane

Gaurang Lakhani[1]([⊠]) [iD] and Amit Kothari[2]

[1] CE/IT, Gujarat Technological University, Ahmedabad, India
gvlakhani1@gmail.com
[2] Accenture, Bengaluru, India
amitdkothari@gmail.com

Abstract. SDN provides flexibility, centralized control, and cost-cutting. SDN decouples the main two functions of a traditional network viz. packet switching and routing. The switch is responsible to forward packets only without any concern about routing decisions or any security checks in SDN. The control plane is responsible for routing decisions. Distributed SDN solves issues of availability and scalability, which are the weakness of a centralized or single control plane. Fault Tolerance and load balancing are the key features of any network. A brief description of our primary research goal of the proposed DCFT (Distributed Controller Fault Tolerance) model is given here. A major focus is given on a coordinator controller election algorithm to provide failsafe through load balancing in the SDN control plane. Implementation of the said algorithm verified with floodlight controller with and without a coordinator, Implementation results reveals that throughput and communication overhead will be increased with coordinator controller, packet delay (latency) will be decreased with coordinator controller.

Keywords: Software Defined Networking · Fault tolerance · Switch migration · Coordinator election · Load balancing · Data plane · Control plane

1 Introduction

Software defined networking (SDN) is innovative method in network management and enable innovation in networking. Current traditional network are multifaceted and difficult to manage especially in the light of changing routing and other quality of service demands by the administrators. SDN controllers are considered as "brain" of the control plane. Controllers connects with network devices through south bound interfaces (SBI) such as openflow protocols. The control plane exposes some features and APIs through the Northbound Interfaces (NBI) to network operators to design various management application exploiting such as a set of REST API. East-West bound API used for inter-controller communication among multiple controllers. Control functionality is removed from network devices that are considered as simple packet forwarding elements. The forwarding decision is flow based rather than destination based [1].

© Springer Nature Singapore Pte Ltd. 2020
N. Chaubey et al. (Eds.): COMS2 2020, CCIS 1235, pp. 234–250, 2020.
https://doi.org/10.1007/978-981-15-6648-6_19

SDN have flow tables. Flow means combinations of match criteria and its associated actions in the set of packet field. All the packets of the same flow will have to follow the same service polices at the forwarding devices. The flow abstraction permits uniting the performance of the different types of network devices such as routers, switches, firewalls, and middleboxes. Flow programming empowers extraordinary flexibility, limited only to the capabilities of the implemented flow tables. The separation of the control plane and data plane can be appreciated by means of well-defined programming interface between switches and SDN controller. Openflow switch has one or more tables of packet handling rules. Each rule matches a subset of traffic and plays out specific activity on traffic. Contingent upon the rules installed by controller application, an openflow switch trained by controller to behave like a router, switch, firewall or perform any other roles [1].

Lack of flexibility, centralized control, and cost are such limitations of traditional networks. Software Defined Networking is a novel way to deal with these issues of traditional networking. SDN decouples the main two functions of a traditional network viz. packet switching and routing. In SDN switch is responsible to forward packets only without any concern about routing decisions or any security checks. The control plane is responsible for routing decisions. Control plane implemented in a distributed fashion where multiple controllers act with synchronization. Openflow [2] APIs are used by SDN to set up forwarding rules and collect statistics in the data plane, which allows controller software and data plane hardware to progress independently. With SDN physical connectivity between two endpoints does not guarantee they can interconnect with each other – the underlying (logical) communication graph be contingent on the network policies reflected by the flow entries installed by the controller. For scalability and reliability, the logically centralized control plane ("network OS") is often appreciated via multiple SDN controllers (see Fig. 1) forming a distributed system. OpenDayLight [4] and Open Networking Operating System (ONOS) [5] and are two such Network OS examples supporting SDN controllers for high availability.

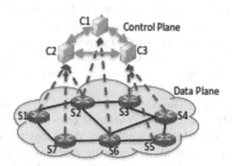

Fig. 1. SDN control plane setup [6]

The main focus of this paper is to propose coordinator controller election algorithm to provide load balancing among distributed SDN controller, provide consistency reliability, scalability, transparency, and immediate deployability in distributed SDN controller using state replication at the cost of little degradation in performance.

The remaining paper is arranged as follows: in Sect. 2 previous paper is discussed, the Objective of the proposed work is given in Sect. 3. Section 4 shows the proposed coordinator election algorithm with a brief description of the DCFT model Evaluation and results in Sect. 5, the conclusion is included in Sect. 6.

2 Related Work

2.1 Architecture of Distributed SDN Control Plane

Our prime research goal is fault management through load balancing in distributed SDN control plane. Architecture of the distributed SDN controller is briefly discussed here.

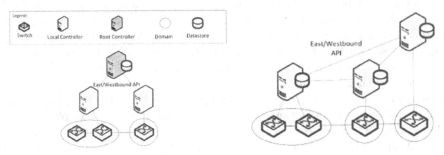

Fig. 2. Hierarchical model [7]   **Fig. 3.** Flat model [7]

Distributed SDN controller share their network information in the SDN controllers. A worldwide network wide state is a product of aggregation from multiple network states. SDN controllers store the worldwide network state in the data store. SDN controllers can use any data store system whether it is relational database, non-relational database, distributed hash table, or distributed file system [7]. SDN adopter can use any schema within their data store. A controller can dominant control the network because it has a perspective of the whole network. Thus to provide a logically dominant control in distributed SDN controller, there must be at least one controller from the group that has a worldwide network state. Our survey summarizes following design choice.

(i) ***Hierarchical model:*** As shown in Fig. 2, one or few SDN controllers in the group have the worldwide network state. Two local controllers maintain the switch of each domain. Meanwhile the root controller accomplishes the management between local controllers. The worldwide network state which is kept in the data store is only available to the root controller. Thus the resident controller should initially question arrange data from the root controller before it can execute any inter domain activity. Because of this procedure this model is also called as client-server model, where the root controller acts as a server and local controller acts as a client. OpenDayLight [4], ONOS [5], Onix [8], and HyperFlow [9] are flat SDN distributed controllers.

(ii) ***Flat model:*** It is also called as horizontal architecture. As appeared in Fig. 3, three SDN controllers control switches in their space and every one of them have an information store and keep up worldwide system state. The entirety of the SDN controller additionally own east/west bound API association with different controllers. Subsequently they can contact and tell other straightforwardly.

Before a SDN controller can build worldwide system state, it should initially get the neighborhood state from every SDN controller in the group. Additionally any progressions occurs inside the space of a controller must be shared to other controller with the goal that they can refresh their worldwide system state to mirror the changes. At the point when the bunch will have the option to play out each system data dispersion effectively, all the SDN controller ought to have the equivalent worldwide system state. Because of this procedure, administrators called this model as shared model since each controller can reach legitimately to different controllers during system data circulation. Others may called this model as repeated state machine on the grounds that the bunch duplicates all nearby system states from SDN controller to each other. Our model followed flat model architecture.

2.2 Related Work Done on Coordinator Election Algorithms in Distributed Computing Environment

Consistency and state replication in distributed SDN is represented by Zhang et al. [6] through Raft in SDN. Complicated interdependency introduced between network OS and network under its control on introducing consensus protocol for maintaining a consistent network state. Which generates new failures and instabilities. The connectivity among these controllers can be provided either in-band or out of band via data plane under their control. In either case (dedicated or virtual) it refers to the network connecting the controllers as the control network. Openflow switches with flow rules installed by the same controller cluster to which it provides connectivity in the network.

Esteban Hernandez [10] has discussed the performance of the OpenDayLight controller under the cluster architecture schema. The author has discussed the protocol of the network in the communication between controllers, different message exchanges between controllers. Message communication is done through the RPC mechanism, the authors proposed the coordinator election algorithm by "request vote" and "append entries". To get the values from the other nodes request vote is used and to replicate log entries, append entries are used by the coordinator. This request vote is in the form of RPC messages. When this RPC message is blank, it is called "heartbeat" messages. The coordinator election process is executed for the arbitrary duration called "term". A term always starts with an election process, where one or more nodes in the candidate state try to become a coordinator. When one of the candidates wins the election and became a coordinator, the term is conserved until it fails. There are also some situations, in which during a term there is not coordinator election, this can be caused by a split vote's situation. In such a situation term will be completed without any coordinator, then a new election taking place with a new term. This ensures that only a node can become a coordinator within a given term. When nodes are started up, they begin in the follower state. They remain in that state as long as they do not receive any message from a coordinator or candidate. If they don't receive any message over a specified interval called "Election Timeout". Then they will change their status to a candidate, assuming that there is no current coordinator.

Authors of [11] have utilized Raft consensus. A raft is a consensus algorithm for managing repeated logs. The consensus is an algorithm that enables controllers to work together as a unique coherent system that is able to handle the failure of some of the controllers. It can be done by replicating the state of the machine of the coordinator. Raft algorithm is divided into coordinator election, log replication, and safety.

Ricardo Mxacedo et al. [12] had represented algorithm based on controller performance. A controller having maximum performance is elected as coordinator. For that, at every regular interval, there is a need to measure the performance of each controller to find the best coordinator which can degrade the performance by overhead.

Scott D. Stoller [13] has used a modified Bully algorithm for coordinator election in which a separate failure detection module is required. We propose load calculation and decision making of the load balancing based on the controller threshold value.

Mazzini et al. [14] proposed dependability of SDN with distributed controllers over leader election algorithm and colored petrinet technique. The master controller will calculate the dependability rate of each node (controllers, switches) and link of the system. This calculation will be based on the proposed RDSDN [15] by the same author. The dependability of the system R (G) will be calculated as the possibility that every pair of the node can send and receive the data. Dijkstra algorithm will be used to calculate the link loss rate. Controller with highest reliability rate among all controllers and their children will be considered as coordinator controller.

We propose a coordinator election based on the load of the controller. All the controllers including the coordinator controller will calculate its own load using separate functions available with each controller, and send their load information to the coordinator controller at regular intervals. The load of the controller will be calculated by accumulating average message arrival rate, flow table entries, and propagation delay.

3 Objective of the Proposed Work

SDN is still in its maturing state so it suffers from issues such as scalability, reliability, and fault tolerance. Following objectives are derived from the reviewed literature:

- To find a suitable coordinator controller election algorithm to balance the load of the distributed SDN control plane.
- Provide more reliability, scalability, transparency and immediate deployability to distributed SDN controller using coordinator controller election algorithm.
- Verify claimed throughput (load balancing rate), latency (packet delay) with simulation results for with coordinator and without coordinator case.

4 Design and Implementation

Our primary research goal is to provide fault tolerance through load balancing in the distributed SDN controller. We have created a model called the DCFT (Distributed

Controller Fault Tolerance) model [1]. Figure 4 has described all the modules used in our model.

A sub-layer called fault tolerance layer, in SDN stack as shown in Fig. 4 is proposed in our model between application (management) plane and control plane by extending the application (management) layer. This layer holds different modules such as switch migration module, DCFT module, fault tolerance module, and transaction management module. The rest of the modules of the DCFT model are coordinator controller election module, Inter controller synchronization, load calculation and decision making modules are resting at the control plane. Out of all these modules, the coordinator controller election module, load collection & decision-taking module are focused on this paper.

The data plane contains forwarding switches as shown in Fig. 4. The control plane did the routing task based on the policy decision of the management plane. Each controller may have no switches with it. Openflow protocol will manage internal communication between controller and switches. Controllers are having three roles master, slave and equal [16]. Openflow protocols 1.5.1 specification [2] included the capacity for a controller to set its part in the multi-controller condition.

DCFT module is the main module of the proposed system, it stores the current state of the system. It will also save changes/updates by switch migration, fault tolerance modules. Publish updates/sync controllers with the help of inter controller messenger,

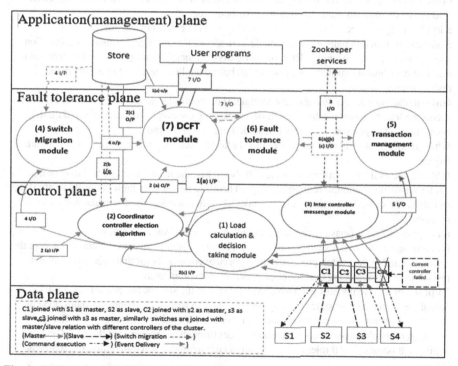

Fig. 4. SDN stack with additional sub-layer of fault tolerance in the DCFT model (Color figure online)

It will receive input from the user program about the state of the controller, the output will be informing the user program about fault management.

Switch migration module provides load balancing and avoids failure on overloading. The overloaded switch will be migrated to a least loaded controller, selected from arraylist, maintained in store. The detail of this module is not presented in this paper due to a lack of space.

Control plane did routing task based on the policy decision of management plane, a load of each controller calculated, coordinator controller will be decided, inter controller messanger will publish update/sync controllers.

Different modules are described below.

Application plane: Store user program, perform event/command ordering, command execution, sharing distributed log records, zookeeper coordinating service is installed at application plane

---

Fault tolerance plane:

3 i/p: subscribe updates of the state of each controller of the cluster

3 o/p: publish/sync update of the state of each controller using zookeeper

4 i/p: overloaded controller from the load calculation module

4 o/p: select the least loaded controller from the arraylist maintained in a distributed data store

4 o/p: select least loaded controller from arraylist maintained in-store, failure of any controller of the cluster due to any reason, orphan switches need to migrated to least loaded controller selected from array list maintained in the distributed log

5 i/p: Events generated by switches on receiving packet or states of the port changes

5 o/p: call transaction management module, provide ACID (atomicity, consistency, isolation and durability properties with NIB, Optimistic Concurrency Control (OCC) and distributed log

6(a) i/p: coordinator (master) controller failed before duplicating accepted events in the distributed log

6(a) o/p: call transaction management module, slave controller accept and buffer all events, no events are lost, first new master must finish processing any events logged by the old master, events marked as processed have their resulting command filtered

6(b) i/p: coordinator(master) controller failed after duplicating the event but before commit request

6(b) o/p: the event was replicated in the distributed log, the master that crashed may or may not have issued the commit request message. Therefore new master must carefully verify if the switch has processed everything it has received, before resending the command and commit requests

6(c) i/p: coordinator (master) controller failed after sending commit request

6(c) o/p: since old master send commit request before crashing, the new master will accept the confirmation that the switch processed the respective commands for that event and will not resend them (guaranteeing exactly-once semantics for commands)

7 i/p: It will receive updates from user programs about the state of the controllers. DCFT module saves the current state of the system, it will also reflect the changes/updates done by switch migration/fault tolerance/transaction management module. The inter controller messenger module provides coordination services through zookeepers via the DCFT module. While fault occurs, it will tolerate fault through fault tolerance and transaction management module

7 o/p: It will inform user programs runs on application plane about occurrence and management of fault

---

(*continued*)

(*continued*)

Application plane: Store user program, perform event/command ordering, command execution, sharing distributed log records, zookeeper coordinating service is installed at application plane

Control plane: 2(a) i/p: Distributed SDN controller from the cluster
2(a) o/p: coordinator controller decided
2(b) i/p: module stores load information, perform load balancing and routing of packets
2(b) o/p: store switch controller mapping information
2(c) i/p: failure of the coordinator can be detected by its slave controller on timeout
2(c) o/p: On failure of the coordinator, the next coordinator will be elected from priority arraylist of coordinator maintained in a distributed log
1(a) i/p N- no of flow table entries, F-average message arrival rate, D-Propagation delay
1(a) o/p $C_{load} = w1*N + w2*F + w3*D$

Data plane: Forwarding packets as per the routing instructions received by the controller

4.1 Load Calculation and Decision Making Module

Proper load balancing gives better fault tolerance, better throughput of the system. Our model gives better load balancing rate, reduce packet delay. In the load calculation module, all the controllers including the coordinator controller calculate its own load and send load information to the coordinator controller. The current packet_in_rate of a controller is considered as a load of a controller. The coordinator controller collects load information and stores it in the distributed database. Coordinator store load information as an array list sorted in ascending order. The first member of the array list is the minimum loaded controller and the last member is a maximum loaded controller without any duplicate entry. After a specified time-interval of every 5 s, the load calculation module calculates the load and sends it to the Coordinator. The time interval can be adaptive or dynamic. The time interval can be set by the aggregate of the current load and the previously calculated load.

4.1.1 Load Calculation Threshold

$T = Tmax/(|CurrentLoad - PreviousLoad| + 1)$
Tmax = initially set interval
CurrentLoad = Controller's Current Load
PreviousLoad = Controller's Previous Load
Load of Controller = packet arrival rate of Controller (packets/Sec) [2].

After receiving the load information coordinator store load of each controller and aggregate load of all the controllers in a distributed data store.

4.1.2 Decision-Making Process

To balance the load of all the controller nodes, a threshold value C is decided to detect overload and under load conditions. Based on this threshold value coordinator decide to balance the load or not.

C = (Average of a load of all the controllers)/(a load of a maximum loaded controller)

$0 \leq C \leq 1$, C is the load balancing rate. If C will be close to 1 load is evenly distributed and if a load is close to 0 uneven load distribution is there. We have selected an initial load balancing rate is 0.7. if the value of C is less than 0.7 than load balancing is required. If the value of C is greater than 0.7 no need for load balancing [8]. In case of overloading few switches need to be migrated from an overloaded controller to an underloaded controller, which is decided by the coordinator controller.

4.1.3 Selection of Destination Controller and Switch to Be Migrated

After the decision taken by a coordinator to migrate a switch the next work to do is to select a destination controller to migrate a switch and selection of a switch to migrate. The selection of a destination controller can be from a sorted array list stored at the distributed data store. The lightest loaded controller has selected whose load is less than the bellow capacity CT. The selection of switch to migrate can be based on a packet in the rate of a switch. The maximum loaded switch should be select to migrate. Before the migration coordinator must check that the migrated switch should not overload the destination controller. It can be checked by the following formula. If the migration can create overload to destination coordinator should choose another switch to migrate.

Load_of_Switch_to_Migrate $\leq$ CT – Load_of_Target
CT = Controller Capacity (packets/Sec).

4.2 Internal Controller Messenger Module

There are two different ways to obtain organize data from other SDN controllers. Polling and, Publish and Subscribe [12].

(i) *Polling:* Each SDN controller intermittently demand for another system data from different controllers in the bunch. For example a SDN demand for another switch data at regular intervals. It will execute the solicitation intermittently in any event, when there is no update occur in the other controller. In this manner it might get same system data as the last one. Along these lines this strategy isn't effective [16].

(ii) *Publish and subscribe*

Each SDN controller can publish/subscribe in the system data from other controller in the group. For example controller c1 needs arrange data from neighboring controller c2, the controller c1 can subscribe in the switch data from c2. Right now goes about as c1 acts as subscriber and c2 goes about as publisher. Later c2 will advise c1 when there is a change with respect to the switch data in the area. Right now c2 will inform c1 just when there is a change accordingly this technique is increasingly proficient for our model [16].

Internal controller messenger module is responsible to provide all the updates of controllers of the cluster to each other. It synchronizes state between the controllers by letting all of them access updates published by all other modules in the controller. ZMQ, the asynchronous messaging service used for internal communication among controllers. Distributed coordination service such as zookeeper [17] glues cluster of the controllers to share the information about a link, topology, etc. it's used for updating the status of the controllers.

4.3 Coordinator Controller Election Module

Coordinator controller performs two roles, one is its ordinary role of routing incoming packets and second is special role, coordinator role, where it has to collect the load of each controller of the cluster and information about switch controller mapping and store it as an array list at the distributed database. All the controllers send their load information and switch information to the coordinator controller. The coordinator controller calculates the aggregate load of all the controllers and stores it in the distributed database. Based on a load of the cluster, the coordinator controller takes the switch migration decision. Controllers can communicate with coordinator using messaging services provided by zookeeper and sync service of floodlight controller.

This module is providing fault tolerance to the coordinator controller. There must be a coordinator controller all the time available in the cluster to take various coordination decisions in case of load imbalance as well as controller failure and to collect and calculate controller statistics. The election module continuously running in the background, when it detects the failure of a current coordinator it starts re-election and elects a new Coordinator. The election module can elect a new coordinator if and only if the 51% of the controllers are active otherwise it sets the controller having id one as the default coordinator.

Controllers of a distributed control plane form a logical cluster. Consider the controllers C1, C2, C3… Cn from Fig. 4, all the controllers are joined with switches in three different roles, master, equal and slave. C1 joined with S1 as master, S2 as a slave, C2 joined with S2 as master, S3 as a slave, similarly controller are joined with a master-slave relationship in the different switches of the clusters.

All controllers of a cluster are assigned a controller id as per they joined the controller cluster viz. C1, C2…Cn. When cluster start, the controller having maximum controller id is elected as a coordinator controller using our election algorithm. Proposed coordinator controller election algorithm

---

Algorithm 1: Coordinator controller election algorithm

---

1. pollTime=5 seconds // Election class is polled every "pollTime"
   seconds such that it checks if a new coordinator present in the network
2. Once the coordinator specified and the follower's role decided, the current coordinator
   is used to managing network vide   publishing and subscribing updates across all nodes
3 pollTime=5 seconds, timeout=6 seconds
4. First, try to get a coordinator
   if (coordinator==none) then coordinator=controllerID1; timeoutFlag=true
5. else if (coordinator.equals (ControllerID)) then
6. roll based function such as initiates publish/subscribe by the coordinator,
   //publish means ask all the nodes to call publish hook, subscribe means ask all the
      nodes to subscribe to updates from all other nodes as well as by calling this in a loop
7. There are different possible states of the controller during the election process,
8. switch (current-state) // current state of the controller
9. {
10. case CONNECT: Network block until the majority of nodes connected
11 case ELECT: check for the new node to connect to, and refresh socket connection,
ensure the majority of nodes connected otherwise, goto CONNECT state.
12 start elections if the majority of a node connected.
13 once coordinator has confirmed by-election it proceeds to coordinate or follow state
14 case SPIN: This is resting state of coordinator after the election
   CheckForCoordinator: This function ensures that there is only one coordinator, set for
   an entire network, none or multiple coordinators causes it to set the current state to
   ELECT.
15. case COORDINATE: This is resting state of coordinator after election keep sending
      heartbeat message and receive a majority of acceptors otherwise, goto ELECT state
16.}
17. check for only "one" coordinator in the network
18. Ask each node if they are the coordinator, all the nodes should get an ACK from only
one of them, if not reset the coordinator.
19. //Election performed
20. if (connected controllers >= majority (51%)) then
21.   if (elected coordinator present == true)
22.   if (no of coordinator ==1)
23.   commit; coordinator elected as controllerID=1
24.   else
25.   call checkForCoordinator function.
26.   else
27. Check for new node to be connect and controller having highest controllerID will
   become Coordinator.
28. Nodes joined after the election: It follows the current coordinator
29. Nodes joined before the election: It participates in the current election process, a
   coordinator will be elected from current active and configured controller
30. Nodes joined during the election: It waits for election to be completed, does not
   participate in the election, and starts following elected coordinator after the election.

(i) *Failure in coordinator controller*

The coordinator is the in-charge of the coordination of all the other controllers, controllers
may have a different number of switches. Failure occurs in the coordinator node leads

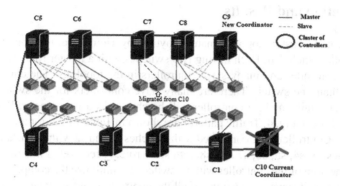

Fig. 5. Failure in coordinator controller, the election of new coordinator controller

to failure of a whole distributed control plane. Failure of coordinator can be detected by using separate functions available with all the controllers in the cluster which will be synchronized with zookeeper services. Coordinator controller fails, aggregate load calculation stopped, a decision of load balancing cannot be taken, which leads towards the failure of an overloaded controller.

To overcome the failure of a coordinator controller we plan to run an election algorithm to elect a new coordinator on a failure of the current coordinator. Controller id decides priority among controllers. After a specified time interval, a check performed that the elected coordinator is active or failed. If the coordinator failed, the re-election starts. A controller having maximum controller id from the cluster, elected as a new coordinator of a distributed control plane. A new coordinator has to migrate switches of the failed controller to a lightest loaded controller by proposed switch migration. All the controllers may have a different number of switches. Figure 5 shows failure in the coordinator controller. C_{10} is a current coordinator, Switch of C_{10} migrated to C_7 (lightest loaded backup controller from the array list). C_9 becomes a new coordinator. Similarly array list from distributed data store updated at every time t seconds.

In our model, the coordinator controller periodically checks the status of the controllers, to perceive the failure of the controller, coordinator controller utilizes controller data, Every particular time coordinator controller checks last refreshed time of controllers If last refreshed time surpasses a certain threshold, coordinator controller think about this controller as failed and proceeds recovery steps.

(ii) *Failure in coordinator controller*

All the controllers are mapped with the no of switches. The controller is responsible for the flow table stored at switch mapped with that controller. If the controller gets failed, we have to migrate its switches to another controller to keep switches functioning.

(iii) *Load imbalance between controllers*

Similarly, load imbalance occurs on the overloading of a controller, the overloaded controller needs to migrate its highest loaded switches to the least loaded controller from an array of a distributed database.

5 Evaluation and Results

We have created a custom topology named mytopo.py. Here in our topology four flood-light controllers included. Each having two switches with a master role. There is only one master controller and many slave controllers in the topology. The controller may have more than one switch. There are many slave controllers for the switches. If the original master fails, a slave controller will be chosen as a new master. We consider custom topology in Fig. 4. Traffic patterns are shown in Table 1 used for all simulations. For example Controller c0 is connected with switches s1 and s2 with the master role and with switches s3, s4, s5, s6, s7 and s8 with slave role. A red dotted line indicating the master connection of the controller with its switch. To minimize the complexity here we have not displayed slave connections of all the controllers and switches. The topology is created using miniedit, a graphical user interface of Mininet.

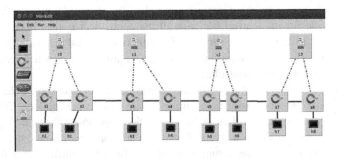

Fig. 6. The topology used in the experiment

5.1 Implementation of Coordinator Election Module

This module provides fault tolerance to the control plane when the current coordinator gets failed and at the same multiple instances of the controller are running. It uses ISyncService in order to store the data. Few updates published by all other modules in the controllers this module synchronizes state between the controllers, In addition, it runs a coordinator election process, in order to enable modules to perform role-based programming in a distributed system with multiple controllers running, in addition, be able to communicate between controllers as well.

In case of failure of the current coordinator there are the following cases:

Case 1: Majority of the controllers are active:
A normal coordinator election takes place and a new coordinator pops up, and the system operates normally.

Case 2: Less than 51% of configured controllers are active:
In this case, the system by default, elect controller 1 as a new coordinator. This is because the coordinator must be available all the time to perform its role.

Case 3: Node joins before the election: It participates in the election, the coordinator is elected amongst the currently active and configured controllers.

Case 4: Node joins during the election: It waits for election to be completed does not participate in the election, following the elected coordinator.

5.2 Experimental Setup

We have used Ubuntu 14.04 with 4 GB RAM, Intel Core i3-2370 M CPU@ 2.40 GHz processor system. The bandwidth of the system is 1 GBps. In four terminal windows, four floodlight controllers are started with similar IP address along with port no 4242, 4243, 4244, and 4245. The default Coordinator will be ControllerID1 but after starting 3 controllers, packet arrival rate (throughput) will be tested by changing the number of the controller node. The throughput and latency mode of the cbench will be used in the flood-light controller to check the throughput (packet arrival rate), latency, communication overhead of the floodlight controller.

TCP flows generation needed to simulate the distribution of network traffic the average flow requests. It's done by hping3. The average packet arrival rate of 500 packets/s. Floodlight controller will be used to process packets received by the switch. To reduce the effect of packet delay and packet loss link bandwidth between switches and hosts to 1000 Mbps. Packet in rate $P = 30$ Bytes/s. we set no of switches managed by one controller is from 2 to 10. All the simulations run for 12 h readings noted at every 20 min.

Table 1. Traffic design used in the experiment

Traffic sequence	Source	Destination
T1	H1	H4
T2	H3	H7
T3	H1	H8

5.2.1 Paket Delay (Latency)

Consider traffic patterns T1, T2 and T3 of Table 2. Traffic T1 generated from host H1 to host H4. Both are connected by controller C1. The simulation experiment starts with a packet delay of 12–14 ms for all traffics. Initially, there is no coordinator, so by default C1 will be chosen as coordinator, as all the four controllers joined with topology and if C1 failed, the coordinator election algorithm will be executed. Figure 9 reveals that packet delay will be decreased in T1 and T2 with the coordinator. Because the proposed algorithm followed the state replication approach. All the controller followed the log replication of the coordinator. The average packet delay of T1, T2 and T3 traffic sequences is decreased by 56.13%.

Table 2. Comparison of with coordinator/without coordinator controller in the cluster

Traffic number	Without Coordinator controller					With Coordinator controller					
	Packet delay (ms)	communication overhead(packet/s)		Throughput (packet/s)			Packet delay (ms)	communication overhead (packet/s)		Throughput (packet/s)		
		Switch-controller	Controller-controller	C1	C2	C3		Switch-controller	Controller-controller	C1	C2	C3
T1	58.1	403	352	423	421	379	28.66	413	362	543	541	499
T2	68.9	374	301	398	444	354	26.74	394	356	518	564	474
T3	55.7	234	202	354	424	388	24.20	267	264	514	544	508

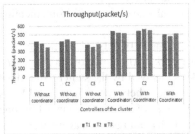

Fig. 7. Throughput of different traffic sequences

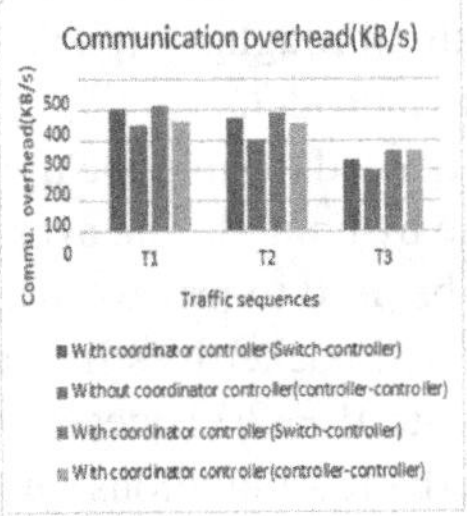

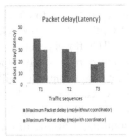

Fig. 8. Communication overhead of different traffic sequences

Fig. 9. Packet delay (latency) of different traffic sequences

5.2.2 Throughput

Figure 7 shows the comparison of the cluster throughput (packet/s) with and without the coordinator controller. Packet_in_rate is considered as the throughput of the system. Table 2 and Fig. 5 reveals that with respect to the topology shown in Fig. 6, packets are captured through Wireshark and analyzed from all the traffic sequences like T1, T2, and T3 at different times. Average throughput will be increased by 22.63%.

5.2.3 Communication Overhead (KB/S)

Figure 8 shows the comparison of the communication delay (KB/s) with and without the coordinator controller. It is calculated between switch-controller and controller-controller for all the traffic sequences T1, T2, and T3. With the coordinator controller, communication overhead between switch-controller will be increased by 7.09 KB/s. and between controller-controller, it is increased by 23.47 KB/s. In the availability of the coordinator controller, the replication state machine approach followed, so log replication carried out at regular intervals resulted increase in communication overhead.

6 Conclusion

This paper proposed a coordinator controller election algorithm in the cluster of distributed SDN controllers. Our primary research goal is to propose the DCFT (Distributed Controller Fault Tolerance) model to provide fault tolerance through load balancing in the distributed SDN controller. The coordinator controller election is one module of the model. To provide a fault tolerance mechanism in the distributed SDN controller cluster, one additional fault tolerance sub-layer will be added in the SDN stack by extending an application plane of SDN. The coordinator controller election algorithm, load calculation, and decision-making modules are described in detail. There are four floodlight controllers in the sample topology (Fig. 4), taken for the simulation. The result of the simulation will be tested for three different traffic sequences as shown in Table 1. Comparison of with coordinator controller and without coordinator controller is demonstrated by Table 2. With the coordinator, Considering an average of all three traffic sequence, the throughput of the cluster will be increased by 22.63%, packet delay(latency) will be decreased by 56.13% and communication overhead will be increased between switch-controller is 7.09 KB/s and between controller-controller is 23.47 KB/s. So by introducing coordinator controller in the distributed SDN controller, consistency, reliability, scalability and immediate deployability of the system are improved at the cost of communication overhead.

Acknowledgements and Conflict of Interest. We are very much thankful of Dr. Bhushan Trivedi, Director, GLS Institute of Computer application, Ahmedabad, Gujarat, India, Dr. Satyen Parikh, Dean, Faculty of Computer Application, Ganpat University, Kherva, Mehsana, India, all our colleagues, friends and reviewers, and organizer of the International conference on computing science, communication and security (COMS2)-2020 the for their comments on our research work and help us to improve this paper. We are hereby declare that we don't have any conflict of interest with any living person about the said research work mentioned in this paper.

References

1. Lakhani, G., Kothari, A.: Distributed Controller Fault Tolerance Model (DCFT) using load balancing in software defined networking. Int. J. Comput. Eng. Technol. **10**(2), 215–233 (2019)
2. "OpenFlow switch specification 1.5.1", p. 74.. https://www.opennetworking.org/wp-content/uploads/2014/10/openflow-switch-v1.5.1.pdf. Accessed 13 Feb 2019
3. Jarraya, Y., Madi, T., Debbabi, M.: A survey and a layered taxonomy of software-defined networking. IEEE Commun. Surv. Tutor. **16**(4), 1955–1980 (2014)
4. Suh, D., Jang, S., Han, S., Pack, S., Kim, T., Kwak, J.: On performance of OpenDayLight clustering. In: IEEE NetSoft Conference and Workshops (NetSoft), pp. 407–410 (2016)
5. Berde, P., et al.: ONOS: towards an open, distributed SDN OS. In: Proceedings of the Third Workshop on Hot Topics in Software Defined Networking, pp. 1–6. August 2014
6. Zhang, Y., Ramadan, E., Mekky, H., Zhang, Z.L.: When raft meets SDN: how to elect a leader and reach consensus in an unruly network. In: Proceedings of the First Asia-Pacific Workshop on Networking, pp. 1–7, August 2017
7. Oktian, Y.E., Lee, S., Lee, H., Lam, J.: Distributed SDN controller system: a survey on design choice. Comput. Netw. **121**, 100–111 (2017)

8. Koponen, T., et al.: Onix: a distributed control platform for large-scale production networks. In: OSDI, vol. 10, pp. 1–6, October 2010
9. Tootoonchian, A., Ganjali, Y.: Hyperflow: a distributed control plane for OpenFlow. In: Proceedings of the 2010 Internet Network Management Conference on Research on Enterprise Networking (2010)
10. Esteban, H.M.: Implementation and performance of an SDN cluster-controller based on the OpenDayLight framework (2016)
11. Suh, D., Seokwon, J., Sol, H., Sangheon, P., Taehong, K., Jiyoung, K.: On performance of OpenDayLight clustering. In: 2016 IEEE NetSoft Conference and Workshops (NetSoft), pp. 407–410 (2016)
12. Macedo, R., de Castro, R., Santos, A., Ghamri-Doudane, Y., Nogueira, M.: Self-organized SDN controller cluster conformations against DDoS attacks effects. In: Global Communications Conference (GLOBECOM), pp. 1–6. IEEE (2016)
13. Stoller, S.D.: Coordinator election in distributed systems with crash failures. Technical report, Indiana University, p. 169, April 1997
14. Mazzini, S., Mohammad, Reza K., Naser, M.: Improving the reliability of software-defined networks with distributed controllers through leader election algorithm and colored petri-net. Wirel. Personal Commun. 109(1), 645–656 (2019)
15. Moazzeni, S., Khayyambashi, M.R., Movahhedinia, N., Callegati, F.: On reliability improvement of software-defined networks. Comput. Netw. 133, 195–211 (2018)
16. Zhou, Y., et al.: A load balancing strategy of SDN controller based on distributed decision. In: 2014 IEEE 13th International Conference on Trust, Security, and Privacy in Computing and Communications (TrustCom), pp. 851–856. IEEE (2014)
17. Hunt, P., Konar, M., Junqueira, F.P., Reed, B.: ZooKeeper: Wait-free Coordination for Internet-scale Systems. In: USENIX Annual Technical Conference, vol. 8, no. 9, June 2010

Signature Based Malicious Behavior Detection in Android

Vikas Sihag[1,2]([envelope]) [iD], Ashawani Swami[1], Manu Vardhan[2] [iD],
and Pradeep Singh[2]

[1] Sardar Patel University of Police, Security and Criminal Justice, Jodhpur, India
{vikas.sihag,spu16cs04}@policeuniversity.ac.in
[2] National Institute of Technology, Raipur, Raipur, India
{mvardhan.cs,psingh.cs}@nitrr.ac.in

Abstract. User's security and privacy are of increasing concern with the popularity of Android and its applications. Apps of malicious nature attempts to perform activities like information leakage and user profiling, detection of which is a challenge for security researchers. In this paper, we try to solve this problem by proposing a behavior based approach to detect malicious nature of applications in Android. Events and behavioral activities of an application are used to generate signature, which then is matched with signature database for detection. Behavioral signatures are designed on the basis of information leakage attempt, jailbreak attempt, abuse of root privilege and access of critical permissions. 260 popular apps of different nature were evaluated in addition to 42 android apps, which were flagged malicious by Government of India. The proposed system shows promising results to detect malicious behaviors. It also defines the nature of malicious activity exploited by an app.

Keywords: Malware · Android · Security · Dynamic analysis · Information leakage

1 Introduction

Android, an open source OS provides us with an interactive platform for running multiple applications. Android OS since its release in 2008, has grown as the most prefered choice in the market with over 2.5 billion active devices worldwide and 74.13% share in December 2019 [16]. Smartphones today being equipped with sophisticated sensors, from camera and microphones to gyroscopes and proximity sensors, creates a new paradigm for user experience. Sensors generates data, which contains sensitive information thus opening new attack surfaces to be exploited by developers with malicious intent. When a malware (malicious app) is installed on an android device, the user is open to serious privacy and security issues such as information leakage and over privilege permission exploitation. Benign and alternative malicious applications are released on the android marketplaces [19,25,27]. These apps are also pushed into the market without third-party reviews [1,5,22]. Google Play Store, Android's official application hosting service has over 2.57 million apps generating about 140 million USD [17].

© Springer Nature Singapore Pte Ltd. 2020
N. Chaubey et al. (Eds.): COMS2 2020, CCIS 1235, pp. 251–262, 2020.
https://doi.org/10.1007/978-981-15-6648-6_20

Spotted in 2010, the first Android Malware was DroidSMS, which would subscribe users to premium SMS services. Since then multiple genres of malware have targeted Android ranging from downloaders to clickers, spyware to banking trojans and adware to ransomware [3,6,12,18,23]. Recently CamScanner a popular document scanning application on Google Play store was identified to be infected with `AndroidOS.Necro.n` dropper, which once installed attempts to install another malware [21]. Recently, 983 cases of known vulnerabilities and 655 zero-days were found among the top 5,000 free apps (each with 1M to 500M downloads) available on Google Play Store.

Applications running on Android performs system interacts at different levels. These system and application interactions can be recorded in the form of logs. Logs are generally classified into either system generated logs or application generated logs. System generated logs record events taking place in the execution of the operating system in order to provide a trail that can be used to understand the activities of the system and to identify problems. Application generated logs are events logged by a running application on the OS. It logs, events, warnings and errors. Information logged in it is determined by the app developer not the OS. Malicious app developers avoid detection by evading logging of its behavior [26]. Application logs are thus less reliable than system logs for behavior detection. Logcat is an operating system debug tool designed for Android. It monitors the system in real-time and creates a dump of system and application log messages, thus making it a suitable choice to collect information from Android OS.

In this paper we try to detect application behavior using log dumps from logcat. The approach is based on system generated logs rather than application logs. As system logs will contain activities and events of all running applications, a filtering mechanism is then employed to constrain on monitoring the selected application only. Behavior based signatures are generated on the basis of malicious activities for purpose of information leakage, jailbreak, abuse of root privilege or access of critical permissions.

Paper Organization: Following Sect. 2 discusses the prerequisites. Section 3 overviews the proposed solution. Section 4 discusses dataset preparation, experimental setup, results and analysis. Related work is covered in Sect. 5. Concluding remarks and future scope are discussed in Sect. 6.

2   Background Information

Android OS has a linux based stacked architecture, with linux kernel closest to the hardware and interact with the device hardware. Stacked representation of Android architecture as illustrated in Fig. 1. Linux kernel is customized for smart devices with power, memory and computational constraints. It includes all the key hardware drivers for camera, keyboard, wireless, audio, screen etc. It is responsible for power management, process management and memory management. Above kernel, HAL provides standard interface to the Java API framework that exposes device hardware capabilities. Each process in Android version 5.0

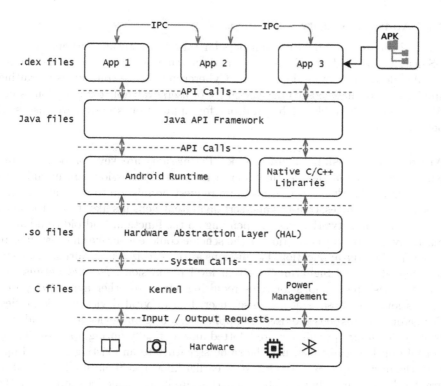

Fig. 1. Android architecture diagram

and above runs with its own Android Runtime (ART), which converts application dex bytecode into native code to be executed. Prior Android versions comprised of Dalvik Virtual Machine, a kind of Java VM optimized for low processing and memory constrained environment. The app works with its own copy of the virtual Dalvik VM. Dalvik for security was designed to efficiently operates multiple virtual machines. Dalvik executable (.dex) file of an application is optimized and run in its Dalvik VM. Most key components and utilities of Android system such as ART and HAL are designed using native codes with C and C++ compatible libraries. Above ART and Native Libraries resides Java API framework. Features of Android are accessed by apps using it to help developers write apps easily and quickly. It includes APIs to design UI, work with databases, handle user interaction, etc. On top of the stack are applications for user interactions. Android contains a set of preinstalled system apps to ensure minimum functionalities of SMS, internet browsing, contact management, calendar, music and more. These system apps provide vital capabilities that developers can access from their app, for instance sharing a message by system messaging app [11,20].

2.1   Android Security Mechanisms

Android due to its popularity, is a popular target of malware authors. Android OS installed with advanced hardwares and softwares generates enormous amount of valuable data for and about users. Cybercriminals are continuously crafting applications to maliciously take advantage of users' valuable data. Various security mechanisms employed by Android for application security are discussed below.

Android Permissions Framework. Permissions are key components and plays a vital role in the identification of malware. Permissions are intended to safeguard the user's privacy. Apps must request permission to user information such as text messages, contacts and certain system elements like the microphone, the camera and network access. Depending on the function, Android could automatically give the authorization or the scheme could encourage the customer to agree or reject the application. Permissions are categorized into Normal, Dangerous, Signature and SignatureOrSystem level permissions. *Normal* permissions are lower-risk permissions for apps requiring access to other apps. *Dangerous* permissions are those which accesses user data or vital device functionalities. Dangerous permissions are used by applications to gain device access and user privacy. *Signature* permission are allotted automatically during app installation only if app being installed has the same signature to an existing installed app with the permission. *SignatreOrSystem* earlier known as Signature|Privileged, is granted by system only to applications that are in a specific location or has the same signature as that of an app declaring it. It is designed for multiple vendors sharing specific features or folders on the system.

Android Sandboxing. Application sandboxing feature creates a contained environment for process to be executed. Each running app is limited to its sandbox, which is quarantined from other apps. An app may get at resources outside its sandbox, only the ones which were permitted by users during installation. Discretionary Access Control (DAC) is used for resource management outside the sandbox. If an app X tries to read application Y's resources, it is prevented because of the lack of user privileges. As apps are digitally signed with the developer's private key, apps with same developer's certificate are assigned same UID for resource and permission sharing. Thus malware authors with developer's key can design an app with the same certificate to access private resources of other apps developed by the developer.

Inter-component Communication (ICC). Android employs ICC mechanism or Binder for apps to communicate with each other or system. It is responsible of request migration from the originating process to the target process. Using ICC an application component can request data access from another component within the same application or other application within the same device or a remote service. For example, a product delivery application may use Map application for device's location by ICC.

2.2   Android Security Threats

Android smartphones being hub of users' private data is always under the lense of app developers. Users now have high probability of facing information leakage such as mobile number, email address, IMSI (International Mobile Subscriber Identifier), IMEI (International Mobile Equipment Identifier), Contact list, and other personal identification information. IMEI or IMSI numbers do not immediately expose user identity, but with malicious service or app having access to it there is always a risk of privacy violation [7,13]. Android security being based on permission model, lacks fine permission control and management.

Apart from threat on user's private information, there is always a threat on exploiting the underlying Android system. Attackers may exploit a vulnerability in the underlying linux sytem to gain root privilege of the device. Attackers with root privileged can easily over powers Android security framework. These attacks can result in unauthorized actions from malicious applications, which thus will cause security and privacy violations.

3   Proposed Solution

Our aim is to design and implement a system, that can collect and select real-time app interactions specific for a target application and check the behavioral activity for malicious nature.

The proposed solution offers a dynamic analysis approach to analyse application behavior. Figure 2 gives overview of the proposed architecture containing an Android system and a server. System generated logs are collected from the Android device at kernel-level. Thus any attempt by malicious application to evade application level logging would be detected. Collected logs are filtered and then matched with signatures for analysis.

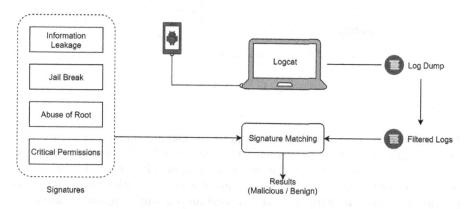

Fig. 2. Work flow of the proposed solution

Logging. Android OS and app activities of different types can be logged using the Android system debugger called logcat. It logs both system and application generated logs as depicted in Fig. 3. A log entry from logcat includes tag and its priority. A tag indicates the component responsible for its generation (for example, OpenGLRenderer). The priority defines the priority level amongst Assert (A), Error (E), Warning (W) and Verbose (V) from high to low.

A log entry format of logcat contains:

```
<date> <time> <PID>-<TID>/<package> <priority>/tag: <message>
```

PID stands for process identifier and TID is thread identifier. Below is a sample logcat entry.

```
14-11 17:31:21.320 74-113/com.example.application I/Application:
IN CLASS: (ENAppn.java:27)
```

Application generated logs are events logged by apps running on the OS. Information logged in application logs is determined by the app developer not the OS. Malicious app developers can easily avoid detection by not logging its activities. Application logs thus cannot be relied upon for behavior detection.

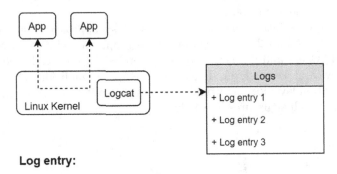

Log entry:

date time PID-TID / package priority / tag: message

Fig. 3. Log collection

Log Filtering. The quantity of logs prevents manual analysis of kernel-level logs. A logging module at the kernel level gather records of log information from all events which take place on the operating system. The collected information consists of entries irrelevant w.r.t. our target activity. Furthermore, given the restricted storage capability on a smartphone the quantity of record information needs to be reduced. We only gather logs associated to interested system calls for malware detection in order to address these issues. Linux OS has around 300 system calls, which can be categorized based on their functionality. Thus system calls responsible for critical activities (such as process, memory and device management) are considered for further analysis. This enables us to acquire log data containing entries of concerned system calls. But it includes system calls related to all processes running on the OS. We therefore further remove entries related to irrelevant process by selecting only the concerned process entries. Using logcat tool process ID of concerned app and child processes are selected for filtering. Critical permissions accessed by application during runtime are captured in logs (Fig. 4).

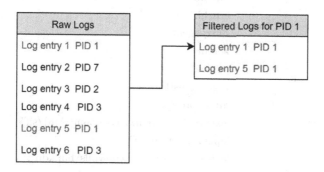

Fig. 4. Log filtering for selected process with PID 1

Signature Matching. The proposed system is based upon pattern matching of signatures with the filtered logs from the above step. Signatures are carefully crafted for high detection accuracy. They if designed to be too specific will lead to high false negative, and if too considerate of various activities will lead to high false positive. Keywords responsible personal information such as mail account, IMEI, phone number, etc. were considered for user's personal identifiable information. For detecting jailbreak application and applications exploiting root privilege, name of known exploit binary files and commands respectively were selected for signatures. And for detecting requested critical permissions at runtime, critical permission request command were listed as signatures. List of signature is given in Table 1.

4   Results and Analysis

A system prototype of the proposed solution was implemented. System logs for the targeted application were generated and filtered, followed by pattern matching with the signatures. Popular applications of different categories were collected.

In total 260 applications were collected from Google Play Store and other Third party app stores for analysis. Selection of applications was done on the basis of popularity. Popular applications from each category (social networking, games, productivity, messaging, etc.) were selected. Apart from the above,

Table 1. Signatures for detecting malicious behaviour

Threat	Signatures and keywords
Information leakage	IMSI and SIM
	IMEI and Android
	CLONE_FILES
	TEL and MAIL
	quattrowirelesssdk
	admob
	adwhirl
	flurryagent
Jail break	asroot
	exploid
	rageagainstthecage
	gingerbreak
Root abuse	^execve("/(system/)?(bin|sbin|xbin)/su"
	^open(".*/iptables"
	^execve(".*/(chmod|chown|ls\b|mkdir|rmdir)"
	busybox
	daemonsu
	kingroot
	kinguser
	supersu
	superuser
	adfree
	greenify
	kerneladiutor
	setcpu
	shootme
	stericson
	titanium
Critical permissions	SEND_SMS_NO_CONFIRMATION
	WRITE_SMS
	READ_LOGS
	INSTALL_PACKAGES
	MOUNT_UNMOUNT_FILESYSTEMS
	READ_PHONE_STATE
	READ_HISTORY_BOOKMARKS
	WRITE_SMS
	READ_SMS
	READ_CONTACTS

42 applications listed malicious by Government of India were also selected for analysis. Analysis results are shown in Table 2 and 3.

Table 2. Analysis results of popular applications

Threat	Number of detection
Information leakage	91
JailBreak	10
Abuse root	15
Critical permissions	277

Table 3. Analysis results of 42 Apps listed malicious by GOI.

Threat	Number of detection
Information leakage	43
JailBreak	12
Abuse root	16
Critical permissions	63

Of 260 applications, 43 applications which taking sensitive data from device and 2 application fetching email data. 21 applications were also detected showing advertisement services. Additionally we have found 10 applications which try to jailbreak the device, 4 applications which is try to root the device, 4 applications run *rageagainthecage* which is used to root the device. Additionally, we found out 16 applications which use superuser activity in the device.

5   Related Work

Takamasa et al. in [8] describe the system architecture for signature pattern based detection of malicious applications for Android. Ma et al. in [13] introduces a novel attack vector called as "shadow attacks", which tries to evade the behavior based detection by partitioning a process into multiple shadow processes. Deguang Kong et al. in [10] describes a system which automatically assess the review to behaviour reliability of mobile applications. According to author, Autoreb uses artificial intelligence to identify linkage between user reviews and privacy compromises. They collected reviews from multiple sources thus to identify issues from reviews towards the application. Burguera et al. in [4] describes the system and framework to perform behavioral analysis of application to detect malware. Crowdroid collected information traces about application from multiple real-time users. It employs crowdsourcing approach to differentiate normal and malicious behavior. It also illustrated similarity between newly generated test malware and real samples. [4] considered system calls as they give low level information. They were able to detect all malicious execution for their self developed malicious apps. Andrea et al. in [15] presents the behaviour based detection system which analyses and correlates function. The functions selected were responsible for package-level, user-level, application-level and kernel-level interactions. A framework based on machine learning is introduced in [11] by Kong and Jin to address permission prediction problem. It captures the relations amongst textual descriptions, permissions, and app category. They tested the approach on 11k applications ranging from 30 categories. [14] and [2] classified malicious and benign applications based on system calls captured using strace tool. They then employ machine learning for classification. Wu et al. in [24] used call frequency and dependency for detection. They then fed LASSO, RF and SVM based machine learning classifiers to achieve accuracy of 93%. System logs and system calls are employed by Jang et al. in [9] for malware detection and familial classification. They reported accuracy of 99% for their approach.

6   Conclusion

We have presented a behavior based android malware detection approach. System generated logs are collected and filtered at runtime for application under analysis to be further matched with generated signatures. Signatures were generated taking into account the application behavior responsible for information leakage, jail break attempt, priviledge escalation attempt and access of critical permissions at runtime. Behavior based detection approaches provides insight into running applications as compared to static analysis approaches and thus need to be employed by market places for detecting behavior deversion of applications from intended behavior. Our approach was found to be effective as it gives considerable insight into malware interactions responsible for security and privacy compromises.

In future, a multi level hybrid approach including static analysis can be envisioned to improve scalability and efficiency of the detection system.

References

1. Bhandari, S., Panihar, R., Naval, S., Laxmi, V., Zemmari, A., Gaur, M.S.: Sword: semantic aware Android malware detector. J. Inf. Secur. Appl. **42**, 46–56 (2018). https://doi.org/10.1016/j.jisa.2018.07.003
2. Bhatia, T., Kaushal, R.: Malware detection in Android based on dynamic analysis. In: 2017 International Conference on Cyber Security and Protection of Digital Services (Cyber Security), pp. 1–6. IEEE (2017). https://doi.org/10.1109/CyberSecPODS.2017.8074847
3. Bose, A., Hu, X., Shin, K.G., Park, T.: Behavioral detection of malware on mobile handsets. In: Proceedings of the 6th International Conference on Mobile Systems, Applications, and Services, pp. 225–238 (2008). https://doi.org/10.1145/1378600.1378626

4. Burguera, I., Zurutuza, U., Nadjm-Tehrani, S.: Crowdroid: behavior-based malware detection system for Android. In: Proceedings of the 1st ACM Workshop on Security and Privacy in Smartphones and Mobile Devices, pp. 15–26 (2011). https://doi.org/10.1145/2046614.2046619

5. Cai, H., Meng, N., Ryder, B., Yao, D.: DroidCat: effective Android malware detection and categorization via app-level profiling. IEEE Trans. Inf. Foren. Secur. **14**(6), 1455–1470 (2018). https://doi.org/10.1109/TIFS.2018.2879302

6. Dash, S.K., et al.: DroidScribe: classifying Android malware based on runtime behavior. In: 2016 IEEE Security and Privacy Workshops (SPW), pp. 252–261. IEEE (2016). https://doi.org/10.1109/SPW.2016.25

7. Doulamis, A., Pelekis, N., Theodoridis, Y.: Easytracker: an Android application for capturing mobility behavior. In: 16th Panhellenic Conference on Informatics, pp. 357–362. IEEE (2012). https://doi.org/10.1109/PCi.2012.22

8. Isohara, T., Takemori, K., Kubota, A.: Kernel-based behavior analysis for Android malware detection. In: 2011 Seventh International Conference on Computational Intelligence and Security, pp. 1011–1015. IEEE (2011). https://doi.org/10.1109/CIS.2011.226

9. Jang, J.W., Yun, J., Woo, J., Kim, H.K.: Andro-profiler: anti-malware system based on behavior profiling of mobile malware. In: Proceedings of the 23rd International Conference on World Wide Web, pp. 737–738 (2014). https://doi.org/10.13089/JKIISC.2014.24.1.145

10. Kong, D., Cen, L., Jin, H.: Autoreb: automatically understanding the review-to-behavior fidelity in Android applications. In: Proceedings of the 22nd ACM SIGSAC Conference on Computer and Communications Security, pp. 530–541 (2015). https://doi.org/10.1145/2810103.2813689

11. Kong, D., Jin, H.: Towards permission request prediction on mobile apps via structure feature learning. In: Proceedings of the 2015 SIAM International Conference on Data Mining, pp. 604–612. SIAM (2015). https://doi.org/10.1137/1.9781611974010.68

12. Lindorfer, M., Neugschwandtner, M., Platzer, C.: Marvin: efficient and comprehensive mobile app classification through static and dynamic analysis. In: 2015 IEEE 39th Annual Computer Software and Applications Conference, vol. 2, pp. 422–433. IEEE (2015). https://doi.org/10.1109/COMPSAC.2015.103

13. Ma, W., Duan, P., Liu, S., Gu, G., Liu, J.C.: Shadow attacks: automatically evading system-call-behavior based malware detection. J. Comput. Virol. **8**(1–2), 1–13 (2012). https://doi.org/10.1007/s11416-011-0157-5

14. Mas' ud, M.Z., Sahib, S., Abdollah, M.F., Selamat, S.R., Yusof, R.: Analysis of features selection and machine learning classifier in Android malware detection. In: 2014 International Conference on Information Science & Applications (ICISA), pp. 1–5. IEEE (2014). https://doi.org/10.1109/ICISA.2014.6847364

15. Saracino, A., Sgandurra, D., Dini, G., Martinelli, F.: Madam: effective and efficient behavior-based Android malware detection and prevention. IEEE Trans. Dependable Secur. Comput. **15**(1), 83–97 (2016). https://doi.org/10.1109/TDSC.2016.2536605

16. Statista: Mobile Operating Systems' Market Share Worldwide from January 2012 to December 2019. https://www.statista.com/statistics/272698/global-market-share-held-by-mobile-operating-systems-since-2009/

17. Statista: Number of Apps Available in Leading App Stores as of 4th Quarter 2019. https://www.statista.com/statistics/276623/number-of-apps-available-in-leading-app-stores/

18. Sun, M., Lui, J.C.S., Zhou, Y.: Blender: self-randomizing address space layout for Android apps. In: Monrose, F., Dacier, M., Blanc, G., Garcia-Alfaro, J. (eds.) RAID 2016. LNCS, vol. 9854, pp. 457–480. Springer, Cham (2016). https://doi. org/10.1007/978-3-319-45719-2_21

19. Sun, M., Wei, T., Lui, J.C.: Taintart: a practical multi-level information-flow tracking system for Android runtime. In: Proceedings of the 2016 ACM SIGSAC Conference on Computer and Communications Security, pp. 331–342 (2016). https:// doi.org/10.1145/2976749.2978343

20. Sun, M., Zheng, M., Lui, J.C., Jiang, X.: Design and implementation of an Android host-based intrusion prevention system. In: Proceedings of the 30th Annual Computer Security Applications Conference, pp. 226–235 (2014). https://doi.org/10. 1145/2664243.2664245

21. Team, K.: Malicious Android app had more than 100 million downloads in google play. https://www.kaspersky.com/blog/camscanner-malicious-android-app/28156

22. Wang, W., et al.: Constructing features for detecting Android malicious applications: issues, taxonomy and directions. IEEE Access **7**, 67602–67631 (2019). https://doi.org/10.1109/ACCESS.2019.2918139

23. Wang, X., Sun, K., Wang, Y., Jing, J.: DeepDroid: dynamically enforcing enterprise policy on Android devices. In: NDSS (2015). https://doi.org/10.14722/ndss.2015. 23263

24. Wu, W.C., Hung, S.H.: DroidDolphin: a dynamic Android malware detection framework using big data and machine learning. In: Proceedings of the 2014 Conference on Research in Adaptive and Convergent Systems, pp. 247–252 (2014). https://doi.org/10.1145/2663761.2664223

25. Xu, K., Li, Y., Deng, R.H.: ICCDetector: ICC-based malware detection on Android. IEEE Trans. Inf. Foren. Secur. **11**(6), 1252–1264 (2016). https://doi.org/10.1109/ TIFS.2016.2523912

26. Zhang, H., Luo, S., Zhang, Y., Pan, L.: An efficient Android malware detection system based on method-level behavioral semantic analysis. IEEE Access **7**, 69246– 69256 (2019). https://doi.org/10.1109/ACCESS.2019.2919796

27. Zhang, M., Duan, Y., Yin, H., Zhao, Z.: Semantics-aware Android malware classification using weighted contextual API dependency graphs. In: Proceedings of the 2014 ACM SIGSAC Conference on Computer and Communications Security, pp. 1105–1116 (2014). https://doi.org/10.1145/2660267.2660359

A Method for Malware Detection in Virtualization Environment

Darshan Tank[1]([⊠]) [iD], Akshai Aggarwal[2], and Nirbhay Chaubey[3] [iD]

[1] Government Polytechnic (Rajkot), Gujarat Technological University, Ahmedabad, India
dmtank@gmail.com
[2] School of Computer Science, University of Windsor, Windsor, Canada
akshai.aggarwal@gmail.com
[3] Ganpat University, Gujarat, India
nirbhay@ieee.org

Abstract. Security of Virtual Machines (VMs) is a major concern with the virtualization environment. Virtual machines are a primary target for an adversary to acquire unethical access to the organization's virtual infrastructure. Traditional security measures are not enough for advanced malware detection. Today's advanced malware can easily avoid detection by using a number of evasion tactics. Process or code injection is one such technique to evade the detection of malware. Various process injection techniques are employed by malware to gain more stealth and to bypass security products. Detection of process injection attack is achieved with little effort on a physical machine as compared to a virtual machine. In this paper, we propose a novel approach to detect malware based on API function calls. API function call information has the ability to trace malware behavior. We found that the presence of certain API function calls may confirm the existence of malware. We implement dynamic malware analysis using the volatility framework.

Keywords: API function call · Hypervisor · Malware detection · Process injection · Virtual machine · Virtualization

1 Introduction

Cloud computing emerging as a future computing model. Virtualization is a key underlying technology to enable cloud computing. Virtualization creates and runs multiple VM or guest operating systems on a single physical machine using Virtual Machine Monitor (VMM) or Hypervisor. Hypervisor facilitates the abstract of physical machine resources such as CPU, Memory, I/O and NIC, etc., among several virtual machines. The sharing of resources increases the security challenges for the cloud service provider. The proliferation of unknown malware and sophisticated rootkits, are more prevalent to tamper the critical kernel data structures. Traditional In-host anti-malware solution is inadequate to ensure the security of the guest operating system, particularly in a virtualized environment [1]. VMI is able to gather the state information of the running VMs while functioning at VMM. Obtaining meaningful state information such as process list,

N. Chaubey et al. (Eds.): COMS2 2020, CCIS 1235, pp. 263–276, 2020.
https://doi.org/10.1007/978-981-15-6648-6_21

kernel driver module, etc., from the viewable raw bytes of the live guest virtual machine memory named as semantic gap [2].

One of the main reasons for using introspection in malware detection is that malware using advanced techniques such as rootkits are not detected using traditional automated malware-detection systems. The other reason is the advanced features that this technology provides, which allows the user to have a deep insight into each action happening in the virtual machine [3].

The rest of the paper is organized as follows: Sect. 2 provides background information on virtual machine introspection, memory mapping under a hypervisor and also introduces the concept of rootkits. Section 3 presents the related work of using the VMI technique to detect and characterize known and unknown malwares. Section 4 outlines LibVMI as a VM Introspection tool. Section 5 introduces volatility as a memory analysis framework. The architecture of our proposed malware detection method is described in Sect. 6. Evaluation and preliminary results are presented in Sect. 7. Finally, the conclusion and future work are discussed in Sect. 8.

2 Background

2.1 Virtual Machine Introspection

Virtual machine introspection is the process of observing the runtime state of virtual machines. Introspection can be achieved either from the hypervisor or from some virtual machine other than the one being supervised. VMI is an art of safeguarding a security-critical application running on virtual machines from security attacks [4]. VMI-based approaches are widely adopted for security applications, software debugging, and systems management. One can introspect the VM from inside or outside of the VM. VMI-based tools may be located inside or outside of the VM. VMI tools can also be used for malware analysis to analyze the behavior of the malware and to detect the latest malware attacks. VMI coupled with existing virtual infrastructure management solutions can become a powerful tool for memory analysis and event correlation. The semantic gap is one of the main restraints of virtual machine introspection [5]. In a virtualized environment, the semantic gap can be defined as the extraction of high-level information of guest OS state from low-level information obtained externally at the hypervisor level [6]. One can do introspection within the virtual machines or outside the virtual machines.

2.2 Memory Mapping

In a normal scenario, there are two levels of memory: virtual memory and physical memory of the physical machine. But when we talk about hypervisors, there are three levels of memory: virtual memory and physical memory of the virtual machine, and physical memory of the host machine. The hypervisors only allocate memory to the virtual machine. By default, hypervisors have no knowledge of what types of activities being performed inside the virtual memory of the virtual machine. To get that information, additional tools have to be installed. Below is a generalized example of memory-sharing within the virtual machine. Figure 1 shows the three levels of memory addressing under hypervisor [7].

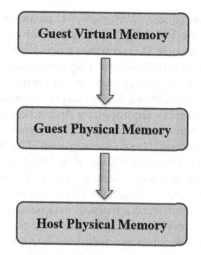

Fig. 1. Memory mapping under the hypervisor

One of the primary objectives of the VMI tools is to translate the memory addresses of the virtual machine's virtual memory: first, from the virtual to the physical memory of the virtual machine, then to the physical memory of the host machine. This will help the hypervisor to access the correct memory area during introspection.

2.3 Rootkits

Rootkits are malwares allowing permanent or consistent, undetectable presence in a computer system. Rootkits can hide specific system resources to achieve the goal of hiding the intrusion into the compromised computer. Rootkits deviate the normal behavior of the system by injecting malicious code into an operating system [8]. Kernel rootkits execute in privileged mode on Ring 0, making it very hard to detect. Kernel rootkits have posed serious security threats due to their stealthy manner. More advanced rootkits can launch Direct Kernel Object Manipulation (DKOM) attacks, which directly modify the core data structure of the OS kernel in memory. Malicious library injection and code injection are also common means for rootkits to subvert the system.

3 Related Work

Researchers and security experts have introduced many ideas and prototypes for malware detection and classification. Malware detection methods can be categorized into two classes: Signature-based static analysis and Behavirol-based dynamic analysis. Static analysis is accomplished without executing the samples while dynamic analysis is performed by executing samples in the virtualization environment. Huseinovic et al. [9] proposed a process monitoring mechanism in a VMware VM running WindowsXP. Hua et al. [10] have designed and implemented a process detection system called VmRecoverySystem. Their proposed architecture uses KVM as a hypervisor which consists of four modules. Tien et al. [11] introduced a VMI method to monitor the presence of malware in the volatile memory of the VM through the analysis of its processes, files, registers, and network activities. Case et al. [12] presented a new kernel-based rootkit detection technique applicable to the Mac OS X system. They have used the most popular memory forensic framework Volatility to analyze the features of malwares.

For detecting malwares in Android, Yang et al. [13] proposed a general tool named AMExtractor for volatile memory acquisition for Android devices. For malware detection in a virtualization environment, Kumara et al. [14] leveraged memory forensic tools such as Volatility and Rekall to analyze the memory state of the VMs, which can address the semantic gap problem existing in VMI. Hua et al. [10] designed and implemented a VMM-based hidden process detection system to investigate rootkits by identifying the lack of the critical process and the target hidden process from the aspect of memory forensics. Tien et al. [15] introduced a memory data monitoring method against the running malware outside the VM, various features were observed from the memory. Kumara et al. [16] proposed an automated multi-level detection system for Rootkits and other malwares for VMs at the hypervisor level. Mosli et al. [17] proposed an automated malware detection method using artifacts in forensic memory images. Kumara et al. [18] proposed an advanced VMM-based machine learning technique at the hypervisor. Machine learning techniques were highly used to analyze the executables that were mined and extracted using MFA-based techniques. Tank et al. [19] presented a review of Mobile Cloud Computing (MCC), its security & privacy issues and vulnerabilities affecting cloud computing systems, analysed and compared various possible approaches proposed by the researchers to address security and privacy issues in MCC. Tank et al. [20] analyzed security issues in an open-source cloud computing project - OpenStack Keystone. Tank [21] identified a need for a lightweight secure framework that provides security with minimum communication and processing overhead on mobile devices. Tank et al. [22] presented a critical study and comparison of virtualization vulnerabilities, security issues, and solutions. Tank et al. [23] discussed Cache Side Channel (CSC) attacks as prominent security threats and introduced a novel approach to detect cache attacks in virtualized environments. Tank et al. [24] explored virtualization aspects of cybersecurity threats and solutions in the cloud computing environment. From the above researches, one can conclude that live memory analysis is an effective way to detect advance malwares.

4   LibVMI - VM Introspection Tool

LibVMI is an open source introspection library. LibVMI focuses on writing and reading memory from VMs. LibVMI is an extended version based on XenAccess Library. LibVMI is designed to work across multiple platforms [25]. LibVMI allows accessing the memory of running virtual machines. In addition to memory access, LibVMI also supports memory events. LibVMI can be utilized to bridge the semantic gap between the hypervisor and guest operating systems [26]. It offers the following features.

- Easily extensible and optimized performance.
- It provides near-native speeds.

- Address the semantic gap problem.
- Access a VM's state from outside of the VM and broad platform support.

5   The Volatility Framework

Volatility is an advanced memory analysis framework. It supports analysis for Linux, Windows, Mac, and Android systems [27]. Various volatility plugins are also developed and maintained by the community to extract information from memory samples. Volatility can be utilized as a memory forensic toolkit to detect advanced malware with a real case scenario [28]. The volatility framework offers the following features.

- An advanced & open source memory analysis tool.
- Support live analysis of virtual machines.
- Runs on Linux, Windows, Mac, and Android systems.
- It can be used to detect advanced malware with a real case scenario.
- Support a variety of file formats.
- Plugins can be developed and distributed independently.

The volatility tool supports a wealth of perceptions into the working of a system [29]. We used Volatility 2.6.1 in our research to extract higher-level semantic information from the live Windows 7 virtual machine. The LibVMI also adds improved integration with Volatility [30].

6   Proposed Malware Detection Method

Malware refers to malicious programs. In this work, we propose a method for malware detection based on examination of API function calls and API function calls sequences. We monitor API function calls and function calls sequences indicative of various types of process injection attacks. The extracted API function calls to be represented as a feature of the machine learning model. Various malware injectors are executed on Windows virtual machines and their runtime memory is acquired. Behavior-based dynamic analysis is carried out using a volatility framework.

Dynamic malware analysis is performed using the Volatility framework. We use impscan [31] and procdump [32] volatility commands. The impscan command is used to extract API function calls from the memory image. The procdump command is used to find the base address of the process. We make use of VirtualAllocEx and VirtualAlloc API functions as Indicators of Compromise (IoC) or malicious activity. The VirtualAllocEx and VirtualAlloc [33] functions allow to allocate memory in the address space of another process. We utilized VirtualAllocEx and VirtualAlloc functions as a precursor to code injection because malware needs to create space in the victim process. Figure 2 shows the generic architecture of our proposed malware detection approach.

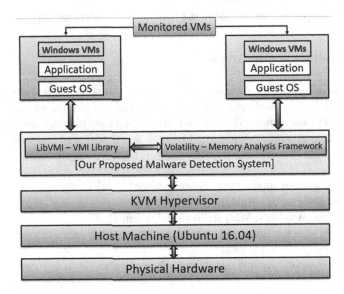

Fig. 2. The architecture of the proposed approach

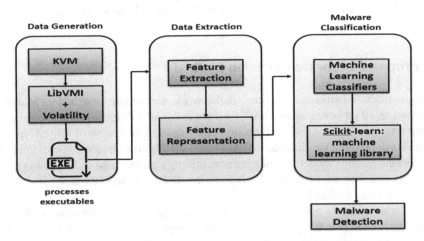

Fig. 3. Work flow of our proposed malware detection process

The work flow of our proposed malware detection process is depicted in Fig. 3. The malwares were executed on Windows virtual machines and their memory is acquired. Dynamic malware analysis is performed using the Volatility Framework. The impscan command from the volatility tool is used to extract API function calls from the dumped memory image. In the memory, the API function calls existed in the Import Address Table (IAT). The impscan command scans the memory image looking for API function calls in the IAT table. The procdump command can be used to find the base address of the process.

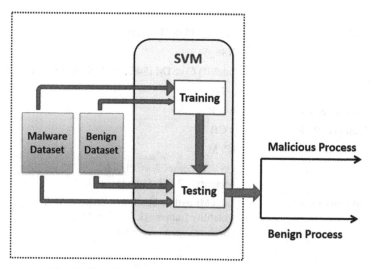

Fig. 4. Classification process using SVM binary classifier

The extracted Windows API function calls utilized as features of the machine learning model. We employed a machine learning method for the classification process. We used scikit-learn, a machine learning library in python. Scikit-learn features various clustering, regression, and classification algorithms including SVM, RF, GB, k-means, and DBSCAN, and is designed to interoperate with the Python numerical and scientific libraries NumPy and SciPy [34]. We applied SVM (Support Vector Machine) supervised machine learning technique for the classification process. It classifies the given sample as either benign or malicious class as shown in Fig. 4.

7   Experimental Setup and Preliminary Results

We used the Kernel-based Virtual Machine (KVM) as our Virtual Machine Monitor (VMM). We perform experiments on the host system, which had the specifications shown in Table 1.

LibVMI python bindings (version-3.4) integrated with the Volatility framework (version-2.6.1) set up on the host operating system. Virtual Machines launched by the KVM hypervisor have Windows 7 and Ubuntu 12.04 guest OS running on it. We gathered experimental data from multiple scenarios. We divided the overall scenarios into two classes, a positive class which represent malware injector scenarios and a negative class which represents standard operations running on a virtual machine.

Table 1. Testbed configurations

Host OS	Ubuntu 16.04.6 LTS
Host OS Type	64-bit
Linux Kernel	Linux 4.15.0-74-generic
Architecture	X86_64
Processor	Intel(R) CoreTM i5-8265U CPU @ 1.60 GHz x 8
Disk	1 TB
Number of Cores & Threads	4 & 8
Physical Memory (RAM)	8 GB
Hypervisor (VMM)	KVM
VM – 1	OS – Windows 7, vCPU - 1 Memory – 2 GB, Storage – 30 GB
Tools /Framework Used	LibVMI python bindings (version-3.4) & Volatility framework (version-2.6.1) (Both are open source tools)

Table 2 highlights all collected scenarios for experimental evaluation. We run various process injection techniques collected from different Github repos to extract data for the positive class. In the idle condition, the virtual machine runs standard operations. We extracted the Windows API function calls from a dumped memory image and utilized it as features of the machine learning model.

Table 2. List of collected scenarios for evaluation

Positive class scenario	Negative class scenario
GitHub - theevilbit/injection [35]	Runs standard operations (Idle Condition)
GitHub - fdiskyou/injectAllTheThings [36]	
GitHub - secrary/InjectProc [37]	
GitHub - marcosd4h/memhunter [38]	
GitHub - stephenfewer/ReflectiveDLLInjection [39]	

The above figures show snapshots captured from live VM. Figure 5 shows a list of active VM on our host & acquiring a memory sample of the live VM. Figure 6 shows the working of the imageinfo command to identify the profile. Figure 7 shows working of procdump command to dump a process's executable and to get the base address of process. Figure 8 shows working of impscan command to extract API function calls from the memory image.

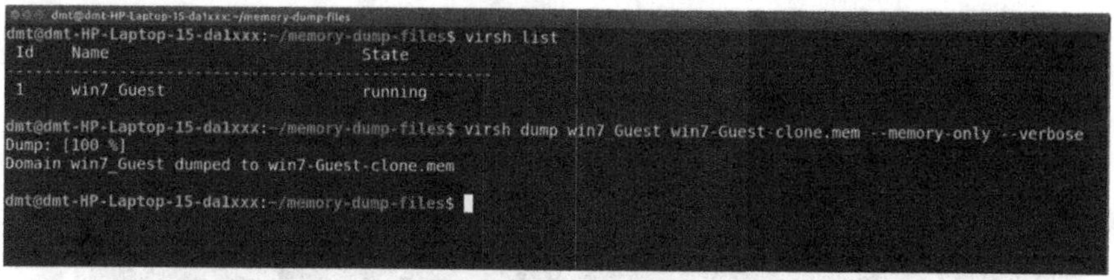

Fig. 5. List of active VM on our host & acquiring a memory sample of the live VM

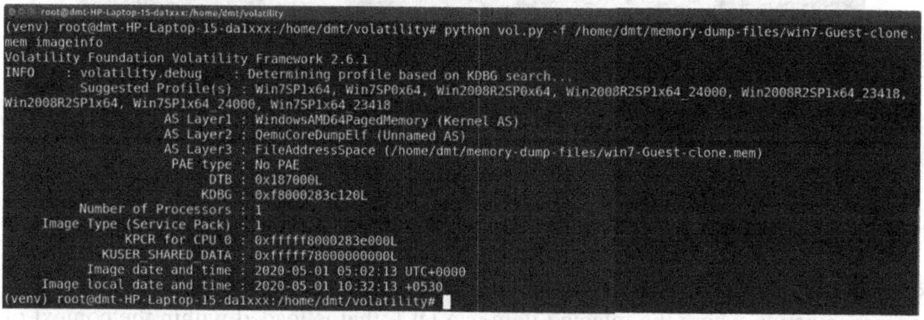

Fig. 6. imageinfo command used to identify the profile

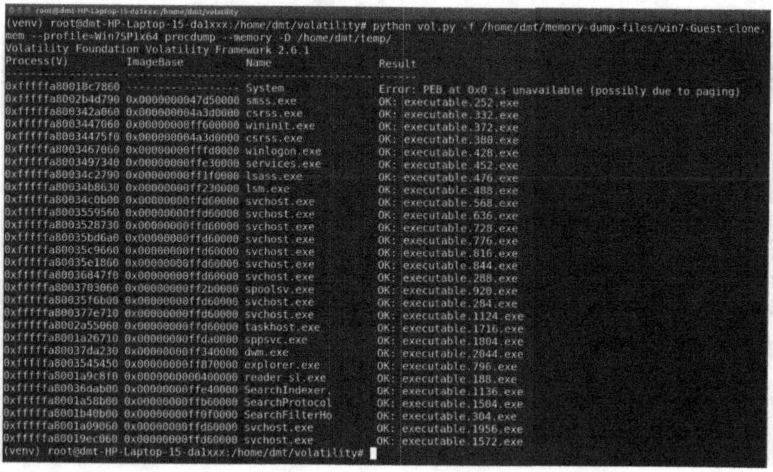

Fig. 7. procdump command to dump a process's executable & to get the base address of the process

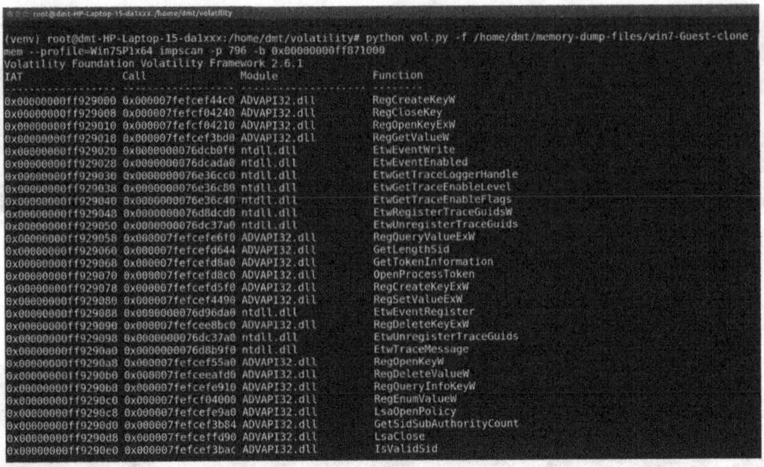

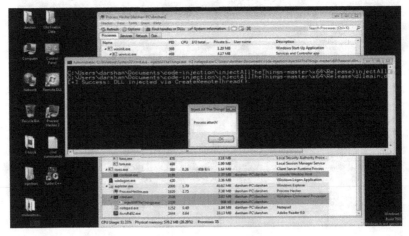

Fig. 8. impscan command to extract API function calls from the memory image

7.1 Experiment: DLL Injection Detection

Remote DLL (Dynamic Link Library) injection or Classic DLL injection is a form of process injection where the injected item is a DLL that is loaded within the context of the remote process. The program that performs the injection is called an injector. In this experiment, we detect the injector process running on a virtual machine (Figs. 9, 10 and 11).

Fig. 9. The injector process is called through command prompt window

Fig. 10. Malicious DLL was loaded in process space

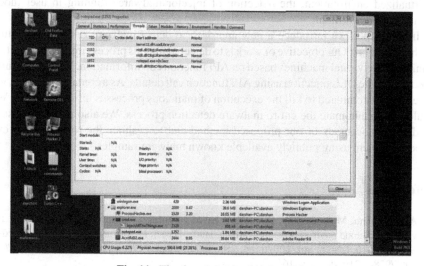

Fig. 11. The thread that loaded the DLL

We examine the captured memory image of VM to detect possible malicious DLL injection activities. The above images show how the injector process injects malicious DLL via the CreateRemoteThread function into the legitimate process. In the above images, the injector process is injectAllTheThings.exe, the injected process is notepad.exe and the injected DLL is dllmain.dll. As shown in the image the corresponding thread that loaded the DLL executes the LoadLibraryW API function.

We identified the malicious injector process by examining the process's API function call information from the captured memory image. Table 3 describes the identified malicious processes.

Table 3. Detection of malicious processes

Captured memory image	Process name	Process Id	Detected as
win7-Guest-clone.mem	injectAllTheThings.exe	2320	Malicious

8   Conclusion and Future Work

The malware leverages various process injection methods. Process injection attacks are the most damaging exploits faced by a large number of internet users today. Process injection or code injection techniques are used by malwares to gain more secrecy and to bypass employed security mechanisms by injecting malicious code that performs sensitive operations to a process that is privileged to do so. Detection of process injection attack is achieved with little effort on a physical machine as compared to a virtual machine. As there is no direct access mechanism to the physical memory of VMs in a virtualized environment, the detection of injector malwares running in user mode memory is more difficult.

In this paper, we introduce a new approach to detect malware running on virtual machine memory. Our objective of work is to detect malicious process injection activities running inside virtual machines based on API function call information. We successfully detected remote DLL injection using API function call details. As a containment plan, we can execute a command to kill the execution of malicious processes inside the VMs. We would like to automate the entire malware detection process. We also plan to measure the detection accuracy of our proposed method and to evaluate the robustness of our proposed system using publicly available known malware samples.

References

1. Ajay Kumara, M.A., Jaidhar, C.D.: VMI based automated real-time malware detector for virtualized cloud environment. In: Carlet, Claude, Hasan, M.Anwar, Saraswat, Vishal (eds.) SPACE 2016. LNCS, vol. 10076, pp. 281–300. Springer, Cham (2016). https://doi.org/10.1007/978-3-319-49445-6_16
2. Zhang, S., Meng, X., Wang, L., Xu, L., Han, X.: Secure virtualization environment based on advanced memory introspection. In: Security and Communication Networks (2018)
3. More, A., Tapaswi, S.: Virtual machine introspection: towards bridging the semantic gap. J. Cloud Comput. 3(1), 16 (2014)
4. Rakotondravony, N., et al.: Classifying malware attacks in IaaS cloud environments. J. Cloud Comput. 6(1), 26 (2017)
5. Dolan-Gavitt, B., Leek, T., Zhivich, M., Giffin, J., Lee, W.: Virtuoso: narrowing the semantic gap in virtual machine introspection. In: 2011 IEEE Symposium on Security and Privacy, pp. 297–312. IEEE, May 2011
6. Fu, Y., Lin, Z.: Bridging the semantic gap in virtual machine introspection via online kernel data redirection. ACM Trans. Inf. Syst. Secur. 16, 1–29 (2013). https://doi.org/10.1145/2516951.2505124
7. Virtual Machine Introspection in Malware Analysis. https://resources.infosecinstitute.com/virtual-machine-introspection-in-malware-analysis/. Accessed 17 Dec 2019

8. Wikipedia contributors: Rootkit. In Wikipedia, The Free Encyclopedia, 12 March 2020. https://en.wikipedia.org/w/index.php?title=Rootkit&oldid=945263481. Accessed 15 Mar 2020

9. Huseinovic, A., Ribic, S.: Virtual machine memory forensics. In: 2013 21st Telecommunications Forum Telfor (TELFOR), pp. 940–942 (2013)

10. Hua, Q., Zhang, Y.: Detecting malware and rootkit via memory forensics. In: 2015 International Conference on Computer Science and Mechanical Automation (CSMA), pp. 92–96 (2015)

11. Tien, C., Liao, J., Chang, S., Kuo, S.: Memory forensics using virtual machine introspection for Malware analysis. In: 2017 IEEE Conference on Dependable and Secure Computing, 518–519 (2017)

12. Case, A., Richard, I.I.I., Golden, G.: Advancing Mac OS X rootkit detection. Digital Invest. **14**, S25–S33 (2015). https://doi.org/10.1016/j.diin.2015.05.005

13. Yang, H., Zhuge, J., Liu, H., Liu, W.: A tool for volatile memory acquisition from android devices. DigitalForensics 2016. IAICT, vol. 484, pp. 365–378. Springer, Cham (2016). https://doi.org/10.1007/978-3-319-46279-0_19

14. Kumara, A., Jaidhar, C.D.: Execution time measurement of virtual machine volatile artifacts analyzers. In: 2015 IEEE 21st International Conference on Parallel and Distributed Systems (ICPADS), pp. 314–319. IEEE (2015)

15. Tien, C., Liao, J., Chang, S., Kuo, S.: Memory forensics using virtual machine introspection for Malware analysis. In: 2017 IEEE Conference on Dependable and Secure Computing, pp. 518–519 (2017)

16. Kumara, M.A., Jaidhar, C.D.: Automated multi-level malware detection system based on reconstructed semantic view of executables using machine learning techniques at VMM (2018)

17. Mosli, R., Li, R., Yuan, B., Pan, Y.: Automated malware detection using artifacts in forensic memory images. In: 2016 IEEE Symposium on Technologies for Homeland Security (HST), 1–6 (2016)

18. Kumara, M.A., Jaidhar, C.D.: Leveraging virtual machine introspection with memory forensics to detect and characterize unknown malware using machine learning techniques at hypervisor. Digit. Invest. **23**, 99–123 (2017)

19. Chaubey, N.K., Tank, D.M.: Security, privacy and challenges in Mobile Cloud Computing (MCC): - a critical study and comparison. Int. J. Innov. Res. Comput. Commun. Eng. (IJIRCCE), **4**(2), 1259–1266 (2016). https://doi.org/10.15680/ijircce.2016.0402028

20. Tank, D., Aggarwal, A., Chaubey, N.: Security analysis of OpenStack keystone. Int. J. Latest Technol. Eng. Manag. Appl. Sci. (IJLTEMAS) **6**(6), 31–38 (2017)

21. Tank, D.M.: Security and privacy issues, solutions, and tools for MCC. In: Munir, K. (ed.) Security Management in Mobile Cloud Computing, pp. 121–147. IGI Global, Hershey (2017). https://doi.org/10.4018/978-1-5225-0602-7.ch006

22. Tank, D., Aggarwal, A. Chaubey, N.: Virtualization vulnerabilities, security issues, and solutions: a critical study and comparison. Int. J. Inf. Technol. (2019). https://doi.org/10.1007/s41870-019-00294-x

23. Tank, D., Aggarwal, A., Chaubey, N.: Cache attack detection in virtualized environments. J. Inf. Optim. Sci. **40**(5), 1109–1119 (2019). https://doi.org/10.1080/02522667.2019.1638001

24. Tank, D. M., Aggarwal, A., Chaubey, N.K.: Cyber security aspects of virtualization in cloud computing environments: analyzing virtualization-specific cyber security risks. In: Chaubey, N., Prajapati, B. (eds.), Quantum Cryptography and the Future of Cyber Security, pp. 283–299. IGI Global, Hershey (2020). https://doi.org/10.4018/978-1-7998-2253-0.ch013

25. Introduction to LibVMI. http://libvmi.com/docs/gcode-intro.html. Accessed 11 Jan 2020

26. Xiong, H. Liu, Z., Xu, W.: Libvmi: a library for bridging the semantic gap between guest OS and VMM. In: Proceedings - 2012 IEEE 12th International Conference on Computer and Information Technology, CIT 2012, pp. 549–556 (2012). https://doi.org/10.1109/cit.2012.119

27. An advanced memory forensics framework. http://volatilityfoundation.org/. Accessed 17 Nov 2019

28. Finding Advanced Malware Using Volatility. https://eforensicsmag.com/finding-advanced-malware-using-volatility/. Accessed 11 Jan 2020

29. Memory Forensics Investigation using Volatility. https://www.hackingarticles.in/memory-forensics-investigation-using-volatility-part-1/. Accessed 11 Jan 2020

30. Ainapure, B., Shah, D., Ananda Rao, A.: Performance analysis of virtual machine introspection tools in cloud environment. In: Proceedings of the International Conference on Informatics and Analytics (ICIA-16). Association for Computing Machinery, New York, NY, USA, Article 27, pp. 1–6 (2016). https://doi.org/10.1145/2980258.2980309

31. GitHub, volatilityfoundation/volatility - Command Reference Mal, https://github.com/volatilityfoundation/volatility/wiki/Command-Reference-Mal. Accessed 08 Jan 2020

32. GitHub, volatilityfoundation/volatility - Command Reference, https://github.com/volatilityfoundation/volatility/wiki/Command-Reference. Accessed 08 Jan 2020

33. VirtualAllocEx function (memoryapi.h) - Win32 apps | Microsoft Docs. https://docs.microsoft.com/en-us/windows/win32/api/memoryapi/nf-memoryapi-virtualallocex. Accessed 08 Jan 2020

34. Wikipedia contributors. Scikit-learn. In Wikipedia, The Free Encyclopedia (2020). https://en.wikipedia.org/w/index.php?title=Scikit-learn&oldid=948478961. Accessed 11 Jan 2020

35. GitHub - theevilbit/injection. https://github.com/theevilbit/injection. Accessed 08 Jan 2020

36. GitHub - fdiskyou/injectAllTheThings: Seven different DLL injection techniques in one single project. https://github.com/fdiskyou/injectAllTheThings. Accessed 08 Jan 2020

37. GitHub - secrary/InjectProc: InjectProc - Process Injection Techniques. https://github.com/secrary/InjectProc. Accessed 08 Jan 2020

38. GitHub - marcosd4h/memhunter: Live hunting of code injection techniques. https://github.com/marcosd4h/memhunter. Accessed 08 Jan 2020

39. GitHub - stephenfewer/ReflectiveDLLInjection: Reflective DLL injection is a library injection technique in which the concept of reflective programming is employed to perform the loading of a library from memory into a host process. https://github.com/stephenfewer/ReflectiveDLLInjection. Accessed 08 Jan 2020

Crime Prediction Using Spatio-Temporal Data

Sohrab Hossain[1][(✉)], Ahmed Abtahee[1], Imran Kashem[1],
Mohammed Moshiul Hoque[2], and Iqbal H. Sarker[2][(✉)]

[1] Department of Computer Science and Engineering, East Delta University,
Chittagong, Bangladesh
sohrab.h@eastdelta.edu.bd
[2] Department of Computer Science and Engineering, Chittagong
University of Engineering and Technology, Chittagong, Bangladesh
iqbal@cuet.ac.bd

Abstract. A crime is an action which constitutes a punishable offence by law. It is harmful for society so as to prevent the *criminal activity*, it is important to understand crime. Data driven researches are useful to prevent and solve crime. Recent research shows that 50% of the crimes are committed by only handful of offenders. The law enforcement officers need early information about the *criminal activity* to response and solve the spatio-temporal criminal activity. In this research, supervised learning algorithms are used to predict *criminal activity*. The proposed data driven system predicts crimes by analyzing San Francisco city criminal activity data set for 12 years. Decision tree and k-nearest neighbor (KNN) algorithms are applied to predict crime. But these two algorithms provide low accuracy in prediction. Then, random forest is applied as an ensemble methods and adaboost is used as a boosting method to increase the accuracy of prediction. However, log-loss is used to measure the performance of classifiers by penalizing false classifications. As the dataset contains highly class imbalance problems, a random undersampling method for random forest algorithm gives the best accuracy. The final accuracy is 99.16% with 0.17% log loss.

Keywords: Crime prediction · Crime · Machine learning · Spatio-temporal activity · Data analytics · Ensemble methods

1 Introduction

Criminal activities are present in every aspect of human life in the world. It has direct impact on the quality of life as well as on the socio-economic development of a nation. As it has become a major concern almost for all countries, governments are prone to use advance technologies to tackle it. Crime Analysis is a sub brunch of criminology which studies the pattern of the crime and criminal behavior and tries to identify the insinuations of such event. A machine learning agent typically uses dataset for predictive analysis where it employs different techniques to find patterns [18, 20, 26]. Besides these, a receny-based analysis and corresponding patterns are also effective in predictive analytics [19]. A machine learning agent can learn about a crime and analyze the pattern

© Springer Nature Singapore Pte Ltd. 2020
N. Chaubey et al. (Eds.): COMS2 2020, CCIS 1235, pp. 277–289, 2020.
https://doi.org/10.1007/978-981-15-6648-6_22

of occurrence of a crime based on the previous reports of criminal activities, and thus find the crime hotspots based on time, type and other factors. This technique is known as classification problem, and it allows predicting nominal class labels [32]. Classification techniques are used in many different domains such as financial market, business intelligence, healthcare, weather forecasting etc. [17]. Law enforcement agencies use analytical information, and employs different patrolling strategies to keep an area secure. In this paper, dataset from San-Francisco open data [1] is used which contains records of criminal activities for the last twelve years. It uses classification techniques such as decision tree, KNN as well as ensemble methods like random forest, adaboost that are well-known in the area of machine learning [25], to find hotspots of crime zone for specific time of day. Later, the results of algorithms are compared, and the most effective approach also registered for future use.

Criminal law and sociology scholars studied the pattern of crime and its relation to socio-economic development. Studies show that notable amount of crimes committed in the micro level of a region. These clusters are knows as hotspots. Researcher claim that a good neighborhood often has few streets or certain areas where higher amount of criminal activities happened compared to other areas. Geographical topology and micro structures are more important for dealing with hotspots. Machine learning can implement the same theory by taking data driven approach to identify hotspots [31]. The main goal of this research is to use various machine learning algorithms to find the clusters, and analyze the previously reported criminal activities to discover hidden patterns. Law enforcement agencies can deal with crimes effectively if they have prior hints about crime activities and information about crime hotspots.

Crimes are being treated as spatio-temporal events. These events can be explained in term of space, time, and attributes where space specifies the location of the crime and time describes the time instant and attributes specify occurred events. Finding spatio-temporal patterns of crime help us to explain the association among crimes, space, and time. Machine learning approaches focus on the analysis of a single attributes such as robberies or on a specific pattern such as crime hotspots [29]. Spatio-temporal outliers, hotspots, coupling, and partitioning are very crucial for crime prediction. Spatio-temporal outliers are events whose attributes varies significantly from other objects in its neighborhood and are used to find unexpected events (e.g., crime). Spatio-temporal coupling occurs in close spatio-temporal proximity. For example, frequent occurrences of robberies occur close to a bar and supermarket on weekends. Spatio-temporal clustering means grouping similar crimes based on time and space. It is used to discover the hidden pattern of criminal activities. Spatio-temporal hotspots are places where the number of events is extremely high. It helps law enforcement organization to detect and limits the criminal activities [13].

2 Related Research

Researches in criminal activities prediction are given priority in all over the world. Most of the researches study relationship among criminal activities, poverty and socio-economic variables like income level [15], unemployment [8], race [4], and level of education [7]. Crime hotspots are located by analyzing demographic data and mobile networks in London [3]. They have implied that anonymized data, collected by mobile networks, contain indicators for predicting crime levels. It combines two data sets – i) 1990 US LEMAS and ii) crime data 1995 FBI UCR, and then applies traditional classification algorithms like naive Bayesian algorithm and decision tree classifier. Thus, 83.95% accuracy has been achieved for predicting a crime category of various areas in USA [9]. However, this paper fails to explain imbalanced classes of crime category, if any. Somayeh et al. [28] used some advanced machine learning techniques by using same databases, where KNN algorithm prediction accuracy is higher (89.50%) than other machine learning techniques. They also used chi-square test to improve the feature selection. Wang et al. [30] proposed a different machine learning technique known as series finder. It find the underlying patterns of criminal activities committed by same person or group of persons.

Clustering is also another common technique used to predict patterns of geographic criminal history and behavior [8]. Remond and Baveja [16] proposed case-based reasoning (CBR) system which filtered out police cases for better prediction. It worked on noisy data, and explained how police reports show only individual criminal activities and do not addresses gang crimes. Social networks are also used as a potential source of criminal activity indicators. Sadhana and Sangareddy [10] used twitter information to find real time criminal offences. They also used the same data set to find the concentration of crime occurrences, and find large scale of hotspots. Thus several techniques [6, 11, 12, 14, 27] are used for analyzing crimes.

3   Dataset Analysis

3.1   Crime Dataset and Attributes

The experiment is conducted on a specific dataset. The dataset is provided by San Francisco (SF) open dataset from SFPD crime incident reporting system [9].

It provides information about crime incidents that occurred in San Francisco from 1/1/2003 to 5/13/2015. The dataset is in a csv file which contains 8,78,049 rows. The

Table 1. Attributes of the crime dataset.

Date time	A timestamp of crime occurrence
Category	Type of crimes. This is the target label for the data. There are 39 types of crimes listed in the data set Crime Description A detailed description of specific type of crimes
Day	Day of week
pDistrict	Police department's district name. There are total 10 police districts in the data
Resolution	How the crime was solved.17 types of resolution are stated
Address	Incident/occurrence street address
X	It signifies the latitude of the location of the crime
Y	It signifies the longitude of the location of the crime

features and label can be determined from the list of attributes in Table 1. The target label needs to be predicted is the category of a crime incident. The attributes crime description and resolution are also related to the target label. Hence, all other attributes apart from these three attributes are used as features.

Table 2. Attributes of the crime dataset.

Category	Frequency
Theft of property	174900
Other offences	126180
Non-criminal	92300
Physical assault	76876
Illegal drug	53970
Theft of vehicle	53781
Damage property	44725
Warrants	42214
Illegal entry	36755
Suspicious activity	31414
Kidnappings	25989
Robbery	23000
Fraud	16679
Forged	10609
Secondary codes	9985
....	......
Trespassing	6

There are 39 types of crimes in the San Francisco crime dataset shown in Table 2. These types are considered as classes. Hence, 39 classes made San Francisco a multi class classification problem. There are few crimes that occur very frequently, and some crimes are really rare. Larceny/Theft is the most common crime with a frequency of 174900, and Trespassing (TREA) is the least common crime with a frequency of 6. There are 14 crime classes that occurred more than 10,000 times and 14 crime classes occurred less than 2,000 times. It resembles that the classes are not evenly distributed.

3.2 Features

From date time stamp, four main features are extracted which are year, month, date, hour.

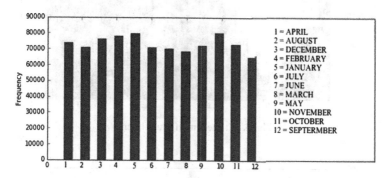

Fig. 1. Crimes in different months

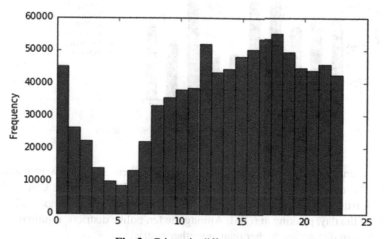

Fig. 2. Crimes in different days

The plots shown in Figs. 1, 2, and 3 indicate the criminal activities occurring throughout of the year. It is observed that summer and winter have less criminal activities compared to other seasons. Most of the crimes occur on Friday, where least crimes occur on Sunday. Crime rates almost gradually increase from Monday to Thursday. This however does not seem indicative of any pattern. The time of crime occurrence depicts an interesting picture (Fig. 4).

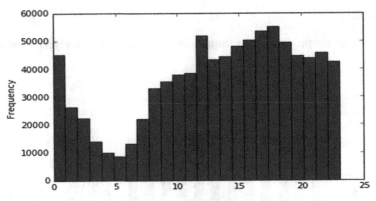

Fig. 3. Crimes in different hours

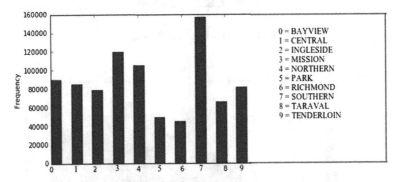

Fig. 4. Crimes in different police districts

Most crimes occur during afternoon to evening where as it is low at midnight to morning. There is an upsurge of criminal activities at 6 PM and 8 PM. Criminal activities are drastically reported around 9 AM, and it continues to show a gradual increase throughout the day, peaking at 6 PM. Among the ten police districts, criminal activities in the southern district are higher than any other districts.

4 Methodology

4.1 Preprocessing

Python library scikit-learn (sklearn) is used for preprocessing the dataset. Some attributes in the csv files contain string values as well as numeric values. In order to use this dataset in machine learning models, the text features need to be converted into a numeric value. Python library numpy is used to convert string into numeric values. Attributes with string data type are "Day", "Category", "Address" columns. Scikit-learn have a preprocessing package that converts string data into numeric data. This package gives an integer value to each unique item after sorting items in ascending alphabetical order. Date-time attribute is also a string data type which is converted into a date-time object, and four different attributes such as "Hour", "Date", "Month" and "Year" are obtained from it.

4.2 Training and Testing Dataset

To avoid over fitting, and getting more realistic accuracy, the dataset is divided into two portions: testing dataset and training dataset. Training dataset contains all features along with the target label. Testing dataset only contains the features from which a machine learning model predicts the target label. Scikit-learn's model selection package contains a class test train split that splits the original dataset into testing and training dataset. The default value of the test dataset size is 25% of the original dataset. This default value is used in the conducted experiments.

4.3 Feature Extraction and Selection

While the given features give sufficient information about a crime incident, new features can be extracted from the given features which might be proven to be useful. Analysis of different features shows that there is a specific pattern in occurrence of crime during different parts of a day. A new feature can be extracted by dividing a day in few different parts rather than considering 24 h. Although, in [22, 23] the authors presented a dynamic time segmentation technique, we consider a static segmentation based on our crime data. Figure 3 shows that crimes start falling after midnight, and rise gradually from afternoon to evening. Therefore, a day can be divided into following parts:

- Early morning: 1 AM–7 AM.
- Late morning: 8 AM–1 PM
- Afternoon: 2 PM–7 PM
- Night: 8 PM–12 AM

With blocks of time introduction, a clearer picture of time can be found which performs better than 24 hour-cycle-time. With blocks of time, a linear data is achieved compared to an arbitrary sequence of occurrence of criminal activities that does not reflect any indication. Principal component analysis (PCA) is a method of linear dimensionality reduction. It projects data in a lower dimensional space and maximizes variances. PCA class of sklearn.decomposition package is used to obtaining variable features from the existing 9 features. An N component in the PCA class indicates the number of new features with lower dimension to be extracted from the old features.

After preprocessing, total number of features is 9. One assumption is made before using any predictive model is that some features might be more useful than others. Too many features can make classification complicated and cause overfitting while more features describe the data better. Sklearn.feature selection module uses univariate statistical tests to find features that are best related to the target label. It can select percentile class of this module takes a percentage input, and returns that percentage of best features. Different percentages of features are used in different models to see which arrangement features gives better performance.

5   Result Analysis

We have used supervised classification method for this experiment. Performances of different machine learning models are discussed below:

5.1   Decision Tree

Decision tree classifier can solve both regression and classification problems. It has many parameters like like n_estimators, criterion, max_depth, min_samples_split, max_features, max leaf nodes, n jobs, random state, verbose, class weight but only two parameters are convenient to use in this case. The number of splits can be made by decision tree, and indicated by *min_samples_splitand*. The function is to measure the quality of a split, is indicated by criterion. Information gain and impurity are the two types of functions which are used for measuring quality of split [21].

Table 3. Classification result for different parameters of Decision Tree.

Split	Function	Accuracy	Log-loss
50	gini	28.26%	8.41
100	gini	29.80%	5.45
300	gini	30.72%	3.31
500	gini	30.45%	2.83
50	entropy	29.24%	8.41
100	entropy	30.43%	5.52
300	entropy	31.17%	3.31
500	entropy	30.56%	2.91
600	entropy	30.46%	2.76

We considered the criteria "gini" for the gini impurity and "entropy" for the information gain [24]. In this case, four columns - split, function, accuracy, and log-loss are used for showing the output in Table 3. The best accuracy is 31.17% when log loss is 3.31, function is entropy, and 300 split. The lowest accuracy is 28.26% when log loss is 8.41%, function is gini, and 300 split. It is observed that split and function have very little impact on accuracy.

5.2   K-Nearest Neighbor

Sklearn.neighbors offers *KNeighborsClassifier* function. KNN has many different parameters like n_neighbors, metric, metric_params, weights, algorithm, leaf_size, p, n_jobs but metric and n_neighbors are very useful among these parameters. Here parameter n_neighbor = 50 is giving us best accuracy score of 28.50% when log loss is 5.04. The lowest accuracy score is 27.91% when n_neighbors = 500, and log loss is 2.62. This shows that log loss is high when accuracy is low. Now, we use feature selection methods to find out whether the accuracy can be improved or not (Table 4).

Table 4. KNN result for different neighbor value.

Features	Log n neighbor	Accuracy (%)	Log Loss
All	30	28.14	6.61
All	50	28.50	5.04
All	70	28.39	4.26
All	100	28.41	3.71
All	200	28.35	3.02
All	300	28.15	2.78
All	400	27.96	2.69
All	500	27.91	2.62

5.3 Adaboost

In adaboost, *base_estimator* and *n_estimator* are two parameters, where *n_estimator* means the number of weak classifier that is used in boosting, and *base_estimator* is used to terminate the boosting. We are going to boost the decision tree result through adaboost ensemble method. Adaboost classifier shows same log loss value but reduces misclassification. Accuracy measurement shows that when we used 100 estimators for decision tree it gives very low accuracy (8.80%) with the log loss 3.10. However, the accuracy is improved when we used the estimator value 10. Predictive ability for both estimator values remains same (Table 5).

Table 5. Result for Adaboost.

Number of trees	Accuracy	Log loss
10	31.22	2.34
50	31.70	2.28
100	31.71	2.28

5.4 Random Forest

Random forest classifier also has various parameters like decision tree but only *min_samples_split, criterion*, and *n_estimators* parameters are used in this paper. We used n_estimators to find the number of trees in the forest, criterion indicates the function which measures the quality of a split, and *min_samples_split* indicates minimum number of samples which is required to split an internal node. Both accuracy and log loss are improved while the numbers of trees in random forest are increased. Ten, 50, and 200 estimator gives accuracy of 31.22%, 31.70%, 31.71% and log loss of 2.34%, 2.28, 2 respectively (Table 6).

Table 6. Random forest's result.

Number of trees	Accuracy	Log loss
10	31.22	2.34
50	31.70	2.28
100	31.71	2.28

5.5 Oversampling Dataset

Oversampling method makes the dataset more balanced by synthesizing new minority class samples [2]. Many functions are available to balance an imbalanced class using oversampling method. In this research, we use SMOTE oversampling technique. In SMOTE, KNN are used for generating synthetic minority classes by operation on feature space. Here, value of k relies on the number of samples need to be created [2].

5.6 Undersampling Dataset

Undersampling is applied to the majority classes in an imbalanced dataset. It undersampled the majority classes by compensating minority classes [5]. It tells the machine learning agents not to become biased and not to ignore the false positives. We use *imblearn* function from *scikit-learn* package to do the undersampling in the imbalance data.

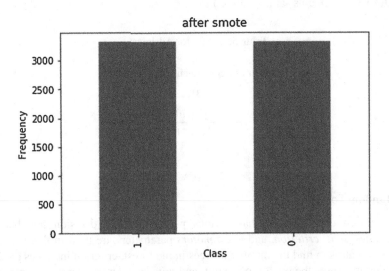

Fig. 5. Class frequencies after random undersampling.

5.7 Random Undersampling

Random undersampling is an efficient and effective technique to balance the data by randomly selecting a subset of data for the targeted classes [5]. Here, random undersampling reduces the frequency of majority class when considering minority class frequency. As a result, classes become balanced, hence same models and parameters can be used. SMOTE oversampling and random undersampling methods are used to boost the result, and made the class more balanced. Figure 5 shows that both classes are balance in the best possible manner. All the classifiers give a better result after introducing oversampling and undersampling methods. Results are improved by a very good margin. After resampling with random undersampling, random forest shows 99.16% accuracy score along with the log loss value of 0.17. Finally, best accuracy score is obtained after applying undersampling (Table 7).

Table 7. Classification result after ENN undersampling.

Sampling	Method	Models	Accuracy	Log loss
Over sampling	SMOTE	Random forest (num of tree = 100)	73.89	0.58
Undersampling	Random undersampling	Random forest (num of tree = 100)	99.16	0.17

6 Conclusion

Machine learning agent can classify a criminal activity using basic details of a crime occurred in an area with time and location. San Francisco dataset has 39 classes, and frequencies of all classes were not equally distributed. As the classes were poorly imbalanced, machine learning agent failed to perform well in the original dataset. From the original dataset, machine learning agents managed to provide a poor accuracy score of 31.71% that is pretty low. So we divided the 39 classes into two classes. One is frequent class and other one is rare class. The frequent class consists of most frequent crimes, and the rare one consists of least frequent crimes. As we expected, machine learning agents performed well in remodeled dataset and resulted accuracy is 68.03%. To overcome the imbalanced problem, we used oversampling and undersampling methods. Machine learning agents can be highly benefited after using these two methods. With an accuracy of 99.16%, random forest performed the best decision making classifier than other machine learning algorithms.

We like to improve our crime prediction accuracy in future. Currently, we use few machine learning techniques like decision tree, KNN, adaboost, and random forest. We plan to use deep learning technique to improve prediction result. In addition, we try to incorporate cybercrime prediction with the real world crime prediction.

References

1. Ang, S.T., Wang, W., Chyou, S.: San Francisco crime Classification. University of California, San Diego (2015)
2. Beckmann, M., Ebecken, N.F.F., Pires de Lima, B.S.L., et al.: A KNN undersampling approach for data balancing. J. Intell. Learn. Syst. Appl. **7**(04), 104 (2015)
3. Bogomolov, A., Lepri, B., Staiano, J., Oliver, N., Pianesi, F., Pentland, A.: Once upon a crime: towards crime prediction from demographics and mobile data. In: Proceedings of the 16th International Conference on Multimodal Interaction, pp. 427–434 (2014)
4. Braithwaite, J., et al.: Crime, Shame and Reintegration. Cambridge University Press, Cambridge (1989)
5. Chawla, N.V., Bowyer, K.W., Hall, L.O., Philip Kegelmeyer, W.: Smote: synthetic minority over-sampling technique. J. Artif. Intell. Res. **16**, 321–357 (2002)
6. Chun, S.A., Paturu, V.A., Yuan, S., Pathak, R., Atluri, V., Adam, N.R.: Crime prediction model using deep neural networks. In: Proceedings of the 20th Annual International Conference on Digital Government Research, pp. 512–514 (2019)
7. Ehrlich, I.: On the relation between education and crime. In: Education, Income, and Human Behavior, pp. 313–338. NBER (1975)
8. Freeman, R.B.: The economics of crime. In: Ashenfelter, O., Card, D. (eds.) Handbook of Labor Economics 3 (c) (1999)
9. Iqbal, R., Murad, M.A.A., Mustapha, A., Panahy, P.H.S., Khanahmadliravi, N.: An experimental study of classification algorithms for crime prediction. Indian J. Sci. Technol. **6**(3), 4219–4225 (2013)
10. Kang, H.-W., Kang, H.-B.: Prediction of crime occurrence from multi-modal data using deep learning. PLoS ONE **12**(4), e0176244 (2017)
11. Kim, S., Joshi, P., Kalsi, P.S., Taheri, P.: Crime analysis through machine learning. In: 2018 IEEE 9th Annual Information Technology, Electronics and Mobile Communication Conference (IEMCON), pp. 415–420. IEEE (2018)
12. Kiran, J., Kaishveen, K.: Prediction analysis of crime in india using a hybrid clustering approach. In: 2018 2nd International Conference on I-SMAC (IoT in Social, Mobile, Analytics and Cloud) (I-SMAC), pp. 520–523. IEEE (2018)
13. Matijosaitiene, I., Zhao, P., Jaume, S., Gilkey Jr., J.W.: Prediction of hourly effect of land use on crime. ISPRS Int. J. Geoinf. **8**(1), 16 (2019)
14. Morimoto, S., Kawamukai, H., Shin, K.: Prediction of crime occurrence using information propagation model and gaussian process. In: 2019 14th Asia Joint Conference on Information Security (AsiaJCIS), pp. 80–87. IEEE (2019)
15. Britt Patterson, E.: Poverty, income inequality, and community crime rates. Criminology **29**(4), 755–776 (1991)
16. Redmond, M., Baveja, A.: A data-driven software tool for enabling cooperative information sharing among police departments. Eur. J. Oper. Res. **141**(3), 660–678 (2002)
17. Sarker, I.H.: Context-aware rule learning from smartphone data: survey, challenges and future directions. J. Big Data **6**(1), 95 (2019)
18. Sarker, I.H.: A machine learning based robust prediction model for real-life mobile phone data. Internet Things **5**, 180–193 (2019)
19. Sarker, I.H., Colman, A., Han, J.: Recencyminer: mining recency-based personalized behavior from contextual smartphone data. J. Big Data **6**(1), 49 (2019)
20. Sarker, I.H., Colman, A., Han, J., Kayes, A.S.M., Watters, P.: Calbehav: a machine learning based personalized calendar behavioral model using time-series smartphone data. Comput. J. (2020)

21. Sarker, I.H., Colman, A., Han, J., Khan, A.I., Abushark, Y.B., Salah, K.: BehavDT: a behavioral decision tree learning to build user-centric context-aware predictive model. Mobile Networks Appl. **25**, 1151–1161 (2019). https://doi.org/10.1007/s11036-019-01443-z

22. Sarker, I.H., Colman, A., Kabir, M.A., Han, J.: Behavior oriented time segmentation for mining individualized rules of mobile phone users. In: 2016 IEEE International Conference on Data Science and Advanced Analytics (DSAA), pp. 488–497. IEEE (2016)

23. Sarker, I.H., Colman, A., Kabir, M.A., Han, J.: Individualized time-series segmentation for mining mobile phone user behavior. Comput. J. **61**(3), 349–368 (2018)

24. Sarker, I.H., Kayes, A.S.M., Furhad, Md.H., Islam, M.M., Islam, Md.S.: E-miim: an ensemble-learning-based context-aware mobile telephony model for intelligent interruption management. AI & SOCIETY, pp. 1–9 (2019)

25. Sarker, I.H., Kayes, A.S.M., Watters, P.: Effectiveness analysis of machine learning classification models for predicting personalized context-aware smartphone usage. J. Big Data **6**(1), 57 (2019)

26. Sarker, I.H., Salah, K.: Appspred: predicting context-aware smartphone apps using random forest learning. Internet Things **8**, 100106 (2019)

27. Mary Shermila, A., Bellarmine, A.B., Nirmala, S.: Crime data analysis and prediction of perpetrator identity using machine learning approach. In: 2018 2nd International Conference on Trends in Electronics and Informatics (ICOEI), pp. 107–114. IEEE (2018)

28. Shojaee, S., Mustapha, A., Sidi, F., Jabar, M.A.: A study on classification learning algorithms to predict crime status. Int. J. Dig. Content Technol. Appl. **7**(9), 361 (2013)

29. Silva, R.A., Pires, J.M., Datia, N., Santos, M.Y., Martins, B., Birra, F.: Visual analytics for spatiotemporal events. Multimedia Tools Appl. **78**(23), 32805–32847 (2019)

30. Wang, X., Gerber, M.S., Brown, D.E.: Automatic crime prediction using events extracted from Twitter posts. In: Yang, S.J., Greenberg, A.M., Endsley, M. (eds.) SBP 2012. LNCS, vol. 7227, pp. 231–238. Springer, Heidelberg (2012). https://doi.org/10.1007/978-3-642-29047-3_28

31. Weisburd, D.: Place-based policing. In: Ideas in American policing. Citeseer (2008)

32. Hossain, S., et al.: A belief rule based expert system to predict student performance under uncertainty. In: 2019 22nd International Conference on Computer and Information Technology (ICCIT), pp. 1–6. IEEE (2019)

Color Image Watermarking in Encryption Domain

Rohit Thanki[1(✉)] and Ashish Kothari[2]

[1] C. U. Shah University, Wadhwan City, Gujarat, India
rohitthanki9@gmail.com
[2] Atmiya University, Rajkot, Gujarat, India
amkothari@aits.edu.in

Abstract. Image watermarking is one of the techniques used for copyright protection of digital images. In this paper, copyright protection of color images using watermarking is presented with the help of data encryption. The main contribution in this algorithm is that the color image converts into an encrypted image using compressive sensing (CS) based encryption and then watermark logo is inserted into the encrypted image to get the watermarked encrypted image. After that, CS based decryption is applied to the watermarked version of an encrypted image to get a watermarked color image. Experimental results of this algorithm show that this technique effectively works for copyright protection of color images and provide better robustness compared to existing algorithms available in the literature.

Keywords: Compressive sensing · Color image · Encryption · Watermarking

1 Introduction

With the growth in social media in recent time, many images are transferred over social media is a very easy task. But sometimes images are transferred without any knowledge the actual creator or owner of it. This situation creates a problem regarding copyright protection of image and it is a very serious crime. The tackle with this crime, one of this technique is a digital watermarking [1]. In this technique, some secret information of creator hides into images or videos to prevent copyright protection of it [2]. Recently, many researchers are presented solution for copyright protection of images using different watermarking algorithms. The details of these algorithms are described as per below.

Savakar et al. [3] proposed hybrid watermarking algorithm based on DWT and SVD for color images. In this algorithm, U, V matrix values of wavelet coefficients of cover image are used for hides watermark into it with the help of PN sequences. This is blind extraction method. This algorithm provides robustness against all kind of attacks. Su et al. [4] proposed schur decomposition based watermarking algorithm for color images. Here, watermark hides into the approximate maximum value of schur coefficients of cover color image using weight factor to get the color watermarked image.

© Springer Nature Singapore Pte Ltd. 2020
N. Chaubey et al. (Eds.): COMS2 2020, CCIS 1235, pp. 290–297, 2020.
https://doi.org/10.1007/978-981-15-6648-6_23

Bal et al. [5] proposed an image watermarking algorithm using cryptography where bit pair matching used for embedding and extraction of watermark image. This algorithm provides good invisibility with good payload capacity. Boris Escalated-Ramirez et al. [6] proposed Hermite transform (HT) based image watermarking algorithm. In this algorithm, the characteristics of HVS which is extracted using HT are used for generation of watermarked image while watermark mask is generated using brightness model. This algorithm provides robustness against all kinds of image watermarking attacks. Darwish et al. [7] proposed hybrid domain color image based intelligent watermarking algorithm using DWT + SVD and genetic algorithm (GA). Here, two watermarks are inserted into the singular values of Y channel and Cb channel of cover image with help of optimized scaling factor. The optimized scaling factor is generated with the help of a genetic algorithm.

Kazemivash et al. [8] proposed an image watermarking algorithm based on firefly optimization and lifting wavelet transform. In this algorithm, first, wavelet coefficients of the host image are selected using firefly optimization. Then, the encrypted watermark is inserted into this selected wavelet coefficients to get a watermarked image. For encryption of watermark, Arnold scrambling uses in this algorithm. Pan-pan et al. [9] proposed geometric feature extraction and LSB substitution based color image watermarking algorithm. In this algorithm, the color image feature is extracted using probability density gradient, Hessian matrix, and SURF feature extraction. After that, this feature divides into bit plane and the watermark is inserted into last bit plane with the help of LSB substitution to get the color watermarked image. Mehran Andalibi et al. [10] proposed an image watermarking algorithm based on wavelet transform and adaptive logo texturization. In this algorithm, first, texture feature of the host image is obtained with the help of HVS. Then adaptive iteration logo scrambling via Arnold transform is applied to the obtained similarity in texture feature. Finally, the watermark is inserted into these features with the help of wavelet based additive watermarking.

In this paper, compressive sensing (CS) based encryption is applied to the Y channel of host color image and converted into an encrypted for watermark content embedding. A logo watermark content along with PN sequence is embedded into the blocks of the encrypted image. In this proposed scheme of paper, logo watermark is inserted into an encrypted version of the color image indicates that this scheme is watermarking in the encryption domain. The paper is organized with Sect. 2 gives cs based encryption and decryption, Sect. 3 gives steps of the proposed scheme, Sect. 4 gives experimental results of the proposed scheme. Finally, Sect. 5 gives the conclusion of the obtained results of the scheme.

2 CS Based Encryption and Decryption

Compressive sensing is one kind of signal processing theory based on linear algebra and sparsity of data. This theory state that 'signal or image can be recovered from its sparse few information'. This theory was introduced by D. Donoho and Candes around 2006 [11, 12]. Initially, this theory was proposed for the compression of data. After a few years of these, many researchers saw the use of this theory in the area of data encryption and decryption [13]. This theory provides simultaneously compression as well as encryption to data. The basic steps for encryption process and decryption process are described in the next subsection.

2.1 Encryption Process

The encrypted image is generated using sparse data of image and measurement matrix in this process. The basic steps of process are as follows:

Step 1: Sparse data (S) of image (I) is generated with help of transform basis function (Ψ).

$$S = \Psi \times I \times \Psi^{'} \tag{1}$$

Where S is sparse data of the image, Ψ is a transform basis function, and I is an original image.

Step 2: Measurement matrix (A) generates with the help of Gaussian normal distribution with mean value is zero and the variance value is one.

Step 3: Encrypted image generates by multiplication of sparse information and measurement matrix according to the below equation:

$$EI = A \times S \tag{2}$$

Where EI is an encrypted image.

2.2 Decryption Process

In this process, the encrypted image can be decrypted with the help of the measurement matrix and CS based recovery algorithms. These recovery algorithms are two types such as L norm based minimization and iterative based algorithm [14]. Here, the orthogonal matching pursuit algorithm [15] is used. The reason behind choosing this algorithm are that it is very simple and high simulation time compared to other recovery algorithms. The basic steps of process are as follows:

Step 1: The decrypted sparse data (x_R) of image from encrypted image (EI) can be get using orthogonal matching pursuit algorithm along with correct measurement matrix (A).

$$x_R = OMP(EI, A) \tag{3}$$

Step 2: After that, the decrypted image (DI) is generated with help of transform basis function (Ψ).

$$DI = \Psi^{'} \times x_R \times \Psi \tag{4}$$

3 Watermarking Algorithm

The watermark logo is inserted into encrypted color cover image to get color watermarked image while extraction of watermark from color watermarked image with the help of correlation properties of PN sequences. This algorithm has divided into processes such as embedding of watermark logo and extraction of watermark. The steps for these processes are described as per below:

3.1 Watermark Logo Embedding

The processing steps for embedding of watermark logo into the cover color image using below steps:

Step 1: The cover color image is taken, and the image converts into YCbCr colorspace using colorspace conversion of RGB to YCbCr.

Step 2: Y channel of the cover color image is chosen for the further process of watermark logo embedding.

Step 3: The encrypted Y channel of cover color image is generated using CS encryption process. Then, this encrypted channel of cover color image breaks into non-overlapping block with the size of 8 × 8.

Step 4: Two highly uncorrelated, random noise sequences are generated using PN sequence generator. The size of each sequence equals to block size.

Step 5: Then, the mask of watermark W is generated based on bits of watermark, size of encrypted channel of cover image and noise sequences using below steps:

- If watermark logo has a value of bit 1, then add noise sequence for one bit is added to that portion of mask.
- Otherwise, noise sequence for zero bit uses for generation of watermark mask.
- This process repeats for all blocks of encrypted channel of cover image.

Step 6: The watermark mask (W) is inserted into the encrypted Y channel of cover color image (EI) using weight factor (α) to get watermarked encrypted Y channel of the cover color image (WEI).

$$WEI = EI + \alpha \times W \tag{5}$$

Step 7: Apply CS based decryption watermarked encrypted Y channel to get watermarked Y channel of the cover color image.

Step 8: Finally, inverse colorspace conversion of YCbCr to RGB is performed to get a watermarked color image.

3.2 Watermark Logo Extraction

The steps for extraction of watermark logo from the watermarked color image are as per below:

Step 1: The watermarked color image is taken, and the image converts into YCbCr colorspace using colorspace conversion of RGB to YCbCr.

Step 2: Y channel of the watermarked color image is chosen for the further process of watermark logo extraction.

Step 3: The encrypted Y channel of watermarked color image is generated using CS encryption process. Then, this encrypted channel of watermarked color image breaks into non-overlapping block with the size of 8 × 8.

Step 4: Two highly uncorrelated, random noise sequences are taken which generates during watermark logo embedding process.

Step 5: The watermark bits' extract from watermarked encrypted Y channel of color image (*WEI*) using the following equations:

$$S_0 = corr2(WEI, N_0)$$
$$S_1 = corr2(WEI, N_1) \tag{6}$$

Where *corr2* is a correlation, N_0 is a noise sequence for zero bit, and N_1 is a noise sequence for one bit.

Step 6: If $S_0 < S_1$, the set watermark bit as one bit. Otherwise, set watermark bit as zero bit. These extracted bits vector to obtain the extracted watermark logo.

4 Experimental Results

This watermarking algorithm is tested and analyzed using standard color image database which is taken from SIPI database [16]. The size of the color image is 256×256 pixels (shown in Fig. 1(a to d)). The binary watermark logo with a size of 50×20 pixels (shown in Fig. 1(e)). The quality of resultant image and performance of the proposed algorithm is measure using quality evaluation parameters [17] such as peak signal to noise ratio (PSNR), normalized correlation (NC), and structural similarity index measure (SSIM) [18]. The PSNR is used for impartibility of the algorithm while NC, SSIM are used for the robustness of the algorithm.

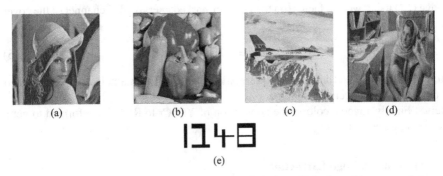

(a)   (b)   (c)   (d)

(e)

Fig. 1. Test color image (a) lena (b) peppers (c) F16 airplane (d) barbara (e) watermark logo

Here, first, Y channel of the color image gets using RGB to YCbCr colorspace conversion. The CS based encryption is applied to the Y channel of a color image to get the encrypted Y channel of the color image. After that, the watermark mask is added to the encrypted Y channel of a color image with help of weight factor α. Then CS based decryption is applied on this resultant image to get watermarked encrypted Y channel of the color image. Finally, YCbCr to RGB color space conversion to get a watermarked color image. The resultant images using this proposed watermarking algorithm is shown in Fig. 2.

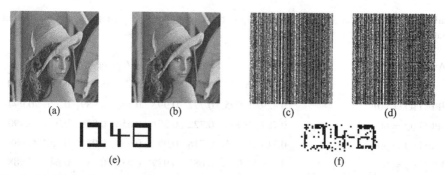

Fig. 2. (a) Original lena image (b) watermarked lena image (c) encrypted Y channel of lena image (d) watermarked encrypted Y channel of lena image (e) original watermark logo (f) extracted watermark logo

Table 1 shows the quality parameters of the proposed watermarking algorithm for different weight factor values are summarized. The result in Table 1 shows that PSNR value is high for low weight factor while NC, SSIM value is high for high weight factor. The robustness of the proposed watermarking algorithm is tested and analyzed using various standard watermarking attacks such as JPEG compression, adding noise, filtering, geometric attacks such as rotation, cropping, blurring and histogram equalization. Table 2 summarized the NC and SSIM value of proposed watermarking algorithm against watermarking attacks. The results in Table 2 indicated that this algorithm provides robustness against watermarking attacks. The algorithm provides less robustness against filtering attacks and rotation attack.

Table 1. Quality parameters of proposed watermarking algorithm for different weight factors

Test images	K = 15			K = 30			K = 45		
	PSNR (dB)	NCC	SSIM	PSNR (dB)	NCC	SSIM	PSNR (dB)	NCC	SSIM
Lena	33.97	0.673	0.989	31.28	0.685	0.991	28.88	0.871	0.997
Pepper	33.78	0.759	0.992	31.26	0.764	0.993	29.14	0.829	0.996
F16 plane	32.33	0.660	0.989	30.40	0.740	0.991	28.62	0.757	0.992
Barbara	31.78	0.751	0.992	30.03	0.709	0.992	28.26	0.840	0.996

The robustness of the proposed watermarking algorithm is compared with the robustness of the recently published watermarking algorithm and summarized in Table 3. Here, the value of NCC is used for robustness performance of watermarking algorithms. The comparison result in Table 3 shows that this proposed algorithm provides better robustness compared to existing algorithms.

Table 2. NC and SSIM values of proposed watermarking algorithm against different watermarking attacks

Attacks	Lena		Peppers		F16 plane		Barbara	
	NCC	SSIM	NCC	SSIM	NCC	SSIM	NCC	SSIM
JPEG (Q = 90)	0.829	0.995	0.772	0.993	0.700	0.989	0.770	0.994
JPEG (Q = 80)	0.787	0.994	0.722	0.991	0.656	0.988	0.670	0.990
JPEG (Q = 60)	0.718	0.991	0.718	0.992	0.639	0.987	0.638	0.988
JPEG (Q = 50)	0.710	0.990	0.687	0.989	0.635	0.986	0.642	0.988
Gaussian noise ($\sigma = 0.001$)	0.849	0.996	0.813	0.995	0.741	0.992	0.833	0.995
Salt & pepper noise ($\sigma = 0.005$)	0.868	0.996	0.809	0.995	0.736	0.992	0.826	0.995
Speckle noise ($\sigma = 0.005$)	0.883	0.996	0.815	0.995	0.753	0.992	0.825	0.995
Median filter (3×3)	0.638	0.986	0.558	0.982	0.532	0.980	0.554	0.983
Mean filter (3×3)	0.452	0.975	0.410	0.972	0.410	0.972	0.526	0.981
Histogram equalization	0.887	0.997	0.849	0.996	0.817	0.995	0.829	0.995
Rotation (90°)	0.481	0.978	0.522	0.980	0.524	0.979	0.504	0.979
Cropping (20%)	0.872	0.997	0.829	0.996	0.756	0.992	0.841	0.996
Sharpening	0.912	0.998	0.845	0.996	0.797	0.994	0.854	0.996
Motion blurring	0.709	0.991	0.598	0.985	0.627	0.986	0.639	0.986

Table 3. Robustness compression of watermarking algorithms

Attacks	Pan-pan et al. [9]	Escalante-Ramirez et al. [6]	Bal et al. [5]	Proposed
JPEG	0.45	0.05	0.650	0.829
Gaussian	0.25	0.215	0.640	0.849
Speckle	Not reported	Not reported	0.840	0.868
Salt & peppers	Not reported	0.13	0.840	0.883

5 Conclusions

In this paper, the watermarking algorithm in the encryption domain has proposed, analyzed and simulated for a color image. Specifically, CS based encryption and decryption are used in this proposed algorithm for copyright protection of color images and results show that this algorithm can be used for this purpose. The comparison of algorithms is also indicated that the robustness of the proposed algorithm provides better than existing watermarking algorithms. This proposed algorithm is indicated that new way of watermark logo embedding.

References

1. Thanki, R.M., Kothari, A.M.: Digital watermarking: technical art of hiding a message. In: Intelligent Analysis of Multimedia Information, pp. 431–466. IGI Global (2017)
2. Borra, S., Thanki, R., Dey, N.: Digital Image Watermarking: Theoretical and Computational Advances. CRC Press, Boca Raton (2018)
3. Savakar, D.G., Ghuli, A.: Robust invisible digital image watermarking using hybrid scheme. Arab. J. Sci. Eng. **44**(4), 3995–4008 (2019)
4. Su, Q., Yuan, Z., Liu, D.: An approximate schur decomposition-based spatial domain color image watermarking method. IEEE Access **7**, 4358–4370 (2018)
5. Bal, S.N., Nayak, M.R., Sarkar, S.K.: On the implementation of a secured watermarking mechanism based on cryptography and bit pairs matching. J. King Saud Univ.-Comput. Inf. Sci. (2018)
6. Escalante-Ramírez, B., Gomez-Coronel, S.L.: A perceptive approach to digital image watermarking using a brightness model and the hermite transform. Math. Probl. Eng. **2018**, 19 (2018)
7. Darwish, S.M., Al-Khafaji, L.D.: An optimized dual watermarking scheme for color images. In: 2018 13th International Conference on Computer Engineering and Systems (ICCES), pp. 640–645. IEEE (2018)
8. Kazemivash, B., Moghaddam, M.E.: A robust digital image watermarking technique using lifting wavelet transform and firefly algorithm. Multimed. Tools Appl. **76**(20), 20499–20524 (2016)
9. Pan-Pan, N., Xiang-Yang, W., Yu-Nan, L., Hong-Ying, Y.: A robust color image watermarking using local invariant significant bitplane histogram. Multimed. Tools Appl. **76**(3), 3403–3433 (2016)
10. Andalibi, M., Chandler, D.M.: Digital image watermarking via adaptive logo texturization. IEEE Trans. Image Process. **24**(12), 5060–5073 (2015)
11. Candès, E.J.: Compressive sampling. In: Proceedings of the International Congress of Mathematicians, vol. 3, pp. 1433–1452 (2006)
12. Donoho, D.L.: Compressed sensing. IEEE Trans. Inf. Theory **52**(4), 1289–1306 (2006)
13. Zhang, X., Ren, Y., Feng, G., Qian, Z.: Compressing encrypted image using compressive sensing. In: 2011 Seventh International Conference on Intelligent Information Hiding and Multimedia Signal Processing, pp. 222–225. IEEE (2011)
14. Thanki, R.M., Dwivedi, V.J., Borisagar, K.R.: Multibiometric Watermarking with Compressive Sensing Theory. Springer, Cham (2018). https://doi.org/10.1007/978-3-319-731 83-4
15. Tropp, J.A., Gilbert, A.C.: Signal recovery from random measurements via orthogonal matching pursuit. IEEE Trans. Inf. Theory **53**(12), 4655–4666 (2007)
16. The University of South Carolina SIPI Image Database. http://sipi.usc.edu/database/databa se.php. Accessed May 2019
17. Kutter, M., Petitcolas, F.A.: Fair benchmark for image watermarking systems. In: Security and Watermarking of Multimedia Contents, vol. 3657, pp. 226–240. International Society for Optics and Photonics (1999)
18. Malpica, W., Bovik, A.C.: SSIM based range image quality assessment. In: 4th International Workshop on Video Processing and Quality Metrics for Consumer Electronics (2009)

Malware Detection Framework Using PCA Based ANN

Khyati Rami[1($\boxtimes$)] and Vinod Desai[2]

[1] Mewar University, Gangarar, Rajasthan, India
khyati.rami@gmail.com
[2] Gujarat Vidhyapith, Ahmedabad, Gujarat, India

Abstract. Different kinds of computer threats exist to damage the computer system, and Malicious programs is one of them. Internet can be the main source to spread some threats. Experts continuously detect those which can slow down the system, or totally damage it. Malware creators have always been a step ahead. To detect malware threat, there are two basic approaches, based on signature and heuristic. For accurate and efficient result of malware detection there are detection techniques based on heuristic method. Polymorphic malwares are growing day by day and heuristic method is combined with machine learning to get more precise and effective detection. Malware detection system using data mining and machine learning methods have been proposed by many researchers to detect known and unknown malware. In this paper we present the ideas behind our malware detection framework by PCA based ANN to detect known and unknown malware. To design the proposed framework we have used MATLAB GUI.ANN is used to detect the presence of malware in CSDMC2019 API dataset. The computational time for ANN classifier is less than 0.2 s compared to NB classifier which has a computational time of 0.82 s.

Keywords: Malware · Malware detection system · PCA · ANN

1 Introduction

Computer threats is created to corrupt confidential information and malicious ways to irritate users, well malware is one of these threats. Malware is increasing at alarming rate to ruin the system. Due to that security incidents is to be grown [1, 2]. Propagation ability of malware is like chain reaction which is dangerous due to none centralized control therefore it is not easy to detect. Malwares are crucial threat to computer security according to studies [3]. Malware intelligent are trying to create program which cannot be traced easily, and time to time they are changing their techniques so malware can be transformed into the malicious code without detection. These simple ideas start first with encryption which go further with oligiomorphic, polymorphic and metamorphic viruses. As per studies existing techniques are found limited therefore combination of the Artificial Intelligence, Machine Learning and Data mining methods are increased efficiency of detection of malware [4]. Signature based detection methods are efficient

© Springer Nature Singapore Pte Ltd. 2020
N. Chaubey et al. (Eds.): COMS2 2020, CCIS 1235, pp. 298–313, 2020.
https://doi.org/10.1007/978-981-15-6648-6_24

to detect known malwares but not enough to detect unknown malware and polymorphic malware due to its signature changes nature. Heuristic based detection methods can trace known and unknown malwares but result can be found high rate of false positive and negative therefor it requires to develop detections methods with accuracy. The heuristic based detection techniques are combined with machine learning method to get accurate and efficient result of malware detection, due to alarming increasing rate of polymorphic malwares. So current condition requires for everyone to find better solution. The paper is organized as follows: Sect. 1 describes the introduction, Sect. 2 describe the literature review, Sect. 3 describe the proposed malware detection system and Sect. 4 describes the results. In this research work ANN is used to detect the presence of malware in CSDMC2019 API dataset. We have tested the proposed malware detection system while connecting it to a mobile OS and transferring a file from mobile OS to desktop OS. We use MALTAB GUI to design the proposed malware detection system, whereas in Sect. 5 we give the conclusion.

2 Literature Review

Mariantonietta La Polla [5] surveys the different threats, vulnerabilities and security solutions for more than decade specifically in the period 2004–2014, by focusing on high-level attacks, which are on user applications. We can group existing approaches keeping in mind to protect mobile devices against different classes of attacks into different categories, based upon the detection principles, architectures, collected data and OS, main focus is on IDS-based models and tools. With this categorization, we aim to provide clear and concise view of the underlying model accepted by each approach. Sujithra M. [6] focused on various threats and vulnerabilities that affect the mobile devices and discussed how biometrics could be a solution to the mobile devices ensuring security. These systems are proved highly confidential portable mobile based security systems which is very much required. Comparing various biometric features such as fingerprint, face, gait, iris, signature and voice. Iris is proved the most effective biometric feature due to its reliability and accuracy. We have also reviewed some research papers based on Malware detection for known and unknown malware. In the following table describe the comparison of studied papers (Table 1).

Table 1. Comparison of studied papers [13]

STUDY	Classifiers	Conclusion
Detecting unknown malicious code by applying classification techniques on OpCode patterns (2012) [7]	ANN,DT,LR,NB,RF,SVM and their boosted version BNB and BDT	Evaluated number of experiments & found that setting of 2-gram, TF, using 300 features selected by DF measure outperformed. The performance of DT and boosted DT was very well as compared NB

(continued)

Table 1. (*continued*)

STUDY	Classifiers	Conclusion
Detecting scareware by mining variable length instruction sequences-2011 [8]	JripSMO,DT,Ibk,NB,Random forest	This paper presents the static analysis method based on data mining which extends the general heuristic detection technique using a variable length instruction sequence mining approach for scareware detection
Accurate Adware Detection using Op-code Sequence Extraction (2011) [9]	ZeroR,Naïve Bayes, SMO, IBk, J48, JRip	Detects adware using data mining & ML method. KNN, and SVM were effective when the data was noisy, KNN's performance is superior incrementally when new training samples are introduced, JRip and J48 algorithms are expensive in term of time consumption to train and generate the model but it is easy to analyze the rules and trees generated to differentiate the non-Malicious and malicious
Detection of Spyware by Mining Executable Files(2010) [10]	ZeroR, Naïve bayes, SMO, J48, Random forest, JRip	Detects spyware by using data Feature set generated by CFBE selection method generally produced better results with regard to accuracy than feature sets generated by FBFE method

2.1 Summary

In the above sections, we have presented a brief review about the malware detection and prevention techniques introduced in the past decades. Day by day the malware writers are improving and evolving camouflage techniques from simple encrypted virus to extreme complex and difficult to detect polymorphic and metamorphic viruses. Based on the literature review we have designed malware detection Model for known and unknown malware.

3 Proposed Malware Detection Framework by PCA Based ANN

A smart host-based system was developed to detect malware on mobile devices and was evaluated. The framework is designed to be light on the system such that it consumes minimum CPU, memory and battery. It continuously samples various features on the device and collects data which is then analyzed using machine learning and temporal reasoning method and the state of the device. The features of the framework are divided into two categories namely Application Framework and Linux Kernel respectively. Features such as Messaging, Phone calls and Applications belong to the former whereas Keyboard, Touch Screen, Scheduling and Memory belong to the latter.

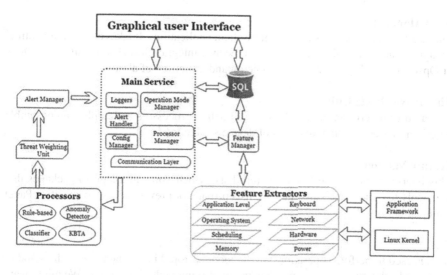

Fig. 1. Malware Detection Framework

The above Framework helps in the detection of malware and in finding the weak points in the Mobile OS. KBTA (Knowledge Based Temporal Abstraction) is normally used for showing the malware behavior in the Mobile OS. The behavior pattern is classified using a Classifier. The data passing through the System is scanned by an Anomaly Detector for incoming anomalies. There are certain preset parameters which are used to dividing the inputs and they are known as Rule Based processes. The above mentioned four processes are used to overcome the malware intrusion.

We now exhibit the work process of our proposed ANN-based malware location framework as appeared in Fig. 1. The entities in Fig. 1 are explained below.

Graphical User Interface

Graphical User Interface (GUI) allows the users to interact with electronic devices with the help of graphical icons and visual pointers such as secondary notation instead of Command Line Interfaces (CLI) which required the user to type commands or use text navigation. CLIs were not very user friendly due to the extensive typing of commands to perform simple operations. Hence GUIs were introduced. The GUI used in this Framework was designed using MATLAB.

Processor

A processor is a logic chip that reacts to and processes the basic instructions that are initiated by the computer. The four basic functions of a processor are fetching, decoding, executing and writing back.

Feature Extractors

This unit is used to extract the useful and required information from the layers. It also contains the necessary hardware and software units in it.

Alert Manager

The Alert manager handles alerts sent by client applications. It takes care of duplicating, grouping, and routing them to the correct receiver integration such as email, Pager Duty, or OpsGenie. It also takes care of silencing and inhibition of alerts.

Threat Weighting Unit

It is used to determine the results from all active processors and applies an ensemble algorithm to derive a final decision of device's infection level.

Feature Manager

This interface allows you to edit feature lists, which you can assign to packages that you apply to cPanel accounts. Feature lists provide or prevent access to specific cPanel features.

SQL

SQL is used to perform operations on the records stored in the database such as updating records, deleting records, creating and modifying tables, views, etc. We might want to stress that the work process is common and can be utilized for authorization based recognition and framework call-based discovery. In disconnected preparing stage, we initially gather true kindhearted and noxious applications. Then, the gathered applications are executed and the information sources are discarded. Utilizing the mapped information as info, we at that point prepared the neural system. In the online identification stage, we dumped the information sources from new applications and the prepared neural system would be utilized to decide if the new application is malware or kind. As authorizations and framework calls contain diverse highlights and have distinctive configurations, we initially present consent based discovery and after that framework call based identification in the accompanying subsections.

3.1 Permission-Based Detection

Step 1: Collecting Information sources and arranging them.

The primary step in the standalone preparing stage is gathering information from the running applications. With the help of credible applications and malware tests, the applications of a similar class should give comparable data such that the data can be used in the irregularity profile. Using these profiles we can classify applications as friendly or malicious.

Step 2: Discarding Data Source Permissions.

With the help of a kind application and corresponding malware tests, the consents asked for by every applications are scrapped. All the consents in an Android Framework are integrated in the AndroidManifest.xml document. For gathering the apk documents a device called Android Asset Packaging Tool (aapt) is used. It helps in recreating the source code and in obtaining the AndroidManifest.xml consents for all applications.

Step 3: Feature extraction.

A set of files consisting of consents requested by an application are collected. For the training part the data is processed as well as mapped to the prerequisite format given by the ANN. To convert the original consent into system readable input a mapping algorithm was designed. In this algorithm an integer is assigned to each feature and the value assigned defines whether it was called for by the application. An application can request only once for a consent. If a consent is requested, its assigned value is 1, else it is 0.

As the ANN acknowledges integers as information, we allocate the consent names to a whole number for preparing the list of authorizations. Outputs such as "01, 02, 03, 06, 09, 15, and 20" are produced by mapping. For example BLUETOOTH is mapped to 12, READ CALL LOG is mapped to 14, and READ CONTACTS is mapped to 8. We can map out this plan to use 2-gram to recognize inclusion by applying two continuous consents in place of one. For instance, we join two consecutive whole numbers and the mapping results are "0102, 0203, 0304, and 0405" where "0102" speaks to the authorizations ACCESS NETWORK STATE and GET ACCOUNTS respectively. After the number grouping, the following stage is to obtain the purpose of each component. It is to be noted that the presence of consent is treated as component esteem. For each element that comes up, its esteem is termed as 1. For those which don't show up, their qualities are termed as 0. After the last two for circles, we get the component vector pointing to the contribution of the ANN as takes after: 1,0,0,0,0,0,0,0,0,1,0,1,0,1,0,0,0,1,0,0,0,1,0,1,0,0,0,0,0,1,0,0,0,0,0,0,0,0,0,0,0,0, 0,0,0,0,0,0,0,0,0, 0,0,0,0,0,0,0,0,0,0,0,0, 0,0,0,0,0,0,0,0,0,0,0,0,0,1,0

Step 4: Classifier learning.

The learning module is used in this step and it is used to build up the neural system for analyzing the application conduct from preparing information. The element vectors are input to the Matlab Neural Network Toolbox which is in Matlab R2016a (8.1.0.604) to execute consent based recognition. The quantity of hubs in a shrouded layer is set to 10 and after that 20. The online identification step is similar to that portrayed in the disconnected preparing stage. Ideally, to group an application, the initial step is to dump the consents and guide the authorization list to the organization required by the ANN. The prepared ANN is used to decide if an application is malware or friendly. The prepared ANN and test information are used as benchmarks for fresh applications. The preparation document has a vaguely different composition from the test file, which houses the component vector related with all applications. The recognition process yields an outcome file which has the order result. The outcome is $+1$ or -1 in this framework. When there is a positive outcome the application is characterized as friendly, whereas in a negative outcome the application is characterized as malicious.

```
Pseudocode for permission based Detection:
Step 1: Begin
Step 2: Gather the information from executing application
Step 3: Dump the permission asked for by every application
Step 4: Utilize Android Asset Packaging (aapt) to recreate the
source code and acquire the AndroidMainFest.xml request for every
application
Step 5: Feature Extraction
Collect set of files with permission
Step 6: Processing and mapping the data to the prerequisite format
of the ANN.
Step 7: Assigning an integer to every feature
Step 8: If permission is requested then feature value=1 else 0
Step 9: Input vector send to Matlab NN Toolbox to execute the per-
mission based recognition
Step 10: If output is +1 then no malware
Else if output is -1 then malware
```

3.2 System Call-Based Detection

The detection system based on system calls has a comparable procedure to the detection system based on permissions. The biggest difference is that it uses a varied data source. In these next few steps, there is a brief introduction to the working of system call-based detection.

Step 1: Data set collection and classification.

The primary step is to gather the data set. The data set has real time friendly applications and malware samples and we segregate them into different groups.

Step 2: System calls recording.

A recognized tool trace is employed to record the system calls requested by the friendly applications as well as the malware samples. Nexus Root Toolkit v1.6.2 is used to avail root permission on Android devices so as to install the trace. Then the trace is run and the system calls made by both the friendly and malware applications are recorded. An Android Debug Bridge (ADB) is used to install the malware on an Android device from a remote computer.

Step 3: Feature extraction.

Each executed application generates a file which contains the system calls and all such files are recorded in a set. The data has to be mapped and processed to prerequisite format provided by the ANN. Each system call is mapped to an integer. As an example, get current process ID – getpid is mapped to 1, readfile is mapped to 3, and readconsole is mapped to 6. We can use 2-gram protocol by using two consecutive system calls as a detection feature instead if one. In order to map the 2-gram, all pairs of continuous integers are combined and generate an outcome similar to "0101 0103 0306 0601 0116 1616 1616 1616 1608" where "0103" denotes system calls getpid and readfile being executed in order. The proportion of density of the system calls is calculated by finding the ratio of the number of each system calls to the total number of system calls generated. Hence we can denote a feature and its value.

Step 4: Classifier learning.

The step 4 of system call based detection is similar to the step 4 of permission-based detection. After this step, the training process of the ANN is complete and is ready to be used for online malware detection. The procedure of the online detection phase is same as the offline training phase. Now, we execute the application, discard the system calls and map the sequence of system calls to the prerequisite format of the ANN to classify the application. Using the ANN trained by the offline training phase, we can identify if a new application is malicious or friendly.

```
Pseudocode for call based Detection
Step 1: Begin
Step 2: collect the dataset
Step 3: record the system calls and obtain root
permission
Step 4: Running trace and capturing the system calls used by the
friendly as well as malicious applications.
Step 5: to install malware utilize Android Debug Bridge (ADB)
Step 6: Feature Extraction record a set of files
Step 7: Processing and mapping the data to the prerequisite format
of the ANN.
Step 8: Assigning an integer to every feature
Step 9: If permission is requested then feature value=1 else 0
Step 9: Input vector send to Matlab NN Toolbox to execute the per-
mission based recognition
Step 10: if output is +1 then no malware
Else if output is -1 then malware
```

4 Simulated Results

Simulated results area is included in the experimental results and performance evaluation of malware detection. The assessment requires two experiments in which one utilizes the public dataset MalGenome and other one is based on a private dataset. MalGenome experiment used k-fold cross validation, otherwise known as the tenfold method. K-fold cross validation utilizes the holdout scheme and runs in a loop, K-fold times. Two segments of dataset are, as the testing set is K subsets and as the training set is K-1 subsets. In the end, the median of all K trials are calculated for getting the result of evaluation. During the newest malware experiment used for both test set. To discover the potential for a forecast relationship, the training set is used as a set of data. Whereas the other test set contributes a principal role in examining how efficient the classifier is. It is worthless by not using the test dataset in the training dataset. Finally, the ideal classifier was determined as the experimental results of both situations. Our data set consists of 1449 apps in total. We collected 1008 top free apps across different category from Google Play to create a benign set. Our malware set consists of 441 apps taken from Android malware Genome Project. We used ApkTotal to make sure that our benign set is free from any malware.

4.1 Results of ANN

In this research work ANN is used to detect the presence of malware in CSDMC2019 API dataset. This dataset is composed of a selection of windows API/System call trace files, intended for testing on classifiers treating with sequences.

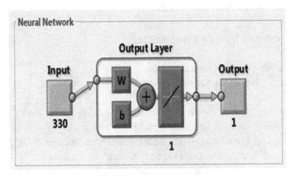

Fig. 2. Structure of Neural Network

We use MALTAB GUI to design the proposed malware detection system which is shown in Fig. 2. The GUI design is flexible and can be comfortable for all the three stages of the proposed system such as malware creation, detection and prevention. Also, we have tested the proposed malware detection system while connecting it to a mobile OS and transferring a file from mobile OS to desktop OS. Once the mobile device is connected it request for the access and the access will be granted if the verification process is successfully completed. The features from the OS will be extracted and using PCA the dimensionality of the extracted features is reduced. The reduced features will be compared with the malware features based upon the training data stored in ANN. If any similarities found between the features the system detects the presence of malware which is created while transferring the data.

Figure 3 shows the structure ANN while training for malware detection after loading the downloaded database and after the completion of feature extraction process and feature reduction by PCA.

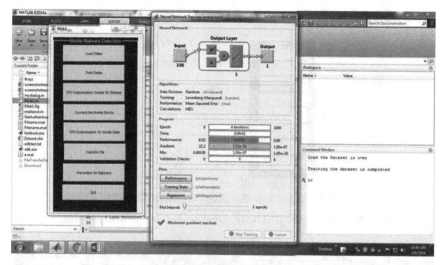

Fig. 3. Screenshot of GUI design window for training ANN

The OS customization initially scans the data in the desktop for malwares. Once the process of desktop OS customization completes the process of file transfer from mobile device will be initiated. As of an initial step a request window will appear to connect the mobile device. Then, the mobile device gets access to the data from the mobile device, it will be correlated and the proposed system loads and scans the data for further processing (Figs. 4 and 5).

Fig. 4. Screenshot of command window

The mobile OS get customized the user id will get verified to initiate the process of file transfer from the mobile device to the desktop system. Then, the verification process completed successfully then the process starts with accessing the files from the mobile device. Once the files are accessed the files from the appropriate device get tracked and transferred via API.

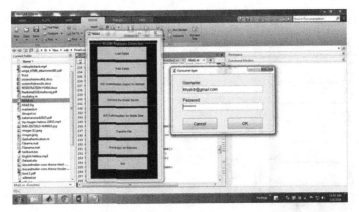

Fig. 5. Screenshot of GUI design window after mobile device access

Fig. 6. Loading files to transfer

Figure 6 shows the screenshot captured while selecting the files which is to be transferred and processed. Again the verification process takes place to improve the system security.

Figure 7 shows the screenshot captured after when the file transfer process get completed and accessed completely. After the completion of file transfer the process of malware detection get initiated again. It checks the presence of malwares occurred during the process of file transfer (Fig. 8).

Fig. 7. File transfer completed

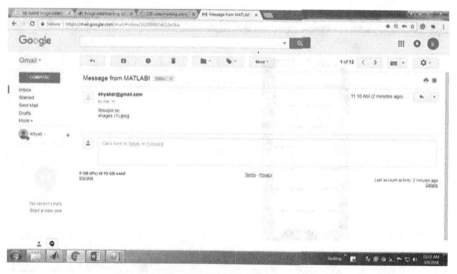

Fig. 8. Intimation of Malware detected via mail

With the presence of malware detected, mail intimation will be directed to the authenticated mail id using MATLAB. The mail also contains the label of the detected malware with the intimation of corrupted file (Figs. 9 and 10).

Trivial hash based deadlock algorithm prevents the overall system and files from the harmful malwares which may create during file transfer (Fig. 11).

Fig. 9. Corrupted file

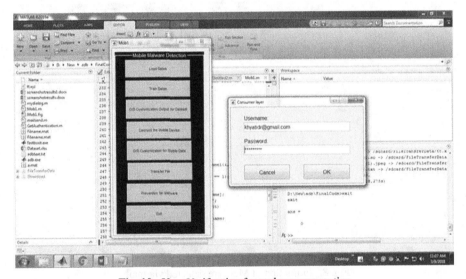

Fig. 10. User Verification for malware prevention

The process from user verification to OS customization will repeat to prevent the entry of malwares in any system. To prevent Malwares using trivial hash deadlock the malware detection process will be initiated and once if detected any suspicious activity the internal and external operations of the system get blocked and no one can access any files from the system.

Fig. 11. User verification succeed

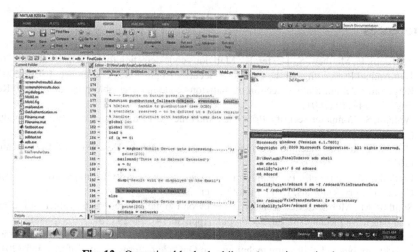

Fig. 12. Operation blocked while malware is received

Now an intimation to reboot the system along with malware intimation will be sent to the users' mail and can operate the system only after rebooting the system. Figure 12 shows the intimation of operations blocked when a malware enters into the system. Then the system is intimated to reboot after detection of malware to prevent further harm to the system. Once the above process gets succeeded the system OS get customized along with the mobile OS and also a successful file transfer was performed and the rebooted system will completely free from malwares and also protected from future malwares.

5 Conclusion

The principal aim of this presentation was to show the efficiency of updating anti-virus tools with new unfamiliar malwares. We can detect new malware by using an updated classifier which can be used for sustaining an anti-virus tool. Labeled files must be modernized for both the anti-virus and its detection model called as classifier. The labeling can be done physically by experts, consequently the aim of the classification is focused effort on labeling files which are likely to be malware or new information added files about benign files.

In this research, evaluation of various machine learning classifiers are to increase the detection of malware outcome for a strong and large collection of file samples and acquire the optimum classifier which can detect mobile malware. The classifiers were Artificial Neural Network (ANN), Bayes network, decision tree (DT) (J48), K-nearest neighbor (KNN) and support vector machine (SVM). Our experiment comprised 49 separate families containing 1,260 Android malware samples included by the MalGenome project samples whereas only 1000 were utilized. There are three phases in the machine learning process: (1) data collection, which captures network traffic; (2) feature selection and extraction; and (3) the machine learning classifier.

References

1. Adelstein, F., Matthew, S., Dexter, K.: Malicious code detection for open firmware. In: 2002 18th Annual Proceedings of the Computer Security Applications Conference, IEEE (2002)
2. Bergeron, J., et al.: Static detection of malicious code in executable programs. Int. J. Req. Eng **79**, 184–189 (2001)
3. William, S.: Computer Security: Principles And Practice. Pearson Education India, Bengaluru (2008)
4. Chumachenko, K.: Machine Learning Methods for Malware Detection and Classification (2017)
5. La Polla, M., Martinelli, F., Sgandurra, D.: A survey on security for mobile devices. IEEE Commun. Surv. Tutorials, **15**(1), First Quarter (2013)
6. Sujithra, M.: Mobile device security: a survey on mobile device threats, vulnerabilities and their defensive mechanism. Int. J. Comput. Appl. **56**(14), 24–29 (2012). (0975–8887)
7. Shabtai, A., Moskovitch, R., Feher, C., Dolev, S., Elovici, Y.: Detecting unknown malicious code by applying classification techniques on OpCode patterns. Secur. Inform. **1**, 1 (2012). http://www.securityinformatics.com/content/1/1/1
8. Shahzad, R.K., Lavesson, N.: Detecting scareware by mining variable length instruction sequences. In: Proceedings of the 10th Annual Information Security South Africa Conference (ISSA11), Johannesburg, South Africa, pp. 18. IEEE, August 2011
9. Raja, K.S., Niklas, L., Henric, J.: Accurate adware detection using opcode sequence extraction. In: Proceedings of the 6th International Conference on Availability, Reliability and Security (ARES11), Prague, Czech Republic, pp. 189–195. IEEE (2011)
10. Shahzad, R.K., Haider, S.I., Lavesson, N.: Detection of spyware by mining executable files. In: Proceedings of the 5th International Conference on Availability, Reliability, and Security. IEEE Computer Society, pp. 295302 (2010)
11. Rami, K., Desai, V.: Survey on security for mobile device: threats and vulnerability. Int. J. Adv. Res. Comput. Sci. Softw. Eng. **5**(12), 446–471 (2015)

12. Smith, T.F., Waterman, M.S.: Identification of common molecular subsequences. J. Mol. Biol. **147**, 195–197 (1981). https://doi.org/10.1016/0022-2836(81)90087-5

13. Landage, J.: Malware and malware detection techniques: a survey. Int. J. Eng. Res. Technol. (IJERT), **2**(12) (2013). ISSN-2278-0181

14. Vaibhav, R., Chen, Y., Jiang, X.: Droidchameleon: evaluating android anti-malware against transformation attacks. In: Proceedings of the 8th ACM SIGSAC Symposium on Information, Computer and Communications Security, pp. 329–334. ACM (2013)

15. Seung-Hyun, S., Gupta, A., Sallam, A.M., Bertino, E., Yim, K.: Detecting mobile malware threats to homeland security through static analysis. Jtheirnal of Network and Computer Applications **38**, 43–53 (2014)

16. Petsas, T., Giannis, V., Elias, A., Michalis, P., Sotiris, I.: Rage against the virtual machine: hindering dynamic analysis of android malware. In: Proceedings of the Seventh European Workshop on System Security, p. 5. ACM (2014)

17. Burguera, I., Urko Z., Simin, N.-T.: Crowdroid: behavior-based malware detection system for android. In: Proceedings of the 1st ACM workshop on Security and Privacy in Smartphones and Mobile Devices, pp. 15–26. ACM (2011)

18. Shabtai, A., Kanonov, U., Elovici, Y., Glezer, C., Theyiss, Y.: "Andromaly": a behavioral malware detection system for android devices. Jtheirnal Intell. Inf. Syst. **38**(1), 161–190 (2012)

19. Schmidt, A-D., et al.: Static analysis of executables for collaborative malware detection on android. In: IEEE International Conference on Communications, 2009. ICC 2009, pp. 1–5. IEEE (2009)

Computing Science

A New Approach to Solve Job Sequencing Problem Using Dynamic Programming with Reduced Time Complexity

Tanzin Ahammad[1] , Mahedi Hasan[1] , Mohammad Hasan[2]([✉]) ,
Md. Sabir Hossain[1]([✉]) , Ariful Hoque[3] , and Md Mamunur Rashid[2]

[1] Chittagong University of Engineering and Technology, Chattogram, Bangladesh
sabir.cse@cuet.ac.bd
[2] Bangladesh Army University of Science and Technology, Saidpur, Bangladesh
hasancse.cuet13@gmail.com
[3] Green University of Bangladesh, Dhaka, Bangladesh

Abstract. The classical algorithm which is dedicated to resolve job sequencing problem with a deadline (JSD) needs exponential time $O(n^2)$, where sorting algorithm [$O(nlog(n))$-(Merge Sort)] must have to use to sort all the jobs in decreasing order of their profit and it is a greedy technique. To reduce the complexity of this classical algorithm, we nullify the sorting algorithm using dynamic programming approach in the proposed algorithm. The time complexity after using this approach reduces to $O(mn)$, where no sorting algorithm [$O(nlog(n))$-(Merge Sort)] needed, which has been shown by proper explanation. Here, we were also given a novel approach to resolve the job sequencing problem using Dynamic Programming and it is a unique approach that always finds an optimal solution. By using this approach, a proper algorithm has been developed in this paper. Besides, finding maximum profit and the sequence of the job to obtain maximum profit, this algorithm gives the sequence of jobs for a specific profit or near a specific profit.

Keywords: Job sequencing problem · Dynamic programming · Sorting · Tabulation · 2D array

1 Introduction

Job Sequencing Problem with Deadline (JSD) is a popular algorithm to find the sequence of jobs to obtain maximum profit. In this problem, normally, deadline and profit of each job are given. The profit is achieved, when the job is completed before the given timeframe. Single unit of time is taken by every job. So, the minimum possible deadline for any job is 1. We have to find a maximum profit if only one job can be scheduled at a time. In the classical greedy algorithm, they have to sort the jobs according to profit, they have to sequence the jobs. In our proposed algorithm, we need not sort the job, using the dynamic programming-tabulation method this algorithm reduced this time complexity for sorting. So, a novel approach to solve the job sequencing problem using dynamic programming also proposed in this paper. Besides, reducing time complexity

N. Chaubey et al. (Eds.): COMS2 2020, CCIS 1235, pp. 317–328, 2020.
https://doi.org/10.1007/978-981-15-6648-6_25

this algorithm gives the sequence of jobs for finding a specific profit or near the specific profit because in all steps total profit is memorized in the first column of a 2D array. This algorithm is unique and always finds an optimal solution. There are various uses of Job Sequencing problems in real life which are described in the related works section such as, network scheduling technique, flow-shop and job-shop scheduling, task scheduling and many more.

2 Related Works

Minimizing the sum of the overheads of delayed jobs in a machine is given in paper [1]. Here, they proposed a method named as "Range-and-Bound". The aim of the paper [2] is to develop an improved polynomial-time approximation algorithm. Paper [3] solved the single processor job sequencing with deadlines. In this paper, they have used dynamic programming type algorithms to get best and optimal solutions.

Job-shop-sequencing problem solved by the "network scheduling technique" covered in paper [4]. In this paper, for obtaining least total execution time, a new network scheduling based method with resource constraints has proposed. This paper is best suited where the resource is limited and the jobs are in arbitrary order. This procedure returns an optimal solution with the minimum duration of time. In addition to these features this algorithm also able to solved those problems that are not possible or difficult to solved using a heuristic algorithm or technique to resolve the Job Shop Sequencing problem.

Another new technique for an optimal solution of the Job Sequencing problem using the "path optimization algorithm" proposed in paper [5]. In this paper, they use the Johnson rule to solve this problem. This procedure finds a sequence of substructure and every time they take the best possible sequence that fills up the criteria for job sequencing problem. This procedure ensures an optimal solution for the job sequencing problem.

Finding minimum finish time for both preemptive and non-preemptive is NP-complete. It is the main objective of the paper [6]. This paper mainly discussed the time and space complexity for job-shop and flow shop scheduling. Also, it discusses the time complexity of different techniques for solving job shop scheduling problems such as a heuristic algorithm for job sequencing, Johnson rule for sequencing job shop problem.

An optimal solution for multi-objective distributed permutation Flow Shop Scheduling problem is discussed in paper [7]. Job sequencing problems are of various types, depending on the number of machines, resources and populations this problem varies. Here, they discussed when the number of populations is of two. Here they used the Taguchi method for solving this problem.

Generating a new job one by one is the proposed method for job sequencing problems in paper [8]. The machine for performing jobs may vary according to their characteristics. This method considers the characteristics of the machine and finds the best- suited machine for every position. For example, first, we chose four machines then next machine five then six. And this technique returns a feasible solution and the large computation may be reduced.

In paper [9], a novel heuristic method called "Time Deviation" for finding Job Sequencing problem is used to minimize the total consumed time. This technique is both applicable for one machine n jobs and n machine m jobs and the time complexity is considerably lower than other proposed techniques. In paper [10] about advanced heuristic technique.

Sequence-dependent set up time means considering the setup time is discussed on paper [11]. In general, we read the papers before we observed that the proposed methodology considers the setup time as processing time but this procedure considers the setup time and analyzes the setup time. But there are some problems with this method. It may not provide an optimal solution.

The technique for job shop for large data is the proposed methodology or procedure in paper [12]. Here Brain k proposed a technique where large data for example data of a company in a spreadsheet is given. This solution generates both optimal and feasible solutions and heuristic solutions.

The intelligence-based genetic algorithm discussed in paper [13]. This procedure is a combination of both heuristic algorithm and the genetic algorithm. When n machines and m jobs are given the heuristic algorithm finds the best-suited job at each line of the machine and then the genetic algorithm is applied. The combination of both heuristic algorithm and the genetic algorithm reduces the complexity of the large data input.

In paper [14], Bożejko et al. proposed a "hybrid single-walk distributed tabu search method" to solve flexible job shop problem. In Paper [15], G.S. Paiva et al. have used graph representation, local search and heuristic methods to solve the Job Scheduling problem. N number of jobs sequencing on a single machine with an obstructive common due window problems has discussed in paper [16]. To solve this problem a new "Backtracking Simulated Annealing (BSA)" algorithm and an efficient coding method is proposed. Paper [17] proposed a new "Tabu Search" algorithm to solve the Job scheduling problems including precedence constraints.

3 Proposed Methodology

To implement this proposed algorithm first read the jobs (means job id, job deadline, job profit for each job). Take a table and fill the first row by 0 and find the maximum deadline. In the table, column numbers are deadline and row numbers are job id, so total columns are maximum deadline and total rows total number of jobs.

For each job, first fill up the present row by the previous row then search maximum deadline/last column no. to 1 and find row's minimum job profit, if row's minimum job profit is less than present job profit, then lock this minimum profits box and put the job id in this box. Sum all the job profit of this row and store it in the first column. If all the jobs are traversed, then print the last row, where 1st value is maximum profit and all other are sequence to obtain this profit. If all the jobs are not traversed, then go the next row and repeat this procedure by searching the last column no. to 1. By this process using the Dynamic Programming and tabulation method, we can find the maximum profit among all jobs and the sequence for obtaining maximum profit. Besides all the other things can be found from the table by applying a specific condition. Here the table stores all the information for each step. We have to apply specific conditions in the table for getting a specific solution (Fig. 1). Let's see the flow chart:-

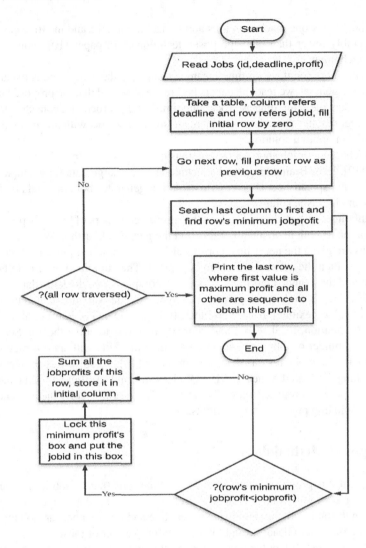

Fig. 1. Flow Chart of our proposed algorithm.

3.1 Pseudocode of Proposed Algorithm

In this research paper, the following algorithm can solve 'The Job Sequencing Problem with Deadlines' and can find the maximum profit with a sequence of the jobs. Here we can also find maximum profit for fixed/flexible number of jobs and also for fixed/flexible deadlines. The following algorithm also gives the solution to obtain a specific profit which jobs had to do in which order if the specific job can't achieve then it can find the nearest profit (less or greater) of the specific profit and can also find its job sequence.

1. READ n and jobs (id, deadline, profit)
2. SET arr [n] to jobs
3. FIND maximum deadline and SET m=maximum deadline
4. SET a[n+1][m+1]={0}
5. FOR i=1 to n
6.   SET s=0,p=INFINITY and l=0
7.   WHILE m>0 DO
8.   SET a[i][j]=a[i-1][j]
9.   IF arr[i].deadline>=j, THEN :
10.   IF arr[i].profit>arr[a[i][j]].profit, THEN :
11.   IF p>arr[a[i][j]].profit, THEN :
12.   SET P=arr[a[i][j]].profit and l=j
13.   ENDIF
14.   ENDIF
15.   ENDIF
16.   SET s=s+arr[a[i][j]].profit and m=m-1
17.   END WHILE
18.   IF l!=0 THEN:
19.   SET s=s-arr[a[i][l]].profit, a[i][l]=arr[i].jobid and s=s+arr[a[i][l]].profit
20.   ENDIF
21.   SET a[i][0]=s
22. ENDFOR
23. FOR j=1 to m
24.   IF a[n][j]!=0, THEN :
25.   PRINT a[n][j]
26.   ENDIF
27. ENDFOR
28. PRINT a[n][0]

4 Experimental Result and Complexity Analysis

4.1 Step by Step Simulation for Sample Input

Here, given an array of jobs. Every job has a deadline and profit, if the job is finished before the deadline, then the profit is achieved. Every job takes single unit of time, so the minimum possible deadline for any job is 1. Find maximum profit if only one job can be scheduled at a time (Tables 1 and 2).

Table 1. Sample input of Dataset.

Job id:	1	2	3	4	5
Deadline:	2	1	2	1	3
Profit:	100	19	27	25	15

Table 2. Initialization step.

Jobid (profit, deadline)	0	1	2	3
0(0, 0)		0	0	0	0
1(100, 2)					
2(19, 1)					
3(27, 2)					
4(25, 1)					
5(15, 3)					

Step 1: Take all the jobs according to jobid in which indicate row number. Take all the deadlines in increasing order as column number. Here every box contains jobid except the 1st column boxes which contain total profit for each row. When jobid = 0, then put 0 in every column of this 1st row. Go to the next row (Table 3).

Table 3. Step 1 simulation.

Jobid(profit, deadline)	0	1	2	3
0(0, 0)		0	0	0	0
1(100, 2)	100	0	1	0
2(19, 1)					
3(27, 2)					
4(25, 1)					
5(15, 3)					

Step 2: Here, first put the previous row values in this row. Then, compare the 1st job's deadline with the column's no./deadline from the maximum/last row deadline 3 to 1. If the 1st job's deadline matches the column no. or greater than the column number then find minimum profit's job (2, 3) among those jobs and if the 1st job's profit is greater than this minimum profit's job(2, 3) (100 > 0), then lock this box (2, 3) and replace this box (2, 3) by 1st job's id. Calculate the sum of all the job's profit of this row and put it in this row's 1st column (100). Go to the next row/job (Table 4).

Table 4. Step 2 visualization

Jobid (profit, deadline)	0		1	2	3
0(0, 0)	0		0	0	0

(continued)

Table 4. (*continued*)

Jobid (profit, deadline)	0	1	2	3
1(100, 2)	100	0	1	0
2(19, 1)	100 + 19 = 119	2	1	0
3(27, 2)				
4(25, 1)				
5(15, 3)				

Step 3: Here, first put the previous row values in this row. Then, compare the 2nd job's deadline with the column's no./deadline from the maximum/last row deadline 3 to 1. If the 2nd job's deadline matches the column no. or greater than the column number then find minimum profit's job (3, 2) among those jobs and if the 2nd job's profit is greater than this minimum profit's job (3, 2) (19 > 0), then lock this box (3, 2) and replace this box (3, 2) by 2nd job's id. Calculate the sum of all the job's profit of this row and put it in this row's 1st column (119). Go to the next row/job (Table 5).

Table 5. Step 3 visualization.

Jobid (profit, deadline)	0	1	2	3
0(0, 0)	0	0	0	0
1(100, 2)	100	0	1	0
2(19, 1)	100 + 19 = 119	2	1	0
3(27, 2)	100 + 27 = 127	3	1	0
4(25, 1)				
5(15, 3)				

Step 4: Here, first put the previous row values in this row. Then, compare the 3rd job's deadline with the column's no./deadline from the maximum/last row deadline 3 to 1. If the 3rd job's deadline matches the column no. or greater than the column number then find minimum profit's job (4, 2) among those jobs and if the 3rd job's profit is greater than this minimum profit's job (4, 2) (27 > 19), then lock this box (4, 2) and replace this box (4, 2) by 3rd job's id. Calculate the sum of all the job's profit of this row and put it in this row's 1st column (127). Go to the next row/job (Table 6).

Step 5: Here, first put the previous row values in this row. Then, compare the 4th job's deadline with the column's no./deadline from the maximum/last row deadline 3 to 1. If the 4th job's deadline matches the column no. or greater than the column number then find minimum profit's job (5, 2) among those jobs, but the 4th job's profit is not greater than this minimum profit's job (5, 2) (25 < 27), so do not lock this job. Calculate the

Table 6. Step 4 visualization.

Jobid (profit, deadline)	0	1	2	3
0(0, 0)	0	0	0	0
1(100, 2)	100	0	1	0
2(19, 1)	100 + 19 = 119	2	1	0
3(27, 2)	100 + 27 = 127	3	1	0
4(25, 1)	100 + 27 = 127	3	1	0
5(15, 3)				

sum of all the job's profit of this row and put it in this row's 1st column (127). Go to the next row/job (Table 7).

Table 7 Step 5 visualization.

Jobid(profit,deadline)	0	1	2	3
0(0,0)	0	0	0	0
1(100,2)	100	0	1	0
2(19,1)	100+19=119	2	1	0
3(27,2)	100+27=127	3	1	0
4(25,1)	100+27=127	3	1	0
5(15,3)	100+27+15=142	3 ———→ 1 ———→ 5		

Step 6: Here, first put the previous row values in this row. Then, compare the 5th job's deadline with the column's no./deadline from the maximum/last row deadline 3 to 1. If the 5th job's deadline matches the column no. or greater than the column number then find minimum profit's job (6, 4) among those jobs and if the 5th job's profit is greater than this minimum profit's job (6, 4) (0 < 15) then lock this box(6, 4) and replace this box (6, 4) by 5th job's id. Calculate the sum of all the job's profit of this row and put it in this row's 1st column (127). Go to the next row/job.

Step 7: If all the jobs/row are traversed, then print the value of the last row, where 1st column of this row (142) which is maximum profit and print all next values of this row (3- > 1- > 5) which is required sequence. Besides, we can find for profit- [127] sequence (3- > 1) 2 jobs needed, for, profit- [119] sequence (2- > 1) 2 jobs needed, if needed profit near 130 then profit– [127] sequence (3- > 1) 2 jobs needed.

4.2 Time Complexity Analysis

In this proposed algorithm time complexity depends on input size. Time complexity directly depends on the number of jobs and the maximum deadline. Let, the number of jobs is n and the maximum deadline is m and the function T(n) denotes the number elementary operations performed by the function. Then the recurrence relation for this proposed algorithm is:

$$\text{For } i = 1 : \quad T(n) = m * T(n-1) + m * c * 1$$
$$\text{For } i = 2 : \quad T(n) = m * T(n-2) + m * c * 2$$
$$\text{For } i = 3 : \quad T(n) = m * T(n-3) + m * c * 3$$
$$\text{For } i = k : \quad T(n) = m * T(n-k) + m * c * k$$

Best Case
When all the jobs are traversed then, best case complexity:

$$T(n) = m * T(n-k) + m * c * k$$
$$= \Omega(m * n), \text{ (without sorting)}$$

Here, all the jobs and deadlines have to traverse. No sorting is needed for this algorithm. The best case of this algorithm is m*n where n is the number of jobs and m is the maximum deadline.

Average Case
The average case complexity of this proposed algorithm has occurred,

$$T(n) = m * T(n-k) + m * c * k$$
$$= \Theta(m * n), \text{ (without sorting)}$$

Here all the jobs and deadlines have to traverse. No sorting is needed for this algorithm. The average case of this algorithm is m*n where n is the number of jobs and m is the maximum deadline.

Worst Case
Here, the recurrence relation:

$$T(n) = m * T(n-k) + m * c * k$$
$$\text{for } i = 1 : T(n) = m * T(n-1) + m * c * 1$$
$$\text{for } i = 2 : T(n) = m * T(n-2) + m * c * 2$$
$$\text{for } i = 3 : T(n) = m * T(n-3) + m * c * 3$$

When all the jobs are traversed, then: $(n = k)$ So,

$$T(n) = m * T(0) + c * m * n \, [T(0) \text{ is some constant c0}]$$
$$T(n) = m * c0 + c * m * n$$
$$= O(m * n), \text{ (without sorting)}$$

So, Best case of this algorithm is m * n where n is the number of jobs and m is maximum deadline.

4.3 Space Complexity

In this proposed algorithm space complexity depends on the input data. Inputs are not constant. So, if there are n number of input jobs and maximum deadline m, then space complexity will be n * m. In this proposed algorithm because of using a 2D array, the space complexity of this 2D array is O(n * m).

4.4 Experimental Result Comparison with Classical Algorithms

Here, experiment results show that for the different number of jobs and different maximum deadlines proposed algorithm execution time is less than the classical algorithm.

Here, Table 8 shows that for the different number of jobs and different maximum deadlines proposed algorithm execution time is less than the classical algorithm.

Table 8. Execution Time Comparison with other classical algorithms.

No.	Number of Jobs	Maximum deadline	Execution time for the proposed algorithm(in μs)	Execution time for the classical algorithms(in μs)
1.	4	2	969.13	1048.67
2.	5	3	952.35	999.95
3.	6	4	993.13	993.56
4.	7	4	1420.4	1566.55

The column in Fig. 2 shows with increasing of both the number of jobs and maximum deadlines execution time increasing but the rate of increasing execution time for new algorithms is less than the classical algorithm.

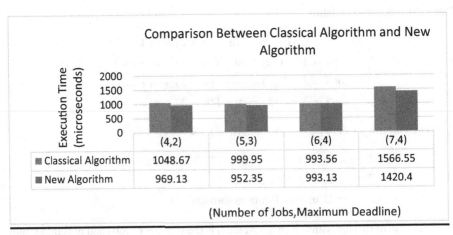

Fig. 2. Comparison Between Classical Algorithm and proposed Algorithm.

The line graph is shown in Fig. 3 with an increasing of both the number of jobs and maximum deadlines execution time increasing but the rate of increasing execution time for the new algorithm is less than the classical algorithm. (Used device in experiment-Intel, CORE I7, 8th Generation, RAM-8 GB, Graphis-4 GB) (Table 9).

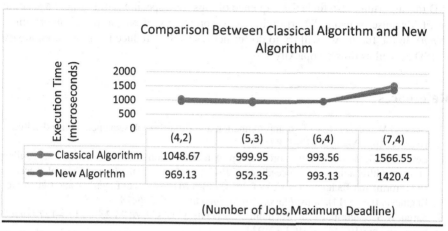

Fig. 3. Execution time comparison graph between classical algorithm and the proposed algorithm.

Table 9. Overall Complexity Comparisons with previous classical algorithms.

Algorithm Name	Best Case time complexity	Average Case time complexity	Worst-case time complexity	Space complexity
JSD	$\Omega(n^2)$	$\Theta(n^2 + nlogn) =$ $\Theta(n^2)$, (with sorting)	$O(n^2 + nlogn) =$ $O(n^2)$, (with sorting)	$O(n)$
Paper [1]	$\Omega(n^2 \log n + n^2/e)$	$\Theta(n^2 + nlogn +$ $n^2/e)$	$O(n^2 + nlogn +$ $n^2/e)$	$O(n^2/e)$
Paper [2]	$\Omega(n^2/e)$	$\Theta(n^2/e)$	$O(n^2/e)$	$O(n^2/e)$
Paper [3]	$\Omega(\min(2^n, nM))$	$\Theta(\min(2^n, nM))$	$O(\min(2^n, nM))$	$O(\min(2^n, nM))$
Proposed Algorithm	$\Omega(mn)$, (without sorting)	$\Theta(mn)$, (without sorting)	$O(mn)$, (without sorting)	$O(mn)$

5 Conclusions and Future Recommendation

The Job Sequencing with Deadline (JSD) is studied and researched by a lot number of researchers. In this paper, we have designed an algorithm by using the dynamic programming approach. By using these approach we have reduced the time complexity

O(mn), where no sorting [O($n log n$)-Merge Sort] is needed, where n is the number of jobs and m is the maximum deadline. So, the time complexity is reduced and a new approach for solving JSD is proposed in this paper. Normally the time complexity for the general JSD algorithm overall O(n^2) where n is the number of jobs. We are able to show that our algorithm is better which gives results faster and it is a new approach. Besides, solving JSD this algorithm also finds the sequence of jobs for a specific profit or near a specific profit. Because of using 2D array the space complexity of our proposed algorithm is O(mn). In the future, we will try to do further research to reduce the space complexity of JSD as well as time complexity.

References

1. Gens, G.V., Levner, E.V.: Fast approximation algorithm for job sequencing with deadlines. Discrete Appl. Math. **3**, 313–318 (1981)
2. Levner, E., Elalouf, A.: An improved approximation algorithm for the ancient scheduling problem with deadlines. In: Proceedings - 2014 International Conference on Control, Decision and Information Technologies, CoDIT 2014, 113–116 (Institute of Electrical and Electronics Engineers Inc., 2014). https://doi.org/10.1109/codit.2014.6996878
3. Sartaj, K.S.: Algorithms for scheduling independent tasks. J. ACM **23**(1), 116–127 (1976). https://doi.org/10.1145/321921.321934
4. Akpan, E.O.P.: Job-shop sequencing problems via network scheduling technique. Int. J. Oper. Prod. Manage. **16**, 76–86 (1996)
5. Singh, P.K.: Path optimization algorithm for network problems using job sequencing technique. Int. J. Distrib. Parallel Syst. **3**(3), 301–309 (2012)
6. Gonzalez, T., Sahni, S.: Flowshop and jobshop schedules: complexity and approximation. Oper. Res. **26**(1), 36–52 (1978)
7. Deng, J., Wang, L.: A competitive memetic algorithm for multi-objective distributed permutation flow shop scheduling problem. Swarm. Evol Comput. **32**, 121–131 (2017)
8. Presby, J.T., Wolfson, M.L.: An algorithm for solving job sequencing problems. Manage. Sci. **13**(8), B-454–B-464 (1967)
9. Karthikeyan, K.: Heuristics algorithms for job sequencing problems. Global J. Sci. Front. Res. GJSFR Classif.-D. **10**, 76–86 (2010)
10. Iqbal, P.: Job sequencing problem using advanced heuristics techniques. In: Proceedings of the International Conference on Applied Mathematics and Theoretical Computer Science, ICPMT, vol. 12, pp. 89–100 (2013)
11. Das, R.M., Man, M.H.: Job-Shop scheduling problem with sequence dependent setup times. Int. Multi Conf. Eng. Comput. Sci. **12**, 67–80 (2008)
12. Baker, K.R.: Solving sequencing problems in spreadsheets. Int. J. Plan. Schedul. **1**, 3 (2011)
13. Norozi, A.: Application of intelligence based genetic algorithm for job sequencing problem on parallel mixed-model assembly line. Am. J. Eng. Appl. Sci. **3**, 15–24 (2010)
14. Bożejko, W., Hejducki, Z., Uchroński, M., Wodecki, M.: Solving the flexible job shop problem on multi-GPU. Int. Conf. Comput. Sci. **9**, 2020–2023 (2012)
15. Paiva, G.S., Carvalho, M.A.M.: Improved heuristic algorithms for the Job sequencing and tool switching problem. Comput. Oper. Res. **88**, 208–219 (2017)
16. Lin, S.W., Ying, K.C., Wu, W.J., Cheng, C.Y.: Single machine job sequencing with a restricted common due window. IEEE Access **7**, 148741–148755 (2019)
17. Wook, J.S., Woo, K.J.: Solving the constrained job sequencing problem using candidate order based Tabu search. J. Inf. Syst. **25**, 159–182 (2016)

Optimizing Complexity of Quick Sort

Md. Sabir Hossain[1] ⓘ, Snaholata Mondal[1] ⓘ, Rahma Simin Ali[1] ⓘ,
and Mohammad Hasan[2](✉) ⓘ

[1] Chittagong University of Engineering and Technology, Chattogram, Bangladesh
[2] Bangladesh Army University of Science and Technology, Saidpur, Bangladesh
hasancse.cuet13@gmail.com

Abstract. Quick Sort is considered as the fastest sorting algorithm among all the sorting algorithms. The idea of selecting a pivot was introduced in classical Quick Sort in 1962. This sorting algorithm takes favorably less time compared to other methods. It needs a complex time $O(nlogn)$ for the best case and $O(n^2)$ for worst-case which occurs when the input array is already sorted or reversely sorted. To reduce the worst-case complexity we provide a strong algorithm where it makes fewer comparisons and the time complexity after using this algorithm becomes a function of logarithm $O(nlogn)$ for worst-case complexity. We experimentally evaluate our algorithms and compare them with classical algorithms and with other papers. The algorithm presented here has profound implications for future studies of handling worst-case complexity and may one day help to solve this occurrence of the fastest sorting method.

Keywords: Quick Sort · Reversely sorted · Time complexity · Best case · Worst case · Logarithm

1 Introduction

Quick Sort is one of the most efficient sorting algorithms. It is capable of sorting a list of data elements comparatively faster than any of the common sorting algorithms. Quick sort is also called as partition exchange sort. It is based on the splitting of an array into smaller ones. Basically it works on the idea of divide and conquer rule. It divides the array according to the partition function and the partition process depends on the selection of pivot. Its worst case complexity made this fastest algorithm a little bit vulnerable. Many authors researched for reducing the worst case complexity $O(n^2)$ either to O(n) or to $O(nlogn)$. In [1] author optimized the complexity of Quick Sort algorithm to O(n) using Dynamic Pivot selection method. The author R. Devi and V. Khemchandani in paper [2] have used Median Selection Pivot and Bidirectional Partitioning to reduce the worst-case complexity. The general Quick Sort algorithm takes $O(n^2)$ time. Here, in this paper, we presented an algorithm which divides the array as half portion to calculate the pivot and then we use this pivot in partition function that divides the main input array. After recursive calling of the quicksort again and again finally we get the sorted output of input array. Although this algorithm is not unique as we took help from various papers and sources. The paper includes some section describing the

© Springer Nature Singapore Pte Ltd. 2020
N. Chaubey et al. (Eds.): COMS2 2020, CCIS 1235, pp. 329–339, 2020.
https://doi.org/10.1007/978-981-15-6648-6_26

whole project more significantly. Section 2 provides the discussion of the related work with associated limitations. Section 3.1 describes the outcomes of this research paper. Section 3.2 includes the preliminaries where the main idea of Quick Sort has been described. Section 3.3 describes the overview of proposed methodology including a diagram explaining the whole process. Section 3.4 shows the algorithm of proposed methodology in details including the pivot selection. Section 5 discusses the experimental results of the proposed method. Finally, Sect. 6 concludes the paper and shows the future directions to this paper.

2 Related Works

Jaja, A. et al. [3] has mentioned the partitioning process of the QuickSort algorithm. The process of a randomized selection of pivot has been discussed in detail. But the limitation is that the proof of randomized Quick Sort is difficult to understand. The basics of Quick Sort where the storage of computers has been given the priority and basic algorithm has been discussed on paper [2]. The key contributions are partition, comparison of quicksort with merge sort and cyclic exchange. But the limitation is that it says nothing about reducing the worst-case complexity of Quick Sort.

Paper [4] also discusses the preprocessing of large data sets using the QuickSort algorithm. Here, the method of random reference selection has been used. Key contributions are the comparison of complexity, handling of the large input set. But the random reference element selection method is difficult to understand and implementation of this method has not yet been discussed and these are counted as big limitations.

Paper [5] has reduced the complexity of the worst case of Quicksort algorithm to $O(n)$ from $O(nlogn)$ for unsorted arrays and Dynamic Pivoting method has been used. The key contribution is the median of five/seven/nine. Random pivot selection, recursive calls, Boolean variable to see if the array is already sorted. The limitation is that as per empirical analysis the proposed algorithm could not run with $O(nlogn)$ complexity. Paper [6] depicts an overview of the pivot selection method. A new pivot selection method Median of five has been introduced. Paper [1] discusses improving the complexity of quick sort algorithm where key contributions are dividing the array into two equal halves and dynamic pivoting. Dynamic pivoting, Recursive calls, Boolean variables are the basic contributions. But the paper could not prove the experimental research.

Many parallel sorting algorithms among which three types of algorithm and their comparative analysis has been discussed by author Sha, L. in Paper [7] and Singh Rajput, I. et al. in paper [11]. The analysis has taken place based on average sorting time, parallel sorting and comparing the number of comparisons. Two versions of Quick Sort the classical and the proposed one has been discussed by Devi, R. et al. In[2]. The worst-case running time of quicksort has been discussed and reduced to $O(nlogn)$ from $O(n^2)$. In paper [8] pivot based selection technique has been discussed and the dynamic selection of pivot has been introduced. In this paper [8], a new dynamic pivot selection procedure has been introduced that allows the database to be initially empty and grow later. Lakshmi, I. et al. in paper [9] discusses four different types of basic sorting algorithm where sorting algorithms are compared according to In paper [6] tried to explain controlling complexity is the simplest way possible and to do this a simple reliability model has been introduced.

Conceptual framework, forward recovery solution, N version programming are the key contributions. But the explanation of controlling complexity is hard to implement and neither assumption is easy in practice.

Schneider, K. et al. in paper [7] described a Multiway Quicksort to make the algorithm more efficient which gives reason to believe that further improvements are possible with multiway Quicksort. Aumüller, M. et al. in paper [8] explained multi-pivot Quick Sort which refers to a variant of a classical quicksort wherein the partitioning step k pivots are used to split the input into k + 1 segments.

Aumüller, M. et al. in paper [9] tried to introduce a model that captures all dual-pivot algorithms, give a unified analysis, and identify new dual-pivot algorithms that minimize the average number of key comparisons among all possible algorithms and explained that dual-pivot quicksort benefits from a skewed choice of pivots. In paper [10], Kushagra, S. et al. proposed a 3-pivot variant that performs very well in theory and practice that makes fewer comparisons and has better cache behavior than the dual-pivot quicksort.

Authors Faujdar N and Ghrera P in paper [11] showed an evaluation of quick sort along with merge sort using GPA computing which includes the parallel time complexity and total space complexity taken by merge and quick sort on a dataset. In paper [12], authors showed an comparison of parallel quick sort with the theoretical one. A special kind of sorting which is double hashing sort can be known with the help of paper [13]. With the help of paper [14], optimized selection sort and the analysis of the optimization process can be understood very well. A dynamic pivot selction method is presented in a very well method on the paper [15].

3 Methodology

The authors of many papers tried in many ways to reduce the complexity of Quick Sort using different ways. In this algorithm worst case of Quick Sort has been modified by calculating mean as the pivot element. The pivot selection method has been done by dividing the array into two sub-array of equal size. Then the maximum and minimum element of both sub-array is calculated. The average value of all these four values is considered as pivot element. Then the partitioning is happening by comparing each element of both sub-array with the pivot element. Thus the loop will be running half of the array only. Here, if the element of the right subarray is smaller than the pivot, the loop variable will increment. Similarly, if the element of the left subarray is greater than the pivot, the loop variable will decrement. After that swap function is called. When the size is equal or less than 3 then the Manual Sort procedure is called which is actually a compare between the elements. As there is no loop in this function, the time is reduced because the recursion function is not called. Thus this algorithm does not lead to the worst case of $O(n^2)$ and it becomes near to $O(n)$ (Fig. 1).

Here in the above flow chart, the algorithm has been presented in short. When the QuickSort function is called, it checks whether the input size is greater than 3 or not. If input size is greater than 3 then it calculates pivot taking the average of maximum and minimum values from both sub-array. After calculating the pivot, the partition function is called where the values are compared with pivot. After completing all the functions, we get a sorted array which is our desired output.

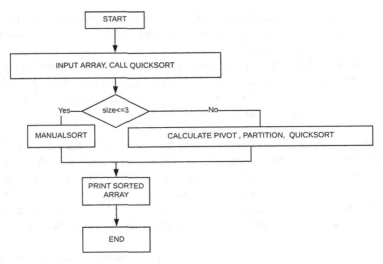

Fig. 1. Flow chart of our proposed algorithm.

3.1 Pseudocode of the Classical Algorithm

The classical algorithm consists of two portions. The main function Quick Sort is called in the first portion where the last element is selected as pivot and passed as an argument in the second portion which is partition function where each element is compared with the pivot i.e. last element.

Algorithm 1: CLASSICAL QUICK SORT.
Classical_Q_Sorter (ARRA,PI,RI)
1. **if** (PI < RI) **then**
2.   qt ← Partition(ARRA,PI,RI)
3.   Classical_Q_Sorter (ARRA,PI,qt)
4.   Classical_Q_Sorter (ARRA,qt+1,RI)

Procedure 1: PARTITION

PARTITION(ARRA,PI,RI)
1. xt ← ARRA[PI]
2. it ← PI-1
3. jt ← RI+1
4. while (True)
5. repeat
6.   jt ← jt-1
7.   until (ARRA[jt] <= xt)
8. repeat
9.   it ← it+1
10.   until (ARRA[it] >= xt)
11. Exchange xt↔ ARRA[jt]
12. return(jt)

3.2 Step by Step Simulation of the Classical Algorithm

Let an array be [9,−3,5,2,6,8,−6,1,3] and obviously not sorted. In the classical Quick Sort last element 3 is considered as a pivot. Each element is compared with pivot and divided into two array where left array is less than pivot and right array is greater than the pivot element. From the divided two array last element is again selected as pivot and again they are divided into sub arrays. This process continues until we get a final sorted array (Fig. 2).

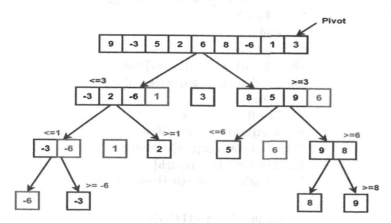

Fig. 2. Step by step simulation of classical Quick Sort.

3.3 Pseudocode of the Proposed Algorithm

This algorithm has three portions. In the first portion, Quick Sort function is called if the size is greater than or equal to 3 otherwise Manual Sort will be called. Then the second portion contains the partition details where each element is compared with the pivot element.

Algorithm 1: QUICK SORT.
QUICK_SORT (arr, low, high)
1. N ← high-low+1
2. **if** N ≤ 3
3.   then call procedure 1 MANUAL_SORT (arr, low, high)
4. **Else**
5.   do a←calculate_pivot(arr,low,high);
6.   q← call procedure 2 PARTITION(arr,low,high,a);
7.   QUICK_SORT (arr,low,q);
8.   QUICK_SORT (arr,q+1,high);

Procedure 1: MANUAL SORT

MANUAL_SORT (arr, low, high)
1.   N ← high-low+1
2.   **if** n ≤ 1
3.   then Return;
4.   **if** n=2 **then**
5.   **if** arr[low] > arr[high] **then**
6.   Exchange arr[low]↔arr[high]
7.   **End if**
8.   **End if**
9.   **if** n=3 **then**
10.   **if** arr[low] > arr[high-1] **then**
11.   Exchange arr[low]↔arr[high-1]
12.   **End if**
13.   **End if**
14.   **if** arr[low] > arr[high] **then**
15.   Exchange arr[low]↔ arr[high]
16.   **if** arr[high-1] > arr[high]
17.   Exchange arr[high-1]↔arr[high]

Procedure 2: PARTITION
PARTITION (arr, low, high, pivot)
1.   i ← low–1, j ← high+1
2.   **DO while**
3.   **IF   TRUE**
4.   **while** arr[i] < pivot
5.   **then** i++;
6.   **End while**
7.   **while** arr[j] > pivot
8.   **then** j--;
9.   **End while**
10.   **if** i ≥ j
11.   **break;**
12.   **End DO while**
13.   Exchange arr+i ↔ arr+j;

3.4   Step by Step Simulation of the Proposed Algorithm

Let, an array be arr [88,77,66,55,44,33,22,11]. Here, the array is not sorted and as the size is greater than 3 it will not call manual sort. So by the pivot selection method this array will be divided into two sub-array of right [88,77,66,55] and left [44,33,22,11]. The max element of the right subarray is 88 and the Min element is 55 whereas the Max element of the left subarray is 44 and the Min element is 11. So the pivot will be the mean of the array. Now each element of two sub-array will be compared with this pivot element and after applying our proposed Quick Sort algorithm to this array, the results we get are shown through a tree below (Fig. 3, Fig. 4and Fig. 5):

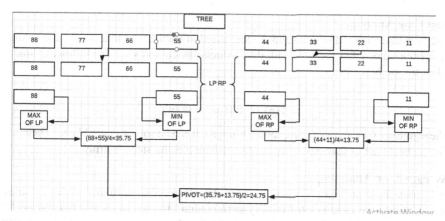

Fig. 3. Tree diagram of PIVOT selection method in Quick Sort.

INITIALLY:

PIVOT	**UNSORTED ARRAY**

AFTER IMPLIMENTING QUICK SORT:

ELEMENT<PIVOT	**UNKNOWN ELEMENT**	**ELEMENT>PIVOT**
i	j	

Fig. 4. Comparison with PIVOT in Quick Sort.

Here, LP = Left Part
RP = Right Part

4 Complexity Analysis

The Best case time complexity of this Quick Sort algorithm is O(*nlogn*), the Worst case time complexity of this algorithm is O(*nlogn*). Analysis of this complexity is described below:

4.1 Time Complexity

Time taken by quicksort, in general, can be written as follows:

$$T(n) = T(k) + T(n - k - 1) + (n)$$

Here, the first two terms are the two recursive call and the last term is the partition of n elements. The time taken by this algorithm depends on the input of the array and the partition process.

Best Case Analysis

The best-case occurs the algorithm is conducted in such a way that always the median element is selected as the pivot and thus reduces the complexity. The following time is taken for the best case.

$$T(n) = 2T(n/2) + (n)$$

The solution of the above recurrence is $O(nlogn)$. It can be solved using Master Theorem. So, the best case of this algorithm is $nlogn$ where n is the size the array.

Average Case Analysis

In average case analysis, we need to consider all possible permutations of an array and calculate the time taken by every permutation. The average case is obtained by considering the case when partition puts $O(n/9)$ elements in one part and $O(9n/10)$ elements in other parts. The following time is taken for this:

$$T(n) = T(n/9) + T(9n/10) + O(n)$$

Although the worst-case time complexity of Quick Sort is $O(n^2)$ which is more than many other sorting algorithms Quick Sort can be made efficient by changing the pivot selection method.

Worst Case Analysis

The proposed algorithm gives a better running time than a classical quick sort algorithm. The pivot selection procedure is repeated for each iteration of the quick until the size of the array becomes less than or equal three. In this case, we go for a manual sort where we compare two elements normally. There might be a situation where a worst-case partitioning will be required. When the array will be already sorted or sorted in descending order then worst case partitioning will be needed. Thus mean is calculated and it always comes between extreme values, so, partitioning splits the list into 8-to-2. Thus, the time taken for the proposed algorithm is:

$$T(n) = T(8n/10) + T(2n/10) + cn$$

The recurrence comes to an end when the condition is $log10/8(n)$. The total time taken becomes $O(nlogn)$. An 8-to-2 proportional split at every level of recursion making the time taken $O(nlogn)$, which is the same as if the split were right down the middle.

Space Complexity

Quick Sort is mainly an in-place sorting algorithm which means it does not need any extra memory. This algorithm works on the 1D array and so it consumes space of n which is basically the size of an array. Thus the space complexity of the full algorithm is $O(n)$ means that the program is running on a linear space algorithm.

5 Experimental Result

In the previous section, we have shown the calculation of the time complexity and space complexity of our proposed algorithm asymptotically. As the new proposed algorithm is not unique, it has some similarities with some sources as all of these are based on the same idea. We have compared our proposed algorithm with these existing algorithms for different input sets in the following sections.

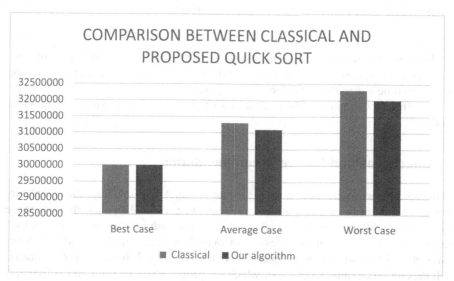

Fig. 5. Runtime comparison chart between the proposed algorithm and the classical algorithm.

Table 1. Runtime(nanosecond) of our proposed algorithm.

Number of input set	Number of elements	Best case	Average case	Worst case
01	25	1000000	1100000	1230000
02	50	2000000	2120000	2230000
03	100	30000000	31000000	32000000

Table 2. Runtime(nanosecond) of the classical algorithm.

Number of input set	Number of elements	Best case	Average case	Worst case
01	25	1000000	1100000	1230000
02	50	2000000	2100000	2220000
03	100	30000000	31000000	32300000

Table 3. Time complexity comparison with previous works.

Algorithm	Best time complexity	Average time complexity	Worst time complexity
Paper[1]	O($nlogn$)	Ω($nlogn$)	O(n^2)
Paper[3]	O($nlogn$)	Ω($nlogn$)	O(n)
Paper [9]:	O($nlogn$)	Ω($nlogn$)	O(n)
Proposed Algorithm	O($nlogn$)	Ω($nlogn$)	O($nlogn$)

Here, we present the run time using time function for three different sizes of input sets. For each input set, we have calculated the best case, average case and worst-case execution time in nanoseconds (Table 1 and Table 2):

In Table 3 we represent the comparison of time complexity with other previous works.

6   Conclusion and Future Recommendation

Many researchers researched on the algorithm of Quick Sort to reduce the complexity and make this sorting algorithm more efficient. We presented an algorithm where we tried to use a different method of pivot selection that reduces the comparison and we successfully turned the time complexity to a logarithmic function. We turned it O($nlogn$) from O(n^2) for the worst time complexity. Obviously, the final choice of implementation will depend on circumstances under which the program will be used. In the future, it seems possible to do further research to calculate pivot in a different way, make the partition process more efficient and handle the worst-case time complexity as perfectly as possible. Moreover, this algorithm is not optimal for large datasets. So in the future, a scope will be created to work with this issue also.

References

1. Latif, A. et al.: Enhancing Quick Sort algorithm using a dynamic pivot selection technique. Wulfenia J. **19**(10), 543–552 (2012)
2. Devi, R., Khemchandani, V.: An efficient quicksort using value based pivot selection an bidirectional partitioning. Int. J. Inf. Sci. App. **3**, 25–30 (2011)
3. Rajput, I.S.: Performance comparison of sequential quick sort and parallel quick sort algorithms. Int. J. Comput. Appl. **57**, 14–22 (2012)
4. Bustos, B.: A dynamic pivot selection technique for similarity search, pp. 105–112 (2008) https://doi.org/10.1109/sisap.2008.12
5. Lakshmi, I.: Performance analysis of four different types of sorting algorithm using different languages. Int. J. Trend Sci. Res. Dev. **2**, 535–541 (2018)
6. Sha, L.: Using simplicity to control complexity. IEEE Softw. **18**(4), 20–28 (2001)
7. Wild, S.: Dual-Pivot quicksort and beyond: analysis of multiway partitioning and its practical potential. Inf. Technol. **60**(3), 173–177 (2018). https://doi.org/10.1515/itit-2018-0012. eISSN 2196-7032, ISSN 1611-2776

8. Aumüller, M., Dietzfelbinger, M., Klaue, P.: How good is multi-pivot quicksort? ACM Trans. Alg. **13**, Article no. 8 (2016)
9. Aumüller, M., Dietzfelbinger, M.: Optimal partitioning for dual-pivot quicksort. ACM Trans. Alg., vol. 12, Article no 18 (Association for Computing Machinery) (2015)
10. Kushagra, S., López-Ortiz, A.: Multi-pivot quicksort: theory and experiments (2013)
11. Faujdar, N., Prakash, S., Professor, G.: Performance evaluation of merge and quick sort using GPU computing with CUDA. Int. J. Appl. Eng. Res. vol. 10 (2015)
12. Abdulrahman Hamed Almutairi, B., Helal Alruwaili, A., Hamed Almutairi, A.: Improving of quicksort algorithm performance by sequential thread or parallel algorithms (2012)
13. Bahig, Hazem M.: Complexity analysis and performance of double hashing sort algorithm. J. Egyptian Math. Soc. **27**(1), 1–12 (2019). https://doi.org/10.1186/s42787-019-0004-2
14. Jadoon, S., Salman, F.S., Rehman, S.: Design and analysis of optimized selection sort algorithm. Int. J. Elect. Comput. Sci. IJECS-IJENS **11**(02), 19–24 (2011)
15. Rathi, N.: QSort-Dynamic pivot in original quick sort. Int. J. Adv. Res. Devel. (2018)

RETRACTED CHAPTER: Software Project Planning Through Comparison of Bio-inspired Algorithms

Jesús Silva[1](✉) , Noel Varela[1] , Harold Neira Molina[1] ,
and Omar Bonerge Pineda Lezama[2]

[1] Universidad de la Costa, Barranquilla, Colombia
{aviloria7,nvarela2,hneira}@cuc.edu.co
[2] Universidad Tecnológica Centroamericana (UNITEC), San Pedro Sula, Honduras
omarpineda@unitec.edu

Abstract. Currently many organizations have adopted the development of software projects with agile methodologies, particularly Scrum, which has more than 20 years of development. In these methodologies, software is developed iteratively and delivered to the client in increments called releases. In the releases, the goal is to develop system functionality that quickly adds value to the client's business. At the beginning of the project, one or more releases are planned. For solving the problem of replanning in the context of releases, a model is proposed considering the characteristics of agile development using Scrum. The results obtained show that the algorithm takes a little less than 5 min for solutions that propose replanning composed by 16 sprints, which is equivalent to 240 days of project. They show that applying a repair operator increases the hypervolume quality indicator in the resulting population.

Keywords: Genetic algorithm · Agile software projects · Multi-target

1 Introduction

During the execution of the project, it is common to note events that affect the plan, which will be called disruptive events [1]. An example of a disruptive event is an employee leaving or a new requirement being added (called user stories in the agile context) [2, 3]. The action of adjusting or updating the original plan after the occurrence of a disruptive event is known as replanning [4]. Because software development is expensive and usually has defined deadlines, project managers must immediately perform replanning to minimize economic and operational impacts and meet defined deadlines [5].

In addition, there are at least three other important objectives that must be assessed in a real project. It is desirable that, when a replanning is carried out, it does not differ

The original version of this chapter was retracted: The retraction note to this chapter is available at https://doi.org/10.1007/978-981-15-6648-6_28

too much from the original one, since it is considered that the initial planning is the best option for the development of the project [6]. Similarly, the history of user (HU) with the highest priority for the release must be assigned to the first sprints and thus develop the most important HU first [7]. In software development, equipment is expensive and the development time of the employees must be used in the best way to avoid wasting it [8]. Therefore, five objectives could be considered when performing replanning: time, cost, stability, release value and wasting development capacity. Therefore, the replanning problem is a multi-objective optimization problem.

This replanning problem can be seen as a generalization of the assignment problem, which is well known to belong to the NP-difficult class [9]. In addition, some of the objectives considered are in conflict, for example, if the development team seeking to minimize the delivery time increases, the project will be more expensive. For this reason, the solution proposed for this problem is based on a multi-objective genetic algorithm, which considers each objective equally important and seeks to result in a set of replanning proposals that serve as support for the project leaders.

2 Bibliographic Review

In this section we will present the most important ideas of some articles, in addition to those focused on agile methodologies, we will also take some that propose solutions to the re-planning problem.

According to the literature review so far, only [10, 11] study the re-planning problem in agile methodologies, which are only introductory and only present the characteristics of the problem, so they do not present a tool to support managers of software projects in the context of agile methodologies. They use heuristics and focus on agile methodologies. In the first [12], a model without replanning is proposed, so it presents a static model, that is, without changes over time. They present a proposed solution to the project planning problem, the authors propose a genetic algorithm and their objectives are the time and cost of the project. They focus on the release phase, but without presenting disruptive events and planning is done for each sprint, but does not consider re-planning from an existing plan. The model seeks to assign employees to tasks. The second [13] only proposes characteristics for the project planning/re-planning model in agile methodologies since it does not present an algorithm or model for the problem. In this paper, only the objectives that they will seek to use are mentioned, which are time, cost, robustness, stability and fragmentation of HU (impact of delayed HU). Being only a proposal, it has no further detail and only mentions general disruptive events.

Most articles found take characteristics of the models developed for traditional methodologies, such as assigning employees to tasks or that planning is done only at the beginning of the project [14].

[15] considers project planning in an agile context, proposes an entire scheduling method to solve it, and only targets the time it takes to develop. We did not find any re-planning, but it presents employee assignment to tasks and does not consider an adequate estimate for HU.

The articles in which the re-planning problem is modeled emphasize that software development is a dynamic system. Changes occur during the execution phase because disruptive events occur. But, without counting the works of [16–18], in all cases they focus on traditional methodologies. They present proposals that seek to solve the problem of planning software projects, but now in a dynamic environment. In [19] we can find a model for the re-planning problem, as a solution proposal implements a genetic algorithm that seeks to minimize project time and cost. Stability is introduced as the objective of the problem and the disruptive events that it considers are two: arrival of new tasks and the movement of employees (when they arrive or leave).

As previously mentioned, the re-planning problem is current and in the last two years we can highlight three documents directed at traditional methodologies, beginning with that of [20], in which the authors seek to minimize time, cost and project stability. The disruptive events that trigger a re-planning are: the arrival or withdrawal of employees to the project, as well as when tasks arrive that were not had in the original planning. The authors seek to model team productivity and how it affects the development of their skills. As in the previous cases, the proposed solution is based on a genetic algorithm [21].

In the study by [11] we found for the first time a multi-objective function proposed in the model, in this way each objective is calculated independently. The proposal presents as a solution to a set of possible re-planning proposals. The objectives to be optimized are: project duration, development time, stability and robustness. They consider the arrival of new tasks, the withdrawal of an employee from the project and when an employee joins, as disruptive events. To validate their work, they used three real-world projects and compared them with the proposals that their algorithm gave as a solution. As in the previous case, [22] also presents a multi-objective function which is made up of: the duration of the project, the cost of development, the stability between plans, the robustness to look for an event-tolerant plan and introduce the objective of employee satisfaction when being assigned to tasks of your liking. As a solution proposal they use an algorithm composed of two heuristics. As a global solution they propose a genetic algorithm which results in a planning proposal, then they try to improve this proposal by applying an AMDE (Angle Modulated Differential Evolution) algorithm. They mention that to validate their algorithm, they were compared with real projects, in addition to cases created for testing [23].

We realize that in addition to time, cost, and stability targets, some of the items consider robustness. This objective is defined as how prone is re-planning to delay delivery dates and cost when a disruptive event occurs. That is, robustness is the ability of rethinking to cope with small changes [24].

To propose a model closer to reality, in the work of [25–27], the authors model the communication necessary between employees to carry out a task. This communication affects the project if many employees are assigned to the same task, because they spend a lot of time communicating. Finally, we find that in more current jobs the productivity and learning curve of employees is modeled, we can see that this characteristic is presented in [28, 29] and improve the model presented in [30].

As we can see, few articles talk about the re-planning problem and only three are focused on agile methodologies. None have characteristics of agile development using Scrum, since they do not use concepts such as sprint speed and story points. Therefore, there is no tool that presents proposals to solve the re-planning problem in agile methodologies.

Our work seeks to propose a re-planning model of projects developed with methodologies agile. The model that we present takes into account five objectives to optimize: time, cost, stability, use of development capacity and release value. These last two objectives are part of our contributions and are explained later.

3 The Problem of Replanning Releases in Agile Software Projects

The research proposes a model for the planning problem in agile methodologies (Scrum), especially focused on the replanning of releases. This will be called the release replanning problem in agile software projects (RPASP). After a disruptive event, the planning should be adjusted as soon as possible and with the least number of changes, so that the cost and time of completion are not affected or, if not, that the increase is minimal, since the increase in cost must be absorbed by the company that develops it and this is translated into loss [31].

Releases are focused on delivering specific functionality and mark the delivery dates of the increments to the system. Each release is divided into one or more iterations, called sprints, as shown in the example in Fig. 1. In the release planning, the user stories needed to fulfill the objective of each release are selected and assigned to some sprint to schedule the order in which they will be developed [31]. When performing a replanning, the assignment of HU to the sprint that best suits the plan is considered, taking into account the duration, priority and dependencies of these.

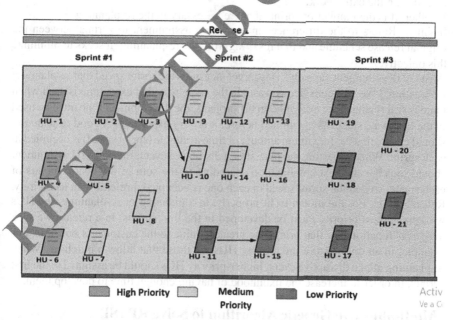

Fig. 1. Representation of an example of release planning, which consists of three sprints.

The re-planning of releases has its own characteristics, which are mainly aimed at making the scheduling of HUs more flexible and agile. Before presenting the model, it is important to introduce some concepts that are important in the agile context, and more specifically in Scrum.

– Story points. In Scrum, the estimation of the effort required to develop user stories rests with the work team. HUs are estimated with a unit called history points, which represents the effort required to develop a HU relative to a reference one. This technique is known as planning poker [33]. In this paper we consider that the team has made an effort estimate for all HUs before release is planned.
– Sprint speed. On the other hand, sprint speed is a historical metric of the ability that the team has shown to fully develop user stories in a sprint.

Our model considers the extra time that a development team can work. If a team works overtime they may have more development capacity in a sprint (sprint speed increases) [29], but the project will become more expensive, since it is necessary to pay extra time. In this work we consider 22.5% of extra work, in an 8-h day this percentage represents 2 extra hours1.

When a disruptive event occurs and a re-planning has to be made, these events are intended to have the least impact on the project, considering the following criteria.

– Cost. It is the cost of the work equipment plus the extra hours that are needed in the re-planning. To calculate it, the regular sprint speed and the sprint speed are obtained considering the extra work.
– Weather. It is the number of sprints that are necessary in the re-planning.
– Stability. Refers to the differences in user story assignment to sprints between the original release schedule and that resulting from the re-planning. It seeks to minimize this objective.
– Waste of development capacity. This target measures the sprint speed that re-planning is "wasting". We will consider as waste in the same way that extra time is used when there is still regular time available. In the projects, the development time must be used in the best way, since, as mentioned before, it is very expensive. A good re-planning should ensure that the maximum amount of time available (sprint speed) is occupied in each sprint. When adjusting the plan after a disruptive event, the new HU assignment should look for the best combination according to the sum of the history points of each sprint, so that the sprint speed in each one is occupied, preferably in its entirety.
– Release value. For the model to fit properly, in a planning or re-planning, the HUs with the highest priority must be developed in the first sprints. In a release we seek to deliver functionality that brings the greatest value to the customer's business. For example, in an online store the priority HUs are those that allow a purchase. When re-planning after a disruptive event, higher-priority HUs should be assigned to the first sprints, in order to increase the likelihood of having enough time to develop them.

4 Multi-objective Genetic Algorithm to Solve RPASP

The mentioned solution seeks to provide project leaders with a set of replanning proposals in a few minutes, since in real projects an expert usually presents a replanning proposal in at least 180 min [16], without guaranteeing that it is a good solution. By modeling the replanning problem as a multi-objective one, the result is ideally a set of solutions that present the best values found for each of the objectives and solutions that present a compensation.

This algorithm calculates the suitability of each of the replanning proposals by implementing the concept of dominance. It is said that a solution x dominates another solution y if x is at least as good as y for all the objectives and is strictly better in at least one of them. The solutions with the best aptitude are those that are not dominated by any other, this is known as non-dominance.

To know the performance of multi-objective algorithms, quality indicators are used, for example, the hypervolume, which results in a value that represents the performance of one algorithm with respect to another. The hypervolume (HV) indicator [13] measures the space covered by the non-dominated solutions with respect to a reference point and this gives some information on the convergence and diversity of individuals in the population. Therefore, one population is better than another if its HV is higher.

There are several methods to solve multi-objective optimization problems: exact, heuristic and metaheuristic. Due to the characteristics of the problem under study, we have used a metaheuristic method, in particular, a genetic algorithm (AG) based on NSGA-II [14].

Genetic algorithms are based on the principles of evolution through natural selection. Broadly speaking, a genetic algorithm considers a function to be optimized, a representation of the solution called the chromosome, genetic operators, and a function that measures the fitness of the chromosome. The search performed by an AG must have a balance between exploiting and exploring the search space. An algorithm for an AG consists of [14]:

1. Representation of the solution as a chromosome.
2. Generation of a population.
3. Repeated application of genetic operators.

For our proposed solution to the re-planning problem, NSGA-II [14] was implemented, which is a multi-objective genetic algorithm that presents elitism and conserves the diversity of the population. Each individual (chromosome) in the population represents a re-planning. NSGA-II implements a rapid classification based on non-dominance, in which all individuals in the population are compared and assigned a level. Each individual's fitness depends on their level of non-dominance, where zero represents the best fitness. The second feature of NSGA-II is an individual's stacking distance. In order to calculate this distance, individuals are increasingly arranged in each of their objectives and the distance between them is measured. This is obtained by calculating the distance that the individual has with his two closest neighbors. If the individual is at one end of the target space, then an infinite distance is assigned to him, since there are no more individuals next to him. After calculating the level of non-dominance and the stacking distance, the selection of individuals that will form part of the population in the next generation begins. As mentioned before, NSGA-II implements elitism so that generation after generation only the individuals with the best aptitude survive, that is, those with the lowest level of non-dominance [17]. The diversity in the new population depends on the stacking distance. When the selection of surviving individuals is being carried out, if two or more individuals have the same level of non-domination, then those who are in a less populated area, that is, the one with the largest stacking distance, are selected.

4.1 Proposed Multi-target Genetic Algorithm

So far, a function was defined for each of the objectives to be optimized: time, cost, stability, waste and release value. Likewise, the function that calculates the aptitude of individuals, which is based on the non-dominance of solutions [13, 14]. Next, the parts of the GA are defined: representation of the solution as chromosome, creation of population and the genetic operators.

- Chromosome. A chromosome is a representation of the shape $a1\ a2\ a3 \cdots an$, where each position i is called a gene and ai is known as an allele. Each gene represents a HU and its value is equal to the sprint it is assigned to in the replanning. The first gene represents $h1$, the second one $h2$ and so on [15].
- Creation of the population. For the creation of the population, the first time the algorithm is executed the individuals are created from the initial planning. This means that from the initial planning a chromosome is built. The other members of the population are variations of this chromosome, which are obtained by mutating the random values of the original schedule [16].

    Selection. It is done with a random binary tournament: two individuals are selected at random from the population and the one with the best aptitude wins. If they are tied in the non-dominance range, then the one with the greater stacking distance is chosen [17].

- Crossing. The crossing will be at a single point and will have a probability of 0.9. This value was selected because it presented the best preliminary results, and it is recommended by the authors of NSGA-II. It should be noted that the two-point cross was also tested, but the results were not satisfactory [18].
- Mutation. To implement this operator, each gene on the chromosome will have a probability of 0.2 of being mutated. A gene to gene mutation is implemented, where the entire chromosome is traversed and each gene has a probability between 0 and 1 at random. If it is less than or equal to 0.2, then a new sprint is assigned, different from the one that was assigned, which is also obtained at random. This value was chosen because it also gave the best results in the preliminary tests [19].

    Due to the probabilistic nature of GAs, when applying one of the genetic operators to an individual it may no longer be feasible. The algorithm looks for all individuals in the population to be, so a repair operator is implemented.

- Chromosome repair. Sometimes solutions leave one or more sprinkles empty. So, although it is a valid chromosome, it is something undesirable in real projects. At this stage of repair, the chromosome is validated and if it has an empty sprint, it is removed. The procedure is as follows: The empty sprint is identified. The HU of the next sprint is run through, to the empty sprint. If there are more empty sprints, the HU are still run to avoid leaving spaces. If there are no more empty sprints, the empty sprint(s) that were run at the end of the replanning is eliminated as a result of the repair [20].

5 Results

Since there are no studies related to the replanning of projects focused on agile methodologies, there are no public test cases to compare this proposal [1, 5, 11, 15, ...]. Therefore, artificial test cases were created and the experiments were divided into two classes. The first one, with small cases, 12 and 17 HU, to test if the algorithm offers coherent solutions. The second class considers larger test cases, from 40 to 100 HU, to know if the repair operator really brings improvement to the performance of the algorithm.

5.1 Experiments with Small Test Cases

Two small test cases were created. The first one, 12 HU and 4 employees, was specially created to show the impact of the objectives. The results for this test case were consistent and small, so the impact of the objectives could be visually observed and the behavior was as expected when simulating some of the disruptive events. The results were similar to the second test case. It consists of 17 HU and 4 employees. The replanning that presented the maximum release value has an empty sprint [3].

The repair, as mentioned above, adjust the history of users so that there are no empty sprints within the replanning. After the implementation, the results shown in Fig. 2 were obtained.

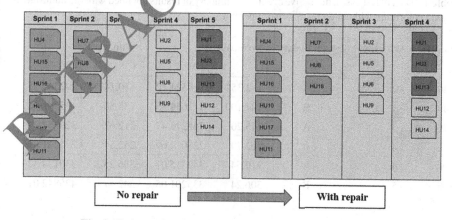

Fig. 2. Release planning after implementing empty sprint repair.

The algorithm results in a set of proposals for replanning, which present a balance in their objectives or present the best value found for any of them.

5.2 Experiments in Large Test Cases

The test cases for this phase were created with the Alba and Chicano test case generator [12], which was configured to randomly create plans with 40, 70 and 100 HU. For the number of employees, 4, 5 and 6 were considered, respectively. By running the test case generator, plans with up to 16 sprints were obtained. In each of the tests, two disruptive events were modeled: one employee leaves and a new HU is added, as these have the greatest negative impact on the planning [19, 20].

To check if the empty sprint repair really contributes to the performance of the algorithm, a test case with a number of HU and employees is obtained with the generator. Then, a disruptive event is simulated and the algorithm is run 10 times. In each execution, the same amount of HU is obtained, the same number of employees, the same disruptive event and the sprint repair is applied. From the 10 repetitions, an average of the algorithm's run time and the maximum values of all the runs for each of the targets are obtained. This procedure is repeated again, but now without the sprint repair.

Now there are 10 repeats with repair and 10 without it, besides two sets of maximum values. From the two sets, a new comparison is made again to get the overall maximums of the 20 runs. The global maximum are the reference points with which the hypervolume of each resultant population is calculated. Finally, the average hypervolume of the 10 populations with repair and the average of the 10 without repair were calculated. The summary of the results of the experiments is shown in Table 1. In the first column is the number of HUs, the second column shows the number of employees and the third column shows the disruptive event: A indicates that an employee leaves and B represents that a new HU is added. The last four columns represent, respectively, the average execution time in seconds (t) and the average of the hypervolume for the algorithm without repair and with repair.

Table 1. Data of test cases, disruptive event and summary of results obtained with the multi-target genetic algorithm, without and with repair operator.

No. HU	No. Employee	Event	No repair		With repair	
			t	HV	t	HV
40	2	A	112.352	168524.12	110.147	192541.65
40	5	B	104.100	112654.35	135.50	135201.42
70	3	A	245.20	265275.47	212.62	320354.24
70	4	B	262.70	223014.69	252.54	295241.85
100	4	A	310.54	342315.01	336.25	330124.32
100	5	B	306.24	335201.05	342.47	425842.01

The results show that the empty sprint repair helped the algorithm reach a higher hypervolume. It can be then interpreted that, when empty sprint repair is applied, the replanning of the result population shows a greater diversity and better results in the target functions. That is, they find better replanning, since, in general, the population converges to better results for the objectives of time, cost, stability, waste and release value. It can be noted that, in most cases, the average execution time increases when the repair is applied, but this is not considerable.

In fact, for the first and fourth experiments, the average execution time with the repair is less than without it. The results show that applying the repair in the algorithm results in a population with a higher HV, therefore, the algorithm has a better performance and does not significantly affect the runtime.

6 Conclusions

This paper presents the replanning of agile software project releases as a multi objective optimization problem. The literature review indicated that there is not much work on optimization problems in agile software development methodologies. Furthermore, a single one that develops its characteristics was not found. So, as a first contribution, the proposal of a model for the problem of replanning releases of agile software projects is presented. Unlike the studies found in the literature review, this model presents specific characteristics of agile development such as: the concepts of history points and sprint speed.

The study introduces the objectives of waste and release value, besides implementing the extra time of development of a team as a configurable parameter, since each team is different.

The problem of re-planning of releases can be considered as a generalization of the allocation problem, which is a problem of the NP-difficult class. Therefore, to solve it, a multi-objective genetic algorithm that implements NSGA-II is proposed. Being a population-based algorithm, it covers the need to quickly obtain release re-planning proposals after a disruptive event occurs. In the results we can see that our algorithm presents a set of proposals to re-plan releases in less than 7 min for the most difficult cases that were tested. The analysis of the results shows that when applying the repair in all cases the HV hypervolume increases and therefore the algorithm has a better performance without hardly affecting the execution time. These solutions present 100 HU, covering 15 of 16 sprints, which we can compare with approximately 240 days of project development. In real projects, an expert generally presents a re-planning proposal in at least 10 min [7], without guaranteeing that it is a good choice.

As future work it is proposed to obtain data from real projects and with that data run the algorithm, simulate disruptive events and verify that solutions are feasible in real projects. Likewise, it will seek to implement other types of heuristics, such as MOEA / D and SMS-EMOA. It will seek to implement a second heuristic to improve the result population (local optimization). Other quality indicators that are important to our results will be investigated and implemented. Finally, it will seek to generate a support tool for real projects.

References

1. Semenkina, O.E., Popov, E.A., Ryzhikov, I.S.: Hierarchical scheduling problem in the field of manufacturing operational planning. In: IOP Conference Series: Materials Science and Engineering, vol. 537, no. 3, p. 032001. IOP Publishing (2019)

2. Phanden, R.K., Jain, A., Davim, J.P. (eds.): Integration of Process Planning and Scheduling: Approaches and Algorithms. CRC Press, Boca Raton (2019)
3. Jahr, M.: A hybrid approach to quantitative software project scheduling within agile frameworks. Project Manage. J. **45**(3), 35–45 (2014)
4. Roque, L., Araújo, A.A., Dantas, A., Saraiva, R., Souza, J.: Human resource allocation in agile software projects based on task similarities. In: Sarro, F., Deb, K. (eds.) SSBSE 2016. LNCS, vol. 9962, pp. 291–297. Springer, Cham (2016). https://doi.org/10.1007/978-3-319-47106-8_25
5. Varas, J.M., et al.: MAXCMAS project: autonomous COLREGs compliant ship navigation. In: Proceedings of the 16th Conference on Computer Applications and Information Technology in the Maritime Industries (COMPIT) 2017, pp. 454–464 (2017)
6. Ge, Y.: Software project rescheduling with genetic algorithms. In: 2009 International Conference on Artificial Intelligence and Computational Intelligence, vol. 1, pp. 439–443. IEEE, Shanghai (2009)
7. Ge, Y., Xu, B.: Dynamic staffing and rescheduling in software project management: a hybrid approach. PLoS ONE **11**(6), e0157104 (2016)
8. Shen, X., Minku, L.L., Bahsoon, R., Yao, X.: Dynamic software project scheduling through a proactive-rescheduling method. Trans. Softw. Eng. **42**(7), 658–686 (2016)
9. Shen, X.N., Minku, L.L., Marturi, N., Guo, Y.N., Han, Y.: A learning-based memetic algorithm for multi-objective dynamic software project scheduling. Inf. Sci. **428**, 1–29 (2018)
10. Song, Y.J., Zhang, Z.S., Song, B.Y., Chen, Y.W.: Improved genetic algorithm with local search for satellite range scheduling system and its application in environmental monitoring. Sustain. Comput. Inf. Syst. **21**, 19–27 (2019)
11. Moosavi, S.H.S., Bardsiri, V.K.: Satin bowerbird optimizer: a new optimization algorithm to optimize ANFIS for software development effort estimation. Eng. Appl. Artif. Intell. **60**, 1–15 (2017)
12. Zheng, Z., Guo, J., Gill, E.: Swarm satellite mission scheduling & planning using hybrid dynamic mutation genetic algorithm. Ac. Astronaut. **137**, 243–253 (2017)
13. Viloria, A., Acuña, G.C., Franco, D.J.A., Hernández-Palma, H., Fuentes, J.P., Rambal, E.P.: Integration of data mining techniques to PostgreSQL database manager system. Procedia Comput. Sci. **155**, 575–580 (2019)
14. Deng, M., et al.: A two-phase coordinated planning approach for heterogeneous earth-observation resources to monitor area targets. IEEE Trans. Syst. Man Cybern. Syst. (2020)
15. Ghoddousi, P., Ansari, R., Makui, A.: An improved robust buffer allocation method for the project scheduling problem. Eng. Optim. **49**(4), 718–731 (2017)
16. Tomori, H., Hiroshi, K.: Control of pneumatic artificial muscles using local cyclic inputs and genetic algorithm. Actuators **7**(3), 36 (2018)
17. Ibraigheeth, M., Fadzli, S.A.: Core factors for software projects success. JOIV Int. J. Inf. Visual. **3**(1), 69–74 (2019)
18. da Silva Arantes, J., da Silva Arantes, M., Toledo, C.F.M., Júnior, O.T., Williams, B.C.: An embedded system architecture based on genetic algorithms for mission and safety planning with UAV. In: Proceedings of the Genetic and Evolutionary Computation Conference, pp. 1049–1056 (2017)
19. Perez, R., Vásquez, C., Viloria, A.: An intelligent strategy for faults location in distribution networks with distributed generation. J. Intell. Fuzzy Syst. **36**(2), 1627–1637 (2019)
20. Viloria, A., Robayo, P.V.: Virtual network level of application composed IP networks connected with systems-(NETS Peer-to-Peer). Indian J. Sci. Technol. **9**, 46 (2016)
21. Plice, L., Lau, B., Pisanich, G., Young, L.A.: Biologically inspired behavioral strategies for autonomous aerial explorers on Mars. In: 2003 IEEE Aerospace Conference Proceedings (Cat. No. 03TH8652), vol. 1, pp. 1–304. IEEE (2003)

22. Barbagallo, D., Di Nitto, E., Dubois, D.J., Mirandola, R.: A bio-inspired algorithm for energy optimization in a self-organizing data center. In: Weyns, D., Malek, S., de Lemos, R., Andersson, J. (eds.) SOAR 2009. LNCS, vol. 6090, pp. 127–151. Springer, Heidelberg (2010). https://doi.org/10.1007/978-3-642-14412-7_7

23. Srivastava, P.R., Varshney, A., Nama, P., Yang, X.S.: Software test effort estimation: a model based on cuckoo search. Int. J. Bio Inspired Comput. **4**(5), 278–285 (2012)

24. Sheta, A.F., Ayesh, A., Rine, D.: Evaluating software cost estimation models using particle swarm optimisation and fuzzy logic for NASA projects: a comparative study. Int. J. Bio Inspired Comput. **2**(6), 365–373 (2010)

25. Tempesti, G.: Architectures and design methodologies for bio-inspired computing machines. In: SNF Professorship Application Research Plan (2003)

26. Chiang, H.S., Sangaiah, A.K., Chen, M.Y., Liu, J.Y.: A novel artificial bee colony optimization algorithm with SVM for bio-inspired software-defined networking. Int. J. Parallel Prog. 1–19 (2018)

27. Camacho, D., et al.: From ephemeral computing to deep bioinspired algorithms: new trends and applications. Future Gener. Comput. Syst. **88**, 735–746 (2018)

28. Chis, M.: Introduction: a survey of the evolutionary computation techniques for software engineering. In: Evolutionary Computation and Optimization Algorithms in Software Engineering: Applications and Techniques, pp. 1–12. IGI Global (2010)

29. Wang, L., Shen, J.: Towards bio-inspired cost minimisation for data-intensive service provision. In: 2012 IEEE First International Conference on Services Economics, pp. 16–23. IEEE (2012)

30. Wang, J., Cao, J., Li, B., Lee, S., Sherratt, R.S.: Bio-inspired ant colony optimization based clustering algorithm with mobile sinks for applications in consumer home automation networks. IEEE Trans. Consum. Electron. **61**(4), 438–444 (2015)

31. Chis, M., (ed.) Evolutionary Computation and Optimization Algorithms in Software Engineering: Applications and Techniques. Applications and Techniques. IGI Global (2010)

32. Sharma, T.K.: Estimating software reliability growth model parameters using opposition-based shuffled frog-leaping algorithm. In: Ray, K., Pant, M., Bandyopadhyay, A. (eds.) Soft Computing Applications, pp. 149–164. Springer, Singapore (2018)

33. Barocio, E., Regalado, J., Cuevas, E., Uribe, F., Zúñiga, P., Torres, P.J.R.: Modified bio-inspired optimisation algorithm with a centroid decision making approach for solving a multi-objective optimal power flow problem. IET Gener. Transm. Distrib. **11**(4), 1012–1022 (2017)

Retraction Note to: Chapters

Nirbhay Chaubey⬤, Satyen Parikh⬤, and Kiran Amin⬤

Retraction Note to:
Chapter "Optimization of Driving Efficiency for Pre-determined Routes: Proactive Vehicle Traffic Control" in: Amelec Viloria, Omar Bonerge Pineda Lezama, Noel Varela and Jorge Luis Diaz Martínez, Computing Science, Communication and Security, CCIS 1235, https://doi.org/10.1007/978-981-15-6648-6_7

The Editors have retracted this article [1] following investigations by Universidad de la Costa and Universidad Tecnológica Centroamericana (UNITEC) which found that the published article contained material translated from another article[2].

Amelec Viloria agrees to the retraction; Omar Bonerge Pineda Lezama, Noel Varela, and Jorge Luis Diaz Martínez have not responded to any correspondence from the editor/publisher about this retraction.

[1] Viloria, A., Lezama, O.B.P., Varela, N., Martínez, J.L.D.: Optimization of driving efficiency for pre-determined routes: proactive vehicle traffic control. In: Chaubey, N., Parikh, S., Amin, K., (eds.) Computing Science, Communication and Security, COMS2 2020. Communications in Computer and Information Science, vol. 1235. Springer, Singapore (2020). https://doi.org/10.1007/978-981-15-6648-6_7

[2] Ledesma, B. Z.: Control Proactivo de Tráfico Vehicular Mediante Machine Learning y Computación Autónoma. Investigation Report at Universidad de Montemorelos (2015)

Retraction Note to:
Chapter "Design of a Network with VANET Sporadic Cloud Computing Applied to Traffic Accident Prevention" in: Amelec Viloria, Omar Bonerge Pineda Lezama, Noel Varela and Jorge Luis Diaz Martínez, Computing Science, Communication and Security, CCIS 1235, https://doi.org/10.1007/978-981-15-6648-6_17

The Editors have retracted this article [1] following investigations by Universidad de la Costa and Universidad Tecnológica Centroamericana (UNITEC) which found that the published article contained material translated from another article [2].

The retracted version of these chapters can be found at
https://doi.org/10.1007/978-981-15-6648-6_7
https://doi.org/10.1007/978-981-15-6648-6_17
https://doi.org/10.1007/978-981-15-6648-6_18
https://doi.org/10.1007/978-981-15-6648-6_27

Amelec Viloria agrees to the retraction; Omar Bonerge Pineda Lezama, Noel Varela, Jorge Luis Diaz Martínez have not responded to any correspondence from the editor/publisher about this retraction.

[1] Viloria, A., Lezama, O.B.P., Varela, N., Martínez, J.L.D.: Design of a network with VANET sporadic cloud computing applied to traffic accident prevention. In: Chaubey, N., Parikh, S., Amin, K. (eds.) Computing Science, Communication and Security, COMS2 2020. Communications in Computer and Information Science, vol. 1235. Springer, Singapore (2020).https://doi.org/10.1007/978-981-15-6648-6_17

[2] Carreño, R.A.O., Becerra, D.A.Z.: Análisis y Simulacion de Computación de Nume Esporádica en VANET's Mediante Uso de Software Libre. Dissertation at Salesian Polytechnic University (2016)

Retraction Note to:
Chapter "Management System for Optimizing Public Transport Networks: GPS Record" in: Jesús Silva, Noel Varela, Erick Guerra Alemán, Omar Bonerge Pineda Lezama, Computing Science, Communication and Security, CCIS 1235.
https://doi.org/10.1007/978-981-15-6648-6_18

The Editors have retracted this article [1] following investigations by Universidad de la Costa and Universidad Tecnológica Centroamericana (UNITEC) which found that the published article contained material translated from another article[2].

Jesús Silva and Erick Guerra Alemán agree to the retraction; Noel Varela and Omar Bonerge Pineda Lezama have not responded to any correspondence from the editor/publisher about this retraction.

[1] Silva, J., Varela, N., Alemán, E.G., Lezama, O.B.P.: Management system for optimizing public transport networks: GPS record. In: Chaubey, N., Parikh, S., Amin, K. (eds.) Computing Science, Communication and Security, COMS2 2020. Communications in Computer and Information Science, vol. 1235. Springer, Singapore (2020). https://doi.org/10.1007/978-981-15-6648-6_18

[2] Arguijo, J.E., León, E.G., Arellano, C.C., García, F.R.: Propuesta de sistema de gestión para optimización de redes de transporte público. Res. Comput. Sci. **148**, 235–245 (2019)

Retraction Note to:
Chapter "Software Project Planning Through Comparison of Bio-inspired Algorithms" in: Jesús Silva, Noel Varela, Harold Neira Molina, Omar Bonerge Pineda Lezama, Computing Science, Communication and Security, CCIS 1235,
https://doi.org/10.1007/978-981-15-6648-6_27

The Editors have retracted this article [1] following investigations by Universidad de la Costa and Universidad Tecnológica Centroamericana (UNITEC) which found that the published article contained material translated from another article [2].

Jesús Silva and Harold Neira Molina agree to the retraction; Noel Varela and Omar Bonerge Pineda Lezama have not responded to any correspondence from the editor/publisher about this retraction.

[1] Silva, J., Varela, N., Molina, H.N., Lezama, O.B.P.: Software project planning through comparison of Bio-inspired algorithms. In: Chaubey, N., Parikh, S., Amin, K. (eds.) Computing Science, Communication and Security, COMS2 2020. Communications in Computer and Information Science, vol. 1235. Springer, Singapore (2020). https://doi.org/10.1007/978-981-15-6648-6_27

[2] Bailon, V.H., Maceda, H.C., Nájera, A.G.: Aplicación de un algoritmo genético multiobjetivo para la replaneación de liberaciones en proyectos ágiles de software. Res. Comput. Sci. **148**, 199–213 (2019)

Author Index

Printed in the United States
by Baker & Taylor Publisher Services